D1074136

Civilizations in History

Second Edition

M. Dale Davis

TORONTO
Oxford University Press
1994

Oxford University Press
70 Wynford Drive Don Mills Ontario M3C 1J9

Toronto Oxford New York
Delhi Bombay Calcutta Madras Karachi
Kuala Lumpur Singapore Hong Kong Tokyo
Nairobi Dar es Salaam Cape Town
Melbourne Auckland Madrid

and associated companies in
Berlin Ibadan

Oxford is a trademark of Oxford University Press

Canadian Cataloguing in Publication Data

Davis, M. Dale, 1947-
Civilizations in history

2nd ed.
Includes bibliographical references and index.
IBSN 0-19-541017-3

1. Civilization. 2. Europe-History. 3. World history. 4. History. I. Title

D21.D38   1993   909   C93-094996-X

Cover Design: Marie Bartholomew
Illustrators: Susan Calverley, Christine Alexiou, Helen Fox
Editor: David Friend
Editorial Assistants: Micaëla Gates, Mia London
Photo Research: Patricia Buckley
Reviewers: George Adams, Stephen Officer

This book is printed on permanent (acid-free) paper ♻.

Printed and bound in Canada

Contents

Acknowledgements

The publisher would like to thank the following educators for their constructive comments in reviewing the manuscript:

George Adams, History Department Head, Notre Dame Secondary School, Brampton, Ontario

Stephen Officer, Head of History and Contemporary Studies, London South Secondary School, London, Ontario

The publisher would also like to thank the Muslim Educational Institute of Ontario for their review of material pertaining to Islam and the Islamic civilization.

Geologic Period	Millions of Years	Event
Precambrian (earliest era)	4500	Creation of the earth
	4000	Formation of the primordial sea
	3500	First signs of life, single-celled algae and bacteria, appear in water
	900	First oxygen-breathing life
Paleozoic (ancient life)	500	First fish with backbones
	400	Amphibians on land
Mesozoic (middle life)	225	Age of dinosaurs
Cenozoic (recent life)	65	Prosimians, earliest primates, develop in trees
	50	Monkeys appear in South America, Africa, and Asia
	30	Apes appear in Africa and Asia
Lower Pleistocene (oldest period of most recent epoch)	5-6	Chimpanzees develop separate line
	4	*Australopithecus afarensis*
	2.5	*First stone tools, Hadar*
	2	*Homo habilis*
	1.7	*Homo erectus*
	1.4	*First use of fire*
	.3	*Homo sapiens*
	.13	*Homo sapiens sapiens*

1

The Origin of Humans

BACKGROUND

The Origin of Humans

People have long attempted to answer questions about the beginning of life. How and when was the world created? What was the origin of humans? Most cultures have some kind of **creation story** or myth that provides explanations. Some cultures appreciate their creation story mainly for its symbolic value. Other cultures believe that their creation story tells exactly what happened. In the western world, the Judeo-Christian tradition has been dominant. The first book of the Bible, called the Book of Genesis, describes how God created the world and all living things. Centuries after this biblical account was recorded in writing, some people became interested in establishing a time frame for the events in Genesis and the rest of the Bible. In 1650, an Irish archbishop named James Ussher studied the Bible carefully and proclaimed that 4004 B.C. was the actual year of human creation. An English biblical scholar, Dr. John Lightfoot, soon after declared that the precise day and time of creation was 23 October at 9:00 in the morning. For the next 150 years, the Ussher chronology was printed in the margins of many bibles.

By the mid-nineteenth century, however, there were some doubts about Ussher's chronology and about the biblical version of creation. Uncertainty arose partly from the discovery of **fossils**. Fossils are rocks that show the imprint of a dead animal or its bones. Scientists discovered that the fossil animals seemed to be different from any known living animals. The most spectacular of these extinct animals was discovered in 1822 by Gideon and Mary Ann Mantell. It was large and heavy-boned, and they called it Iguanodon. Richard Owen of the British Museum coined the term *dinosaur* from the Greek for "terrible lizard" to describe this new type of creature. Under Owen's direction, a life-size reconstruction of Iguanodon was put on display at London's famous Crystal Palace exhibition in 1853. The Iguanodon and other fossils forced people to reconsider their ideas about how the world began. They had assumed that all life on Earth appeared suddenly, as the book of Genesis recounts, and that there had been few changes since then.

Religion

Here is the story of the creation of the world as it is given in Genesis: "In the beginning God created the heaven and the earth." During the next six days, God gave shape and form to the new creation. He created man in his own image from the dust on the ground, breathing into his nostrils to give him life. The man, named Adam, lived in the Garden of Eden, which God had planted for him. Adam was given authority over all the animals, but God sensed that he was lonely. God caused Adam to sleep, took a rib from his side, and created the first woman, Eve.

Bishop Ussher's date of 4004 B.C. for the creation of the Earth was based on the lifespans of the people in the Bible. By working backwards from the date of Jesus' birth, which was known, he calculated the number of generations extending to Adam. When Ussher's date was printed in the Bible, many people (including Darwin) came to believe it was part of the original scripture. This meant that the age of the earth, pegged at about 6000 years, became a cornerstone of Christian faith.

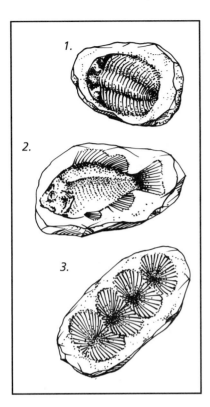

Fossils. A trilobite (1) and an early fish (2) and tree (3).

The fossil remains of dinosaurs and the concept of extinction were not in harmony with the Christian view of creation or with the time frame that had been devised.

Some years earlier, in 1831, a young naturalist named Charles Darwin had made a five-year, around-the-world voyage on board H.M.S. *Beagle*. He carefully studied living animals and fossil remains in South America and the Galapagos Islands. Building on the scientific discussions and discoveries of the early nineteenth century as well as his own travels and research, Darwin soon developed a controversial set of ideas. He believed that the earth was very old, and that species adapted and changed over long periods of time. These ideas were consistent with fossil evidence, but were contrary to how the Bible was being interpreted at the time.

Unwilling to confront the criticism he knew he would face, Darwin did not publish his work. But in 1858 Darwin received a letter from another naturalist, Alfred Russel Wallace. Working in the jungles of Malaysia, Wallace independently identified the same processes of change worked out by Darwin. Darwin rushed to complete his work, entitled *On the Origin of Species*, and published it in 1859. Although Darwin shared the credit with Wallace, Darwin's name has been the one most closely linked with the theory of evolution, and Wallace's contributions have been overlooked.

Darwin's book presented an explanation of how new types of animals develop. In nature, organisms produce several offspring, each possessing a different, unique set of characteristics. Some individuals have characteristics that give them a competitive advantage. They are better able to obtain food, mates, and territory, or to resist disease. These individuals survive, reproduce, and pass on their characteristics to their offspring. Less successful individuals die before they reproduce, and their inappropriate characteristics appear less frequently within the population. As Darwin put it in a later work, there is a natural selection of those individuals best suited to survive.

This ability of species to change is crucial because the environment is always changing. Throughout the centuries, climates grow warmer and cooler, precipitation patterns change, and, as a result, so do animals' habitats. Some species are able to adapt to new conditions. Through natural selection, parents pass along useful characteristics to their offspring. Over generations, small physical changes are spread throughout the population, and the species survives. With enough small changes over a long period of time, the survivors become different from their ancestors. Species that cannot adapt to changing conditions eventually become extinct. It was Darwin's theory of gradual change that became popularly known as **evolution**.

Darwin's ideas outraged most religious believers. Although he had not discussed humans in his book, the implications were clear. If Darwin was correct, humans were much older than the six thousand years ascribed to them by the Christian church. The notion that humans might have evolved from another (presumably "lower") species was frightening. Most people

The Evolution of a Theory

In everyday conversation, the word *theory* is commonly used to refer to an idea that is tentative, unproven, or unreliable. Science uses the word *theory* differently. In science, a theory is the best possible explanation of all the available facts. A theory is not the final truth, but it is the best account of how something happens, according to what is known at the time. A theory thus represents an informed opinion based on thorough research and understanding. As new information is discovered, it must be related to the theory. If the theory accommodates the new information, it continues to act as the most appropriate framework. If the new information does not fit, a new theory must be developed.

Darwin's theory of evolution is really quite remarkable. It has survived the discovery of genes and the unravelling of the DNA molecule. These discoveries provided the key to heredity and the means by which small changes take place at the molecular level through time and random mutation. Although Darwin did not know about genes and DNA, the theory he developed was able to encompass the new information. Darwin also predicted that fossils would be found that showed animal species in transition. Although the pattern of evolution is more complicated than Darwin imagined, transitional fossils of birds, reptiles, and mammals have indeed been discovered. To scientists, evolution is the central fact of biology. As new facts are discovered, the theory is tested to see if it needs to be modified.

Indeed, Darwin's theory has been slightly revised by some of today's scientists. The fossil evidence suggests that sometimes evolution takes place more quickly than Darwin believed. In 1972, Stephen Jay Gould and Niles Eldredge proposed an explanation for this speed, called **punctuated equilibrium**. According to this view, the origin of new species occurs among groups that have become isolated from their main populations due to some relatively rapid geographical change. The isolated population must adapt rapidly to its new environment if it is to survive. Such changes may give it a better chance of survival in other regions as well. The new species spreads, quickly dominating the main populations that did not evolve. This sudden replacement of one species by a new one means that no fossils of the transition between the two species exist.

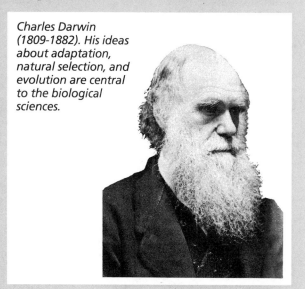

Charles Darwin (1809-1882). His ideas about adaptation, natural selection, and evolution are central to the biological sciences.

refused to believe this idea, but some wondered whether Darwin was on the right track in tracing the path of human development. More evidence was required.

The Fossil Record

A major source of evidence for evolution is the **fossil record**. To the scientist, the fossil record is a layered calendar in stone that shows the changes in animal development over time.

To form a fossil, an animal's body must lie undisturbed. The ideal location is at the edge of a river or lake. If enough rain falls, the water level rises and the skeleton is covered with silt and mud. Sometimes, the mud then hardens and, when the bones decay, an impression of the skeleton is left in the stone. In other cases, the skeleton is partly or wholly dissolved by water seeping through the stone, the hollow fills with minerals, and the skeleton is duplicated in stone. Because fossilization occurs in different ways, fossils come in a variety of types and shapes that represent bones, footprints, and tissue. Unfortunately fossils are rare. Usually when an animal dies, scavengers or passing herds move its bones. Hot weather and wind quickly break up the remaining pieces of bone, leaving nothing to fossilize.

After the publication of Darwin's book, several fossil finds suggested that humans are indeed much older than was originally thought. In 1891, Eugene Dubois discovered a tooth and skullcap along the Solo River in Java. At the same site, two years later, he found a thighbone. When combined with later

How Fossils Form.

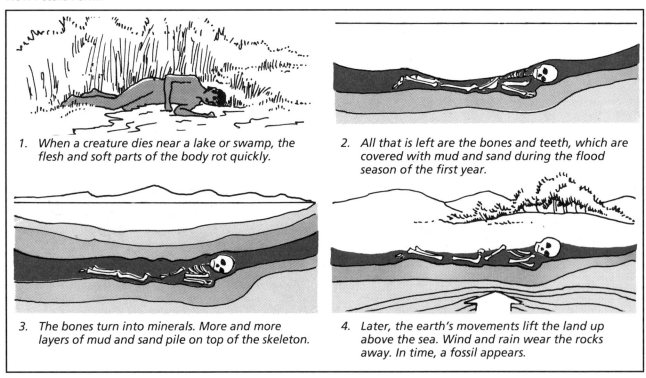

1. *When a creature dies near a lake or swamp, the flesh and soft parts of the body rot quickly.*

2. *All that is left are the bones and teeth, which are covered with mud and sand during the flood season of the first year.*

3. *The bones turn into minerals. More and more layers of mud and sand pile on top of the skeleton.*

4. *Later, the earth's movements lift the land up above the sea. Wind and rain wear the rocks away. In time, a fossil appears.*

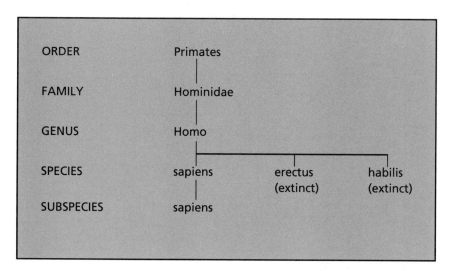

ORDER	Primates		
FAMILY	Hominidae		
GENUS	Homo		
SPECIES	sapiens	erectus (extinct)	habilis (extinct)
SUBSPECIES	sapiens		

The Biological Classification of Homo sapiens sapiens.

Science

Scientific names are an important part of the classification system used to describe living things. They are derived from Latin words and have at least two parts to them. Consider the term *Homo erectus*. The first part of the name, *Homo*, tells the **genus** of the organism. Living things that have a unique set of characteristics in common are grouped into a single genus. The second part, *erectus*, tells the **species**. Organisms of the same species can interbreed; organisms from different species cannot. A genus usually contains several different species.

finds from Europe, Africa, and Asia, a picture of a muscular, heavyset human relative emerged. It was eventually given the scientific name **Homo** (human) **erectus** (upright), based on its ability to walk upright, as present-day humans do. Scientists guessed that Homo erectus was about five hundred thousand years old, but, during the early twentieth century, there was no way to prove such a claim.

Scientists now became curious to know what species preceded Homo erectus. A possible answer to that question came in November 1924, when Dr. Raymond Dart received three crates from the limeworks at Taung, Botswana, delivered by a geologist friend. Among the rocks was the tiny fossil brain and skull of a six-year-old child. The hole where the spinal cord entered the brain was underneath the skull, which suggested the creature walked upright. In addition, its teeth were shaped like those of a modern human. The brain, however, was smaller than the brain of Homo erectus. In fact, it was nearer in size to that of an ape. The evidence suggested that this child would have been almost, but not quite, human. It became known as the "Taung Child," and Dart gave it a separate scientific name, **Australopithecus africanus** (southern ape of Africa). The age of Australopithecus was estimated at over a million years, but again there was no way to prove this. A technique known as **relative dating** established that fossils found in rock layers deeper in the ground were older than fossils found in layers nearer the surface, but this technique cannot give a date in years.

The importance of Australopithecus was immediately questioned when Dart published his findings in 1925. The leading anthropologist of the day, Sir Arthur Keith, declared that Australopithecus was not a human forerunner but belonged instead in the family of apes. Indeed, Australopithecus was long overshadowed by another find made earlier in the century.

This profile of a field site shows how relative dating works. Fossils from different times are layered in sequence in the fossil record.

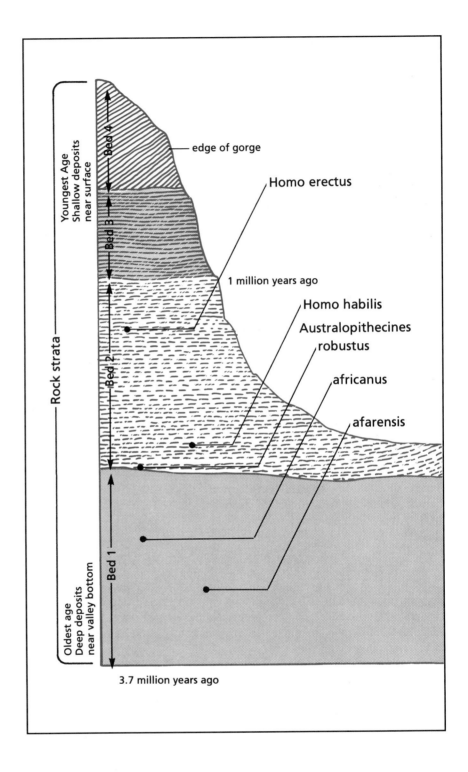

Piltdown Man: An Embarrassing Setback

In 1911, an amateur archaeologist named Charles Dawson made a startling discovery in a gravel pit at Piltdown, England, where he had been working for almost a decade. Dawson found a braincase comparable in size to that of a contemporary human. It was similar to cranial fragments found at the same site three years earlier. The project continued, and Dawson and another archaeologist uncovered an ape-like jaw with worn-down, human-shaped teeth. In 1912, Dawson proclaimed that a new human species had been found, and **Piltdown Man**, as it was popularly known, became a sensation. That this remarkable discovery was made in England at a time when England was a major world power gave the new find unwarranted credibility. The original Piltdown fossils were locked in a safe and access to them was extremely limited. Even so, most leading British scientists eagerly accepted Piltdown Man into the family of human ancestors. Keith had found his "first Englishman"! Years later, when Dart argued that Australopithecus was a human ancestor, Keith criticized him by pointing out that Piltdown's characteristics (large brain, ape-like jaw) were the reverse of Australopithecus's characteristics (small brain, human-like jaw).

In 1953, however, fluorine tests released by the British Museum showed that Piltdown Man was a fake. The bones of a modern man and an orangutan had been chemically treated and filed to give the appearance of fossils. It has been suggested that university students did it as a prank to fool their professors. The most intriguing evidence concerning the forgery, though, is an anonymous essay in a diary that describes the Piltdown find but is dated two days *before* the official announcement of the discovery. The diary belonged to Sir Arthur Keith!

Scientists had been fooled before. The very year that Piltdown Man was "discovered," the discovery of 2-million-year-old human remains in California had been exposed as a fraud. Similarly, "Nebraska Man," announced in 1922 on the basis of a single molar tooth, in six years was proven to be a fragment from an extinct pig! Despite such embarrassments, faith in science remained because scientists continually checked one another's work, developed better methods, and were willing to expose a hoax when it was uncovered.

The Pattern of Primate Evolution

Hoaxes aside, what can scientists tell us about the pattern of primate evolution? Many gaps still exist in the fossil record, but a general line of development has emerged.

The invention of new dating methods has been crucial. Until the 1950s, only relative dating was possible. Since then, however, a technique known as **absolute dating** (or **chronometric dating**) has been developed, based on the phenomenon of radioactive decay. Using the known rate for an isotope of potassium to change into argon gas, the age of volcanic

Timeline of Primate Development.

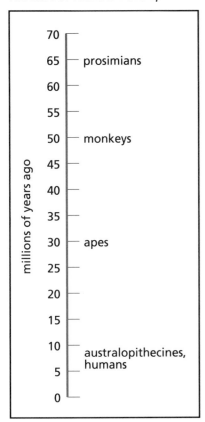

material in years can be determined. If a fossil is found close to this material, then the age of the fossil is known. Scientists usually conduct several tests until a consistent result from a pure sample is obtained.

The primate order, which includes prosimians, monkeys, apes, the australopithecines, and humans, slowly began to appear after the decline of the dinosaurs 65 million years ago. From the outset, the prosimians, small, tree-dwelling creatures, developed features common to all primates. They had clutching hands and binocular vision to distinguish depth and colour. Their descendants still live in the remote jungles of the world.

Between 50 and 45 million years ago, monkeys evolved from some of the prosimian lines into more than 150 different types. Their mastery of the treetops ensured their survival. Between 30 and 20 million years ago, the monkeys of Africa and southern Asia continued to change in response to their environment into several types of prehistoric apes. Scientists have intensely debated what happened next and how humans eventually evolved.

Darwin did not argue, as some people claim, that humans descended from species of apes that are alive today. He believed that humans and apes had a common ancestor at some time in the distant past. The fossils placed this point of divergence at 10-20 million years ago, when prehistoric apes known as the dryopithecines ("oak apes") lived in the shrinking African forests. Several kinds of prehistoric apes have been championed as our direct ancestor, but doubt has been raised about each candidate in recent years.

Beginning in the late 1960s, however, biochemist Vincent Sarich and microbiologist Allan Wilson pioneered techniques that compare blood proteins of living apes and humans. Since they began their work, additional **microbiological techniques** have enabled scientists to identify differences in the amino acids that make up blood proteins, and even to note differences in DNA and RNA molecules. From these complicated procedures, a **biological clock** has been worked out that shows humans and modern apes shared a common ancestor between 5 and 8 million years ago. Fossil specialists were initially unconvinced by this work. As the tests became more precise and consistent, and as new fossils supported the work of the microbiologists, this date became widely accepted.

Apparently, sometime around 5 or 6 million years ago, one species of prehistoric ape started down an evolutionary path that led to our own species. Many fossils exist of the different species that arose during the course of that evolution, although the relationship among the fossils is open to debate. But the major transitions are clear. The capacity to walk upright on two legs is one of them. This ability separates all apes, prehistoric and modern, from the australopithecines and humans. Although apes often appear to walk on two legs, they can do so only for brief periods. They always return to a four-legged stance. Significantly, the same muscles apes use to climb trees are the ones that humans use to walk. This means that the transition to an upright stance might not have been as difficult as

Differences Between Apes and Humans.

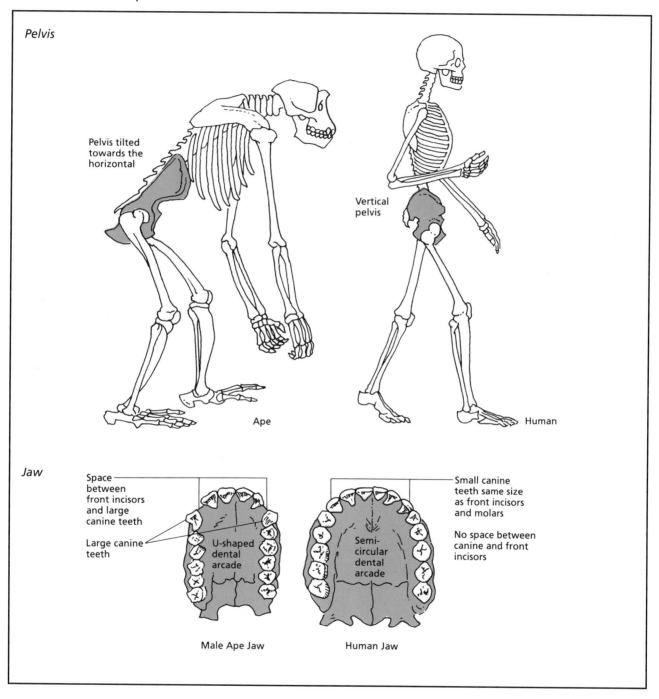

Pelvis

Pelvis tilted towards the horizontal

Vertical pelvis

Ape

Human

Jaw

Space between front incisors and large canine teeth

Large canine teeth

U-shaped dental arcade

Small canine teeth same size as front incisors and molars

No space between canine and front incisors

Semi-circular dental arcade

Male Ape Jaw

Human Jaw

Relationship Between Brain Size and Body Weight.

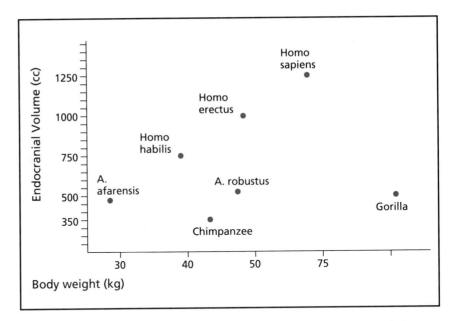

scientists used to believe. During the 1950s, scientists guessed that an upright stance might have been encouraged by the need to peer over tall grass on open ground. Today, other factors are thought to be more important. Walking upright freed the hands for using tools and carrying food to home base. It also enabled body heat to dissipate more easily.

The transition from a smaller to a larger brain was also important. Humans have a larger brain than any other primate; our large brain is one of our distinguishing characteristics. The average adult brain is about 1350 cm^3, over three times the size of the brain of a chimpanzee. Current fossil evidence suggests that humans began to develop larger brains about 2 million years ago. These early humans had a precision grip, made possible by a thumb set across from the fingers of the hand. This combination of a large brain and a precision grip enabled humans to make and use stone and probably wooden tools and weapons. Thus, superior intelligence became a means for human survival.

Australopithecus and Homo

Once the Piltdown forgery was revealed, many scientists had to alter their ideas about the course of human evolution, and they acknowledged that the australopithecines were a possible human ancestor. From the 1950s onward, many important fossils have been discovered, and there has been an effort made to determine which fossils are Australopithecus and which are Homo, and to discover how the fossils are related. The branch of science concerned with such matters is called **paleoanthropology**, the study of ancient humans. The Leakey family (Mary, her husband Louis, and their

Science

It used to be that fossil hunters would work in isolation. Mary and Louis Leakey, for example, spent three lonely decades working the fossil beds of the Olduvai Gorge in Tanzania. Then, in the late 1960s, F. Clark Howell introduced the idea of teams of experts working a single site. Such teams might include a geologist to study rocks, a palynologist to study fossil plant pollen, a pedologist to study soils, a paleoanthropologist to study fossil humans and their tools, and a photographer to make a visual record of the results.

The Great Rift Valley

The earth's crust is divided into several plates that actually float on the molten rock beneath them. These plates move very slowly, a phenomenon known as **continental drift**. The pulling apart and grinding together of plates causes earthquakes, volcanoes, and changing landforms.

Beginning about 25 million years ago, eastern Africa slowly began to pull away from the rest of the continent. Gradually the Great East African Rift Valley was formed. It runs south from Turkey, through Israel, the Afar Triangle, and Lake Turkana, to the region of the Zambezi River. The Great Rift Valley is currently as wide as 80 km and up to 300 m deep, and many important archaeological sites are within this area. Rivers have eroded gorges and exposed fossil-bearing sediments that scientists are now studying.

The relatively rapid and dramatic changes in altitude and drainage over short distances created diverse environments—parkland, forests, savanna, and lakes. Species were forced to adapt quickly to new conditions; it is likely that the first upright walkers evolved as a result.

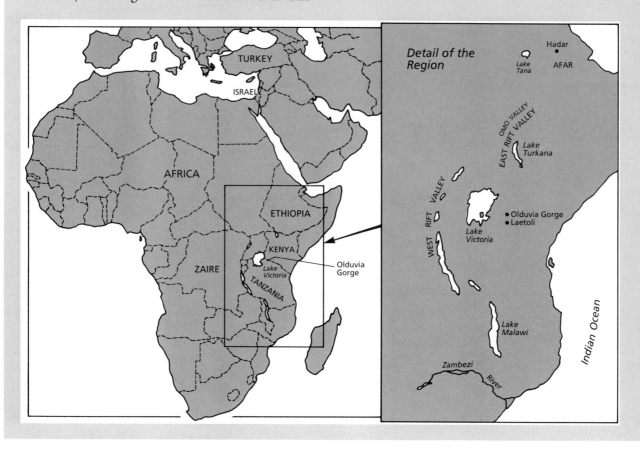

sons Richard and Jonathan) and Donald Johanson have been the chief paleoanthropologists of the late twentieth century.

Donald Johanson and his team, working near Hadar in the Afar region of Ethiopia, made several of the spectacular finds that ushered in a golden age of paleoanthropology in the 1970s and 1980s. In 1973, Johanson found a small knee joint of an upright walker; in 1974, the 40-percent-complete skeleton of an Australopithecus nicknamed "Lucy" became international news; in 1975 the remains of thirteen individuals, the so-called "First Family," were unearthed. These finds were securely dated at between 3 and 4 million years old.

The Afar region of Ethiopia is located in the **Great Rift Valley** of east Africa. The Leakeys also worked in the Great Rift Valley, but in Tanzania, 1500 km to the south of Johanson's finds. There they found fossil jaws and footprints that were the same age as the fossils Johanson discovered. Years earlier, in 1961, Jonathan Leakey had found a fragmentary skull that dated at 1.75 million years old. His father named the new species **Homo habilis** (handy human). In 1972, at Lake Turkana, Richard Leakey found another, much more complete, Homo habilis skull with a brain clearly larger than that of any australopithecine. The skull was given the laboratory number 1470 and was dated at about 1.9 million years old.

The Issue Emerges

The Leakeys and Donald Johanson are attempting to trace the actual path of human evolution. In essence, they are searching for the earliest human. They have formulated hypotheses based on the evidence outlined above and on a great deal of other evidence as well. But their interpretations of the evidence are quite different. The Leakeys believe that Homo habilis is the earliest known human, and that the much older Australopithecus fossils represent an evolutionary branch separate from humans. In other words, they believe that Australopithecus did *not* evolve into Homo. In Johanson's view, however, Australopithecus *is* a direct human ancestor. The following sections give the reasons behind each perspective. Which view is correct—or have the experts been fooled again?

PROBLEM QUESTION

Whose ideas about the origins of humans are more convincing: Donald Johanson's or Richard Leakey's?

ALTERNATIVE ONE: Blueprints from the Past

Based on *Lucy's Child* (1989) by Donald Johanson and James Shreeve, and *Blueprints* (1989) by Donald Johanson and Maitland Edey

The discovery of Lucy, an australopithecine, in 1974 was of crucial importance to the science of paleoanthropology. At 3.5 million years, she

---

More to Consider

In 1992, scientists determined that a piece of skull found in Kenya in 1967 is 2.4 million years old and should be classified in the genus Homo. This 8 cm scrap of bone is the oldest Homo fragment discovered so far. Unless an older species of Homo is identified, it is most likely a Homo habilis.

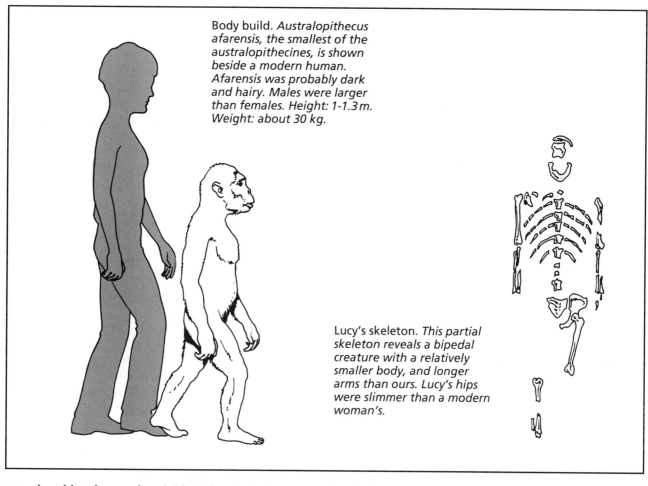

Body build. *Australopithecus afarensis, the smallest of the australopithecines, is shown beside a modern human. Afarensis was probably dark and hairy. Males were larger than females. Height: 1-1.3 m. Weight: about 30 kg.*

Lucy's skeleton. *This partial skeleton reveals a bipedal creature with a relatively smaller body, and longer arms than ours. Lucy's hips were slimmer than a modern woman's.*

Australopithecus afarensis.

was the oldest known hominid. (A hominid is an organism belonging to the family *Hominidae.* In the biological classification system, family is the level immediately above genus.) This date was obtained by cross-referencing five techniques: geology, fission-tracking, paleomagnetism, biostratigraphy, and potassium argon. Significantly, Lucy's skeleton was 40 percent complete. Humans are symmetrical creatures. A missing bone from one side can be duplicated from its mirror image on the other. This means that 80 percent of Lucy's skeleton can be reliably reconstructed. Usually skeletons are found in fragments or in isolated pieces, but with Lucy, a largely complete individual was available for study.

Lucy's partly worn wisdom teeth indicated she was an adult between twenty-five and thirty years old. Her knee joint and pelvis proved that she was the earliest-known upright walker. Lucy had a relatively small brain, the smallest of any hominid yet discovered. This surprised scientists who, at the time, believed that a larger brain would have evolved before the upright stance.

Johanson returned to Ethiopia's Afar region in 1975. His team made a striking discovery of several hundred teeth and pieces of bone at site 333. At least four children and nine adult males and females were identified. All thirteen individuals were killed in a single catastrophe—perhaps a flash flood—at the same moment. This discovery provided an opportunity to see large and small adults as well as children within a single group. Johanson dubbed the find "the First Family." They could be compared with Lucy, since all of them lived at about the same time.

Working with his colleague, Tim White, Johanson spent over two years analyzing the numerous fossils brought back from Ethiopia. White noticed that these fossils were similar in date and type to those that Mary Leakey's team had found at Laetoli in Tanzania. In addition, Mary Leakey had found the fossilized footprints of three hominids who were upright walkers. They were from a slightly earlier time than Lucy and the First Family. White had worked with the Leakey team and had helped to excavate and preserve the footprints. He was convinced that the fossils the two teams had found were from the same species, and he in turn convinced Johanson.

The fossil sites in Ethiopia and Tanzania are both located in the East African Rift Valley. Johanson and White believed that hominids walked up and down the Rift for over a million years, living along river banks and lake shores. In their view, Lucy, the First Family, and the Laetoli footprints and fossils were all linked, and warranted the naming of a new species, *Australopithecus afarensis*. In 1979, Johanson announced his conclusions.

When all of the existing fossil evidence was examined, it seemed to Johanson that the root stock of all the australopithecines and the Homo line was Australopithecus afarensis. In essence, this species was the origin of humans. Johanson believed that afarensis was the only hominid that lived before 3 million years, but additional finds in the 1980s placed the earliest member of the group at over 4 million years.

According to Johanson, the evolutionary history of humans can be summarized as follows. Between 3 and 2 million years ago, Australopithecus afarensis evolved in different directions in different regions of Africa. There was Australopithecus africanus, mentioned earlier, and also Australopithecus *robustus* and *boisei*, both of whom were larger. All became extinct. But in east and northeast Africa, afarensis evolved into Homo habilis by at least 2 million years ago, Homo erectus by 1.7 million years ago, and Homo sapiens by about three hundred thousand years ago.

Controversies

Working in Olduvai Gorge in 1986, Johanson and White found the remains of a female Homo habilis about the size of Lucy, which they nicknamed Lucy's Child. The proportions of her legs and upper arms are in between an ape's and a human's, which is exactly what would be expected. Nonetheless, Lucy's Child presents a problem to those who interpret fossils. Her arm proportions are *more* apelike than those of Lucy. If Homo habilis is indeed a descendant of Australopithecus afarensis, why are habilis's arm proportions *less* like a human than its predecessors?

Questions

1. Why was the discovery of Lucy so important?
2. How did the discovery of the First Family enable Johanson to develop and expand the importance of Lucy?
3. What influence did Tim White have on Johanson's views of human origins?
4. Why was the East African Great Rift Valley important to Johanson and White's views?
5. What were the stages—the different lines of development—that Johanson now believes are part of early hominid evolution?

ALTERNATIVE TWO: The Making of Humans

Based on *The Making of Mankind* (1982) by Richard Leakey, *A Guide To Koobi Fora* (1988) by Meave Leakey and Richard Leakey, and *Origins Reconsidered* (1992) by Richard Leakey and Roger Lewin

In 1979, Johanson announced his evidence for the new species Australopithecus afarensis. Mary Leakey strongly disagreed. She believed that the fossils she had found in Tanzania were more like a type of Homo, and that they differed in important respects from those Johanson had found in Ethiopia. This dispute began a bitter and continuing feud between Johanson and the Leakey family. The Leakeys had always contended that the human line (Homo) was very ancient. Although Louis, Mary, and their son Richard had their own interpretations, all agreed that the australopithecines were *not* ancestral to Homo.

In Richard's view, the lineage that leads to modern humans probably began with a species of bipedal prehistoric ape about 7.5 million years ago. It seems likely that this founding species eventually evolved into *several* new species, a process known as *adaptive radiation.* Fossil sites between 7.5 and 4 million years have not yet been excavated. When such evidence is uncovered, it will probably show that the Homo line emerged first, and that Australopithecus was an intriguing side branch that ultimately became extinct.

According to Richard Leakey, the First Family discovered by Donald Johanson should not be collectively classified as Australopithecus afarensis. What Johanson calls males are twice as big as the so-called females of the First Family. It is true that there was a large difference in size between male and female australopithecines, but the *extreme* difference in size in the remains Johanson discovered more logically suggests that the fossils represent two species rather than one.

The large fossils (and the footprints at Laetoli) are most likely from the Homo line. What was happening with Homo that far back is not clear at present. Too few fossils of the Homo line have been found between 3 and 2 million years old to unmask the real pattern of human evolution.

These fossilized hominid footprints were found by Mary Leakey (shown here) and her team at Laetoli.

Controversies

The difference in brain size between Australopithecus afarensis (400-425 cm³) and Homo habilis (650-800 cm³) is very important. A 50 percent increase in brain size in a million years (or less) is most unlikely. This disparity makes it difficult to accept afarensis as the root stock for the genus Homo.

Until that problem is corrected, the large fossils Johanson uncovered cannot be confidently categorized. The later stages of Homo's evolution are better known. Between 3 and 2 million years ago, global cooling formed the arctic icecap and brought drier climates to the rest of the world. This, in turn, led to the fragmentation of the East African habitats and presented an evolutionary challenge. Homo adjusted to these climate and habitat changes by learning to use stone tools. As a result, the Homo brain began to expand. Evidence shows that both these developments were occurring about 2.5 million years ago. Larger brains require more food energy, so Homo added meat to its diet. About 1 million years ago, Homo erectus migrated out of Africa and spread throughout the temperate regions of the world. Homo sapiens evolved from Homo erectus in Africa, Europe, and Asia about three hundred thousand years ago.

The smaller fossils in Johanson's First Family are probably examples of Australopithecus afarensis who, like the famous Lucy, lived between 3 and 4 million years ago. As many as four species of australopithecines may have evolved in slightly different ecological niches from afarensis. This evolutionary branching again can probably be attributed to the climate changes. At first, the different species of Australopithecus thrived, but eventually each one became extinct. Their disappearance could be linked to the success of Homo erectus and other animals, whose expanding populations might have encroached on australopithecine habitats, decreasing the amount of available food.

Questions

1. Why did a bitter feud develop between the Leakey family and Donald Johanson?
2. According to Richard Leakey, why can the fossils of the First Family not be collectively classified as Australopithecus afarensis?
3. Why is the difference in brain size between afarensis and Homo habilis significant?
4. Are Leakey's arguments about the ancestry of the Homo line convincing? Explain your answer.

ANSWERING THE PROBLEM QUESTION

It is very difficult for a person with limited expertise in an area to choose between viewpoints developed by experts. But there are steps you can take to help you make a choice. Once you understand the views of each author,

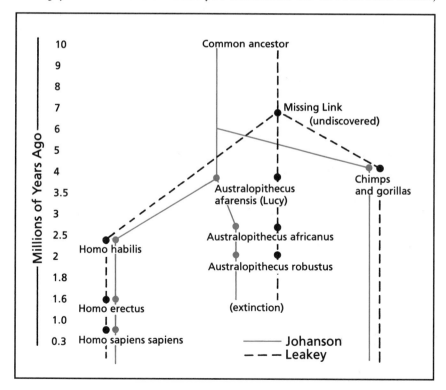

Johanson's and Leakey's Views of Human Evolution.

compare them carefully. Where the two authors agree, there is a good chance the information is reliable. Where they disagree, a way must be developed to see which one is on the right track.

For example, you might focus on the key characteristics that distinguish humans from all other living primates. What does the fossil evidence say about the emergence of these characteristics? When viewed in this way, does the evidence seem to tie in with either of the two theories presented?

Taking a different line, review the two explanations and look for key arguments. Can you identify any weak spots? Are important questions left hanging?

THE STORY CONTINUES . . .

The First Tool Makers

The earliest hominids yet discovered appeared over 1.5 million years before stone tools were developed. They probably used or made tools out of sticks and perhaps out of bone, but these perishable materials left no artifacts to be found. The earliest known tools, therefore, are made of stone and were found at Hadar (2.5 million years) and in the Omo Valley (2.1 million years), both of which are located in Ethiopia, and at Lokalelei (2.5 million years) on the western shores of Lake Turkana. They are classified as **Lower Paleolithic** (Earliest Stone Age), which refers to stone tools over two hundred thousand years old. Tools are presumed to be the result of human activity, but no fossils of Homo have ever been found in close proximity to these earliest examples. Most scientists believe that Homo habilis was responsible for the production of the tools, since the oldest Homo remains extend to about 2.4 million years.

Homo erectus, which evolved from Homo habilis about 1.7 million years ago, was significantly different. Where habilis stood between 1 and 1.5 m in height, with a bulky body and arm proportions between apes and humans, Homo erectus had the height, slimmer body, and arm proportions of modern humans. An almost complete Homo erectus skeleton of a twelve-year-old boy, found by Kamoya Kimeu in Kenya in 1984, was 1.62 m. The boy would have been 1.8 m tall if he had reached adulthood. Erectus was also more intelligent, having a brain size between 800 and 1100 cm^3. Fossil evidence shows that the brain's speech centre was more pronounced in erectus, suggesting that erectus had more sophisticated vocal skills. Clearly, major changes had taken place in the transition from habilis to erectus.

The tool technology of erectus reflected these evolutionary advances. A new type of Lower Paleolithic tool industry known as **Acheulian** emerged about 1.5 million years ago and is typified by the teardrop-shaped hand axe. Such stone tools (and probably other tools made of wood) gave early humans additional control over the way they lived by

Science

Since the 1960s, the amount of evidence from prehistoric sites has greatly increased; there are significant remains from over a thousand individuals found at hundreds of sites. It is important to keep in mind, however, that scientists have relatively little information about how human ancestors actually lived their lives millions or even tens of thousands of years ago. Scientists use the direct evidence they have as the basis for reasonable speculations about how prehistoric humans might have behaved. But all descriptions of prehistoric life contain speculation. Theories about early human behaviour are continually being rethought and revised as new evidence is found or as better explanations are offered. For example, as our views about women have changed in modern times, so have our assumptions about the roles of women among prehistoric humans.

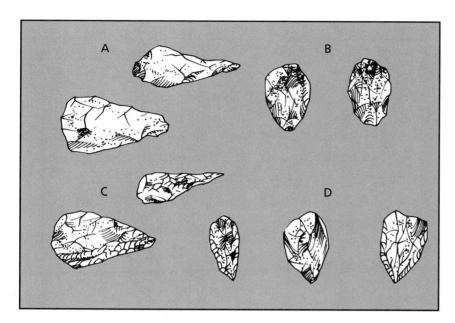

Stone Tools. A) Hand-axes were used by Homo erectus in Africa 500 000 years ago. B) At the same time, Homo erectus in south-east Asia were using less sophisticated chopping implements. C) The hand-axes of 250 000 years ago had become flatter, with straighter edges. D) Neandertal Man often worked with flakes of stone rather than larger pieces. The two scrapers and the spearhead were made 70 000 years ago.

helping them with their hunting and enabling them to skin animals and build small shelters.

Among the most important influences in the development of Homo erectus was fire. The earliest use of fire has been dated at 1.4 million years ago in Kenya. Homo erectus learned to save and use the coals from fires started by lightning and lava flows. This led to both physical and cultural changes. As cooked meat was added to the diet, for example, the size of the large molars once needed to grind tough food was gradually reduced. Fire's warmth meant that Homo erectus could live in colder parts of the world. Fire also provided security. By lighting up the darkness, erectus was able to fend off wild animals.

At the campsite, women, children, and the elderly tended the fire and gathered the fruit, nuts, and vegetables that were the essential part of the group's diet. Homo erectus males were the hunters. Initially, they probably had limited success in killing even small animals, but their techniques improved, and by five hundred thousand years ago, large-scale elephant hunts were occurring in Europe.

The use of technology gave Homo erectus a competitive advantage. Presumably, tool manufacture and use are linked to brain size and intelligence. Increases in intelligence leading to improved tool use were encouraged by natural selection. Over thousands and thousands of generations, this selection led to the physical and mental development of the brain. Homo erectus was physically capable of making only slow and clumsy speech, but it is likely that these prehistoric humans were verbalizing their experiences. The critical ability to use language was beginning.

Fossil Bearing Sites.

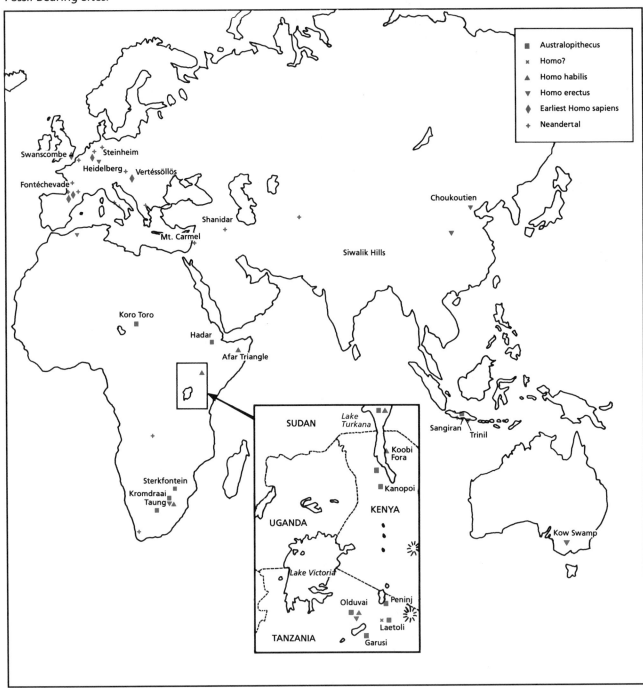

The Emergence of Homo Sapiens

Traditional interpretations of fossil evidence suggested that all modern humans could trace their beginnings back to about 1 million years ago. At this time, Homo erectus first left Africa and eventually reached Asia, Europe, and Indonesia. In each area, Homo erectus continued to evolve into **Homo sapiens** (human the wise) in response to local conditions. Thus, regional lines of development produced Asians, Europeans, and Indonesians. This view of Homo's development is known as the **multi-regional model**.

Many of the fossils found between four hundred thousand and one hundred and thirty thousand years ago show transitional characteristics. A skull from Arago, France, (four hundred thousand years old) possesses both erectus and sapiens features. This skull is larger, more rounded, and has smaller brow ridges than a typical Homo erectus skull. Yet its features are more angular and less refined than those of Homo sapiens. The Swanscombe skull (two hundred and fifty thousand years old), found in the interglacial gravels of the Thames estuary in Kent, England, is one of the earliest fossils to show clear sapiens features—a larger, rounded skull and smaller browridges and teeth.

During the 1970s, however, a new time frame for the development of Homo sapiens was proposed. The microbiologists who had demonstrated that humans and apes diverged between 5 and 8 million years ago applied their techniques to the origin of Homo sapiens. Allan Wilson and his team developed a new way of tracing humanity's development by using genetic material outside the cell nucleus called **mitochondrial DNA** (MDNA). These rod-like structures are inherited only in the female line. They do not change as they are passed from mother to daughter to granddaughter and so on unless they are affected by random mutations. Wilson's studies indicated that MDNA mutates at a regular rate of 2 to 4 percent per million years. If the differences in MDNA among populations living the world over could be determined, the constant rate of mutation could be used to determine the time period in which these accumulated differences began. This **molecular clock** would establish the date from which populations diverged from a common ancestor.

Under Wilson's guidance, Rebecca Cann and Mark Stoneking tested MDNA samples and did studies of women from Europe, Asia, Africa, New Guinea, and Australia. They found that human populations were remarkably alike. Their MDNA varied only half of 1 percent, with the greatest variation occurring in people of African descent. Cann and Stoneking concluded that Homo sapiens emerged from a small band of Africans between one hundred and fifty thousand and two hundred and fifty thousand years ago. These dates are quite different from the previous figure of 1 million years given by paleoanthropologists. When these results were announced in 1987, they became known as the **Eve hypothesis**, and, later, as the **Out of Africa model**.

Controversies

News of the Eve hypothesis shocked those scientists who had relied mainly on the finding of fossils to identify human ancestors. Some paleoanthropologists continue to dispute the dates provided by the microbiologists, while others argue that the fossils support the Eve theory. This professional controversy will no doubt continue with much heated debate.

"Neither the genetic information of living subjects nor the fossilized remains of dead ones can explain in isolation how, when, and where populations originated. But the former evidence has a crucial advantage in determining the structure of family trees: living genes must have ancestors, whereas dead fossils may not have descendants. Molecular biologists know the genes they are examining must have been passed through lineages that survived to the present; paleontologists cannot be sure that the fossils they examine do not lead down an evolutionary blind alley."

Allan Wilson and Rebecca Cann, microbiologists

"Mitochondrial DNA is useful for guiding the development of theories, but only fossils provide the basis for refuting one idea or the other. At best, the genetic information explains how modern humans might have originated if the assumptions used in interpreting the genes are correct, but one theory cannot be used to test another. The fossil record is the real evidence for human evolution, and it is rich in both human remains and archaeological sites stretching back for a million years. Unlike the genetic data, fossils can be matched to the predictions of theories about the past without relying on a long list of assumptions."

Alan G. Thorne and Milford Wolpoff, paleoanthropologists

According to Cann and Stoneking, Homo erectus evolved into different types of Homo sapiens in Africa about two hundred thousand years ago. One successful line, perhaps between one hundred and thirty thousand and one hundred thousand years ago, developed into our modern subspecies (**Homo sapiens sapiens**). The relatively small population of 4000 individuals successfully survived in new environments and spread out of Africa. By sixty thousand years ago, these fully modern humans appeared in Java. It took the next twenty thousand years for them to reach China. By 35 000 B.C., they had arrived in Europe and Australia, while between 30 000 and 12 000 B.C. they crossed the Bering land bridge to populate the Americas. (For an alternate theory and date of arrival in Australia, see the sidebar on page 25.) Wherever and whenever they arrived, these Homo sapiens sapiens replaced the slightly less advanced types of Homo sapiens. Cann believes that an influx of new diseases arrived with Homo sapiens sapiens, which contributed to the demise of their competitors. Others have argued that Homo sapiens sapiens pushed local Homo sapiens populations to extinction through violence or through better technology, food gathering, and shelter

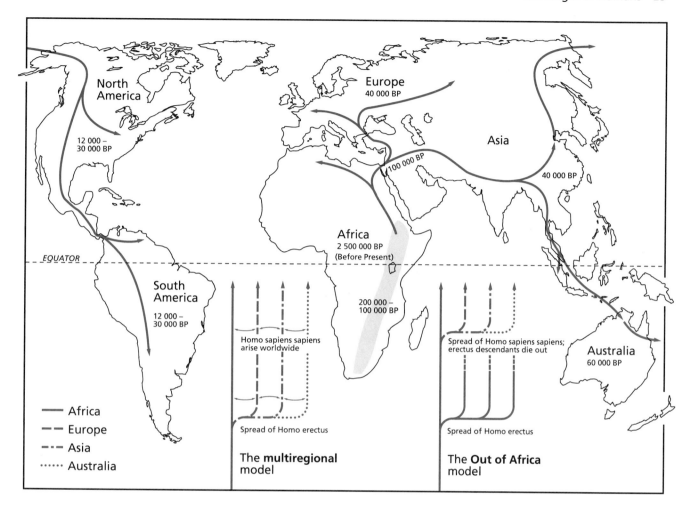

The Origin of Modern Humans.

The multiregional model:
115 000 years ago Homo sapiens sapiens arose simultaneously from Homo erectus populations around the world.

The Out of Africa model:
115 000 years ago a small population of sapiens sapiens arose in Africa and spread, displacing descendants of Homo erectus around the world.

building. Perhaps Homo sapiens was absorbed into Homo sapiens sapiens through interbreeding.

Among those who either perished or became absorbed was a type of Homo sapiens whose remains were found in the Neander Valley of Germany in 1856. This was the famous **Neandertal Man**, who was at first seen as an oddity rather than a possible human relative. A similar specimen found in Spain eight years earlier had been largely ignored. As more and more finds were made over the next century, it became clear that Neandertal Man had ranged from Europe to the Near East, Africa, and Asia during the final stage of the Ice Age.

The Neandertals lived in Europe between one hundred and thirty thousand and thirty thousand years ago. They were shorter in height than Homo sapiens sapiens, and had shorter arms, much heavier bones, and

Homo habilis
Height: 1.2-1.5 m
Weight: 50 kg

Homo erectus
Height: 1.5-1.8 m
Weight: 40-72 kg

Homo sapiens sapiens
Height: 1.69-1.77 m
Weight: 68 kg

Three Species of the Genus Homo.

greater physical strength. In addition, a Neandertal skull is broader, has a sloping forehead, and is slightly larger. Their tools were more advanced than those used by Homo erectus, but did not develop much further, perhaps because Neandertal was struggling against the cold of the Ice Age climate. There seems to have been a definite Neandertal culture. Evidence suggests that they buried their dead, cared for the sick and the elderly, and probably developed some kind of language. In Europe, they co-existed with Homo sapiens sapiens for at least five thousand years before they disappeared as a distinct group for reasons that are not clear.

The earliest Homo sapiens sapiens yet discovered were found in South Africa, and date from between one hundred and thirty thousand and one hundred thousand years ago. If the Out of Africa model is valid, these remains might represent the founding population of modern humans. The fifteen individuals found at Jebel Qafzeh in Israel, whose remains are ninety to one hundred thousand years old, could be the vanguard of the sapiens sapiens who were about to spread throughout the globe and dominate other species of Homo.

Although Homo sapiens sapiens have existed for over one hundred thousand years, it was not until about forty thousand years ago that a cultural explosion occurred, which led to new types of stone and bone tools, as well as the creation of art and elaborate burial rituals. In Europe, Homo sapiens sapiens are represented by **Cro-Magnon**, named after the French

Cro-Magnon artists worked by the light of tallow lamps made of stone to create the cave paintings in Lascaux, France. Rocks on the cave floor provided the black and red pigments.

cave in which the original find was made in 1868. Cro-Magnon became the finest hunter of the Paleolithic era. They made spear points from reindeer antlers and developed the spear-thrower, a wooden or bone lever that functions as an extension of the arm and increases the power of the throw. Blade point manufacture was raised to an art form. Rawhide snares were used to trap foxes, three-pronged spears to catch fish, dugout canoes for travel, and animal leather was sewn with a bone needle to provide warm clothing. The gathering of plants was well organized, stopping just short of seed planting.

Cro-Magnon was the first European to develop fine art. Although cave art started slightly earlier in Africa, Cro-Magnon left impressive drawings at sites such as the Lascaux Caves in France and the Altamira Caves in Spain. They usually show deer, horses, bison, and animals that are now extinct. Even more intriguing are the figurines of clay, ivory, and stone found from France to Russia. They are called **Venus figurines** because of the exaggerated curves used to show the female body. Some date to about 30 000 B.C. Experts suspect that they may represent fertility symbols that were connected with the worship of a mother goddess.

There is additional evidence of Cro-Magnon religion. The skeletons of two boys who died twenty-three thousand years ago were found laid head-to-head in a grave in Sungir, Russia. Finely made beads, ivory jewellery, and mammoth-tusk spears and daggers were found with the bodies. This suggests they were laid to rest according to some ritual, perhaps in preparation for an afterlife.

More to Consider

Scientists have long been puzzled about why sapiens sapiens's cultural development took so long to occur and why it happened so suddenly. Then, in 1988, archaeologists Alison Brooks and John Yellen found some bone harpoons in Zaïre. They were crafted as well as any of the paleolithic tools found in Europe, but they dated from forty thousand years earlier, to eighty thousand years. As well, new dating methods indicated that Homo sapiens sapiens reached Australia sixty thousand, not thirty-five thousand, years ago. This would mean that the ancestors of the Australian aborigines were sailing open-ocean vessels about twenty thousand years before the cultural explosion occurred in Europe. Perhaps future evidence will confirm that sapiens sapiens's cultural advance began much earlier than has been supposed.

When God was a Woman

Venus figurines have been interpreted by Merlin Stone and others as evidence of a widespread **matrilineal culture**. A matrilineal culture is one in which lines of descent are traced through the female, not the male, side. In a matrilineal culture, women occupy important social and religious positions.

Stone speculates that Upper Paleolithic (Later Stone Age) peoples might not have understood the relationship between sex and procreation, just as some of the tribal peoples of today do not. Mothers were seen as the sole producers of children, and children would therefore take their mother's name. Studies of Paleolithic sites show that these cultures practised ancestor worship. They probably traced their history back through a line of women to the creator, a female god, the divine ancestress. It is possible that these cultures led to the goddess-worshipping societies of the Near and Middle East in Neolithic (New Stone Age) times.

Venus of Willendorf, 27 000 years old.

As the Neandertals of Europe slowly disappeared, Cro-Magnon, the innovator, survived. Rapid cultural development would follow.

SUMMARY

Where did human beings come from? Most peoples have creation stories that provide an answer to this question. For people in the Judeo-Christian tradition, the biblical stories in the Book of Genesis explain the origin of humans. Until the nineteenth century, Christians generally believed that the world was created only a few thousand years ago, and that humans and all other life had been created instantly and had not changed much over time.

In the nineteenth century, people began to question that view of the world's history. Charles Darwin published his revolutionary work, *On the Origin of Species*, in 1859, arguing that the earth had existed much longer than was thought, that some species had changed over time, and that other species had become extinct. He proposed a process called natural selection: organisms with advantageous characteristics are more likely to survive and pass along those characteristics to their offspring. Darwin's theory of change in species became known as evolution. His ideas were generally ridiculed because they violated several fundamental Christian beliefs of the time. As fossils were discovered and studied, however, his theories began to be accepted.

At first scientists had no convincing method for assigning dates to the fossils that were found. But as techniques of relative dating and absolute dating have been refined, scientists have formulated a relatively clear picture of humanity's evolutionary history, based on many important fossil discoveries. A number of microbiological procedures have been equally important. By comparing the blood proteins of humans and apes, scientists have been able to map out a probable evolutionary time frame.

Sixty-five million years ago, the dinosaurs vanished, and gradually the primates appeared. Monkeys evolved between 50 and 45 million years ago, and they in turn evolved into prehistoric species of apes between 30 and 20 million years ago. Based on the findings of microbiologists, scientists now believe that humans began to evolve from a species of prehistoric ape between 6 and 5 million years ago.

The change from ape to human took millions of years and involved a couple of important transitions. One was the development of the upright stance; the other was the enlargement of the brain. The ability to walk on two legs was present at least 4 million years ago in a species known as Australopithecus afarensis. Fossils show that afarensis had an upright stance but not the large brain that characterizes the species of the genus Homo. The large brain seems to have developed about 2 million years ago and is present in the first Homo species known to us, Homo habilis.

The paleoanthropologist Donald Johanson found many Australopithecus fossils in Ethiopia during the 1970s and 1980s. He believes that Australopithecus afarensis evolved into several other species of Australopithecus that became extinct, and also into the species Homo habilis. This path would make Australopithecus a direct human ancestor.

The Leakey family, also notable paleoanthropologists, disagree with Johanson's interpretation of the fossil evidence. In their view, the ancestor of Homo habilis is a Homo species that has not yet been discovered, not Australopithecus afarensis. They believe that the Australopithecus species are just a side branch from the main branch of human evolution. The debate between Johanson and the Leakeys cannot be absolutely resolved without further evidence.

In either case, it seems that habilis appeared over 2 million years ago. Habilis had a large brain and a precision grip, and was thus able to make and use tools. Tool use gave habilis a competitive advantage and encouraged the further development of the brain.

Habilis evolved into the species known as Homo erectus about 1.7 million years ago. Erectus was quite different from habilis. Habilis was short and had long arms. Erectus was about as tall as modern humans and had arms the same length as ours. A larger brain made erectus more intelligent, and consequently erectus had more sophisticated tools. By about 1.4 million years ago, this new species had learned how to use fire and was living in temporary campsites. Women, children, and the elderly tended the fire and gathered most of the food—fruit, nuts, and vegetables. The males were hunters, although at first their rare kills provided very little of erectus's food. Probably erectus was able to use language to a small extent.

In the 1970s, the microbiologists Rebecca Cann and Mark Stoneking studied the mitochondrial DNA (MDNA) from women around the world and concluded that Homo erectus evolved into Homo sapiens about two hundred thousand years ago in Africa. According to the Eve hypothesis, also called the Out of Africa model, as their theory is known, Homo sapiens then evolved into our own subspecies, Homo sapiens sapiens, between one hundred and thirty thousand and one hundred thousand years ago. Some paleoanthropologists dispute the Eve hypothesis and continue to look for fossil evidence that will show that Homo sapiens is older than the microbiologists believe.

The remains of the oldest known sapiens sapiens were found in South Africa and date from between one hundred and thirty and one hundred thousand years old. At least forty thousand years ago, and probably much earlier, sapiens sapiens developed a sophisticated culture. Bone and stone tools were refined, artistic practices were broadened, and religious rituals were made more elaborate. Sapiens sapiens had moved outward from Africa by that time. As they spread, they either exterminated or interbred with the less advanced types of Homo sapiens they encountered. In Europe, Neandertal Man, a type of Homo sapiens, lived alongside Cro-Magnon, a type of homo sapiens sapiens, for at least five thousand years, but it was the Cro-Magnons who dominated and survived.

2
The Rise of Civilization

Date	Event
B.C.	
100 000-40 000	Homo sapiens evolves into Homo sapiens sapiens--Cro-Magnon
16 000	Earliest agriculture occurs in the Nile Valley
10 000	Rapid extensive flooding occurs in the Gulf of Mexico from glacial meltwater
9500	Earliest domestication of cattle occurs in southern Europe and Egypt
c. 9000	Neolithic Era begins
8000	Jericho emerges as a settlement of at least two thousand people
3800	First city-states develop in Sumer
3400	Wheel originates in Sumer Earliest-known pictographic writing appears in Sumer
3000	*Approximate date of Noah's flood according to Creationist writers*
2800	Sumerian writing evolves into cuneiform script
2600	Plough developed in the Middle East Variety of gods and heroes glorified in *The Epic of Gilgamesh* in Middle East
2300	Sargon rules all Mesopotamia, creating the earliest-known empire
2100	Ur-Nammu establishes Third Dynasty, Sumer's last empire Oldest-known legal code developed by Ur-Nammu
1750	Under Hammurabi, Babylon becomes centre of Mesopotamian world
1000-700	Assyrians conquer Mesopotamia First-known library established at Nineveh
700-612	Rebellion causes dissolution of Assyrian Empire

2

The Rise of Civilization

BACKGROUND

The First Cities

Upper Paleolithic Homo sapiens sapiens improved on their ancestors' way of life. They ate better and had better clothes and tools. Dwellings made of wood, animal bones, and skins enabled them to stay in one place for weeks or even months. Yet, despite these changes, their lives remained basically nomadic. In addition to gathered foods, they depended on a diet of meat, which meant that they had to follow migrating animals.

The last Ice Age occurred during the final stages of the Paleolithic Era, which must have made life a challenge for Homo sapiens sapiens. A cooler climate resulted in the southward expansion of glaciers into several present-day temperate zones. With an enormous volume of water locked up in continental ice sheets, sea level dropped upwards of 100 m and exposed land bridges between islands and continents. About 10 000 B.C., the climate of the earth warmed, the sea level rose as the ice melted, and the land bridges were eliminated.

This period marked the transition from the Paleolithic to the **Neolithic** (New Stone Age) Era. Neolithic culture was characterized by a variety of activities and accomplishments: the domestication of animals and the introduction of agriculture, weaving (including basket making and rope making), stone polishing, pottery making, and the construction of lasting habitation, which led to a sedentary life. No location developed all of these features at the same time. Each development emerged gradually from local circumstances and needs. New practices may have been tried, abandoned, and retried many times before lifestyles were permanently and significantly altered.

There is evidence that the domestication of animals *may* go back thirty thousand years. Some cave paintings of that period show a line that could be a harness across the muzzle of a horse. In France, a fifteen-thousand-year-old horse-head carved in stone seems to be embraced by a harness of rope. Cattle were probably domesticated in Kenya at about the same date.

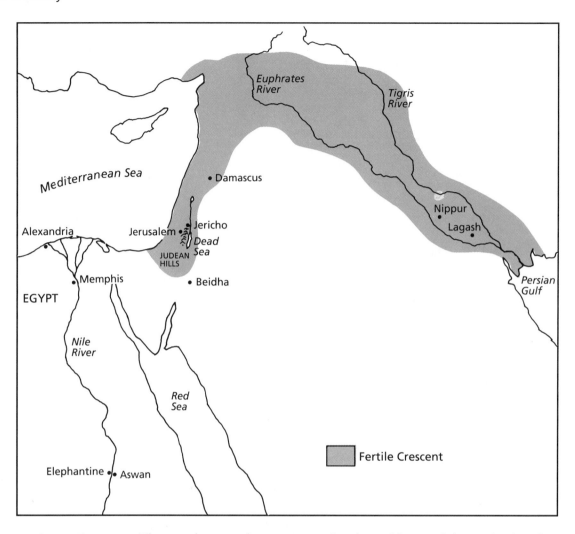

The Fertile Crescent. The Fertile Crescent in the Middle East is a region of relatively high precipitation. Here archaeologists have found the most conclusive evidence of early plant (particularly barley and wheat) cultivation and animal domestication. Seven thousand years ago, the Tigris and Euphrates rivers flowed separately into the Persian Gulf because the sea penetrated much farther inland.

These early examples are suggestive, but widespread domestication first became entrenched in the **Fertile Crescent** between 8000 and 5000 B.C.

The precise date for the beginning of food production is also difficult to determine. Gathering wild fruits and nuts became almost systematic by the late Upper Paleolithic Era. Experimentation with seed growing probably took place in several locations before the techniques of agriculture were mastered and used by succeeding generations. Kernels, grinding stones, and stone blades with silica from plants, all dating to between 18 000 and 12 500 B.C., have been uncovered at various Egyptian sites. It remains uncertain, however, if the stage of true agriculture, which involves deliberate planting and harvesting, was reached this early. This promising beginning was lost when a series of Nile floods about 10 000 B.C.

forced the prehistoric Egyptians to turn to fishing and hunting, which were more reliable.

At **Jericho**, in present-day Israel, several elements of what has been called the "Neolithic Revolution" gradually came together. In typical middle-eastern fashion, successive occupants of the Jericho site built and rebuilt on the same ground. Original structures were covered with later ones. This building and rebuilding created an enormous mound known as a **tell**, several examples of which dot the region. The tell at Jericho was first explored by Kathleen Kenyon between 1951 and 1958, and her excavations reached all the way to the lowest level. Jericho's earliest inhabitants were the Natufians, a hunter-gatherer society that built temporary shelters there between 9500 and 9000 B.C. They lived a semi-nomadic existence ranging from the Nile Delta to the Judean Hills, and they may have incorporated elements from communities along the Nile into their settlement at Jericho. Although they were nomads, the sickles they left behind suggest they harvested wild plants.

Between 9000 and 8000 B.C., the later inhabitants of Jericho practised true agriculture, though it was only in its infancy. Other sites in Syria and Iraq show similar patterns at about the same time. At Jericho, the proportion of sheep and goats compared to wild gazelle had increased noticeably by 8000 B.C., and the trend continued more dramatically over the following thousand years.

Jericho's most striking feature, however, was the wall, 2-3 m thick, that enclosed the 5 ha (hectare) site. The wall and the massive 10 m watchtower near one of the two town gates indicate that the two thousand or so residents of Jericho feared attack.

The First City-States

Civilization is a slippery term. The dictionary defines a civilization as "an advanced society." But what does it mean to be "advanced"? The Mayan civilization did not have cities as we think of them, but they did build gigantic ceremonial complexes and had a marvelous understanding of mathematics. The Minoan civilization established a sophisticated trading network and possessed a system of writing, but seems not to have kept records of its own history. Obviously, it is not possible to be precise about the ingredients that make up a civilization. In the simplest terms, a civilization is what results when large numbers of people work together to sustain themselves. Usually they settle in one area. They devise systems to co-ordinate their efforts and organize the tasks to be achieved. These systems become increasingly complex legal codes, formalized religions, monetary systems, systems of government, and written languages. People's work becomes specialized; they provide one another with goods and services and are mutually interdependent. Often there are cities containing marketplaces, storehouses, temples, residences, administrative buildings, and sites for manufacturing. It

More to Consider

In nomadic societies, men hunted while women gathered the fruits, nuts, and grains essential for survival. It thus seems likely that a female developed agriculture. Since agriculture was the central feature of the Neolithic Revolution, the status of women was probably very high. This prestige was reflected in the dominance of the Mother Goddess throughout the Neolithic world.

More to Consider

On Elephantine Island at Aswan, Egypt, archaeologists have unearthed a town gate that predates Jericho. Mud-brick dwellings that surround the gate have not yet been accurately dated. The results may indicate that, as far as we know, the world's first town was situated along the Nile.

Jericho

The site for Jericho was probably selected because of its location on a natural trade route. It is easy to imagine that travellers were lured by the natural spring (which still nourishes the ground) and the convenient supplies of salt from the Dead Sea, used to preserve meat.

Trade was conducted in Jericho as early as 8500 B.C., and by 7000 B.C. Jericho's water and food supplies would have made it a logical stop for traders. Since there was no money, they would have done their business using a **barter system**—one good exchanged for another. Traders from the north offered **obsidian** and greenstone in return for the hematite (iron ore) and sea shells of the south. Significant amounts of all of these objects have been unearthed at Jericho.

Obsidian, a volcanic glass, was fashioned into razor-sharp tools and weapons, and was also used as a mirror or to make fine works of art. It was one of the most valued materials traded among the widespread towns of the prehistoric Middle East. City dwellers living near obsidian-producing volcanoes probably stockpiled obsidian to exchange for farm produce. Evidence suggests that trade in obsidian began as early as thirty thousand years ago. By tracing the obsidian found in objects uncovered during archaeological digs, scholars have been able to establish four distinct (but overlapping) trade routes.

Other minerals—salt, hematite, copper, and soapstone—accelerated trade around 8000 B.C. This may well explain the sudden growth in the number of cities from then on.

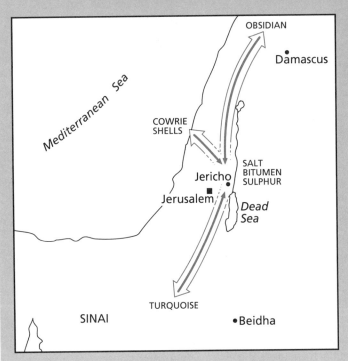

Jericho was an important trading centre.

The obsidian blade shown here originated in Greece in the fifth or sixth century B.C.

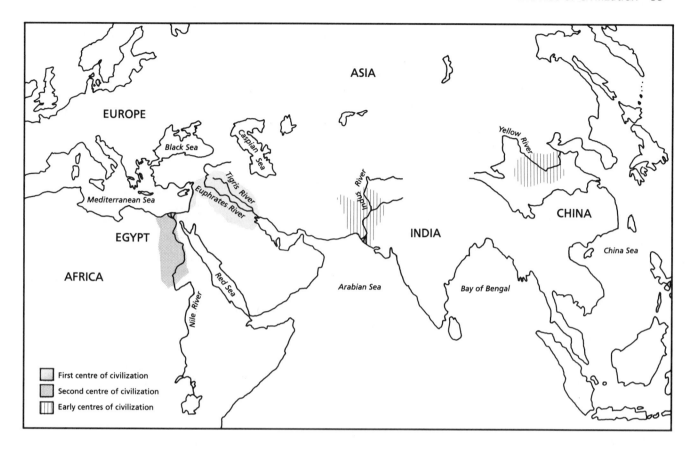

First Centres of Civilization.

is not necessary, however, for all the characteristics listed above to be present in any one civilization.

The emergence of the first civilizations was gradual and intermittent; there was no fixed or predetermined sequence. Urban centres could develop only when people refined their ability to produce food on a scale large enough to produce surpluses. A critical development was the invention of irrigation, especially in areas of marginal rainfall. Civilizations arose first in major river valleys because the fertile soils could support large population densities. The first **cradles of civilization** were the Tigris and Euphrates rivers and the Nile River. A bit later, civilizations developed along the Indus River and the Yellow River.

Mesopotamia, "The Land Between the Rivers," was the name the Greeks gave to the Tigris-Euphrates Valley. The Mesopotamian civilization consisted of several societies that grew up in the same region and had many features in common. Between 6000 and 5000 B.C., the first arrivals came from the highlands of present-day Iran and settled near the Tigris at Tell el-Ubaid. In the ruins of their reed and mud-brick houses, archaeologists have

Religion

The practice of believing in many gods, as the Sumerians did, is known as **polytheism**. The Sumerians worshipped as many as four thousand gods and goddesses. Each city-state took a special deity as its protector. Sumerian gods and goddesses were **anthropomorphic**, which means they had the characteristics and appearance of humans. They were thought to reside in the temples built for them.

The ruler of each city-state and the many advisers worked within the walled enclosure of the ziggurat. On behalf of the gods, they exercised great power over the allocation of land, the maintenance of irrigation canals and ditches, and the collection of grain. When a ruler is regarded as a representative of a god, the system of government is called a **theocracy**.

discovered pottery with geometric and animal designs, and tools made of copper.

The **Sumerians** settled the Plain of Sumer in southeastern Mesopotamia about 4000 B.C. Farms prospered, villages and towns grew, and by 3500 B.C. full-fledged cities emerged at Ur, Kish, Lagash, and Nippur. The Sumerians developed the first true civilization between 3500 and 3000 B.C., the culmination of thousands of years of urban, economic, and social development in the region.

Their building skills enabled the Sumerians to construct large temples. These temples began as one-room rectangular buildings, often built on raised platforms. When one temple collapsed, another was constructed upon the ruins. As the temples grew higher and higher, they took on a step-like appearance. Sumerian architects deliberately adopted this shape when they built new, even more impressive temples, which became known as **ziggurats**. Ziggurats were specially engineered to compensate for the optical illusion that causes straight lines to appear curved when viewed from a distance. As a result, a ziggurat's lines would have looked impressively straight and true. (Much later, the Greeks employed similar techniques when they built the Parthenon.) Each ziggurat was dedicated to a goddess whom the Sumerians believed owned the city.

Although the first Sumerian homes were made of bundled reeds, they learned how to bake and glaze clay bricks for larger structures. Sun-dried mud-bricks erode easily, however, and few of the temples have survived.

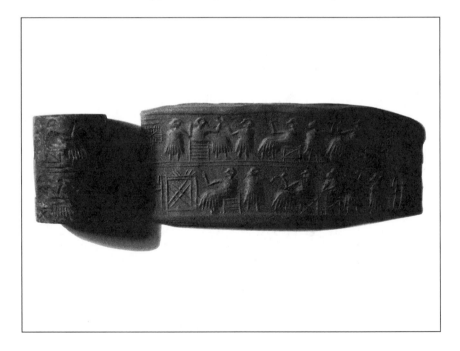

Early Sumerian royalty was buried in tombs containing a variety of riches and artifacts. This photograph shows a cylinder seal made out of lapis lazuli on the left. When the seal was rolled across a soft material, it created the banquet scene shown on the right.

Only the still-imposing ziggurat at Ur, which dates from the third millennium, hints at the past grandeur of the region.

By 3000 B.C., the Plain of Sumer was speckled with about a dozen independent **city-states**. Each city-state consisted of the city plus the surrounding farmland, and had a population of between twelve thousand and thirty-six thousand people. As rivalries developed among the cities, leading citizens were appointed to rule in times of crisis. Sustained rivalries eventually enabled these temporary leaders to rule as kings.

Urban life in the city-state became increasingly complex. There were merchants, artisans, priests, slaves, debtors, creditors, leaders, as well as the farmers and herders who worked the surrounding agricultural land. A central authority controlled a variety of officials and tax collectors, and also the workers who built dams and canals to tame the floodwaters of the rivers. New methods of irrigation were created, and the invention of the plough and the wheel increased yields and the ability to transport heavy loads. Along with the growing complexity came the need to record transactions, ideas, and techniques. In 3200 B.C. at Uruk, a whole system of pictographic writing was invented. Although a few of the symbols may have existed earlier, the system did not develop slowly, symbol by symbol, but was created in its entirety from the start.

The pictographs were initially traced on small tablets of wet clay, but the raw clay tended to tear as the diagram was made. By 2800 B.C., the Sumerians had learned to use a stylus that left a clean, wedge-shaped impression. This script, the first true writing, was called **cuneiform** (after the Latin *cuneus*, a wedge). Human experience was no longer entrusted only to memory. It could be recorded.

Because trade was of crucial importance to the state, so the earliest writing was not used for epic poetry but for account books and transaction

Science

Our present-day practice of dividing the hour into sixty minutes and a minute into sixty seconds comes from the Sumerians, who divided a circle into 360 degrees and based their mathematical system on the number 60.

Cuneiform script was inscribed with a stylus onto wet clay tablets.

records. Rulers, priests, and merchants were the first to benefit from the new invention.

Origins of Flood Legends

It is from the prehistoric era, before the birth of writing, that stories emerge from peoples all over the world about a **universal flood** or **Great Deluge** that destroyed civilization. Written accounts came sooner in some cultures than in others. There are an estimated 220 different cultural traditions of a great flood. Although they vary in detail, the flood stories have some common characteristics: one person is warned of the approaching catastrophe; everyone else disregards the warning; the flood destroys civilization with the exception of the chosen one and the chosen family; animals provide information about conditions after the flood; and the survivors always land on a mountain to start afresh.

The most familiar flood legend in Western culture is the biblical account of Noah. After forty days and nights of rain, Noah's ark, with its cargo of animals, came to rest on Mt. Ararat, located in contemporary Turkey. Historian Sir James Frazer argued in his book *Folklore in the Old Testament* that the story of Noah probably originated in an earlier Babylonian epic. Others have estimated that it was first written down by Hebrew scholars between the tenth and fifteenth centuries B.C.

Scientific creationists believe that the biblical account of the flood must be accepted as the absolute truth, and that physical evidence supports this view. They point out that 75 percent of the earth's surface is covered with sedimentary rock formed by water-borne silts and sands. Throughout the world, there are rock formations with fossils of fish, insects, and animals that seem to have been overwhelmed by a flood and buried in its debris. Fossils have been found near the top of Mt. Everest, the world's highest mountain. Cube-shaped salt crystals the size of grapefruit exist at 2500 m on the slopes of Mt. Ararat, presumably formed when sea water dried and receded. Similarly, pillow lava, formed when molten material contacts water, is found above 4000 m on the same mountain. Creationists argue that a universal flood offers the best explanation for these phenomena.

Geologists admit that flooding occurred along the banks of the Tigris-Euphrates rivers. They believe, however, that the evidence suggests the floods were local events only. In 1928-29, Sir Leonard Wooley sank several shafts into the ground at the ancient Mesopotamian city of Ur. In one large shaft he found a layer of clean clay 3.7 m thick. Wooley was convinced he had found proof of the Great Deluge, but shafts in other parts of the city showed no signs of flood deposits. Geological investigations at several other Mesopotamian sites have provided similar indications of relatively limited flooding.

More to Consider

The Bible gives no precise date for the flood. By cross-referencing the Bible with information in Sumerian and Assyrian records, scholars have determined that the flood supposedly occurred between 3000 B.C. and 2800 B.C. Some biblical authorities favour a date of about 2300 B.C.

The Story of the Great Deluge

The Sumerians had the earliest-known legendary account of a great flood. Archaeological excavations at Nippur unearthed fragments of a flood story that dates to a minimum of 2200 B.C. and perhaps as far back as 3400 B.C. The hero's name was Ziusudra ("lifelong days"), and his huge boat endured seven days and nights of flood and windstorms. This story was handed down, with changes, through several succeeding empires—from the Sumerians to the Akkadians, then to the Babylonians, and finally to the Assyrians.

During the British excavations of the Assyrian city of Nineveh in the 1850s, twenty-five thousand clay tablets were unearthed from the crumbled library of King Assurbanipal (668-626 B.C.). In 1872, the British Museum employed George Smith, an enthusiastic amateur, to piece together the rather carelessly collected tablets. Smith soon came across the story of the flood. An upwelling of publicity brought him enough money to go to Nineveh in search of more tablets.

What Smith uncovered within a week of his arrival was the 3500-line poem known as *The Epic of Gilgamesh.* The hero of the poem is Utnapishtim ("he found life"), whose ship was tossed by the flood for six days and nights before it landed on Mt. Nisir.

Does the general consistency in the flood stories from these cultures, and from many others around the world, prove that there is an important kernel of truth behind the legends? The answer is important. If the legends are accurate and all of human civilization was indeed wiped out by a Great Deluge, it would mean that the development of civilization before the flood was virtually a dead end. Humanity would have been forced to begin again, but without the material advantages that centuries of civilized life had produced. It would mean that later civilizations were born out of a global catastrophe. The impact of such an event would have been branded deep into people's consciousness and would have altered the way they looked at the world and their future in it. Confidence in the permanence of civilization and in humanity itself would have been hard to regain.

And if the stories are in fact only legends, why are there so many different accounts all over the world? Might there be other reasonable explanations for the widespread occurrence of this one narrative?

A word-for-word translation of five lines from The Epic of Gilgamesh, *discovered by George Smith.*

127   6 ur·ra   ù 6 mu·šá·a · ti
      6 days   and 6 nights

il · lak šá·ru a·bu·bu me·hu·u · i · sáp pan KUR
blows the wind, the flood, the southstorm sweeps the land.

129 si·bu·ú u · mu·i·na ka·šá·di .... šu·ú abu·bu qab·la
     the 7ᵗʰ day, when it came, ... the flood, the battle

šá im·tah · su   ki ma ha·a·a·al · ti
which he had fought   like an army,

131 i · nu · uh A · AB · BA uš·ha·ri· ir·ma im·hul·lu a·bu·bu ik·la
     grew quiet the sea, and was still the storm, the flood ceased.

The Issue Emerges

The debate between scientific creationists and geologists (and other scientists) is not just a debate about alternative views of history. It is also a debate about what conclusions can logically be drawn from the same set of facts, and about what methods of analysis can legitimately be called scientific. Henry Morris and Duane Guish, co-founders of the Institute for Creation Science, argue that their methods are the same as those used by all modern scientists. They have simply reached a different conclusion. Their opponents claim that scientific creationists base their arguments on faith rather than on scientific principles.

One of the most fascinating aspects of the debate centres on the existence of Noah's ark. Many efforts have been made to find the ark, or even a fragment of it. The assumption is that physical evidence of the ark legitimizes the biblical story of the flood (as well as all the other events described in the Bible, including the creation of humans).

Is scientific creationism a scientific or a religious alternative? Are the disagreements between scientific creationists and mainstream scientists a question of interpretation or of fundamentally different methods? Here are two contemporary viewpoints from opposite sides of the issue.

THE PROBLEM QUESTION

What can scientific creationists and mainstream scientists tell us about the existence of Noah's ark on Mt. Ararat?

ALTERNATIVE ONE: Scientific Creationism and Noah's Ark

Based on *Scientific Creationism* by Henry. M. Morris (1974), *In Search of Noah's Ark* by David Balsiger and Charles Sellier (1976), "Scientific Creationists and Error" by Robert Schaderwald (1986), and *Noah's Ark* by Patricia Kite (1989)

Before the flood, the climate of the earth was much more uniform than it is now. There is evidence of broad-leaved forests in Egypt and in the semi-arid American West. Admiral Byrd found petrified forests 160 km from the South Pole. It is also known that Australian and South American deserts were once swamps.

These facts can be explained by the presence of a canopy of water vapour 1 to 3 km thick that covered the earth. The canopy was translucent to the light of the stars but created a greenhouse effect. Daytime temperatures were kept at 21° C, and evening temperatures were only 1-2° C cooler. The canopy and increased amounts of carbon dioxide kept the heat in and radiation out. People and animals lived for much longer as a result. Adam, for example, lived for 930 years; Methuselah for 969 years; and Noah for 950 years. Little if any rain fell. The small cooling change from day to night provided enough moisture through condensation to water plant life.

George Dodwell, astronomer at Adelaide Observatory in Australia, has calculated that the earth's axis shifted significantly in 2345 B.C., about the time of the flood. A shift of this size may have been caused by the close passage of, or a collision with, a large meteorite. The impact caused seabeds to rise, earthquakes to spread, volcanoes to form, and water to emerge from beneath the crust. The landscape, which had been almost featureless, was now completely transformed. Great mountains rose. The water canopy collapsed, producing forty days and nights of rain and creating vast oceans. Without the water canopy as protection, more radiation reached the earth's surface, reducing lifespans for all organisms. The variety of climates that exist today were created.

Everything that was not carried in the ark was destroyed by the flood. The rain stopped after forty days, but it took much longer for the flood to recede. Two hundred and twenty-four days passed before the first land was exposed and the ark came to rest "on the mountains of Ararat." This means that the floodwaters were at least 5000 m deep, judging from the present elevation of the mountain. The large capacity of the ark would have been more than enough to comfortably accommodate two of every species. Feeding them might appear to have been a difficult task for Noah and his family (eight people). It seems likely, however, that conditions aboard the ark triggered a hibernation instinct, so most of the animals slept.

Two hundred people, in twenty-three different sightings, have claimed to have seen the ark. The most significant evidence was provided by Fernand Navarra. After unsuccessful climbs of Ararat in 1952 and 1953, Navarra found what he felt was the ark. He removed a 1.5 m

Mt. Ararat.

Earth's surface

Better swimmers	Humans always found near surface
	Mammals always found above reptiles
	Reptiles always found above amphibians
	Amphibians always found above fish
	Fish with backbones (vertebrates) always found above invertebrates
	Marine animals without backbones (invertebrates)
	Simple spherical-shaped organisms
Poorer swimmers	Deepest Sediments

Creationists believe that the fossil layers were caused by the Great Deluge around 3000 B.C. The layers shown on the Creationists' Column are a reflection of swimming ability.

wooden section from the glaciated mountainside just below the 4000 m mark, where trees had never grown. Apparently, part of the ark had fallen during a storm or snowslide from its previous position at 4200 m. An expedition led by Navarra in 1969 found additional wood fragments on the ice-covered slopes of the mountain. Tests for the degree of coal formation, gain in wood density, cell modification, and degree of fossilization indicated an age of between 4400 and 5000 years.

As the floodwaters receded, all the sediment carried by the flood began to settle, burying the creatures drowned by the disaster. This created the fossil layers geologists study today. It is a record in stone of the single greatest catastrophe in human experience. All the creatures found in the fossil record—including dinosaurs—existed at the same time in the period before the flood. They all originated during God's perfect creation between six and ten thousand years ago. Evidence of this is provided by the fossilized human footprints mixed with dinosaur tracks that have been repeatedly identified in the Paluxy riverbeds near Glen Rose, Texas, since the 1950s.

The different layers of the fossil record can be explained very simply. During the flood, the corpses of all the organisms were tossed in the waters and then sank. Logic suggests that their position in the fossil record would depend on where they drowned, their ability to swim, and their shape and weight. Thus, the deepest sediments would contain simple organisms whose spherical shape caused them to settle first. The next layer would be marine animals without backbones—invertebrates—who lived near the bottom of the sea. The vertebrates would be found next because they would escape burial, for a time, by swimming. Above these fish would be the amphibians and reptiles who lived at the boundary of water and land. Because of their herding instincts, the higher forms of land animals would be found in large numbers in the upper layers of the fossil record. Few humans and birds would be found, owing to their mobility. The bodies of any organisms that escaped being buried by sediment would be exposed on the ground after the flood receded and would decompose without a trace. The fossil record reveals exactly this pattern.

Following the flood, Noah's family and the animals that were saved became the ancestors of all present-day human and animal populations. Physically and mentally, humans have always been humans. The fossil record shows no transitional forms. Though the australopithecines have been cited as human ancestors, they were probably just prehistoric apes that became extinct. Fossils such as Homo erectus likely represent the negative results of inbreeding, poor diets, and a hostile environment, rather than a stage in human development.

QUESTIONS

1. a) Describe the climatic and geographic conditions that existed throughout the globe before the flood.
   b) What was the human lifespan like before the flood?
   c) Why is 2345 B.C. a significant date in the flood theory?
2. How and why did climate, geography, and lifespans change when the water canopy collapsed?
3. a) Who survived the flood?
   b) Why was it relatively easy to care for the animals on the ark?
4. Why were the expeditions of Fernand Navarra to Mt. Ararat in 1955 and 1969 important for creationists?
5. What evidence do creationists present to illustrate that the fossil record is the result of the Great Deluge?
6. Creationists argue that Noah's family are the ancestors of modern human populations. Do you agree with this conclusion? Give reasons for your answer.
7. Creationists claim there are no transitional forms in the fossil record. Would a scientist agree? Explain your answer.

ALTERNATIVE TWO: Scientists Examine the Evidence for Noah's Ark

Based on "Arkeology: A New Science in Support of Creation?" by Robert A. Moore (1981), *In the Beginning* by Dr. Chris McGowan (1983), and "A Survey of the Taylor Site Evidence" by Glen J. Kuban (1986)

It is unlikely that the size of the ark as described in the Bible would have been large enough to hold all of the animals. However, assuming that it was, where would Noah have stored the food required for the journey? In one day, an African elephant eats about 160 kg of food. In ten months, the duration of the flood according to creationists, a pair of elephants would consume 96 t. And this is only one of the thousands of species the ark would have been carrying. How would Noah have kept the meat fresh for the carnivores before the days of refrigeration? And how would Noah and his family have disposed of all the waste the animals produced?

Another problem would have been the supply of drinking water. The floodwaters would have been contaminated with dead bodies and, therefore, would not have been drinkable. The ark must have been equipped with freshwater storage tanks. These would have taken up even more space.

Although the Bible makes no mention of taking sea life aboard, the tremendous volume of fresh water added by the Deluge would have killed most saltwater organisms. Since they exist today, Noah must have

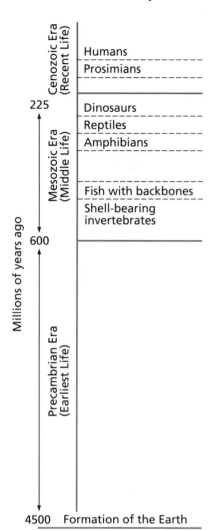

Fossil Locations on the Geologic Column. Only the first appearance of each creature is shown on this geologic column, which covers 4.5 billion years. Fossils of each type have also been discovered at higher levels.

included them on the passenger list. The necessary aquariums would have added to the space problem.

Although Fernand Navarra discovered wood on Mt. Ararat in 1955 and 1969, his finds are inconclusive. Navarra and his son Raphael were by themselves when they discovered hand-tooled wood in 1955. Two of Navarra's fellow climbers, Colonel Sahap Atalay and J.A. deRiquier, accused Navarra of depositing the wood so that it could be "found" later. Navarra located wood on the 1969 expedition only after he had had the chance to be alone on the glacier. When the wood was radiocarbon tested in a number of laboratories, the results converged on the eighth century A.D. This is about 3000 years too late for the Great Deluge.

The end of the flood raises even more questions. Where, for example, did all the water go after the flood? It could not have become locked in the polar icecaps because they account for only about 2 percent of the world's water, both fresh and salt. If all the ice were to melt today, the sea level would rise only about 40 m. This is a lot less water than would have been required to cover the highest mountain peak. Food would have been another problem. All life on earth was destroyed by the flood. After they disembarked from the ark, what would the people and animals have eaten while new plants were growing? Yet another puzzling question involves the distribution of animals today. How did animals such as the kangaroo, the polar bear, and the panda get from Mt. Ararat to Australia, the arctic, and China?

At the time of the flood, usually given anywhere between 2300 and 3000 B.C., the human population would have been reduced to the eight members of Noah's family. Numbers would have remained small for generations. Yet the archaeological evidence in Mesopotamia and elsewhere in the world shows no such drastic, worldwide decrease in population at or near the flood date. In fact, at this time civilization was blossoming in Mesopotamia.

The fossil record and geologic column we study today are not, as the creationists argue, the result of the Great Deluge. Relative and absolute dating techniques show that the fossil record covers millions and billions of years. It is true that simple sea creatures appear first in the fossil record, followed by fish, amphibians, reptiles, and mammals at succeedingly higher levels. But it is *not* true that simple sea creatures appear only in the bottom layers. They are also found in younger rocks because they continued to live long after their first appearance. This contradicts the idea of sudden burial by sediments. Human fossils are rare not because people were good swimmers, but because they did not live and die in fossil-forming locations. In the past two decades, fossils have been discovered that support the idea that humans evolved gradually from Australopithecus to Homo erectus to Homo sapiens.

Rumours of giant fossilized human footprints intermingled with dinosaur tracks along the Paluxy River in Texas began early in the twentieth century. In the 1980s, Glen Kuban studied the coloration, relief, and fissure patterns of the prints. His conclusion was that the so-called human prints were really a badly eroded portion of a three-toed dinosaur track. The Paluxy River tracks are the "Piltdown Man" of creationism.

QUESTIONS

1. What problems would Noah and his family have faced on the ark in caring for their cargo of animals?
2. Why does it seem unlikely that there was a global flood 5000 m deep?
3. Why do scientists not accept Fernand Navarra's claim that he found a piece of Noah's ark?
4. What problems would Noah and the animals have experienced after the ark landed on Mt. Ararat?
5. Creationists argue that the geologic column of fossils and rocks is the result of a single, devastating, worldwide flood. Scientists argue that the geologic column illustrates the story of the earth and the development of life over the last 4 billion years. Which argument is more convincing? Explain your answer with evidence.
6. Creationists argue that there are no fossils from earlier transitional forms of humans. Scientists argue that there are. Which point of view is more persuasive? Again, explain your answer with evidence.
7. How does Glen Kuban interpret the footprints along the Paluxy River in Texas?

ANSWERING THE PROBLEM QUESTION

For some Christians, the criterion needed to solve this problem is simple—faith in the word of God. Faith overrides all other considerations.

In a *scientific* analysis, though, it is not acceptable to point to some supernatural agency as an explanation of puzzling facts. Creationists argue that their belief in the Great Deluge described in the Bible is not based on faith alone, but is supported by scientific evidence. Your task, then, is to weigh that evidence and to judge the conclusions drawn from it. There are at least two areas you should consider as you try to answer the question. First, what is the geological evidence for a flood of the size and duration described in the Bible, at the alleged date? Second, is there any direct physical evidence of the ark? You must decide, based on what you have read, which criteria are the most important and, from there, which viewpoint about Noah's ark is most convincing.

THE STORY CONTINUES . . .

Sargon and the Birth of Empire

During the third millennium B.C., city-states in Sumer were constantly at war. One city gained ascendancy only to lose it to another. The turmoil

More to Consider

The Semitic languages are among the oldest in the world, apparently originating between 8000 B.C. and 6000 B.C. Peoples who speak one of these languages are known as Semitic peoples.

There is no clear archaeological evidence about where the Semitic peoples came from; perhaps they began as nomads on the Arabian Peninsula. They were some of the earliest peoples in Mesopotamia, and lived alongside the Sumerians. Sargon was raised among the Sumerians but had a Semitic background, and was the first Semitic king of Mesopotamia.

Today, over 200 million people speak one of the Semitic languages, which include Arabic and Hebrew.

finally ended in the late twenty-fourth century B.C. A **Semitic** leader named Sargon gained control of one of the city-states of northern Sumer by means that are not clear. He developed a military force equipped with bronze weapons and chariots pulled by donkeys. This army of lancers, archers, and chariots first conquered the neighbouring land of **Akkad**, then upper Mesopotamia, and eventually the entire Fertile Crescent.

From his new capital of Agade, Sargon ruled the world's first empire, confidently calling himself "King of the Four Quarters." The Akkadians borrowed many aspects of the Sumerians' culture, including their irrigation techniques, cuneiform writing, and even their gods.

Ur-Nammu and the Third Dynasty of Ur

Mesopotamia was invaded in 2200 B.C. by the Gutians, but they were overthrown by a Sumerian revolt in 2112 B.C. Soon afterwards, a ruler named Ur-Nammu established the **Third Dynasty**. Under his enlightened rule, literature, agriculture, trade, and architecture flourished.

Cities that had decayed during the Gutian conquest were revitalized. The Sumerian city of Ur, for example, became a metropolis that was home to between thirty and forty thousand people. It was ringed by two broad canals that linked up with the Euphrates River. The thick walls that surrounded the city were pierced by gates and a third canal that harboured foreign trading ships. Houses, shops, and bazaars crowded the vast enclosure. Built on the ruins of earlier structures, a great ziggurat rose almost 25 m from a base that measured 61 m by 43 m. Every mud-brick bore the stamp of the king's name. The ziggurat, visible from 30 km away, overlooked the swampy lands of the river valley. The patchwork of fields that spread between irrigation canals provided a secure agricultural base for Ur, and the city provided sanctuary for farmers in time of attack.

A model of the ziggurat at Ur. The base and the ramps are still intact, but the upper three stages no longer exist.

Ur-Nammu is also famous for providing the world's earliest-known **legal code**. It was issued in an attempt to bring peace and stability. Based on Sumerian tradition, the laws were written on clay tablets for all to see. The only copy left is badly damaged, and only five of the laws can be deciphered. Three of the five are particularly interesting, because they state that an offender who causes physical injury to another should be made to pay a fine. In the societies of that time, physical punishments were more common than fines.

Ur-Nammu's Third Dynasty was the last for Sumerian kings. Sumer's agricultural lands had been overworked and were full of salts that had accumulated as a result of the irrigation techniques. The Sumerians were not able to overcome a challenge that faces urban societies to this day: how the needs of city life can be met without permanently damaging the environment. Nomadic tribes began entering, then invading, Mesopotamia after 2000 B.C. About 1950 B.C., the Elamites conquered the city of Ur and levelled its imposing walls to their foundations.

The Babylonians

Groups of nomadic peoples continued to move into Mesopotamia in the aftermath of Ur's collapse. In about 1850 B.C., the Amorites built the village of **Babylon** on the Euphrates River. Babylon grew into a magnificent city-state, with a great ziggurat dedicated to the god Marduk. The Amorite king Hammurabi, who came to the throne about 1750 B.C., proved to be one of the great leaders of the ancient world. He was an outstanding warrior who eventually conquered all Mesopotamia and ruled an empire the equal of Sargon's. Babylon became the administrative and cultural capital of the Mesopotamian world under Hammurabi's shrewd guidance.

Hammurabi is best known for drawing up a uniform code of laws for his vast empire. It was one of the earliest attempts to guarantee that people should live by the law rather than by impulse. The laws were engraved on stone slabs and pillars called **stelae**, which were then distributed to cities throughout the empire for all to see and obey. Much of Hammurabi's code used the principle of "an eye for an eye, a tooth for a tooth," though applications and punishments varied with a person's rank in society.

The Assyrian Empire

Following Hammurabi's death, internal rebellion and foreign invasion led to the decline and fragmentation of the Babylonian empire. In 1595 B.C., the Hittites of Anatolia invaded and looted the Fertile Crescent using their superior iron weapons and horse-drawn chariots. When the Hittites left, the Kassites, about whom little is known, conquered and occupied Mesopotamia for almost five centuries. Despite the dominance of the Kassites, Mesopotamia was continually exposed to foreign incursion and internal strife.

Institutions

The roots of Ur-Nammu's code can be traced back to about 2350 B.C. King Urukagina of Lagash issued an important cuneiform inscription concerning new measures of justice. Oppressive taxation, begun in war but continued in peacetime, allowed officials to take animals and food from farmers. Urukagina fired the abusive tax collectors, gave amnesty to those wrongly imprisoned, and made decrees protecting citizens from the government. This inscription contains the earliest-known use of the word *freedom*.

The Code of Hammurabi

In 1901, French archaeologists excavating at ancient Susa in Iran uncovered a black pillar over 2.5 m high. It was engraved in cuneiform writing and turned out to be a law code from the eighteenth century B.C., issued by the Babylonian king Hammurabi. It consisted of 282 regulations. The importance of agriculture was reflected in the many laws that relate to the maintenance of canals and the cultivation of fields. Other laws reveal the nature of the class structure and describe the application of punishments. Although the code of Hammurabi is not the oldest law code, none exceeded its scope until the sixth century A.D.

Here are some of the regulations contained in the code:

1. If a man has accused another of laying a nertu [death spell?] upon him, but has not proved it, he shall be put to death....
3. If a man has borne false witness in a trial, or has not established the statement that he has made, if that case be a capital trial, that man shall be put to death....
6. If a man has stolen goods from a temple, or house, he shall be put to death; and he that has received the stolen property from him shall be put to death....
14. If a man has stolen from a child, he shall be put to death....
21. If a man has broken into a house, he shall be killed before the breach and buried here....
22. If a man has committed highway robbery and has been caught, that man shall be put to death....
24. If a life [has been lost], the city or district governor shall pay one mina of silver to the deceased's relatives....
42. If a man has hired a field to cultivate and has caused no grain to grow on the field, he shall be held responsible for not doing the work on the field and shall pay an average rent....
53. If a man has neglected to strengthen his dike and has not kept his dike strong, and a breach has broken out in his dike, and the waters have flooded the meadow, the man in whose dike the breach has broken out shall restore the grain he has caused to be lost....
55. If a man has opened his runnel for watering and has left it open, and the water has flooded his neighbour's field, he shall pay him an average crop....
128. If a man has taken a wife and has not executed a marriage contract, that woman is not a wife....
138. If a man has divorced his wife, who has not borne him children, he shall pay over to her as much money as was given for her bride-price and the marriage-portion which she brought from her father's house, and so shall divorce her....
143. If [a woman] has not been discreet, has gone out, ruined her house, belittled her husband, she shall be drowned....
195. If a son has struck his father, his hands shall be cut off....
196. If a man has knocked out the eye of a patrician, his eye shall be knocked out.
197. If he has broken the limb of a patrician, his limb shall be broken.
198. If he has knocked out the eye of a plebian or has broken the limb of a plebian, he shall pay one mina of silver.
215. If a surgeon has operated with the bronze lancet on a patrician for a serious injury, and has caused his death, or has removed a cataract for a patrician, with the bronze lancet, and has made him lose his eye, his hands shall be cut off....
229. If a builder has built a house for a man, and has not made his work sound, and the house he built has fallen, and caused the death of its owner, that builder shall be put to death.
282. If a slave has said to his master, "You are not my master," he shall be brought to account as his slave, and his master shall cut off his ear...

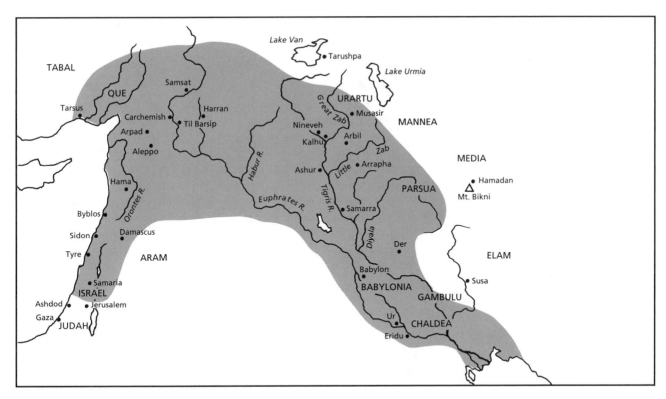

The Assyrian Empire c. 700 B.C.

The next important empire was **Assyrian**. From their city-state of Assur in the Tigris Valley, the Assyrians began to move outwards after the eleventh century B.C. They adopted the iron weapons and two-wheeled chariots of the Hittites and made superior bows, arrows, slings, and lances. Enemies were not only defeated, they were shown no mercy. One Assyrian king proudly proclaimed: "I cut off their heads and like heaps of grain I piled them up." Another commented: "I skinned alive all their chief men. Their young men and maidens I burned in the fire."

The Assyrians created the most feared and militant empire the Western world had ever experienced. After they captured Babylon, about 700 B.C., their control stretched through the Fertile Crescent to southeastern Anatolia and the Egyptian Nile Delta. If an uprising brewed among the conquered peoples, the troublemakers were deported and dispersed to distant sectors of the empire.

Using the wealth they plundered in their conquests, the Assyrians built an impressive capital at **Nineveh**. Under the leadership of King Assurbanipal, Nineveh became the jewel of the ancient world. The world's first library, containing twenty-two thousand clay tablets written in the cuneiform of Sumer and Babylon, preserved invaluable records of Mesopotamian history.

During the seventh century B.C., conquered peoples began to rebel against Assyrian dominance. A coalition of forces captured and destroyed Nineveh and divided the Assyrian Empire among themselves in 612 B.C.

SUMMARY

About 10 000 B.C., the earth's climate began to warm and the last Ice Age ended. The Paleolithic Era gave way to the Neolithic Era. Nomadic patterns continued, but some peoples became sedentary and developed new technologies—agriculture, domestication of animals, and building construction being the most important. The tell at Jericho is an important archaeological site because it reveals the story of this kind of development.

The first civilizations arose in river valleys, known as cradles of civilization. A civilization is an advanced society that possesses complex systems by which people co-ordinate their efforts for the common good. In the valley of the Tigris and Euphrates rivers (the land of Mesopotamia), the Sumerians established the world's first true civilization about 3500 B.C. The city-states of Sumer each had a ziggurat, a large temple in the shape of a stepped pyramid. The Sumerians perfected new irrigation techniques, and they also invented the plough, the wheel, and a whole system of pictographic writing called cuneiform. One of the earliest written stories describes a vast flood that covered the world and destroyed almost all life. Geological evidence suggests, however, that floods were local, not global, events.

The Sumerian city-states were frequently at war until sometime late in the twenty-fourth century B.C., when a conqueror named Sargon took control not only of Sumer but also of the whole Fertile Crescent. Sargon's empire was short-lived, but in 2112 B.C., a Sumerian named Ur-Nammu established the Third Dynasty. The first legal code dates from this time. After 2000 B.C., Mesopotamia was invaded by various nomadic tribes who destroyed some Sumerian cities.

The next Mesopotamian empire was created by the Amorite king Hammurabi, whose rule began about 1750 B.C. The centre of the empire was the city of Babylon, built on the Euphrates River. Hammurabi's empire was as large as Sargon's, and the whole territory was subject to one set of laws, contained in the legal code for which Hammurabi is famous. The empire disintegrated after his death.

Mesopotamia remained fragmented until the Assyrians asserted themselves hundreds of years later. By 700 B.C. they had captured Babylon, and Assyrian influence eventually reached beyond the Fertile Crescent. Nineveh became their most impressive city, and was the location of the world's first library. The empire did not last long after the taking of Babylon.

3

Egyptian Civilization: Puzzle of the Pyramids

Period	Date BC	Event
Prehistoric	18 000	Earliest harvest of wild plants occurs in the Nile Valley
	5200	Megalithic cultures begin in Europe
	5000	Africans bring true agriculture to the Nile
	4500	Isolated agricultural communities emerge along the Nile Mud-brick buildings first constructed
Early Dynastic	3100	Upper and Lower Egypt united by Narmer First Dynasty established, with capital at Memphis Trade begins with Mediterranean and Red Sea areas via boat, and with Nubia and African coastal settlements overland Stonehenge I
Old Kingdom	2650	Third Dynasty Age of the Pyramids
	c. 2571-2548	*Great Pyramid of Khufu (Cheops in Greek)*
	2200	Seventh Dynasty
First Intermediate	2100	Disunity begins; pharaohs lose authority while nobles, priests, and officials gain power Stonehenge II
Middle Kingdom	2040	Eleventh Dynasty; central authority is restored
	2000	Stonehenge III
Second Intermediate	1650	"Hyksos" enter Delta and slowly gain control of Egypt Decay of central authority
New Kingdom	1550	Eighteenth Dynasty Thutmose III expands Egyptian Empire to Euphrates River Akhenaten makes religious reforms
	1334	Tutankhamun ends radical changes of Akhenaten
	1288-1220	Ramses II builds the great temple at Thebes, the rock-cut temple at Abu Simbel, and hypostyle hall at Karnak
	1100	Twenty-first Dynasty
Late Dynastic	525	Persians conquer and rule Egypt
	332	Alexander the Great gains control of Egypt
Ptolemaic	30	Rome conquers Egypt

3

Egyptian Civilization: Puzzle of the Pyramids

BACKGROUND

Egypt and the Nile

Shortly after the rise of Mesopotamia, the civilization of ancient Egypt developed along the Nile. The Nile was Egypt's lifeblood. It flowed through vast stretches of scorching desert, forming a narrow band of fertile ground 1.5 to 22 km wide. When floodwaters overflowed the river's banks and then receded, they deposited a black fertile soil that the ancient Egyptians called *kemet*. This "gift of the Nile" provided some of the richest soils in the world for Egyptian farmers. It was capable of sustaining three crops per year.

Agriculture was possible only where the river made its deposits of alluvium or where irrigation canals funnelled water. The Egyptians used the oxen-powered water wheel and the *shaduf* to move water from one level to another. The *shaduf* is a pivoted pole with a bucket hung from one end and a stone weight hung from the other. With these two simple tools, the Egyptians extended their network of canals and increased the available farmland. Where the water supply ended, a person could place one foot in a rich field of grain and the other in absolute desert. On either side of the river valley, the desert was so vast that it could not be easily crossed. It protected Egypt from foreign invasion and restricted outside influences.

Though the Nile was not as volatile as the Tigris and Euphrates rivers, its floods could fluctuate significantly. Floodwaters sometimes reached upwards of 16 m. At such levels, the mud-brick homes of the Egyptians who lived at the edge of cultivation could easily be washed away. When the flood ran low, starvation could result. To gauge the flow of the river, the Egyptians used **nilometers**. These were horizontal notches marked at regular intervals into rocks above the river. Egyptian officials used nilometer readings to estimate what the crop yields would be downstream, and to set taxes accordingly. Farmers used the readings to determine when planting could begin.

Science

In 4000 B.C., the Egyptians became the first people (as far as we know) to discover that the solar year has 365 days. They noticed that when the star Sirius was aligned with the rising sun, the Nile flood level was at its peak. They counted the number of days between recurrences of these events and determined the length of the year.

The Egyptian calendar was divided into three seasons: Inundation, Seed, and Harvest. Each season consisted of four thirty-day months, with five "extra yearly" days added to the end of Harvest. But a calendar with only 365 days is about one-quarter of a day short every year, or one day every four years—hence, our own tradition of leap year. As the error in the Egyptian calendar accumulated, the real harvest moved out of step with the Harvest season. This prompted one Egyptian to comment that "winter comes in summer, and the months come about turned backwards."

*In Egyptian hieroglyphics, some symbols are pictures of what they represent (**pictographs**), and other symbols stand for a particular sound (**phonograms**). The idea for hieroglyphics probably came to the Egyptians from contact with Mesopotamia, where the Sumerians had developed their own pictographs. Writing was an essential part of Egyptian life even though most Egyptians did not master the skill.*

After Egypt's demise, hieroglyphic writing gradually disappeared. It remained a mystery until a special rock slab was unearthed in the Egyptian Delta town of Rosetta during Napoleon's campaign in 1799. The writing on the stone was deciphered by Jean-François Champollion in 1822. By matching the Greek message at the bottom with the hieroglyphics shown on the top, he was able to decode the Egyptian inscription and identify the symbols.

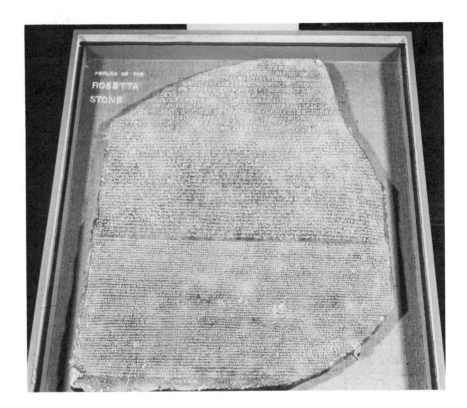

The Nile was important in many other ways. It provided water for drinking and for the growing of grain from which bread was baked. A type of paper was made from the papyrus reed that grew in the river. Beginning about 3000 B.C., written records were kept on this material in Egypt's own picture-script, known as **hieroglyphics**. The tough, buoyant reeds also served as material for building the barges and boats that were used on the Nile. Water transport could move downstream easily with the flow of the river, and upstream travel was aided by the prevailing winds, which blew against the current. The Nile thus functioned as a central "highway" running the length of Egypt.

Egyptian civilization occupied the lower 1200 km of the Nile Valley. The city of Cairo stands at the junction of the Valley and the Delta, where the Nile enters the Mediterranean Sea after a journey of 6741 km. In antiquity, the Nile had seven major channels in the Delta, and silt deposits annually covered about 15 000 km^2. Regular surveys of the Delta were made to ensure that land was properly divided among the farmers.

Creation, Gods, and Eternity

The Egyptians, like other peoples, believed that the most important gods were those associated with the creation of the cosmos. Although several creation

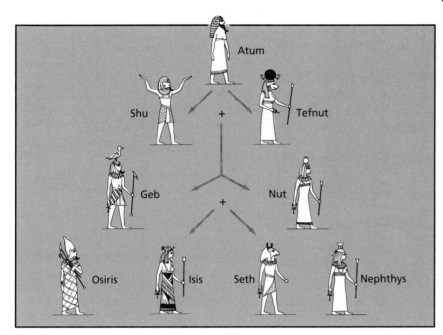

The origin of the gods as told by the priests of Heliopolis c. 2400 B.C.

stories were told, the earliest and most widely accepted was composed by priests of the city Heliopolis between 2480 and 2137 B.C. According to this story, the earth began with the emergence of the primeval mound from Nun, the waters of chaos. Standing on the mound was the creator-god Atum. (In later periods, Atum was linked with another important deity, the sun-god Re, and was given the name Atum-Re.) From Atum, who was self-created, came the other gods and goddesses, including Shu (air), Tefnut (moisture), Geb (earth), Nut (sky), and Osiris, Isis, Seth, and Nephthys.

These last four deities originated in other cities. Making Atum their grandfather was a way for the priests of Heliopolis to put their city and their god first. Other cities (Memphis, Hermopolis, and Thebes, for example) developed their own creation stories. Most of the stories do not mention the creation of humans. Because Egyptian religion grew out of local traditions and varied from region to region, it cannot be encompassed by any single system or account. But in every region, religion was central. In the fifth century B.C., the Greek traveller and historian Herodotus observed that the Egyptians "are religious beyond measure more than any other nation."

During Egypt's prehistory, chieftains in each village claimed mystical powers. They usually took up residence near the temple of the village deity so that its blessing could be invoked. To encourage their soldiers in battle, chieftains used animal figureheads to represent desirable characteristics, such as the speed of the falcon or the fearsomeness of the crocodile. Similarly, local deities initially looked like animals, to symbolize their special qualities.

With the passage of time, the idea of gods with human forms gradually emerged. Anubis, the jackal-headed guardian of the tomb, and Horus, the falcon-headed god, had human bodies. Osiris, who represented the yearly life cycle of the Nile, was shown entirely as a human image.

Egyptian religion can seem confusing because of the large number of gods and goddesses, and the many forms each can take. But the Egyptians of a particular community usually worshipped only one god or a local triad of deities. A god revered in one town might not be recognized in another. The background of the king also influenced which gods were worshipped. For example, if a leader from Thebes became king, the importance of Theban deities rose accordingly. "Great" or national gods were created, recognized in all communities alongside local gods.

Myths associated with local deities gradually became intertwined to produce a legend about a primal struggle for power. The god Osiris was the key figure. It was believed that Osiris had once ruled Egypt with his wife and sister, Isis. Osiris was then murdered by his jealous brother, Seth, who dismembered Osiris's body and scattered the parts to eliminate all traces. Isis, however, remained loyal. She carefully collected the pieces and put Osiris back together. After his resurrection, Osiris retired to become lord of the underworld. Horus, son of Osiris, was left to do battle with Seth and, judged to be victorious, was given the crown of Egypt. This story of death, resurrection, and triumph established that Egypt would forever be ruled by a single king. While he lived, the king was the embodiment of Horus, and when he died he became Osiris, master of the afterlife.

The story not only provided a religious foundation for the power of the king, but reinforced the tradition of preserving dead bodies. This tradition was very old, and probably started as a result of natural processes. Initially, an Egyptian was buried in a pit dug into the ground. The dry, hot sand absorbed about three-quarters of the body's moisture, preventing decay. Some authorities have argued that, when these bodies were exposed by wind or scavengers, the Egyptians hit upon the idea of artificial preservation. In any case, once the bodies were removed from the natural dehydrating effects of the desert and placed in small tombs, they quickly decayed. To counteract this decay, the Egyptians wrapped corpses in resin-soaked linen.

The Egyptian process of preserving corpses is known as **mummification**. A royal mummy had jewellery placed under the wrappings. This explains why tomb robbers recklessly stripped the mummies when they found their coffins in burial chambers. Combined with the dry, hot Egyptian climate, this and other methods of mummification preserved even Stone Age corpses to a remarkable degree. The three-thousand-year-old mummy of Ramses II in the Cairo Museum still has dried skin, hair, and teeth intact.

Mummification and the Afterlife

Egyptians practised mummification to preserve the bodies of the deceased. Their abilities improved steadily and peaked during the New Kingdom. In the most elaborate types of mummification, the internal organs were removed, dried, and wrapped separately. They were stored in containers known as **canopic jars**.

The Greek historian Herodotus describes the range of options for mummification that a rich purse could buy:

There are a set of men in Egypt who practise the art of embalming, and make it their proper business. These persons, when a body is brought to them, show the bearers various models of corpses, made in wood, and painted so as to resemble nature. The most perfect is said to be after the manner of him whom I do not think it religious to name in connection with such a matter; the second sort is inferior to the first, and less costly; the third is the cheapest of all. All this the embalmers explain, and then ask in which way it is wished that the corpse should be prepared. The bearers tell them, and having concluded their bargain, take their departure, while the embalmers, left to themselves, proceed to their task. The mode of embalming, according the most perfect process, is the following:—They take first a crooked piece of iron, and with it draw out the brain through the nostrils, thus getting rid of a portion, while the skull is cleared of the rest by rinsing with drugs; next they make a cut along the flank with a sharp Ethiopian stone [obsidian], and take out the whole contents of the abdomen, which they then cleanse, washing it thoroughly with palm wine, and again frequently with an infusion of pounded aromatics. After this they fill the cavity with the purest bruised myrrh, with cassia, and every other sort of spicery except frankincense, and sew up the opening. Then the body is placed in natrum [**natron**, sodium carbonate dissolved in water—a salt bath] for seventy days, and covered entirely over. After the expiration of that space of time, which must not be exceeded, the body is washed, and wrapped round, from head to foot, with bandages of fine linen cloth, smeared over with gum, which is used generally by the Egyptians in the place of glue, and in this state it is given back to the relations, who enclose it in a wooden case which they have had made for the purpose, shaped into the figure of a man. Then fastening the case, they place it in a sepulchral chamber, upright against the wall.

Mummification was a way of preserving the soul, not only the body. The Egyptians believed that there were several aspects to each person's spirit. When a person was conceived, the artisan-god Khnum created a spiritual double for him or her, known as the *ka*. Ghostly in form and stored in the heart, the *ka* could be freed from the owner during sleep. Upon death, the *ka* left the body to journey to the underworld and to be judged by Osiris. The Egyptians referred to their tombs as "houses of the *ka*." Each morning the *ka* returned to the tomb, beckoned by the body in which it had lived. At pyramids and temples, priests brought offerings of food and drink for the *ka* each day. Perfume, clothing, and furniture were left in the tomb for the *ka* to enjoy. Even early pit graves contained small objects such as pots, beads, and food that must have been intended for use in the afterlife.

A second spiritual element was the *ba*, represented by a human-headed bird. It is usually described as a person's vital life force. If the body remained intact, the well-being of the *ba* was insured. The *ba* left the body at the moment of death and could leave and enter the tomb freely using the body as a perch.

Induced by magic spells performed over the body, the *akh* was the "shining spirit" into which a person was transformed at death so that she or he could exist in the afterlife. The mummies of Egyptian rulers were buried in increasingly large tombs, which peaked in size during the Pyramid Age. The average Egyptian, on the other hand, continued to be buried in a pit grave that was nothing more than a hole covered with dirt. But even the average Egyptian was mummified. All of this effort was expended on mummification because the Egyptians believed that, if the body could be preserved, the essential elements of the spirit—the *ka*, *ba*, and *akh*—would continue into eternity.

Painted and gilded mummy case of the musician-priestess of Amun, Djed-maat-es-ankh, ninth century B.C.

The pharaoh's ba *hovers over his body.*

The Founding of the World's First Nation-State

People harvested wild plants in the Nile Valley at least as early as 18 000 B.C., but agriculture (deliberate planting and reaping) became an integral part of Egyptian life only about 5000 B.C. It arrived from an outside source. As African agriculturalists were forced off the drying lands of the Sahara, they came first to the Faiyum, then to the Nile. The rich soils provided undreamed-of food surpluses to support the rapidly growing population.

By about 4500 B.C., agricultural communities were developing along the Nile, consisting of houses made of mud-brick, like those in Mesopotamia. This material was well-suited to a dry climate and lasted a surprising length of time. As tribal groups developed, fighting among them occurred over the valued strips of river land. Eventually, the final 1200 km

Ancient Egypt.

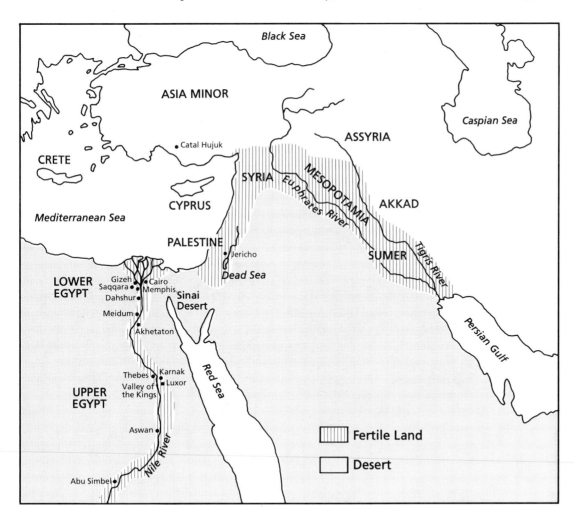

course became divided into provinces called *nomes* by the Greeks. Two main kingdoms were formed. **Upper Egypt** stretched from Cairo to the south, and was divided into sixteen *nomes*. The region of Nubia greatly influenced Upper Egypt's cultural traditions, especially those of kingship and burial. **Lower Egypt** encompassed the Delta region, which was known as a "land of more peril than productivity" because floodwaters continually washed away the communities that were perched on sandy mounds above the low-lying, marshy lands. Lower Egypt was divided into ten *nomes*.

Tradition says that Egypt was unified for the first time when King Menes of Upper Egypt swept north with his armies and captured Lower Egypt. There is no mention of Menes in the archaeological record. Perhaps his exploits are recorded under another name, or perhaps they were actually performed by two other kings, Narmer and Aha. In any case, around 3100 B.C., the first **nation-state** was born—an independent community of people spread over a wide area and united under one government. A new capital was established at Memphis, the junction of the two lands. As a result of the dependable Nile and the protecting deserts, life in the new land was stable, and the first nation developed largely on its own terms, with few outside pressures and influences. Change was limited and carefully controlled.

The lists of kings worked out by a priest named Manetho in the third century B.C. form the basis for dividing Egyptian history into thirty **dynasties**. Archaeologists have grouped together dynasties with common characteristics to create broader classifications: the Early Dynastic Period (circa 3100-2650 B.C.), the Old Kingdom (circa 2650-2134 B.C.), the Middle Kingdom (circa 2040-1640 B.C.), and the New Kingdom (circa 1550-1070 B.C). Lapses in central authority that interspersed eras of accomplishment are known as intermediate periods.

The Kingdoms and Dynasties of Egypt.

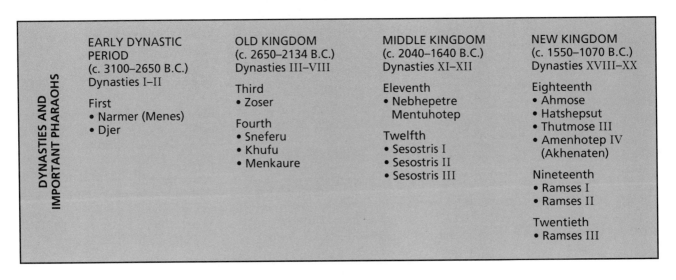

DYNASTIES AND IMPORTANT PHARAOHS	EARLY DYNASTIC PERIOD (c. 3100–2650 B.C.) Dynasties I–II	OLD KINGDOM (c. 2650–2134 B.C.) Dynasties III–VIII	MIDDLE KINGDOM (c. 2040–1640 B.C.) Dynasties XI–XII	NEW KINGDOM (c. 1550–1070 B.C.) Dynasties XVIII–XX
	First • Narmer (Menes) • Djer	Third • Zoser Fourth • Sneferu • Khufu • Menkaure	Eleventh • Nebhepetre Mentuhotep Twelfth • Sesostris I • Sesostris II • Sesostris III	Eighteenth • Ahmose • Hatshepsut • Thutmose III • Amenhotep IV (Akhenaten) Nineteenth • Ramses I • Ramses II Twentieth • Ramses III

As the stature and power of the rulers, or **pharaohs**, increased during the early years of unification, more and more titles became associated with royalty. In the tradition of the Osiris myth, the pharaoh was associated with Horus. To this was added the title "Favourite of the Two Goddesses" (the vulture and cobra) and, by the Second Dynasty, "King of Upper and Lower Egypt."

Among the pharaoh's most important functions as god-king was to maintain a natural harmony that the Egyptians called *maat*. *Maat* is usually defined as justice, truth, order, and righteousness, but it also referred to the cosmic order of the Creation. Only after the Creator "put *maat* in the place of chaos" did he emerge from the primeval mound.

The Old Kingdom (c. 2650-2134 B.C.): Age of the Pyramids

Their religious beliefs inspired the Egyptians to erect monuments to their pharaohs. The monuments became increasingly spectacular as the pharaohs' power grew and as building skills improved. Some are so large and grand that they continue to amaze and mystify us today. Clues about the development of these monuments came in 1912, when James Quibell began excavations at Saqqara. He found several massive mud-brick tombs, known as **mastabas**.

During the First Dynasty, mastabas of sun-baked mud-bricks were built at Abydos. Characterized by a flat roof with sloping sides, these tombs contained compartments for an array of grave offerings that included food, furniture, tools, and weapons that might be useful to the king in the afterlife. The burial chamber underneath was carved out of the bedrock and reached through a vertical shaft. Burial pits for courtiers and attendants encircled the mastabas at Abydos. There is evidence that as many as 580 royal servants of king Djer of the First Dynasty were killed to accompany and assist him in the afterlife. This practice was later abandoned, and only the royal family was buried near the king.

Soon after, the royal cemetery was moved to Saqqara near Memphis. The imposing mastabas there were as long as 65 m, as wide as 37 m, and as high as 12 m. They were subdivided into many chambers, some containing myriad burial goods for use in the afterlife. The burial chambers were dug into the bedrock and could only be reached through the roofs, most of which, by the time they were excavated, were unstable and had collapsed. Early mastabas were finished in wood trimmed with strips of gold; later ones were stone-lined and even more elaborate.

During the Old Kingdom, the Egyptians developed another, more monumental, burial chamber for royalty—the **pyramid**. One after another of these imposing structures was built; as a result, the Old Kingdom is also known as the Age of the Pyramids. But no one knows exactly why the Egyptians started building them. Maybe the pyramid shape was chosen for symbolic rather than practical reasons. Some authorities associate the pyramid

Religion

One of the rituals depicted most frequently on temple walls is the pharaoh offering *maat* (shown as a goddess in a feathered headdress) to the gods. This offering enabled his subjects to be at one with the gods and to enter the afterlife. In everyday life, *maat* translated into an existence of "blessed uneventfulness" with few surprises.

Controversies

In 1935, Walter Emery found objects in twelve mastabas at Saqqara that gave the names of all eight kings of the First Dynasty. The same names were found in the burial chambers at Abydos, which had been discovered by Flinders Petrie in 1899. Since Emery's find, there has been an ongoing debate about where the kings of the First Dynasty were actually buried.

Stonehenge

The Egyptians developed a great civilization and built remarkable structures that reflected the extent of their knowledge. At the same time, and even earlier, the uncivilized peoples of Europe were also building. Western Europe became dotted with over fifty thousand unusual stone constructions called **megaliths**, which consisted of single boulders or groups of boulders placed in a pattern. They are usually found within 100 km to 200 km of the ocean. The oldest megaliths date to 5200 B.C., while the youngest were constructed as recently as 1500 B.C. The building then came to an abrupt end for unknown reasons.

Many **megalithic tombs** have survived along the coastal areas of Sweden, Britain, Ireland, France, Spain, Portugal, and Italy. Most are covered by mounds of earth and are known as **barrows**. The largest prehistoric mound is Silbury Hill in Britain, which measures 163 m wide at the base. The flat-topped peak is over 38 m high. Although its dimensions are clear, its exact purpose is unknown.

Perhaps the most ambitious builders were the temple builders of Malta. They had completed thirty monuments by 3000 B.C. Their multi-roomed tombs had chambers measuring 30 m across in complex, clover-leaf arrangements. These contained burial catacombs for as many as seven thousand people at a single site.

The most famous of all the megalithic monuments is **Stonehenge**. It is located on Salisbury Plain in southern England. An outer ditch with a bank immediately inside surrounds the monuments and forms a circle 95 m across. As visitors approach the site, however, it is the stand of 45 t megaliths that catches the eye. For hundreds of years, people assumed that Stonehenge was conceived of by Druid priests of the fourth century

B.C. In fact, Stonehenge was in ruins for seven centuries before the Druids arrived!

Stonehenge was built in at least three major stages, and several minor ones, over a period of sixteen hundred years. The first stage, Stonehenge I, was begun about 3100 B.C. by a tribal people who lived by farming different crops and trading in stone axes. Their tombs were collective graves in which no one received special consideration. These people laid out the fifty-six Aubrey Holes (named after the person who discovered them) that are evenly spaced about 5 m apart, just inside the ditch. On the outside of the site they placed the Heel Stone, a 31 t megalith, in a very precise position.

Stonehenge II was begun around 2100 B.C. Eighty bluestones were transported 365 km and placed in a double circle. The third phase, which produced Stonehenge as it is known today, was started about 2000 B.C. During this phase, Stonehenge's Sarsen Circle, consisting of posts and lintels (crosspieces), was built. Each post weighed about 25 t, while the lintels weighed 7 t apiece. Within this circle, the builders erected the Sarsen Trilithons, five pairs of enormous post-and-lintel constructions arranged in a horseshoe configuration. Special stones the size of a football were used to hammer each post and lintel.

Stonehenge is a very complex structure. The precise positioning of the stones has caused great debate. When a person stands in the very centre of the monument facing the entrance, his or her straight line of vision overlooks four upright stones at and beyond the outer circle and focusses on the all-important Heel Stone. The view along this axis is aligned with the sunrise over the Heel Stone on 21 June, the summer solstice. The fifty-six Aubrey Holes appear to mark the fifty-six-year cycle of the moon as it rises and sets at different points over the horizon. This positioning meant that eclipses of the sun and the moon could be predicted.

Archaeologists and others have not reached a firm conclusion about the purpose of Stonehenge. Many modern-day investigators have argued that the placing of the Heel Stone and Aubrey Holes is so exact that the builders must have had an advanced understanding of astronomy and mathematics. Yet these people could neither read nor write.

Over the centuries, megalithic monuments have suffered a common fate. As they were abandoned, natural processes weathered and eroded them. Christians often dismantled them in the belief that they were destroying pagan monuments. Farmers moved the stones as they cleared the land, and villagers claimed the material for local construction. Still, Stonehenge and other ruins show that prehistoric peoples were capable of great feats of design and engineering, even though they had not developed a true civilization.

The Sarsen Circle, the trilithons, and the bluestones as they would have looked upon completion.

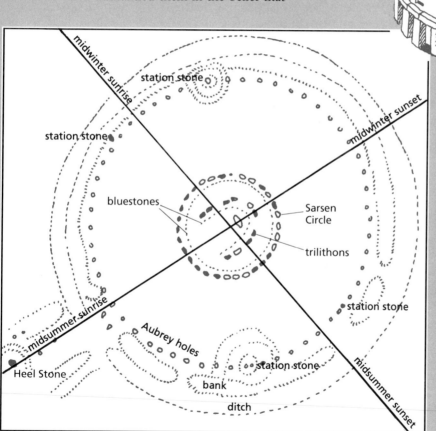

Stonehenge, top view. Stonehenge in its final form was a complex structure. Inside the original ditch and chalk embankments were fifty-six Aubrey Holes, forming an inner circle 87.78 m across. This circle was overgrown by the final phase. Four station posts were positioned within these holes on opposite sides. There was also a smaller (29.56 m) ring of large Sarsen posts and lintels. Inside this ring was still another circle of smaller bluestones. Huge trilithons made of two stone posts and one lintel were then arranged inside in a horseshoe pattern, along with a final group of bluestones.

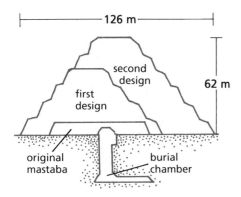

The Step Pyramid at Saqqara (c. 2650).

shape with the primeval mound of creation. Others point out that early writings describe the pharaoh's ascent to heaven via a stairway formed by the sun's rays, and that the profile of a stepped pyramid is also the hieroglyph for stairway. Furthermore, the sheer height of the pyramid would place the pharaoh closer to his destination.

It was during the time of pharaoh Zoser (2650-2631 B.C.) that the first pyramid was constructed. He established a powerful centralized administration strong enough to subdue local squabbling totally. His most trusted advisor was Imhotep, a mathematician, doctor, writer, and architect. Zoser instructed Imhotep to build his burial monument. The size and scale of the end result eclipsed anything yet constructed in Egypt. How Zoser increased his authority to the extent that large numbers of workers could be organized and fed until the project was completed is unclear.

Imhotep chose a site 3.2 km west of Memphis on a rocky plateau at Saqqara. The initial design was a rectangular mastaba built not of mud-brick but of stone. Several additions and alterations occurred, however, resulting in a design of six mastabas placed on top of one another. The underground burial chamber, which was lined with pink granite, was supplemented with a maze of passages as the project expanded. A large granite plug sealed the **sarcophagus** (stone coffin), which was literally quarried into the end of the chamber.

Imhotep's monument to Zoser was the first of eighty-seven pyramids built along the west bank of the Nile between 2650 and 1640 B.C. Originally, the Step Pyramid of Saqqara was covered with a smooth surface of limestone to form a pyramid on a rectangular base. At 62 m high, it was the world's first large public building made completely of stone, and it formed the centrepiece of a vast, walled complex that was larger than those

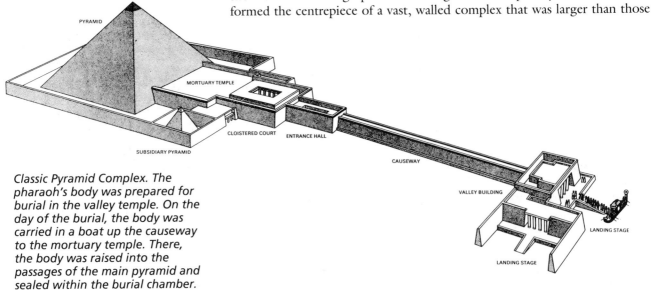

Classic Pyramid Complex. The pharaoh's body was prepared for burial in the valley temple. On the day of the burial, the body was carried in a boat up the causeway to the mortuary temple. There, the body was raised into the passages of the main pyramid and sealed within the burial chamber.

of subsequent pyramids. Under Zoser, the Egyptian state had reached its classic form.

Soon after, pharaoh Sneferu (2595-2571 B.C.), founder of the Fourth Dynasty, oversaw an even grander project. At least two pyramids were under construction at the same time—the pyramid of Meidum and the Bent Pyramid of Dahshur. Unlike the pyramid of Saqqara, both were conceived as pyramids, not mastabas, from the start. Today, the pyramid of Meidum is a pile of rubble surrounding the still-standing central core. Some believe the pyramid collapsed because the angle was too steep, while others believe that it was never finished. The Bent Pyramid is unusual because the slope of the sides becomes more gentle near the top. At approximately the same time, the Egyptians built the Red Pyramid at Dahshur. It featured a square base and uniformly sloping sides, and was thus the first true pyramid.

The largest pyramid ever built was achieved under the rule of Khufu (2571-2548 B.C.), known to the Greeks as pharaoh Cheops. Khufu's monument, called the **Great Pyramid** because of its size, is part of the Gizeh group of monuments, which also includes two other pyramids and the Giant Sphinx. The Great Pyramid is made of 2.5 million stone blocks averaging 2.5 t each. Its staggering dimensions never disappoint even the most expectant visitor. The square base, covering a 6 ha area, is aligned almost exactly with the main points of the compass. Somehow, blocks of granite weighing 53.5 t were moved from Aswan, over 700 km away, to line the burial chamber. Other pyramids had burial chambers dug into the bedrock, but Khufu's was located above ground in the centre of the monument. It was reached by a complicated series of passages, including the 9 m high Grand Gallery, which ran at a steep angle of twenty-six degrees. Originally the entire outer casing was finished in highly polished limestone blocks, fitted together without mortar within millimetres of each other. Today, only a few casing stones remain at the edge of the base.

The Issue Emerges

The Great Pyramid of Khufu was better built, larger, and made with bigger blocks than any pyramid before or since. Yet there was no record of how it was planned or executed until the Greek historian Herodotus provided the classic explanation, two thousand years after the pyramid's construction. He was told that the Great Pyramid was completed by the labour of one hundred thousand workers over twenty years. Many alternative theories have since been advanced to account for the seemingly miraculous construction of the pyramid.

Erich von Däniken has suggested that the earth was visited by astronauts from outer space. Their offspring became the human race as it is known today. Eventually they left for the stars, to return at a later, unspecified date. "Primitive" people remembered them as "gods" who possessed

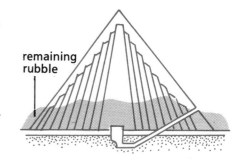

Collapsed Pyramid at Meidum (Sneferu, c. 2600).

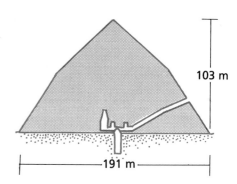

Bent Pyramid at Dahshur (c. 2600).

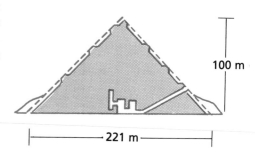

Red Pyramid at Dahshur (c. 2600).

Khufu's Burial

According to tradition, Khufu's dead body was moved by boat from the palace at Memphis to the Valley Temple in Gizeh at the edge of the Nile. It was there that purification, mummification, and other religious rituals occurred. After ten weeks, the mummy was ready for burial. Priests led a procession up a ramp that led to the Mortuary Temple within the pyramid complex. To reflect the belief that the spirit of the dead pharaoh boarded the sun's heavenly boat and travelled across the sky each day in the company of Re, Khufu was towed in a funerary boat that rested on a wooden sledge. Additional mourners followed, shouldering a larger boat intended for his voyage into the underworld. Khufu's Great Ship was found buried beside his pyramid. From the Mortuary Temple, following further ceremony, the mummy was taken to the pyramid and raised 18 m to pass through the entrance. Once the mummy was moved along the complex of inner passages into the burial chamber, the corridors were sealed in an attempt to protect Khufu for an eternity against tomb robbers.

Legend has it that the Great Pyramid was first entered again in A.D. 820 by Caliph Siamum, an Islamic leader, who believed that an emerald of tremendous size lay just inside. He and his workers almost gave up the task of finding the opening but, while they were probing the north face, the sound of falling stone indicated the presence of inner passages. Once the outer casing was removed, they quickly discovered the original passage. They worked their way to the burial chamber, but there was no emerald, nor was a pharaoh found lying in the granite sarcophagus. This left the impression that either Khufu's body was never placed in the pyramid, or it had been spirited away! Possibly the threat of grave robbers prompted Egyptian priests to remove the pharaoh's body after the burial ceremony and place it in less pretentious surroundings. Not a single body has been found in any of the other eighty-six pyramids along the Nile.

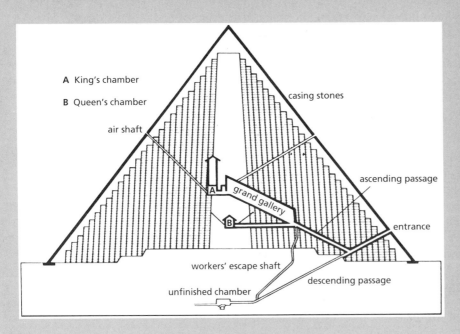

The Great Pyramid is the only one with the burial chamber in the heart of the structure above ground level.

A King's chamber

B Queen's chamber

air shaft

casing stones

grand gallery

ascending passage

entrance

workers' escape shaft

descending passage

unfinished chamber

far superior knowledge and skills. Before the "gods" left, they used their knowledge to help with a variety of projects. Von Däniken's hypothesis explains the breathtaking achievements of many early societies, including those of Easter Island, Mexico, South America, and ancient Egypt, and, of course, the mystery of the Great Pyramid.

More recently, Joseph Davidovits proposed the idea that the Egyptians may have possessed an advanced knowledge of chemistry, allowing them to cast the large blocks of stone from moulds on the building site. Little technology would have been required. This hypothesis eliminates the apparent difficulty of transporting huge blocks over long distances.

Is there any substance to either of these radical views, or is the more traditional, "heave-ho" explanation that Herodotus first described a better hypothesis?

THE PROBLEM QUESTION

Is the construction of the pyramids more convincingly explained by von Däniken, Wilson, or Davidovits?

ALTERNATIVE ONE: Chariots of the Gods?

Based on *Chariots of the Gods* by Erich von Däniken (1968)

If we meekly accept the neat package that Egyptologists serve up to us, ancient Egypt appears suddenly and without transition with a fantastic ready-made civilization. Great cities and enormous temples, colossal statues with tremendous expressive power, splendid streets flanked by magnificent sculptures, perfect drainage systems, luxurious tombs carved out of the rock, pyramids of overwhelming size—these and many other wonderful things shot out of the ground, so to speak. Genuine miracles in a country that is suddenly capable of such achievements without recognizable prehistory!

Fertile agricultural land exists only on the Nile Delta and on small strips to the left and right of the river.... Could [the large number of labourers] have lived on the scanty yields of agriculture in the Nile Delta?

I shall be told that the stone blocks used for building the temple were moved on rollers. In other words, wooden rollers! But the Egyptians would scarcely have felled and turned into rollers the few trees, mainly date palms, that then (as now) grew in Egypt, because the dates from the palms were urgently needed for food and the trunks and fronds were the only things giving shade to the dried-up ground. But there must have been wooden rollers, otherwise there would not be even the feeblest explanation of the building of the pyramids. Did the Egyptians import wood? In order to import wood there must have been a sizeable fleet, and even after it had been landed in Alexandria the wood would have to be transported up the Nile to Cairo. Since the Egyptians did not have horses and carts at the time of the building of the Great Pyramid, there was no other possibility. The horse and cart was not introduced until about...1600 B.C. Of course the scholars say that wooden rollers were needed....

It is well known that the ancient Egyptians practised a solar religion. Their sun god, Re, travelled through the heavens in a bark [a boat]. Pyramid texts of the Old Kingdom even describe heavenly journeys by the king, obviously made with the help of the gods and their boats. So the gods and kings of the Egyptians were also involved with flying....

Is it really a coincidence that the height of the pyramid of [Khufu] multiplied by a thousand million—98 000 000 miles [157 711 400 km]—corresponds approximately to the distance between the earth and the sun? Is it a coincidence that a meridian running through the pyramid divides continents and oceans into two exactly equal halves? Is it coincidence that the area of the base of the pyramid divided by twice its height gives the celebrated figure, 3.14159? Is it coincidence that calculations of the weight of the earth were found and is it also coincidence that the rocky ground on which the structure stands is carefully and accurately levelled?

There is not a single clue to explain why the builder of the pyramid of...the Pharaoh Khufu chose that particular rocky terrain in the desert as the site for his edifice.... [I]t would certainly have been more practical to locate the building site nearer the eastern quarries in order to shorten transport distances.... Since there is so much to be said against the textbook explanations of the choice of site, one might reasonably ask whether the "gods" did not have their say here, too, even if it was by way of the priesthood. For the pyramid not only divides continents and oceans into two equal halves, but it also lies at the center of gravity of the continents. If the facts noted are not coincidences—and it seems extremely difficult to believe that they are—then the building site was chosen by beings who knew all about the spherical shape of the earth and the distribution of continents and seas.

Today, in the twentieth century, no architect could build a copy of the pyramid of [Khufu], even if the technical resources of every continent were at his [or her] disposal.

2 600 000 gigantic blocks were cut out of the quarries, dressed and transported, and fitted together on the building site to the nearest thousandth of an inch. And deep down inside, in the galleries, the walls were painted in colours.

The site of the pyramid was the whim of a pharaoh.

The unparalleled "classical" dimensions of the pyramid occurred to the master builder by chance.

Several hundred thousand workers pushed and pulled blocks weighing twelve tons [10.9 t] up a ramp with (non-existent) ropes on (non-existent) rollers.

The host of workers lived on (non-existent) grain.

They slept in (non-existent) huts which the pharaoh built outside his summer palace.

The workers were urged on by an encouraging "Heave-ho" over a (non-existent) loudspeaker, and so the twelve-ton blocks were pushed skyward.

If the industrious workers had achieved the extraordinary daily rate of ten blocks piled up on top of each other, they would have assembled the 2 600 000 stone blocks in the magnificent stone pyramid in about 250 000 days—664 years. Yes, and don't forget that the whole thing came into being at the whim of an eccentric king who never lived to see the completion of the edifice he had inspired.

We know next to nothing about the how, why, and when of the building of the pyramid. An artificial mountain some 490 feet [150 m] high and weighing 6 500 000 tons [5 900 000 t], stands there as evidence of an incredible achievement, and this monument is supposed to be nothing more than the burial place of an extravagant king! Anyone who can believe that explanation is welcome to it....

Reprinted from *Chariots of The Gods?* by Erich von Däniken, by permission of Souvenir Press Ltd.

Controversies

If, as most experts claim, the Great Pyramid was built within the twenty-three years of Pharaoh Khufu's reign, one 2.5 t block would have to be cut, transported, and fitted into place every two minutes. This figure is based on a twelve-hour work day, three hundred days a year. Von Däniken claims that this rate could not be achieved with construction techniques available today. How then did the Egyptians do it over 4500 years ago?

QUESTIONS

1. What is the picture of ancient Egypt that Egyptologists describe, according to von Däniken?
2. Why does von Däniken ask the question, "Could [the large number of labourers] all have lived on the scanty yields of agriculture in the Nile Delta?"
3. What problems does von Däniken see with the possibility that wooden rollers were used in construction?
4. a) What technique does von Däniken use when he questions a series of so-called "coincidences" about the Great Pyramid of Khufu?
   b) Who, according to von Däniken, chose the building site of the Great Pyramid?
   c) Is von Däniken's writing technique convincing? Explain your answer.
5. a) What is the traditional explanation of how the Great Pyramid was built?
   b) Why does von Däniken object to this explanation?
6. Who, by implication, gave the Egyptians the knowledge and technology to build the pyramids?

ALTERNATIVE TWO: Who Built the Great Pyramid?

Based on "Who Built the Great Pyramid? by Margaret Sears (1990) and "The Chariots Still Crash" by Clifford Wilson (1975)

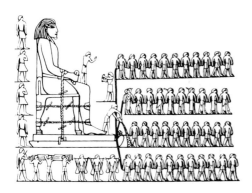

Djehutihotep.

In separate articles, Margaret Sears and Clifford Wilson argue that plenty of evidence shows that the Egyptians built the Great Pyramid themselves, using teams of workers to move the blocks into position. The bulk of the limestone came from a quarry located on the Gizeh plateau, south of the pyramid. The fine white limestone employed in the casing came from Tura across the Nile. The granite used in the king's burial chamber was ferried by boat from Aswan, about 700 km upriver. Obviously, the construction of the Great Pyramid involved an enormous commitment, but the Egyptians were inspired by religious conviction. For example, the site for the pyramids (the west bank of the Nile) was determined by the religious belief that the setting sun in the west was the dwelling place of the dead. During Khufu's reign, Egypt was rich, united, and at peace with its neighbours. Under an authoritarian god-king, all attention could be focussed on the critical task of building a tomb that would endure.

How did the Egyptians cut and move the stone blocks? They used wooden rollers, rafts, and sleds like those on display in the Cairo museum. Coniferous wood was imported from Phoenicia at the time of Sneferu. Clearly wood was available when required, because Khufu's wooden funerary boat was found buried beside the pyramid, along with quantities of rope. A picture from the later tomb of Djehutihotep shows 152 men moving a huge statue of the pharaoh on a wooden sled. In the picture, to lessen the friction of the 53.5 t load, a liquid is being poured along the route. French architect Henri Chevier has shown that one man harnessed to a rope can move a 1 t block on a slippery path of Nile mud. With teams of workers, the 2.2 t blocks that make up most of the pyramid could have been moved easily into place. Using pulleys and ropes, workers could drag the stone up embankments of earth. Once the project was complete, the earth could simply be removed.

The tools for cutting the stone included copper chisels, dolerite hammers, and wooden wedges. Much of the rock has a natural cleavage; it splits evenly along a straight line when prompted with a wedge and chisel. The precision fit of the outer casing blocks was such that the blade of a knife could scarcely fit between them. This feat was accomplished by trimming the blocks before they were hauled into place. Stonemasons would have cleaned up and smoothed the outer limestone surfaces once the structure was complete and the earthen ramp removed. Yale Egyptologist Mark Lehner discovered a series of evenly spaced bore holes on the plateau that could have been used to hold survey poles. This technique could have helped the builders to ensure that the lines of the pyramid were kept straight.

Many of the blocks used in the Great Pyramid were marked with practical instructions such as "this side up," while others name the quarry teams that worked on them—"Vigorous Gang" or "Enduring Gang," for example. Some crews demonstrated their sense of humour by inscribing messages such as "How drunk is the king?" The quarries across the Nile still contain unfinished blocks the same size and shape as the ones in the Great Pyramid.

In 1988, Lehner and Zahi Sawass of the Egyptian Antiquities Organization began a series of continuing excavations to locate the settlements of the workers who built the Great Pyramid. Near one of the Gizeh pyramids, ruined walls 80 m by 450 m enclose a series of galleries now filled with sand. Excavation of some of the galleries has revealed bits of flint blade, copper, sandstone rubbers used to polish stone, and grinding pigments, all of which date to the Old Kingdom. Non-local stones such as granite, quartzite, and basalt, commonly used in buildings and tools, were also uncovered. A thumb-size model of a large statue seemed to confirm that these galleries were storage rooms for materials used in royal craft production. Three hundred metres south of the Sphinx, another excavation uncovered buildings that contain implements used to store grain and make bread and beer. This granary dates to the time of pharaoh Menkaure, and its isolated location suggests it could have been used by those working on his pyramid. Further excavations may yet reveal the dwellings of those who worked on Khufu's Great Pyramid.

Well-organized teams could have completed the Great Pyramid within Khufu's lifetime. Ramps from the quarry to the pyramid could rise around the perimeter with each level of blocks. The Bent Pyramid has marker stones indicating that it was half finished in about a year. Modern calculations indicate that the Great Pyramid could have been built in less than a decade.

QUESTIONS

1. Where did the stone to build the Great Pyramid come from?
2. According to the above viewpoint, why was Khufu able to organize enough workers to do the job?
3. What evidence proves that wood and rope were available for construction?
4. What tools and techniques do Wilson and Sears say were used to shape and move the large stone blocks?
5. How do they explain the close fit of the stones and the straight lines of the Great Pyramid?
6. Does there seem to be evidence that large numbers of workers were present in the area of the Gizeh pyramids? Explain your answer.
7. How long would it have taken to build the Great Pyramid according to Wilson and Sears?

ALTERNATIVE THREE: An Enigma Solved

Based on *The Pyramids—An Enigma Solved* by Joseph Davidovits and Margie Morris (1988)

According to the heave-ho theory, the Egyptians used ramps to help them move the heavy stones and other materials to the right level. Remains of small ramps have been found at Saqqara and Gizeh, but they were probably used for climbing rather than as a means to raise heavy stone blocks. It would require 140 workers to raise an average pyramid block on a ramp with a 1:3 ratio. To sustain the fourteen hundred blocks per day needed for the construction of the Great Pyramid, 52 500 workers making four trips per day would have been required. This seems highly unlikely. Some of the largest blocks are found at elevations thirty stories high. Getting them there would have required much more labour than the modest calculations above suggest. There are no murals of the time showing the ramps and sleds that were supposedly used to move the blocks. (The earliest-known relief showing a statue being dragged is dated to eight hundred years after the Great Pyramid was finished.) Wooden rollers would have made the task easier, but the earliest evidence of their use by the Egyptians dates to 750 B.C., about eighteen hundred years later than the time of the Great Pyramid.

Aside from the problem of the ramps, the heave-ho theory has many other weaknesses. Evidence proves that the Egyptians knew how to dress blocks using stone and copper tools. Yet copper is a soft metal unsuitable for cutting hard stone, particularly on the scale required for the Great Pyramid. Davidovits points out that Khufu's Pyramid contains an amount of stone equal to that used in *all* of the monuments produced from the New Kingdom onward. In addition, the limestone of the Old Kingdom pyramids was twice as hard as the soft limestone and sandstone used in the majority of New Kingdom construction. The type of bronze needed for tools able to cut pyramid limestone was only available eight hundred years after the Great Pyramid was built! Furthermore, modern studies by D.D. Klemm, a geochemist from the University of Munich, have shown the limitations of quarrying. Several methods of quarrying were used by the Egyptians, and later by the Romans, but there is no evidence that *any* of the methods were employed before 1600 B.C.

In Davidovits's opinion, the blocks of the Great Pyramid are actually high quality concrete—synthetic stone—*cast directly in place*. He claims that each block is about 90-95 percent limestone rubble and 5-10 percent cement. Suitable ingredients were plentiful. The aluminum and silicon binder that would have been necessary was available in the silt of the Nile River. Natron salt is abundant in the deserts and salt lakes. It reacts with lime and water to produce caustic soda, the crucial component for this method of stonemaking. Lime could have been obtained by heating limestone in simple hearths. The Sinai mines were rich in other minerals that would have facilitated rock formation and rapid setting of the wet concrete.

Davidovits believes the workers mixed these ingredients in wooden moulds. True, the trees along the Nile are not appropriate for making

Science

The earliest-known remains of high quality cement have been found at Jericho (c. 7000 B.C.), Tel Ramid, Syria (c. 6000 B.C.), and Catal Hujuk, Turkey (c. 6000 B.C.). It is likely that travellers brought this technology to Egypt. The ancient cement in pyramid blocks at Gizeh has remained intact for over forty-five hundred years. In contrast, Portland Cement (invented A.D. 1824), the basis of modern construction, began to crack after only fifty years when it was used in restoration work at Gizeh.

large moulds. But Egypt began to import suitable woods—such as cypress, cedar, and juniper—from Lebanon as early as the predynastic era. Once set up, the moulds could be waterproofed with a thin layer of cement, which would then become part of the block. This layer can be seen on the bottom of the blocks in the Great Pyramid.

Once cast, a block hardened within hours. The mould was removed while the block was relatively soft. Moulds were oiled beforehand to ease the blocks' removal. (Herodotus reported that the builders of the Great Pyramid smelled of rancid oil.) The moulds could have been easily disassembled so that one or more faces of a block could be used as a part of the mould for the next block, which explains how the stones could be fitted so close to one another.

It is extremely difficult to distinguish artificial from natural limestone. But Davidovits maintains that at Gizeh there is compelling evidence proving that most blocks for the three main pyramids were cast, not quarried. Chunks of stone can be seen incorporated into the blocks. Lines left by the moulds appear on the surface of the large blocks, which took longer (three days) to set. These lines are wavy, characteristic of most types of concrete, and not horizontal, characteristic of natural limestone. Unlike natural limestone, most pyramid blocks have no strata at all. The density of pyramid blocks is different from that of the blocks found in the quarries. In addition, quarry blocks contain cracks filled with calcite, whereas similar cracks are missing from pyramid blocks. Carved blocks exhibit tool marks; pyramid blocks do not. Pyramid blocks were set to ten standard lengths and laid in different patterns throughout the pyramid. Such regular blocks could not have been cut, stored, and selected on the scale required. In natural stone, fossil shells are layered horizontally; in the pyramid blocks, they are jumbled throughout. But a greater number of shells settled at the bottom of the mould, leaving a weathered matrix at the top of the block. This resulted in severe erosion on top, leaving a sponge-like pattern of holes in many blocks.

According to Davidovits, the Egyptians of the Old Kingdom were highly skilled in the ancient art of chemistry known as *alchemy*. We know they had techniques for making wine, beer, and vinegar. They mastered the chemistry of mummification. Davidovits is certain that the Egyptians also had the alchemical expertise to cast concrete blocks. During the Old Kingdom, the prestige of the god Khnum, the Divine Potter who was one of the creators of the universe, reached its peak. Khnum was also associated with alchemical stonemaking.

The implements needed to make the pyramids of the Old Kingdom were simply those used to lay sun-dried mud-bricks: hoes to scrape up fossil-shelled limestone; baskets to carry ingredients; troughs to prepare the mix; and ladders, squares, plumb lines, levels, trowels, and wooden moulds. There can be little doubt that the Egyptians, in effect, *poured* their pyramids! But when they developed metallurgy and the wheel, they began to work with stone in new ways. And as the Old Kingdom declined, the old knowledge of alchemy was lost.

QUESTIONS

1. What problems exist with the heave-ho explanation of how the Great Pyramid was built?
2. a) In Davidovits's opinion, how was the construction of the Great Pyramid accomplished?
   b) What evidence suggests that the cement used in the ancient world was stronger than modern cement?
3. a) What materials were needed to cast a block?
   b) Where did these materials come from?
4. Do you think Davidovits produces enough evidence to prove that the stone in the pyramid was manufactured? Explain your answer.
5. What difficulties of pyramid construction could be avoided using the technique of casting stone blocks?
6. Is there more evidence to support the heave-ho method of pyramid construction or more evidence to support Davidovits's ideas? Again, explain your answer.

ANSWERING THE PROBLEM QUESTION

The very existence and magnitude of the Great Pyramid instantly challenges the mind to imagine how it was built so long ago. Von Däniken questions several traditional assumptions about pyramid construction. He does not deny that the Egyptians built the Great Pyramid, but argues that extra-terrestrials may have provided the know-how required to meet the construction schedule. In some cases, the facts he cites differ from those given by Sears and Wilson. When you encounter disagreements about basic information, consult other sources to determine which of the original claims is accurate.

In answering the problem question, you will have to consider the materials used and the process of construction. How were the large amounts of limestone removed and transported from the local quarry? How was the polished limestone of the outer casing quarried and shipped across the Nile? How were the enormous granite blocks removed from the bedrock and transported from Aswan? Were the tools of Egyptian technology and their labour practices advanced enough during the Old Kingdom for them to have quarried, transported, shaped, and polished the finished product? How could ramps have been used to move heavy stone upward as the height of the pyramid soared? Or was the burden of transportation greatly reduced by the Egyptians' ability to pour a mixture into a wooden mould and produce the stone right on the spot?

Absolute answers to all of these questions will probably never be found. But you should be able to establish some criteria and rank the three explanations according to how well they satisfy your requirements. Having done that, which theory do you prefer?

THE STORY CONTINUES . . .

The Shape of Egyptian Society

The pyramids have attracted admiration and attention for thousands of years. But what do we know about the society that created them? Not surprisingly, Egyptian society was structured much like a pyramid. At the peak was the pharaoh, the god-king and the focus of all loyalty and appreciation. The royal family, the vizier (the chief minister), and the courtiers shared some of the pharaoh's pre-eminence and enjoyed the ceremony of palace life. The next level of the social pyramid was occupied by the ruling class. Within this group, the priesthood had the most prestige. In theory, the pharaoh was the high priest of the nation. Duties at the temples, however, were usually carried out by a chief priest, who commanded great power and exercised control of the wealth from temple treasures. A pharaoh had the power to appoint a new chief priest, but the office usually remained within one family and was passed from generation to generation. It was the priests who knew how to perform rituals that pleased the gods—daily sacrifices, spells to sustain the fertility of the land, and prayers that made possible the transition from this life to the afterlife.

The ruling class also included an aristocracy of rich landowners, public officials, and, particularly from the Middle Kingdom onward, military commanders. Usually the vizier, who advised the pharaoh on the administration of the nation, was chosen from this elite, as were provincial governors and tax collectors. A family from the ruling class lived in an impressive residence, probably a vast walled enclosure that contained as many as seventy rooms. Its main entrance, often framed with 4 m high columns, led to a spacious courtyard and hallway, off which large, high-ceilinged rooms were arranged on two levels. To keep cooking odours at a distance, the kitchen was located away from bedrooms and servants' quarters. Courtyards were landscaped with gardens, trees, and lotus-laden pools and fountains stocked with fish. An open, refreshing atmosphere was ensured. Ventilation was considered crucial. Rooms were built facing away from the sun where possible, and windows were kept small. The terrace on the second floor was covered with a roof supported by columns, allowing a pleasant breeze to circulate and keeping the family cool when they slept on this level on summer nights.

Decoration was rich but (compared with tomb interiors) simple. Plastered walls were painted with patterned trim or scenes of flowers, fruits, or birds. Furniture woods had to be imported from Syria and Lebanon, but Egyptian cabinetmakers did work of the highest quality. They aimed for and achieved an elegant combination of beauty and comfort. Stylized bodies of lions and jackals formed the lower portions of armchairs; folding chairs had birds' heads at the crosspieces. The legs of the beds were carved to resemble animal legs. Furniture was finished in ebony, ivory, gold, and semi-precious stones. Cushions were padded with cotton or feathers and covered with leopard skin.

To provide these and other luxuries, as well as goods that were more essential, there was a middle class of merchants, traders, and artisans. By the Middle Kingdom, their numbers were significant. They gathered around the temples and palaces in royal cities such as Memphis and Thebes, living and working in single-storey, mud-brick homes similar to those found in the villages along the Nile.

Among the most prestigious members of the middle class were the scribes, whose profession was literacy. They are often depicted in a seated position working with their palettes, water cups, and brushes. Training involved five years of intense work, beginning at the age of nine, but the rewards were worth it. A scribe could anticipate a life free from taxes, enter the priesthood, and hold the highest appointed offices in the land. Accurate records were essential for the efficient operation of government, particularly for the tabulation of taxes collected and the outflow of expenses. It was the scribe who recorded the heroic deeds of the pharaoh as well as day-to-day events—births, deaths, and marriages.

The working classes of Egyptian society were by far the most numerous. Their single-storey homes formed an unbroken façade along the village streets. Most homes were furnished simply with benches, beds, and reed mats. There would also be baskets, cooking pots, and utensils for grinding grain. Peasant farmers planted and harvested with the unending cycle of the Nile. During the flood season, they were often required to work on temples and palaces for their pharaoh. They were housed in construction villages consisting of square mud-brick dwellings. Peasants were also obligated, periodically, to maintain irrigation canals and to serve in the military. When the flood-waters receded, farmers began to plant wheat, barley, fruit, and vegetables. Each season, tax collectors took over half of the crop for the pharaoh.

Particularly during the Middle and New Kingdoms, prisoners of war were brought to Egypt as slaves. Most suffered a hard life, but some lived as free peasants and others served in the houses of the rich. Slaves did much the same work as was required of the peasants.

Egyptians of all classes had similar ideas about fashion and appearance, although the ruling class obviously had more resources to devote to these aspects of social life. For all Egyptians, it was socially essential to wash before and after each meal. Tomb paintings show attendants hanging up clothes and pouring water over ruling-class women. Priests took several baths each day. In an attempt to achieve total purity, they shaved their bodies, including their eyelashes and eyebrows. Egyptians generally felt disgust for peoples who were less hygienic.

Facial hair was viewed with disdain. Many Egyptian priests and ruling-class men shaved their heads and ridiculed the beards worn by foreigners. Only in certain circumstances were beards permissible. Short, round, imitation beards on a well-shaven chin were worn for ritual purposes. A long square beard was reserved for a king. The pointed tapering beard could be worn only by a god.

From the Old Kingdom onward, ruling-class men and women owned at least one wig made from real hair. (Peasants, when they could afford them, had wigs made from wool that was dyed black.) A woman of distinction could either wear a wig or style her hair in long braids. She might also use an eye make-up called *kohl*, which could be coloured black, blue, or green.

The Middle Kingdom (c. 2040-1640 B.C.)

Great as Egypt's wealth and system of labour were, the colossal task of building the pyramids had exhausted resources by the end of the Sixth Dynasty in the twenty-first century B.C. Priests, nobles, and officials had gained local loyalties and land grants while organizing work crews for public construction. As a result, the pharaoh lost much of his power and stature. It was the Theban pharaoh Nebhepetre Mentuhotep (2060-2010 B.C.) who reunited the country, launching the Middle Kingdom. Egypt prospered after a century of internal strife, and the breakdown of central authority was reversed.

During the Twelfth Dynasty, the increased power of the pharaoh led to a new era of commercial expansion, backed by the creation of a new army. Canals were built, more land was brought under cultivation in the Faiyum, and trade was extended from Nubia to Palestine and Syria. But the pharaohs did not fully recover the levels of prestige enjoyed by their predecessors, and Egyptian society changed as a result. Immortality, previously a royal privilege, became attainable by all Egyptians; faith in Osiris assured a person's survival after death. Similarly, every Egyptian now enjoyed equality before the law, although some class distinctions remained.

During the Thirteenth Dynasty, Egypt appeared to be unified, but this was superficial. In reality, a series of weak pharaohs were unable to maintain a firm grip on the many peoples spread along the reaches of the Nile. The expansion of the Hittite Empire in the eastern Mediterranean pressured outsiders to spread into the Delta in large numbers by about 1650 B.C. Earlier arrivals, interested in the growing wealth of the Middle Kingdom, had been kept under control by a firm central government. This time, the **Hyksos**, or "rulers of foreign lands," managed to gain control, although no one knows exactly how. Their horse-drawn chariots, bronze weapons, and powerful bows were superior to Egyptian military technology. It seems, however, that they conquered the country mainly through sheer force of numbers, and a Hyksos ruler became pharaoh in 1674 B.C. The

Egypt during the Twelfth Dynasty.

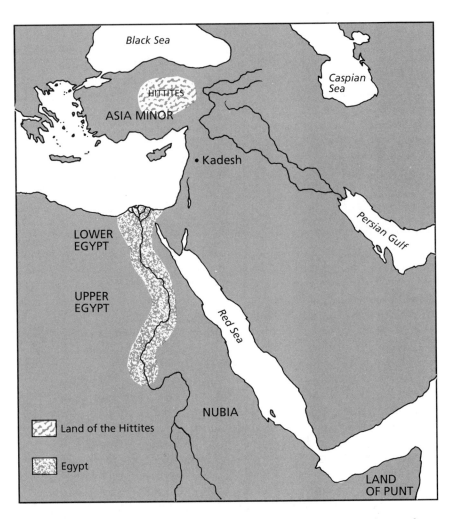

Asiatic Hyksos adopted almost every aspect of Egyptian culture, from administration to hieroglyphic writing, but foreigners they remained. Their presence was resented by native Egyptians.

The New Kingdom (c. 1550-1070 B.C.)

A national resistance movement under Theban leadership struggled for decades against the Hyksos intruders. Led by Ahmose (1550-1526 B.C.), they were finally successful in establishing the Eighteenth Dynasty in 1550 B.C. This success marked the beginning of ancient Egypt's final period of greatness. The New Kingdom, as the era was called, was a time of strong pharaohs including Thutmose III (1490-1436 B.C.) and Ramses II (1288-1220 B.C.). They used the superior bows and chariots introduced by the Hyksos to help create the first Egyptian Empire outside the Nile Valley.

Queen Hatshepsut (1503-1482 B.C.) was the most powerful female pharaoh in Egyptian history. During her reign, defence was strengthened, trade was bolstered, and the country improved. This is her mortuary temple.

Their control extended southward into the Sudan and eastward into the Sinai and western Asia. Tributes collected throughout the empire greatly enriched the New Kingdom.

When Thutmose II died, Queen Hatshepsut, "a god's wife," assumed the authority of the pharaoh. For the next thirty years, Hatshepsut dominated Egyptian life, while her stepson, Thutmose III (who would later become a great military pharaoh), played a secondary role. Her burial temple reveals that she sent (and possibly led) an expedition into what is now Somalia. This was the "land of Punt," where exotic leopard skins, ostrich feathers, hardwoods, and myrrh could be obtained. The same temple also shows how the Egyptians cut and transported obelisks from Aswan for the Temple of Amun in Thebes. Hatshepsut is often depicted in portraits and statues dressed in male clothing, including the narrow decorative beard male pharaohs occasionally taped to their chins. Peace and prosperity dominated her reign.

Amenhotep IV (1353-1334 B.C.), the "heretic pharaoh," was another important leader. He became pharaoh at the age of twelve and married his father's Mesopotamian widow Nefertiti, who was eighteen. In the fifth year of his reign, Amenhotep insisted that the sun-god Aten was more important than all other deities. He dedicated a new city to Aten at the site of Amarna, halfway between Memphis and Thebes.

To Amenhotep, the purest religion was the worship of the sun itself, creator of the world and the source of all life. Accordingly, Amenhotep

More to Consider

Archaeologists discovered the bricks from Akhenaten's temple during the 1920s. Many of the stones bearing the names or portraits of the royal couple were broken or mutilated. Canadian Egyptologist Donald Redford heads the Akhenaten Temple Project, which has recovered one hundred thousand of the original stones from Karnak and other sites.

changed his name to Akhen*aten* and that of the city of Amarna to Akhet*aten*. All temples dedicated to other gods were closed, which horrified the Egyptian priests. The name of the previous sun-god, Amun, was removed from the face of all public buildings.

With Akhenaten's death in 1334 B.C., the religious revolution that he and Nefertiti had imposed quickly collapsed. Subsequent generations attempted to deny their existence by eliminating all traces of their influence. The great temple built by Akhenaten at Karnak was dismantled, and many of the bricks hidden within the pylons of the nearby Temple of Amun.

Egyptologists continue to debate Akhenaten's importance. During his reign, impressive temples were built, but the empire stagnated. For some, Akhenaten was the pioneer of **monotheism**, the worship of a single god. Others believe that he was simply trying to regain the divine status enjoyed by pharaohs in earlier times.

Akhenaten's successor was the boy-king Tutankhamun (1334-1325 B.C.), whose tomb was discovered only after years of expensive and patient searching. By virtue of their size, the pyramids of the Old Kingdom had been open invitations to grave robbers. From the Middle Kingdom onward, attempts were made to hide the burial place of the pharaoh. Chambers were cut into the solid rock of a desolate location, across the Nile from Luxor and Karnak, called the Valley of the Kings. The entrances were sealed and disguised with debris. Most of the tombs, however, were still broken into and looted soon after they were closed.

By the end of the nineteenth century A.D., many excavators were convinced that the Valley of the Kings had been fully explored. Even so, a wealthy English aristocrat named Lord Carnarvon sponsored an archaeologist named Howard Carter to search for an undiscovered tomb. Clay jars with seals bearing the name Tutankhamun had been recovered by a previous excavation in 1907. Carter felt that the real tomb was still to be found, but excavations from 1917 to 1921 yielded nothing. Only after much pleading by Carter, who pointed out the need to excavate a small, unchecked area below the tomb of Ramses VI, did Carnarvon reluctantly agree to finance the digging for one more season.

On 5 November 1922, Carter's team found the first of sixteen steps that led to a tomb entrance. In the days, weeks, and eventually, ten years of work that followed, the world became familiar and fascinated with "Tut's tomb," as it was called. Travellers from every continent came to witness the process, much to the annoyance of Carter, who hated the publicity. The fabulous treasure of over five thousand items dazzled the imagination. There were exquisite thrones of inlaid gold, sculptures of alabaster, and jewellery of precious and semiprecious stones. The highlights were the inner coffin, made of over 100 kg of solid gold, and the death mask that rested on the head of the mummy itself. These artifacts provided a wealth of information about Egyptian life.

Surprisingly little is known about Tutankhamun himself. It seems likely that the priests of Amun pressured the young pharaoh to reverse Akhenaten's religious revolution and to reopen the temples dedicated to other deities. He moved the capital from Amarna to Thebes and changed his name, which had been Tutankhaten, to Tutankhamun in honour of the previous sun-god. After a nine-year reign, Tutankhamun died at the age of eighteen. The magnificent burial of this relatively insignificant pharaoh gives a tantalizing hint of the riches that must have been associated with more important leaders. Although thieves had broken into Tutankhamun's tomb, it was still largely intact when discovered by Carter. It is this fact that gives Tutankhamun's name the kind of immortality that the ancient Egyptians cherished.

During the Nineteenth Dynasty, Ramses II emerged as one of Egypt's greatest warrior pharaohs. The Hittite Empire in northern Syria posed a threat to Egyptian interests beyond the Nile. Ramses met this challenge and took his army north to the Orontes River. When forced to retreat after a surprise attack by the Hittites at Kadesh, temple inscriptions credited him with a victory! He led his armies into Syria a second time, caught the Hittites embroiled with other problems, and negotiated the first nonaggression treaty in history. The Egyptians and the Hittites agreed not to attack each other and to provide assistance if attacked by another. Syria was evenly divided, with the Hittites gaining the north and Egypt the south.

Ramses II then embarked on one of the most ambitious building programs of any pharaoh. He enlarged the already impressive temples at Luxor and Karnak at Thebes. A sacred lake for religious rituals was excavated beside the temple of Amun-Re at Karnak. The addition of a hypostyle hall (a hall supported by pillars) extended the temple to a length of over 350 m. Among his other projects were the rock-cut temples built for himself and his favourite wife, Nefertari, at Abu Simbel.

The New Kingdom lasted until the eleventh century B.C., but internal and external pressure resulted in its gradual decline. Defensive battles against a mysterious group of marauders known as "the peoples of the sea" were successful but costly. Control of Egypt moved to the high priests, who dominated the weak successors of Ramses III. With the arrival of the Iron Age in Europe and in the Aegean, military power spread northwest, and Egypt eventually fell to a series of better-equipped armies. The country was dominated by Libyan, Nubian, Assyrian, and Greek dynasties. The fall of Egypt to Augustus Caesar in 30 B.C. marked the end of the classic age of civilization and achievement. Eternal monuments were swallowed by the desert, and even the spoken language was lost.

SUMMARY

Although the Nile River flows through desert, the silts deposited by its annual flooding make agriculture possible along its banks and on the Delta

The gold death mask of Tutankhamun.

More to Consider

When the Aswan Dam was planned in 1964, it was clear that the two temples would be submerged beneath the rising waters of Lake Nasser behind the dam. A four-year project sponsored by the United Nations succeeded in lifting the statuary and rooms of the original temples about 60 m above the original site that Ramses selected.

at the river's mouth. Agriculture began in the Nile Valley about 18 000 B.C. but was not firmly established until 5000 B.C. Villages were constructed after 4500 B.C. as farming practices and irrigation techniques improved.

The civilization of ancient Egypt developed all along the lower 1200 km of the Nile, and at first was divided into two kingdoms. Lower Egypt comprised the Delta region, which ended at about the point on which the city of Cairo sits today. Stretching south of Cairo along the Nile Valley was the kingdom of Upper Egypt. According to tradition, the two kingdoms were brought together around 3100 B.C., and the world's first nation-state was established. Because the Nile Valley was surrounded by vast deserts, the new nation was unusually stable and grew with few outside influences into a great civilization.

The Egyptians were led by a pharaoh who was regarded not only as a king but as a god. The pharaoh, his family, and his chief minister, the vizier, were at the peak of the society. Beneath them was the ruling class. Priests had the highest status, but the ruling class consisted of wealthy landowners, public officials, and military commanders as well. This segment of society lived in large residences and enjoyed a life of comfortable surroundings and other luxuries. The middle class of Egyptian society was made up of merchants, traders, and artisans. Scribes, who kept records for the state, also belonged to the middle class, but had more prestige. Middle-class Egyptians lived in simple, single-storey houses that were almost the same as the dwellings the working classes occupied in the villages. The working classes made up the largest part of Egyptian society. They worked the fields and were also expected to serve in the army, maintain irrigation canals, and build the palaces and pyramids for which the Egyptians are famous.

The Egyptians were a very religious people, but there was no single system everyone accepted. Each community had its own cluster of gods it worshipped and its own religious stories to tell. When a particular community or city became powerful, its gods and stories became popular throughout the kingdom. Atum, Amun, Re, and Osiris are a few of the deities whose worship became widespread. The idea of immortality was important in ancient Egypt. There was an assumption that the pharaoh would rule the afterlife when he died. To guarantee the pharaoh's immortality, his body was carefully preserved through a process of mummification. Eventually, all Egyptians, not just pharaohs, were believed to be immortal and were mummified, although not with as much ceremony.

Early pharaohs were buried in large rectangular tombs known as mastabas. Each mastaba was divided into several chambers, including a special burial chamber that contained the pharaoh's mummified body. About 2650 B.C., the architect Imhotep designed Pharaoh Zoser's tomb, which started out as a mastaba but, due to design changes, ended up as a pyramid. The pyramid design was the standard for a thousand years (2650-

1640 B.C.), through the Old and Middle Kingdoms. Eighty-seven were built in total.

The Great Pyramid, erected for pharaoh Khufu around 2550 B.C., was the grandest of them all. The average weight of the stone blocks used was 2.5 t, and two-and-a-half million blocks were required. The burial chamber inside was made of enormous granite blocks weighing 53.5 t apiece. The outside was finished with limestone casing stones, put precisely in place to create a smooth, almost seamless surface. Only a few of the casing stones remain today.

Many people have wondered how something as massive as the Great Pyramid could have been built using the relatively simple technology the Egyptians possessed. There are no records from the time of construction; the first description of building methods came two thousand years later. The heave-ho theory is most widely accepted. According to this view, the pyramids were built by a large labour force using boats, wooden sleds, and rollers to transport the blocks; levers and ramps to move them into position; and stonecutting tools to shape and place them. Other theories have also been proposed. Erich von Däniken believes that the Great Pyramid was made possible through the knowledge brought by visitors from space. Joseph Davidovits speculates that the Egyptians might have used their knowledge of alchemy to create artificial stone, or concrete, casting the blocks right on the spot using wooden moulds.

The building of the pyramids consumed Egypt's resources, and the unity of the nation broke down during the twenty-first century B.C. Central authority was reinstated by Nebhepetre Mentuhotep (2060-2010 B.C.), and the Middle Kingdom began. During the Thirteenth Dynasty, the Hyksos, "rulers of foreign lands," moved into Egypt in great numbers and to a large extent took over. A Hyksos leader became pharaoh. But Egyptians resented this dominance and overthrew the newcomers. The New Kingdom began about 1550 B.C., and under strong pharaohs such as Thutmose III and Ramses II, the Egyptian nation-state extended beyond the Nile Valley for the first time in its history.

A number of interesting rulers led Egypt during this period. Queen Hatshepsut (c. 1470 B.C.) broke the tradition of male pharaohs and took the throne for thirty years. A later pharaoh, Amenhotep IV (1353-1334 B.C.), completely revised the Egyptian religion, changing his name to Akhenaten to reflect his beliefs. Tutankhamun (1334-1325) followed Akhenaten. He was a boy when he became pharaoh, and his reign was short and unremarkable. Today, however, he is among the most famous of the pharaohs because his tomb was discovered in A.D. 1922 with most of the burial goods intact. In the Nineteenth Dynasty, Ramses II was an aggressive warrior and an equally ambitious builder. He led the Egyptians into war with the Hittite Empire to the north, and eventually negotiated a peace treaty with them to stop the conflict.

By the eleventh century B.C., Egypt was in decline. The "peoples of the sea" were continually attacking the Egyptians and sapping their resources. The peoples to the northwest of Egypt gained in military strength, and Egypt was conquered again and again by more technologically advanced armies.

4

Bronze Age Greece and the Mystery of Atlantis

Archaeological Time Period	Date B.C.	Event
Paleolithic (Old Stone Age)	2 500 000	Earliest use of stone tools
	9600	Plato's date for destruction of Atlantis
Neolithic (New Stone Age)	9000	
	7000	Neolithic farmers on Crete
Copper Age	5000	
	3100	Unification of Upper and Lower Egypt
	3000	Proposed approximate date for biblical flood
Bronze Age	2600	Outsiders from Cyclades arrive on Crete Trade, pottery making, and metalworking flourish
	2000	Old palace period on Crete
	1700	All palaces destroyed by earthquake and rebuilt
	c. 1500	*Volcanic eruption on Thera ends Minoan civilization* *This may be the actual date for the destruction of Atlantis*
	1450	Knossos inhabited by Mycenaean "squatters"
	1380	Knossos destroyed for last time
	1347	Tutankhamun rules in Egypt
	1300	Fortified citadel at Mycenae becomes the most powerful of Mycenaean palace-states in the Aegean
Iron Age	1100	Sea peoples sack and destroy all Mycenaean palace-states
	750	Homer composes *Iliad* and *Odyssey*
	600	Solon visits Egypt and hears story of lost civilization
	355	Plato writes his dialogues
	A.D.	
	1900	Arthur Evans excavates Knossos

4

Bronze Age Greece and the Mystery of Atlantis

BACKGROUND

Discovery of a Lost Age

Historians and archaeologists rely on many kinds of evidence to learn about the past—fossils, bones, ruins, and artifacts, for example. Written records are particularly valuable, but in many cases are difficult or impossible to obtain. Sometimes archaeologists have to piece together fragments of information taken from unrelated sources. Written records from ancient cultures can be difficult to interpret, and there is always the question of whether the information is accurate. For these reasons, history is filled with gaps, mysteries, speculation, and controversy.

The **Bronze Age** of the Aegean, which paralleled the development of ancient Egypt from about 3000 to 1100 B.C., was an era of remarkable accomplishment that was lost to history for over twenty-five hundred years. It survived only as a legend passed on by word of mouth until Homer recorded it in his poems some four or five hundred years later. For centuries, his narratives were regarded mainly as entertaining stories. In the late nineteenth and early twentieth centuries, however, Sir Arthur Evans and amateur archaeologist Heinrich Schliemann made striking discoveries of a missing civilization, and Homer's poetry was seen in a new light.

Evans's pioneering efforts on the Aegean island of Crete, in combination with recent archaeological work, have provided information about the growth of a remarkable, independent cultural tradition. Crete was originally inhabited by Neolithic farmers from coastal Mediterranean societies, who lived in settlements of caves and mud huts. By 2800 B.C., building skills in the Aegean had improved to the point where boulders were used to construct rough, circular, multiple graves called *tholoi*. About 2600 B.C., as the Pyramid Age flowered in Egypt, a brilliant Bronze Age culture emerged quickly on Crete with better technology for stone and metalworking, and a unique tradition of pottery and art for which Crete is famous. It seems likely that a new wave of settlers with

Dating Periods of Human Development

The history of human development has been divided into many different periods, each of which has been given a special name. These names, and the dates that go with them, function as convenient guideposts, but they are misleading as well. On a historical timeline, a particular period can seem to be a precise thing, with clear starting and finishing points. In actuality, however, one era does not simply end and another begin like the switching off and on of a light. Eras blend into one another. Some of the achievements from one era are modified and built upon in succeeding eras. Other achievements are only partially preserved. Still others are forgotten altogether and lost.

The names given to the major divisions of history often reflect an important type of technology that we know was used during that period. For example, the term *Paleolithic* (Old Stone Age) is used for the period when crude stone tools were in use, while the term *Neolithic* (New Stone Age) has been given to the time when stone was finely crafted into tools and artifacts. The Copper Age was the period when people learned how to fashion copper into different implements. During the Bronze Age, copper and tin were mixed through a more advanced process of metallurgy to make a bronze alloy.

Although one part of a society may use the new technology of an age, other parts of the society may continue to use the previous technology.

Different societies sometimes take generations to reach the same stage of development. Often, the resources needed for new techniques are controlled by the people who are most powerful. Today, for example, the level of industrialization varies greatly within individual nations and around the globe. Moreover, archaeologists discover only those objects that can withstand the passage of time, so some technologies remain unknown to us. Obviously, then, the name given to a period of history is a partial, general description only.

advanced abilities was responsible. Probably they travelled by boat from the Cyclades—the numerous Greek islands of the Aegean Sea. These peoples had developed their own cultures, but had found themselves limited by the few resources and small size of the islands on which they lived. The larger island of Crete gave them more opportunities. Products made in Crete during this period have been found throughout the Middle East, Egypt, and the Cyclades, suggesting that a vigorous trading system was created in a relatively short time.

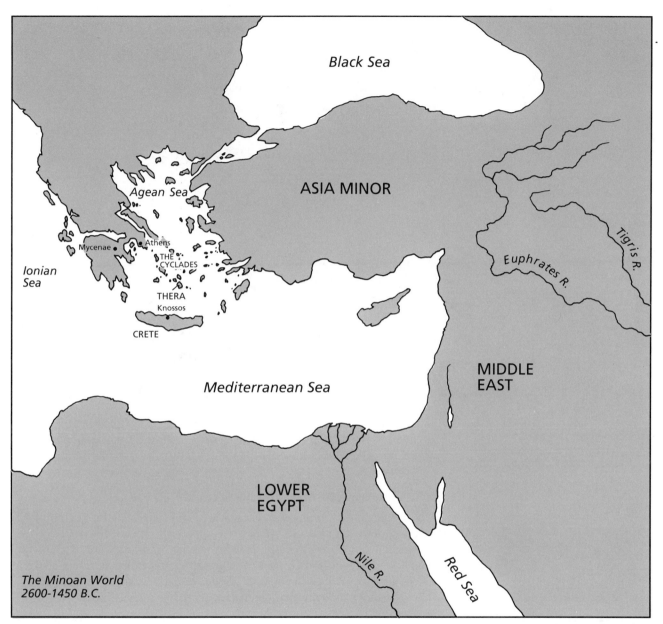

Black Sea

ASIA MINOR

Agean Sea

Ionian
Sea

Mycenae

Athens

THE
CYCLADES

THERA

Knossos

CRETE

Euphrates R.

Tigris R.

MIDDLE
EAST

Mediterranean Sea

LOWER
EGYPT

Nile R.

Red Sea

*The Minoan World
2600-1450 B.C.*

Minoan trade reached into Egypt and the Middle East.

Sir Arthur Evans's excavation of the palace at Knossos. The distinctive Minoan columns are narrower at the base than they are at the top.

Pithoi *jars were storage containers of the ancient world.*

Many small villages were established on Crete during the next five hundred years. By 2000 B.C., the political power of the island became concentrated in eight centres, each with an impressive palace, the largest of which was **Knossos**.

The Flowering of Minoan Civilization

The archaeologist Arthur Evans excavated this palace at the beginning of the twentieth century, and called the Cretan civilization **Minoan**, after the mythical King Minos. Evans discovered that facilities were available at Knossos to accommodate over four hundred jars, called *pithoi*, that were often taller than a person and had a large storage capacity for grain and oil. These facilities indicate that the palace served as a distribution centre for agricultural produce.

The palace had a central courtyard surrounded by a maze of hundreds of rooms. There were separate chambers for royalty, administrators, civil servants, and artisans. Many of the buildings were several stories high and finely finished with closely hewn masonry and superbly engineered drainage systems. Water was brought to Knossos through terracotta pipes extending 15 km. Within the palace, a series of open and closed channels directed water flow, and each rain gutter was designed with right-angled turns and baffles to reduce the speed of the water as it drained.

The Minoans developed a system of writing, but left no record of individuals or dates as in ancient Egypt, or any indication of their system of government. Based on the illustrations in **frescoes**, the numerous altars at palace sites, and the evidence of wealth and food redistribution, the general population was probably ruled by a small elite dominated by a priest-king. The system certainly seems to have been effective. There were few squabbles among the eight Minoan centres because the people needed to work together to obtain maximum output from the land. The lack of palace fortifications suggests that the dominating strength of the Minoan navy in the Aegean left the Minoans little to fear from their neighbours.

The **double-headed axe** was a prominent fixture in Minoan culture. Such axes have been found as artifacts, and were also depicted on pottery and in what appear to be shrines. Just as the cross would later have deep meaning for Christians, the double-headed axe seems to have symbolized something important to the Minoans.

Of equal interest is the respect granted to the bull. Its horns were represented in architecture, while the animal itself was depicted in a variety of activities. One of the most famous frescoes found by Evans shows male and female youths somersaulting over a large, charging bull. Archaeologists have suggested this was either a ritual for all youths or perhaps a demonstration by a special class of athletes.

Frescoes indicate that the Minoans saw or idealized themselves as a graceful, slender people with long hair that curled as it hung down the back. Males are shown with red skin and females with white throughout Minoan art. Women seem to have had a free and prominent role in Minoan society. Many of the deities at shrines were either female or accompanied by female figurines, which suggests that goddesses and gods were equally important. Animals, and possibly humans, were sacrificed to both female and male deities.

Most of the art in Minoan culture was miniature in size, as opposed to the monumental work done in Egypt and Mesopotamia. The markings on beads and finger-size cylinders and the elaborate engravings on gold and silver jewellery and gold vases and cups often portray with amazing skill the same pictures found in the larger wall paintings. Again in contrast to the Egyptians, not a single piece of writing is found on palace walls or in tombs.

The End of Minoan Civilization

This advanced and prosperous Bronze Age civilization suffered a wide-scale catastrophe in 1700 B.C. when all Minoan palaces on Crete were destroyed simultaneously. Walls were toppled, *pithoi* jars fell through floors, and the unique narrow-based, wide-crowned columns were charred and broken.

Religion

According to a famous Greek myth, there once was a king of Crete named Minos. His wife gave birth to a monster that was half-man, half-bull—the Minotaur. King Minos was ashamed and locked the Minotaur in a labyrinth beneath the palace at Knossos. Seven young men and seven young women were brought from Athens every year to be sacrificed to the Minotaur.

Ariadne, Minos's daughter, fell in love with Theseus, one of the youths who was going to be sacrificed. To save Theseus from the Minotaur, she learned the secret of the labyrinth from Daedalus, the man who built it. Following Daedalus's advice, she gave Theseus a ball of thread. He took it with him into the maze and left a strand trailing behind him as he explored the twisting passages. He found the Minotaur, killed him, and followed the thread back to the entrance of the maze. He and Ariadne then escaped from Crete.

A fresco is a special kind of painting on a wall or ceiling. The paint is applied when the plaster is still wet and so becomes part of the wall when the plaster sets. Images shown in frescoes, paintings, sculptures, and other works of art contain a great deal of information about the culture that produced them.

Bull vaulting, shown in this fresco, was either a ritual activity or a Minoan sport.

Ladies in Blue. The elegance in female dress, illustrated in this fresco, suggests that Minoan society was cultured and prosperous.

Most archaeologists have concluded that an earthquake caused the disaster. Despite this setback, the civilization recovered quickly. The Minoans built even larger palaces on the old sites, incorporating and improving upon earlier achievements in art and architecture.

Minoan civilization came to an abrupt and tragic end when another cataclysm struck between 1500 and 1470 B.C. An enormous volcanic eruption on the island of Thera created tsunamis (tidal waves) and spread volcanic ash across much of the Aegean, including a large part of the island of Crete. Only Knossos, largest of the Minoan palaces, escaped general destruction. By 1450 B.C., only Knossos was occupied; but "squatters," as Evans called them, had replaced the Minoan builders. The palace itself was destroyed for the last time in 1380 B.C., possibly by outsiders from the mainland or by rebellious Cretans who resented foreign occupation of their soil. The Minoan civilization ended about a century before the boy-king Tutankhamun came to the throne of Egypt, and was virtually forgotten. Archaeologists are still looking for records that will reveal more about the Minoans, but clues are scarce.

The Issue Emerges

It is possible that one very significant record of the Minoan civilization exists in the works of the Greek philosopher Plato. Writing over one thousand years after the fall of Knossos, he presented a detailed description of a land he called **Atlantis**, a lost paradise. According to Plato, Atlantis existed nine thousand years before the time of Solon, a Greek political leader who lived around 600 B.C. Atlantis was supposedly founded by Poseidon, the god of the sea, who gave the kingdom to Atlas, one of his sons. (At the time Plato was writing, it was customary to trace important places and people back to the gods.) Atlantis was an island, but it controlled a much larger empire.

The main city of the island, known as the Metropolis, was laid out in a circle 25 km in diameter, and was ringed with walls and canals. One enormous canal connected it to an irrigated, agriculturally rich plain some 368 by 544 km in size. The central hill supplied hot and cold springs to the city, and private citizens as well as nobles bathed in warm baths during the winter. Walls were made from red, white, and black stones quarried locally, and the inner enclosure, which contained the royal palace, was lined with valuable metals. The people of Atlantis worshipped Poseidon. As well, they sacrificed a bull every five or six years for religious reasons. Beyond the city, Atlantis used its military power of ten thousand chariots and twelve hundred ships to control the island and its coastal empire, both of which were located beyond the Pillars of Hercules.

Plato's account of Atlantis is found in two of his dialogues, and four times the claim is made that the story is true. In both dialogues, details about Atlantis come from Critias, who was a real person. According to

More to Consider

At Akrotiri, on the island of Thera, archaeologist Spyridon Marinatos unearthed a Minoan community that dates to the same time period as the reconstructed palaces on Crete. It had been buried in volcanic ash. Continued excavation, which is expected to last into the twenty-first century, may push the origin of this site even further into the past.

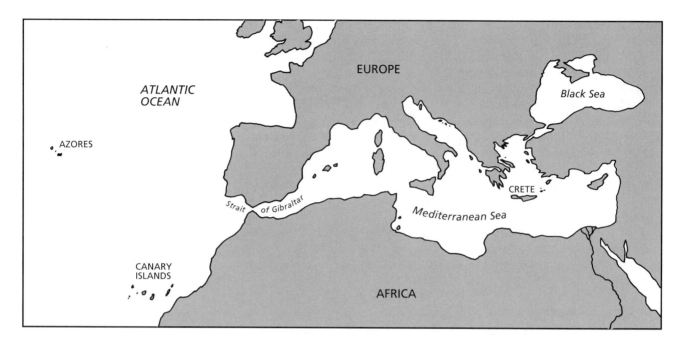

Was Atlantis located in the Atlantic Ocean, beyond the Pillars of Hercules (the Strait of Gibraltar)?

Plato, Critias received his information from his grandfather and from lost documents once in his family's possession. These documents, in turn, were based on what Solon had learned from Egyptian priests. Solon did travel the Mediterranean about 600 B.C., and the Roman historian Plutarch later quoted a fragment of Solon's poetry that describes the Nile. It seems possible that the Egyptians did tell Solon the story of Atlantis, and perhaps gave him a written account.

One aspect of Plato's Atlantis has captured people's imaginations. Atlantis, a great sea power, launched an attack on Athens and Egypt when suddenly

> there occurred violent earthquakes and floods; and in a single day and night of misfortune the island of Atlantis disappeared in the depths of the sea.[1]

Does Plato's story of Atlantis and its sudden destruction have some truth to it? As was mentioned earlier, Plato located Atlantis "beyond the Pillars of Hercules." Most observers have taken the Pillars of Hercules to mean the Strait of Gibraltar, which would place Atlantis somewhere in the Atlantic Ocean. Others, including Plato's student Aristotle, felt that Plato simply made up the entire story. Recent investigators have tried to identify

---

1. Francis Hitching, *The World Atlas of Mysteries*, (London: William Collins Sons and Co. Ltd., 1978), p. 137.

Atlantis as Crete and Thera, contending that Plato's story is one of the rare records of the Minoan civilization.

PROBLEM QUESTION

Is it most likely that the land of Atlantis was a continent in the Atlantic, a fictional kingdom invented by Plato, or the island of Crete?

ALTERNATIVE ONE: The Secret of Atlantis

Based on *The Secret of Atlantis* by Otto Muck (1976)

Otto Muck believes that Plato's story in the dialogues is true, and he explains why in *The Secret of Atlantis*. If by the Pillars of Hercules Plato meant the Strait of Gibraltar, then Atlantis would have been about 1200 km west of Europe in the vicinity of the Azores. Crude pottery and weapons discovered on these islands suggest that the area was once inhabited by Neandertal Man, the precursor of Cro-Magnon. In other words, the Azores have been inhabited for a very long time.

In France and Spain, archaeologists have uncovered weapons, artifacts, and cave paintings of red-skinned people that they credit to Cro-Magnon. They have not discovered how this advanced Cro-Magnon culture arose, however. It seems possible to Otto Muck that Cro-Magnon originated in Atlantis. They travelled to Europe from the west, moving inland along the rivers that drain into the Atlantic. According to this view, European Cro-Magnon culture is evidence of the existence of Atlantean colonies.

There is also evidence that suggests there were connections between Atlantis and other parts of the world. The striking similarities between the Egyptian pyramids and those of Central and South America are puzzling. But even more fascinating, according to Muck, is the connection between the Basques of Spain and the Mayan Indians.

An early Basque missionary in Guatemala was surprised to discover that an isolated tribe of pure Mayans understood his language. There were other similarities between the Basques and these Mayans, including their hooked-nose appearance, the digging sticks both used to loosen the earth for planting, and a sport known to Basques as pelota. This game, played with a small, hard ball and wicker rackets fastened to the players' hands, is practically identical to one that Mayans played at the time of the Spanish conquest.

Otto Muck presents other evidence to prove an inhabited continent once existed in the middle of the Atlantic. Some species of eel have a remarkable life cycle. They are born in the Sargasso Sea, southwest of the Azores. For three years they float with the Gulf Stream all the way to Europe, where they make their way up freshwater rivers and streams. When they are ready to mate, ten to fifteen years later, they make the long trip back to the Sargasso. According to Muck, this journey is instinctive, but long ago the eels migrated to the freshwater rivers of Atlantis, which were only a short distance away. Although the continent has disappeared, the eel's instincts continue to guide them along the Gulf Stream until they reach fresh water.

For more support, Muck refers to the oceanography of the Atlantic. The floor of the ocean is divided by a ridge 1800 m high. This ridge runs from Iceland almost to the Antarctic Shelf. In the area Muck claims Atlantis once occupied, there is a massive bulge almost 1100 km long and 400 km wide. Known as the Azores Plateau, it has submarine volcanic peaks that break the ocean's surface. According to Muck, the size and shape of this plateau are amazingly similar to Plato's description of Atlantis.

Muck thinks it is possible that the same phenomenon that created the two enormous gouges on the ocean floor known as the Puerto Rico Trench might also have contributed to the disappearance of Atlantis. Plato refers to a "deviation in the courses of the stars, and the destruction by fire of everything on earth." This deviant star, according to Muck, was an asteroid. Judging from the immense scars on the ocean floor, he estimates its diameter to have been about 10 km. Muck describes the catastrophe this way:

> At a height of about 400 km, the asteroid began to be surrounded by the red ... hydrogen light. The hotter the asteroid became, the whiter and more brilliant was the light.... Its gaseous tail became immense.... After entering the densest part of the atmosphere ... it burst.[2]

At this point, two enormous pieces plunged into the ocean; one created the Puerto Rico Trench; the other penetrated the earth's crust and started a chain reaction of volcanic eruptions and earthquakes. In the vicinity of Atlantis, these natural reactions were stupendous. Huge clouds of steam and ash rose from the red-hot magma that gushed from the earth's crust into the Atlantic. This erupting magma created a depression into which Atlantis began to sink. In twenty-four hours, just as Plato reported, the continent had completely vanished. All that remained, according to Muck, were the lava-covered peaks that we now call the Azores.

The effects of the asteroid's impact were not confined to the vicinity of Atlantis. The destruction was widespread. Each catastrophe triggered another around the globe. One of the most devastating effects was a deadly gas that took its toll wherever the wind carried it. The disappearance of tens of thousands of Siberian mammoths can be attributed to the gas. Vegetation found in the stomachs of these animals indicates that Siberia then had an ice-free environment. It was only when the impact of the asteroid tilted the earth that the climate abruptly changed.

The asteroid's impact was also responsible for the Great Deluge mentioned in the Bible. According to Muck, water condensed from the enormous clouds of steam and ash, creating flood conditions. The magnitude of the destruction, Muck explains, is why the memory of Atlantis was lost. Those who survived the catastrophe and their descendants struggled to live under an immense cloud of volcanic ash that hovered over northern Europe. It took about three thousand years before even the rudiments of civilization were again acquired. By this time, 4000 B.C., all that had survived of the land of Atlantis was its name.

Questions

1. Why does Muck think that Atlantis was located in the Atlantic Ocean?
2. a) What evidence does Muck present to prove that the Cro-Magnon were from Atlantis?
   b) Did Cro-Magnon develop the kind of Bronze Age civilization that the people of Atlantis supposedly possessed? (See "The Origin of Humans," p. 25.) Explain your answer.
3. How does Muck use the flow of the Gulf Stream and the mating habits of European eels to support the existence of Atlantis in the Atlantic?
4. a) What connections can be found between cultures on both sides of the Atlantic that suggest Atlantis may have provided a link between Europe and Africa, and the Americas?
   b) Is this evidence convincing? Explain your answer.
5. What evidence does Muck present to suggest that the area surrounding the Azores may have been the former site of the Atlantean continent?
6. How is the argument about a large asteroid striking the earth related to the disappearance of Atlantis in a single day and night, as described by Plato?
7. When Muck explains other mysteries, such as the disappearance of the Siberian mammoths, is the case for Atlantis weakened or strengthened? Explain your answer.
8. Why, according to Muck, was Atlantis forgotten for such a long time?

ALTERNATIVE TWO: Plato's Atlantis

Based on "Appendix on Atlantis" by Desmond Lee (1977)

In "Appendix on Atlantis" (which is contained in *Timaeus and Critias*, a translation of two of Plato's dialogues), Desmond Lee addresses two questions. First, could Minoan Crete have been overwhelmed by earthquakes and volcanic explosions? The geological and archaeological evidence suggests that it was. The island of Thera (now called Santorini) lies on a major fault line. According to Lee, no doubt exists that an explosion occurred on the island in the last half of the fifteenth century B.C. It is difficult to assess events before and following the event, but there does seem to be a connection between the explosion and the destruction of Minoan sites in Crete in the latter part of that century.

The explosion of Thera would have been similar to the 1883 explosion of Krakatoa, but on an even grander scale. Because the Krakatoa explosion occurred in the recent past, we know a lot about it. For six or seven years before the explosion, earthquakes occurred in the area. Molten rock accumulated and finally blew a great hole in the earth. Most of Krakatoa disappeared.

The effects were almost beyond belief. The explosion was heard 5000 km away in western Australia. Clouds of volcanic ash turned day into night within a 250 km area. The resulting massive tidal wave had a reach of 80 km, at which point the waves averaged a height of 15 m. One wave tossed a small warship, anchored in a harbour, 3 km inland.

The size of the crater at Thera is four times larger than the one at Krakatoa. The distribution of volcanic ash and the size and extent of the tidal waves would have been accordingly bigger. Core samples taken from the seabed do indeed show widespread distribution of ash. The 20 cm depth of ash found in central and eastern Crete would have destroyed all vegetation and made the area uninhabitable. The size and extent of the tidal wave can only be estimated. But, as Lee points out, it would have smashed ships and harbours at the very least. The explosion at Thera was, in all likelihood, associated with earthquakes. The damage at Crete—the collapse of buildings followed by fire—was the kind of destruction earthquakes cause. Desmond Lee suggests that the earthquake that damaged Crete was the same major earthquake associated with the explosion at Thera.

Lee asks a second question: could any inkling of this catastrophe have reached Plato? The destruction of Atlantis, according to Plato, occurred nine thousand years before Solon, long before the Minoan civilization even existed. Lee points out, however, that Plato may have misunderstood the numbers he encountered. If the figures Plato provides are divided by ten, the date given for Atlantis's destruction corresponds to the end of the Minoan empire. Plato may have mistranslated his source or made an error in multiplication.

Lee also says that the Egyptians could have known about Crete, and could have heard about the volcanic explosion of Thera. They might even have experienced some of its effects. It is possible that the Egyptians told this story to Solon, and that it was passed along to Plato generations later. But Desmond Lee believes that, if Plato used this story at all, it was only for the drama of the catastrophe. There are no other similarities between Atlantis and Minoan Crete. Plato told the story of Atlantis not as history, but to make a philosophical point. He invented most of the details to support his overall argument. In fact, Lee suggests that Plato's account of Atlantis could be regarded as the first example of science fiction.

Questions

1. Why does Lee compare the volcanic explosions on Krakatoa and Thera?
2. Why does Lee believe that the eruption of Thera and the end of Atlantis could have happened at about the same time?
3. How, according to Lee, did the ash, tidal wave(s), and earthquake affect Crete?
4. What was the end result of the Thera explosion for Minoan civilization?
5. a) What evidence does Lee provide to prove that Plato could have known about the Thera explosion?
   b) According to Lee, what was Plato's reason for using Atlantis in his writing?
   c) When Plato wrote the dialogue about Atlantis, what was his main concern?
6. What classification does Lee give Plato's story of Atlantis?

ALTERNATIVE THREE: Atlantis: The Truth Behind the Legend

Based on "Atlantis" by Edward Bacon (1974)

For some years now, it has been apparent to scholars that the Atlantis described by Plato was similar to the Bronze Age civilizations of the Aegean and the Near East, such as the Minoans, the Mycenaeans, the Hittites, the Egyptians, and the Babylonians, between about 2500 and 1200 B.C.

According to Plato, Atlantis was exceptionally rich and fertile, with level plains and well-wooded mountains. The land was intensively cultivated and produced two crops a year with the aid of hot and cold springs. Politically, Atlantis was a federation of ten kings, led by the descendants of Atlas, meeting in the ancient metropolis for conferences and a ritual bull-game. Technologically, Atlantis was extremely advanced. The people had written laws. They possessed a knowledge of metalworking, including the use of gold, silver, and bronze. They had an exceptional grasp of the engineering and architecture involved in the construction of temples, walls, long canals, tunnels, and harbour works. The inhabitants worshipped a number of gods, of whom Poseidon was the chief, and they also practised a bull cult. Socially, there was considerable stress on the good life, with public baths not only for men and women, but also for horses. Edward Bacon argues that, in all these details, Atlantis resembles Minoan Crete.

But according to Plato, the story of Atlantis was recorded by Egyptian priests around 9600 B.C., thousands of years before the Minoan civilization. In fact, based on the archaeological evidence, no place as advanced as Atlantis could have existed at that early date. In 9600 B.C., the people of Atlantis would not have been able to attack the Athenians, because Athens would not exist for centuries. Metalworking had not been discovered anywhere in the world. The agriculture of Atlantis was an impossibility, given that the first and simplest farming communities date from, at the earliest, 7000 B.C. The horses that supposedly bathed in Atlantis were unknown in Europe until the Bronze Age. It would seem, then, that Plato's Atlantis was a myth, an imaginary kingdom he created to illustrate certain political theories.

Or, as Bacon proposes, was there something wrong with Plato's date? Perhaps the Egyptian priests or Solon wrongly substituted nine thousand for nine hundred years. If there was such a mistake, and the true date of the disaster was ten times smaller than Plato suggests, then Atlantis's destruction would have occurred around 1500 B.C. instead of 9600 B.C.—about the time when the Minoan civilization abruptly declined. Exactly the same mistake could have been made with the figures Plato uses to describe the size of Atlantis. If the dimensions he gives for the Royal City of Atlantis are divided by ten, the size of the city shrinks to something very closely approximating the central plain of Crete, the heartland of Minoan civilization.

If Plato's figures are adjusted as Bacon recommends, then Atlantis is not necessarily an impossible kingdom, thousands of years more advanced than it could have been. A connection *could* be made between Atlantis and the Minoans. Accomplishments and events that would be out of place in 9600 B.C. are perfectly suited to 1500 B.C. For example, Minoan Crete was a prosperous power in close contact with Athens and Egypt, and could well have been in conflict with them, as Plato claims Atlantis was. It is still necessary, though, to account for the destruction of Atlantis in a single day and night.

Bacon's explanation involves the explosion of the island of Thera. Today, Thera consists of three islands. These lie around a great expanse of water from the centre of which rise two relatively modern volcanic islets. The great expanse of water is in fact a gigantic volcanic crater, known as a *caldera,* formed by a colossal explosion.

The most striking recent example of such a disaster is the explosion of Krakatoa in Indonesia in 1883. This explosion was heard nearly 5000 km away, thirty-six thousand people perished, and the sound waves travelled around the world three times. Tidal waves crossed the entire Pacific and were still strong enough to break anchor chains in Valparaiso, Chile. Volcanic dust rose to a height of 8 km and some of it fell as far away as Japan.

The magnitude of such an eruption can be calculated based on the size of the caldera. The caldera of Thera has a volume about five times that of Krakatoa; the violence of its explosion must have been something like five times as great. Its effects in the landlocked and island-studded Aegean and its wider effects in the whole eastern Mediterranean must have been catastrophic beyond imagination. It caused the disappearance of the greater part of the previously circular island, which had already been rendered uninhabitable by deposits of pumice and ash up to 60 m deep. It also produced tidal waves that must have swept many kilometres inland in nearby Crete, with wholesale destruction and loss of life.

In Bacon's view, we have two curiously similar accounts, one of which is Plato's. The other, the sum of the discoveries of archaeologists and geophysicists, tells us that the great empire of Minoan Crete suffered a series of natural disasters—fires, earthquakes, and floods—in the late sixteenth century B.C., which brought about the end of the civilization; and that, around 1500 B.C., a fertile island some 100 km north of Crete blew up and caused widespread devastation throughout the Aegean and eastern Mediterranean.

These two accounts of unparalleled disaster are so similar in nature, location, and date that Bacon believes they must be different accounts of the same disaster. And when an archaeological expedition, led by Professor Marinatos of Athens in 1967, uncovered Minoan remains deep under the pumice of Thera, the final link was added. The identification of Thera with the ancient metropolis of Atlantis, and of Minoan Crete with the Royal City and empire of the Atlanteans, thus became virtually inevitable.

Questions

1. Does the Atlantis that Bacon describes appear to be a civilization of the Stone Age, the Copper Age, the Bronze Age, or the Iron Age? Explain your answer.
2. a) Why does Plato's date of 9600 B.C. for Atlantis seem impossible to Bacon?
   b) Does Lee agree with Bacon's conclusion about the date?
   c) How would Muck react to the conclusions of Bacon and Lee about the date of Atlantis?
   d) Which argument do you find the most convincing?
3. How does Bacon's argument about a mistake by a factor of ten relate to the size of Atlantis and to the size of the central plain of Crete?
4. Identify the similarities and the differences in the descriptions of volcanic explosions given by Lee and Bacon.
5. What is Bacon's overall conclusion about the existence of Atlantis?

ANSWERING THE PROBLEM QUESTION

In choosing the best explanation of Atlantis, consider several factors. For example, the story of Atlantis, told by word of mouth and through written translations, passed through many hands—from Egyptian priests to Solon, from Solon to Critias the Elder, and from Critias the Elder to Critias and Plato. Even if the story was based on a real event, how many changes in the original version were made by exaggeration or accident before it reached Plato? And once Plato heard the story, did he simply use it as the framework for one of his philosophical speculations?

Then there is the fascinating challenge of trying to determine the exact location of Atlantis. Plato's reference to the Pillars of Hercules would seem to place Atlantis in the Atlantic Ocean. Is the argument that Muck presents about the impact of an asteroid and the subsequent sinking of the land surrounding the Azores convincing? The geological evidence must be examined. On the other hand, maybe the location Plato provides is incorrect or misleading.

Consider another factor. Can we assume that an error of a factor of ten was made during the original translation of the story? If there was, then the date of the Thera explosion closely matches the time period of Atlantis, and the size of the city and empire of Atlantis approach that of Thera and Crete.

Could the catastrophe of the fifteenth century B.C. on Thera have destroyed Atlantis in a day and a night, or should Plato not be taken literally on this point? What are the characteristics of such volcanic eruptions, and what were the precise effects of the Thera explosion on the Aegean world?

You should evaluate, rank, and apply these criteria, and any criteria of your own, to the problem of the existence of Atlantis.

THE STORY CONTINUES . . .

The Rise of the Mycenaeans

While the Minoan civilization of Crete flourished, dominating a relatively peaceful Aegean community, another group of people, known as the **Mycenaeans**, began to develop small, independent kingdoms on the mainland. Although the explosion on Thera disrupted the Minoan world, their civilization lasted until 1450 B.C., when Knossos was finally abandoned. Most likely, it took thirty to fifty years for the smothering volcanic ash to destroy agricultural production. At this time it seems as though at least one group of Mycenaeans (the squatters to whom Evans referred) occupied Knossos and exploited its fading power for what they could.

Why the palace at Knossos was destroyed in 1380 B.C. remains a mystery. By then, each of the small Mycenaean kingdoms of Pylos, Mycenae, Athens, Thebes, and Tiryns had grown into a **palace-state**—a united community centred on a fortified palace used as a defence and as a residence for the rulers. Unlike the peaceful Minoans, the new powers often competed against each other and conflict ensued. Possibly the destruction of Knossos was the result of a battle among Mycenaean palace-states for more territory or larger trading networks.

The Mycenaeans replaced the Minoans as the prime influence in the Aegean and beyond. They controlled the Cyclades, and established colonies in Rhodes, Miletus, and Cyprus. They set up trading posts in Asia Minor, and

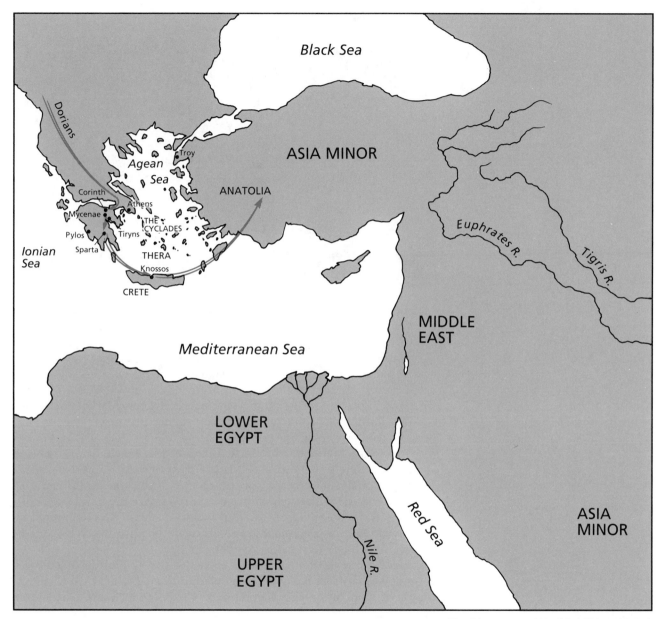

The Mycenaean World 1450-1100 B.C.

The entrance to the tomb of Agamemnon.

extended travel from Troy to Egypt. Based on the crowding in grave sites by the year 1300 B.C., it seems possible that the Mycenaean population approached that of the Golden Age of Athens some nine hundred years later.

The focal point of power was Mycenae, and its location possessed several advantages. Most of Greece is mountainous; arable land is scarce. But Mycenae was adjacent to the plain of Argos, which provided space for villages and fertile soil for farming. The Mycenaeans enriched themselves by making crafts from ivory imported from Syria, manufacturing bronze weapons, and producing fine pottery.

Crowning a hilltop that overlooked the area was the **citadel**. Its massive stone blocks were so impressive that later Greeks thought it was the work of the giants, or Cyclops, that the poet Homer described in the *Odyssey*. The Lion Gate, a triangular-shaped stone that rests over the entrance to the citadel, features a carving of two lions beside a column slightly tapered in the Minoan style. The entrance lies on a steep incline that would have made any attack on the fortress extremely difficult.

Inside the walls, fourteen graves contained twenty-four unnamed royal corpses. Not far from the citadel a number of circular-shaped tombs, much larger and more finely built than those on Crete, can be found. The largest of these, called the Treasury of Atreus, is entered through a corridor that slopes upward toward an enormous gateway, inside which the tomb rises in the shape of a beehive to a height of about 14 m.

The Collapse

Although Mycenae was powerful, the extensive, thick-walled fortifications suggest that the Aegean world was unstable and insecure. As it turned out,

B.C.

1450	Mycenaeans occupy Knossos after Minoan collapse
1380	Palace of Knossos destroyed for the last time, possibly as a result of conflict among Mycenaeans
1300	Fortified citadel at Mycenae becomes the most powerful of Mycenaean palace-states in the Aegean
1288	Kadesh: Hittite and Egyptian empires fight an inconclusive battle
1250	Mycenaeans move into trading areas vacated by Hittites and Egyptians in eastern Mediterranean
1200	Sea peoples end Hittite empire
1100	During previous century, sea peoples destroy all Mycenaean palace-states

Mycenaean Chronology.

the fear of attack was fully justified. All of the great Mycenaean palace-states were burned, pillaged, and destroyed over the course of a century, from 1250 to 1150 B.C. Why did this happen? The answer is not clear.

Archaeologists' speculations about what happened to the Mycenaeans are based on what is known about other empires that collapsed about the same time. During the last five hundred years of the Bronze Age, a powerful empire controlled by the Hittites grew on the Anatolia Plateau (in what is now Turkey). The Hittites' main rival to the south was the revitalized Egypt of the New Kingdom. In 1288 B.C., under Pharaoh Ramses II, the Egyptians marched north with thirty-five hundred war chariots to fight the Hittites for control of what is now the Lebanese coast. The battle at Kadesh was inconclusive and exhausted the resources of both sides. The armies withdrew from the disputed area. By 1200 B.C., the Hittite Empire had been sacked and burned, and the Egyptian Empire had been greatly weakened from attacks by mysterious invaders referred to as the "peoples of the sea" in Egyptian inscriptions.

Although the origin of the sea peoples is clouded in generalities, the development of their power is clear. At first, they were allies of the major powers. Neither the Hittites nor the Egyptians were a sea-going people, so in wartime they recruited navies from surrounding coastal centres. Later, however, these sea peoples turned on their former allies, usually joining the side that seemed most likely to succeed. Eventually, they disposed of the major land-based empires.

Initially, the warlike Mycenaeans exploited the vacuum of power and set up trading posts in the now-open Lebanese coastal region. It is quite possible that some Mycenaeans had actually joined various groups of sea people on their increasing number of raids. This action would have created much of the uncertainty and tension reflected in the extensive fortifications of many Mycenaean palace-states.

The Greek poet Homer's epic poetry supports this idea of Mycenaean raiders, although it is difficult to sift fact from fiction in his work. In his poem, the *Iliad*, a combined force of Greeks from the Mycenaean world attacks Troy, a powerful and wealthy city on the northwest coast of Asia Minor. Heinrich Schliemann, a wealthy German industrialist and amateur archaeologist, took this tale of heroic battles literally. In 1876, his excavations at the site of an ancient city uncovered a wealth of artifacts and fabulous treasures of gold and silver vases and jewellery. He believed he had discovered Troy, until then regarded as purely mythical. Critics pointed out that the city Schliemann had exposed was only one of nine stacked on top of each other, and that he had picked the wrong one as the city of the Trojan Wars. Undaunted, Schliemann again took Homer as a literal source and again found an incredible number of gold and bronze objects, this time at five royal grave sites at the citadel of Mycenae. He labelled one gold mask the death mask of Agamemnon. (Agamemnon was one of the Greek leaders, according to Homer.) This find, he claimed, demonstrated that much of Homer's writing was factual. Archaeology has since proven that the mask predates the era of Troy. Despite the shortcomings of Schliemann's work, it does seem that there is at least some truth behind Homer's epics.

Perhaps the Mycenaeans and the sea peoples did conduct some raids together, but the collaboration did not last. As the strength of the sea peoples increased, they disrupted the trade in goods and grain on which the Mycenaean world depended. Finally the sea peoples, playing no favourites, sacked Mycenaean palace-states. There is no archaeological evidence to indicate that they occupied the area for any length of time. It seems they were content to strike, loot, and leave.

By 1000 B.C., the Mycenaean culture had disappeared. Mainland Greece was gradually controlled by an illiterate, less-advanced group called the Dorians. Their society, dominated by a king and tribal council, achieved little that endured. In fact, their presence marked the beginning of a three-hundred-year period known as the "Dark Ages," from which no records of the once-flowering Mycenaean culture survived.

SUMMARY

From about 3000 to 1100 B.C., Bronze Age cultures rose and fell in the Aegean region of the Mediterranean. Knowledge of these cultures was almost entirely lost for twenty-five hundred years.

The Minoan civilization of Crete was established by about 2600 B.C. and thrived for over a thousand years. But our discovery of the Minoans is

Homer

For thousands of years, Homer has been regarded as a great poet, but almost nothing is known about Homer. We will probably never discover exactly when or where he lived. The best guess is that he resided in one of the Greek colonies of Asia Minor sometime during the eighth century B.C.

Homer's poems were among the first Greek poems to be written down. Until that time, Greek poetry had been memorized and passed from generation to generation by word of mouth. Homer's long poems are actually made up of many shorter ones that had been composed in some cases hundreds of years earlier. The skill with which he combined these poems and contributed to them was immediately recognized as genius.

Homer's poetry was meant to be read aloud; he would have recited his work at important festivals, probably accompanied by music. The *Iliad*, for example, could have been recited in about fifteen two-hour sessions, spaced out over three days.

The *Iliad* and the *Odyssey* are generally regarded as **legends**; they are not true stories, but are based on actual historical events. For example, the Greek leaders Agamemnon and Nestor may have been real people. But Homer's poetry is also rich in **myth**, fictional stories about gods, goddesses, heroes, and supernatural occurrences. Most of the main Greek myths are associated with centres of Mycenaean civilization.

The *Iliad* preserves many details of the Mycenaean world. By Homer's day, the Mycenaean strongholds had disappeared or were only backward communities. Why did Homer glorify an age more than four hundred years in the past rather than his own? Mycenae was broken by the sea peoples, and its survivors scattered to distant lands by the Dorian invasions that came afterwards. Homer was remembering the time before the downfall. Perhaps he himself was a descendant of the displaced Mycenaeans.

Homer's poetry is remarkable not only in itself, but also for what it represents. As unreliable as it is, it is still one of the few records we have of the Mycenaean period. And it preserves the stories of poets even older than Homer, which might have been lost if Homer's epics had never been written down.

Lines 410-418 from Book II of Homer's Iliad.

βοῦν δὲ περιστήσαντο καὶ οὐλοχύτας ἀνέλοντο·
τοῖσιν δ' εὐχόμενος μετέφη κρείων Ἀγαμέμνων·
" Ζεῦ κύδιστε μέγιστε, κελαινεφές, αἰθέρι ναίων,
μὴ πρὶν ἐπ' ἠέλιον δῦναι καὶ ἐπὶ κνέφας ἐλθεῖν,
πρίν με κατὰ πρηνὲς βαλέειν Πριάμοιο μέλαθρον
αἰθαλόεν, πρῆσαι δὲ πυρὸς δηΐοιο θύρετρα,
Ἑκτόρεον δὲ χιτῶνα περὶ στήθεσσι δαΐξαι
χαλκῷ ῥωγαλέον· πολέες δ' ἀμφ' αὐτὸν ἑταῖροι
πρηνέες ἐν κονίῃσιν ὀδὰξ λαζοίατο γαῖαν."

*They stood in a circle about the ox and took up the scattering
barley; and among them powerful Agamemnon spoke in prayer:
"Zeus, exalted and mightiest, sky-dwelling in the dark mist:
let not the sun go down and disappear into darkness
until I have hurled headlong the castle of Priam
blazing, and lit the castle gates with the flames' destruction;
not till I have broken at the chest the tunic of Hektor
torn with the bronze blade, and let many companions about him go
down headlong into the dust, teeth gripping the ground soil."*

very recent. Only at the beginning of the twentieth century did Arthur Evans conduct his excavations of the palace ruins of Crete. He found that the Minoans possessed advanced technology. They worked in stone and metal, and also crafted beautiful pottery and art. After 2600 B.C., they created a trading network that distributed their goods throughout the Middle East, Egypt, and the Cyclades.

Eight major centres, each with its own palace, had developed on the island by 2000 B.C. The largest was Knossos, which featured a central courtyard with hundreds of chambers clustered around it. The elaborate water supply and drainage systems and the remains of well-made buildings reveal that the Minoans were excellent engineers. We know very little about specific people or events in Minoan history because their system of writing apparently was not used to keep these kinds of records. We do know that women had a prominent role in the community and that goddesses and gods were equally important.

The castles of Crete were not strongly fortified, which suggests that the Minoans were peaceful and that the Aegean region was secure. The end of the Minoan civilization came not through war but through natural disaster. About 1700 B.C. there was probably a major earthquake that destroyed all the palaces at the same time. The Minoans recovered, and built structures that were even more impressive. But a later calamity was too much for them. The volcanic island of Thera exploded sometime between 1500 and 1470 B.C., and the resulting tidal waves were probably devastating. In the following years, the ash from the eruption spoiled the island's agriculture. Only the palace at Knossos survived the initial destruction, but it was inhabited by people who were not Minoan, and was finally destroyed about 1380 B.C.

The Minoans seem to have been forgotten by the peoples who succeeded them; few records of their presence exist. Some scholars have maintained that Plato's description of Atlantis actually refers to the Minoans. For a long time, Atlantis was presumed to be a fictional civilization created by Plato as part of a philosophical argument. But many of the characteristics of Atlantis are characteristics of the Minoans as well. Like Crete, Atlantis was destroyed by a sudden disaster. Plato says that Atlantis disappeared in 9600 B.C., thousands of years before the Minoan culture actually developed. It is conceivable that Plato or someone before him made an error in calculating the dates for Atlantis. But others argue that Atlantis was indeed mythical, or that it did exist but was not related in any way to Crete.

During the time the Minoans flourished on Crete, other Bronze Age cultures matured on the mainland of what is now Greece. Palace-states were founded in Pylos, Mycenae, Athens, Thebes, and Tiryns. These peoples are collectively known as the Mycenaeans because Mycenae was powerful at the time. The heavy fortifications of Mycenae's citadel are a good indication that frequent military conflicts occurred among the Mycenaean peoples.

After the Minoan civilization was extinguished, the Mycenaeans controlled the Aegean. Homer's *Iliad*, though written several hundred years after this period, probably depicts the Mycenaeans in action. The poem describes the Mycenaean seige of a coastal city named Troy. It is by no means a wholly factual record, but the archaeologist Heinrich Schliemann, using it as a guide, uncovered important finds at Mycenae and at a city that he identified as Troy. Subsequent research has proven that some of Schliemann's assumptions were wrong, but it does seem that Homer's poetry contains fact as well as fiction.

The Mycenaeans probably collaborated with groups known as the "sea peoples," whose navies had conducted earlier raids against the major land-based empires of the eastern Mediterranean—the Hittites and the Egyptians. The Mycenaeans and the sea peoples shared the Aegean for awhile, but apparently this peace did not last. In the space of one hundred years, between 1250 and 1150 B.C., all of the Mycenaean palaces on the mainland were burned and ruined. There is no clear information about how and why this destruction occurred, but most likely the sea peoples turned on the Mycenaeans and looted their cities. By 1000 B.C., the Mycenaean civilization was broken. The Dorians, who had no system of writing and were less technologically developed, moved into and took control of mainland Greece, and almost all knowledge of the Mycenaeans vanished.

Date B.C.	Event
1100	Sea peoples destroy and sack all Mycenaean palace-states Dark Ages begin
800	Greek city-states emerge
776	First Olympics are held
750	Homer composes the *Iliad* and the *Odyssey*
650	Age of Tyrants in city-state government
620	*Sparta suppresses the Messenian Rebellion and develops best army in Greece*
520	*Persian Empire dominates vast region from the Indus River to the eastern Aegean*
490	*Greeks defeat Persians at Marathon*
480	*Three hundred Spartans fight to the death against Persia at Thermopylae* *Athenian navy defeats Persians at Salamis*
479	*Sparta defeats Persians at Plataea*
477	*Delian League formed to protect Greek city-states from Persian attacks*
465	*Greeks defeat Persians again* *Athens turns Delian League into an Athenian Empire*
447	*Construction of Parthenon begins*
445	*The Thirty Years' Peace is declared between Athens and Sparta*
431	*Peloponnesian War begins between Sparta and Athens*
429	*Pericles dies during plague*
416	*Athenians massacre Melians*
404	*Sparta wins Peloponnesian War and occupies Athens* *Sparta demolishes the Long Walls from Athens to the port of Piraieus*
399	Socrates, tried and condemned to death, drinks poison
377	Second, more democratic, Athenian League is formed
376	Athens defeats Spartan navy at Naxos
371	Thebes defeats Spartan army at Leuctra using new military tactics
338	Philip II of Macedonia defeats Athens and Thebes at Chaeronea Philip II imposes unity on Greek city-states
336	Philip II is assassinated Alexander assumes his father's role

5

The Ideals of Sparta and Athens

BACKGROUND

The Rise of City-States

The geography of Greece helped to determine the characteristics of Greek civilization. Most of Greece has little land suitable for agriculture. The mountainous interior often extends to an irregular coastline, leaving only isolated pockets of farmland. During the Dark Ages (1100-800 B.C.), a series of individual towns, called **city-states,** emerged in these pockets. Most had populations of less than fifteen thousand.

Each **polis** (the Greek word for city-state) was a separate political unit. The polis included areas of farmland that could be defended from attack. At the centre of the polis was the **agora,** or marketplace, where people gathered to converse and to shop. Usually, a fortified hilltop called an **acropolis** provided sanctuary for residents during a battle. Residents were intensely loyal to their particular city-state.

This extreme civic loyalty was in some ways a drawback, because it inhibited any large-scale co-operation among the many city-states, which were already divided by geography. There was unity only during the religious or athletic festivals held at Delos, Delphi, or Olympia. The rest of the time, the city-states squabbled and fought among themselves. Neighbours conquered neighbours, and the victors had additional mouths to feed, which strained already inadequate supplies of food.

To solve the problem of food shortages, the Greeks put their developing seafaring skills to use, and about 750 B.C. they began to colonize fertile areas beyond mainland Greece. Over the next two hundred years, colonization took place on an unprecedented scale. Greek colonies spread from the Black Sea and the Dardanelles to the coastal areas of what are now Italy, France, and Spain. The solution was only temporary as economic pressures continued to grow along with the population, but it did result in the first age of progress since 1100 B.C., the time of the Mycenaean downfall.

Religion

In Homer's epic poetry, the Greek gods are shown taking part in human battles, seducing and having children with mortal men and women, and plotting and arguing among themselves. The Greeks did not accept Homer's stories as literal truth, but they did believe the gods were larger-than-life beings with great abilities and human personalities and failings. They created festivals for and dedicated cities to Zeus, Hera, Athena, Ares, Poseidon, Apollo, Artemis, Aphrodite, and the other gods of Mount Olympus. The Greeks thought the gods could be worshipped and appeased through proper ceremonies, such as ritual sacrifices and the celebration of special occasions. For example, the Olympic Games, first held in 776 B.C., combined widely accepted religious beliefs with the Greek love of physical fitness and fair play.

More to Consider

Hoplites were foot soldiers armed with swords, shields, helmets, and 3 m long spears. Some of them also had armour breastplates. Hoplites were effective because of the innovative way they worked together. They would stand in a densely packed pattern of lines known as a **phalanx**. Each soldier in a line used his shield to guard his own left side and the right side of the man beside him. Only the soldier at the right-hand end of each line was vulnerable. When attacked on horseback or on foot, the hoplites would stand firm and use their long spears to slaughter the enemy. But when a phalanx broke its formation, the individual hoplites were easy victims.

Oligarchy versus Democracy

The way Greeks governed themselves changed during this period of expansion. Influential landowners and aristocrats, who could afford to buy equipment to defend the cities, gradually replaced the kings. There was pressure to reform this new system, however. Ordinary farmers were dissatisfied because they were usually deeply in debt and many lost their land. In addition, as battle tactics came to require large armies of infantry, or **hoplites**, the warriors and the merchants who financed them demanded a greater say in affairs.

Government by city-state aristocrats was replaced by government by a single individual, who was known as a **tyrant**. A tyrant was someone who took power illegally, instead of in the manner approved by the state. But many of the measures that tyrants introduced were beneficial. During what is known as the Age of Tyrants, from 650 to 500 B.C., rulers codified laws, developed industry and commerce, and even broke up large estates and divided them among the peasants. Although some Greek city-states kept this system, others changed to rule by a small group (an **oligarchy**) or by all citizens (a **democracy**). **Sparta**, a city-state located on the Peloponnesus of Greece, developed the best example of government by oligarchy. Unlike their neighbours who colonized beyond the mainland, the Spartans secured land by enslaving fellow Greeks in their own province of Laconia and in the bordering province of Messenia. Because twenty-five thousand Spartans had to control a mainland empire of two hundred and fifty thousand Greeks, they trained and maintained an army of the best foot soldiers in all of the Aegean world. The Spartan ideal became selfless devotion to the common good of the state at any cost.

Most of what is known about Sparta comes from written sources left by its chief rival, the city-state of **Athens**, located on the peninsula of Attica. In contrast to Sparta, Athens adopted a type of democratic government, and was in constant contact with outlying colonies and city-states. It encouraged and depended on the trade and commerce passing through the nearby

The Greek Phalanx. Sparta developed this method of warfare.

GREEK GOVERNMENT

Sparta: Oligarchy
Rule by the few

2 KINGS

Priestly and judicial functions
Elected by the Assembly

5 EPHORS (overseers)

Presided over the Senate and the Assembly
Put legislation before the Assembly: "Yes" or
"No" vote decided by the loudest yell as judged
by the ephors
Had the most political power
Elected annually by the Assembly

SENATE

Elected by the Assembly for life
Prepared legislation for the Assembly and advised
the kings

ASSEMBLY

Free male citizens over thirty
Elected kings, ephors, and Senate
Voted on legislation but could not initiate it

Athens: Democracy
Rule by the many

COUNCIL OF FIVE HUNDRED

Chosen by lot from citizens over thirty
Divided into ten groups of fifty
Carried on day-to-day business and prepared legis-
lation and topics for Assembly discussion
New president elected every day

BOARD OF TEN GENERALS

Elected by the Assembly for one year

JURY OF SIX THOUSAND

Selected by lot from free citizens over thirty

JUDICIAL BOARD OF NINE ARCHONS

ASSEMBLY

All male citizens over eighteen
Open meetings, public discussion of all issues
Passed all laws, determined foreign policy, and
directed military operations
Decision of majority was final
Three obels paid for attendance

port of Piraieus. Some Athenians, including Plato, admired the order and self-discipline achieved by Sparta, and others, such as the philosophers Aristotle and Socrates, were critical of the chaos and instability in their own democratic system.

Obviously, there were extreme differences between Spartan and Athenian societies, and all the other Greek city-states were similarly individual. For the most part, each was proud of the system of government it had evolved; each believed that its own civic values were superior. Both the Athenians and the Spartans came to view the conflict between the two states as battles between "right" and "wrong" ways of life. The Greek city-states remained fragmented. Only the threat of a common enemy could unite them, and then only temporarily.

The Persian Wars

While the Greek city-states were completing their colonizing, a great empire suddenly developed, attaining its full extent after 559 B.C. Cyrus II of Persia established the actual imperial structure, but it was during the reign of Darius I, beginning in 522 B.C., that the **Persian Empire** was expanded to its limit. The 4000 km expanse of the empire, from the Indus River to the eastern Aegean, had a population of ten million. It had a common language, a standard coinage, and a single ruler. The Persians borrowed heavily from each of their subject peoples in art and architecture and were flexible in recognizing local laws and traditions, but they maintained a great pride in their own homeland bordering the Persian Gulf. To the Persians, the Greek city-states were barbarian outposts on the fringe of their immense civilization.

Conquest had been the key to Persian expansion and, in 546 B.C., the need for naval bases and trading centres led them to capture Greek outposts on the Ionian coast. In 499 B.C., Athens and Eretria supported the Ionian cities in a revolt against Persia, who crushed the enterprise brutally. Persia chose to invade the Greek mainland to punish the enemy and perhaps in hopes of additional conquest. Given the divisions that had existed among Greek city-states, the chances of victory for the invincible Persian army appeared great indeed.

The Persians, under Darius, struck first in 490 B.C., easily taking the Eretrian force of about forty thousand, and then landing at Marathon, about 40 km north of Athens. There, only ten thousand Athenians and about one thousand other Greek soldiers were left to face the twenty thousand Persians. Sparta claimed that it was celebrating a religious festival and could not send troops. Despite the odds against them, the Greeks attacked at dawn, catching the Persians off guard and without their cavalry. The brilliant victory, in which 6400 Persians were killed while only 192 Greeks were lost, changed the course of Greek history by showing both that Persia could be defeated and the advantages of unity among city-states.

More to Consider

According to legend, the Athenians learned about the Greek victory at Marathon when a lone messenger ran the 40 km distance and delivered the news. From this feat of long-distance running, legendary or not, comes the term *marathon*.

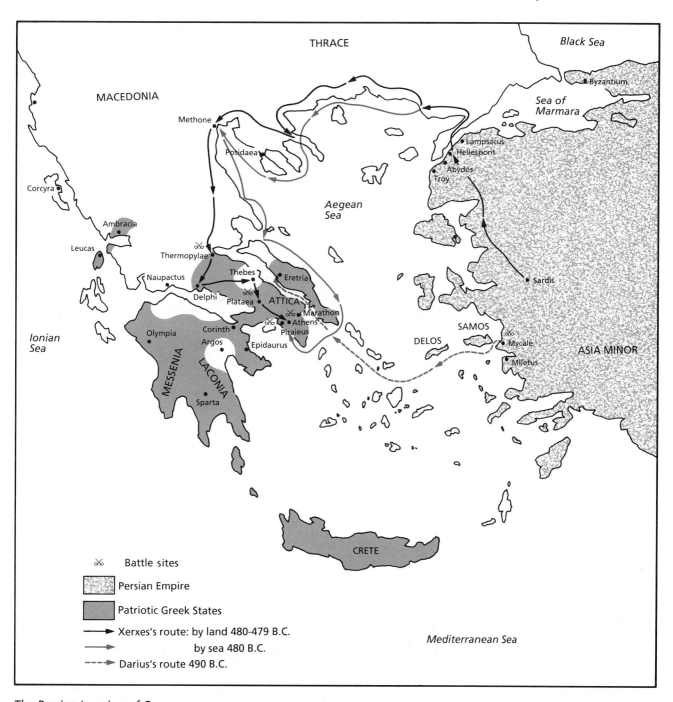

The Persian Invasion of Greece.

A decade later Darius's son, Xerxes, organized an expedition of one hundred and fifty thousand soldiers and five hundred warships to seek revenge. The Greeks, including the Spartans, stood firm at the narrow pass of Thermopylae until a traitor showed the Persians a secret road by which the Greeks could be attacked from the rear. Left to defend the pass, three hundred Spartans—the best soldiers in Greece—and seven hundred Thespians fought to the death. Their sacrifice gave the main Greek force time to prepare a battle plan. Athens had to be abandoned to the Persians, who sacked and burned the city. In the bay off the island of Salamis, the Athenian navy defeated the Persian navy in a decisive, hard-fought battle. Shortly thereafter, the Spartans again proved their military superiority by defeating the Persians at Plataea.

Although Spartan forces returned to the Peloponnesus after the war, the fact that a group of tiny city-states had defeated the might of the Persian Empire added to an overall sense of Greek unity. A new confederacy, known as the **Delian League**, was organized under Athenian leadership to protect its members against attacks from the Persians. Initially, membership was voluntary, with each state contributing money that Athens used to build a strong navy, but the three hundred members of the Aegean community soon fell under Athenian domination.

Although the League did prove its value when another Persian military thrust against Greece was soundly defeated in 465 B.C., the organization in essence became an Athenian empire, with Athenian officials and troops "defending" many of the smaller city-states, which were forced to provide money and soldiers for the glorification and strengthening of Athens. The threat of additional expansion by Athens, and the contrast between Athenian democracy and Spartan oligarchy, led to several military clashes between the two city-states until an uneasy **Thirty Years' Peace** was declared in 445 B.C.

The Greek Trireme. This type of manoeuvrable ship was very successful against the awkward craft of Xerxes's Persian fleet at Salamis. The men on board included 170 rowers, 30 crew members, and 18 soldiers who used metal-tipped rams to puncture and sink enemy ships. Two eyes were painted on the bow of the trireme so that the vessel could "see" its way.

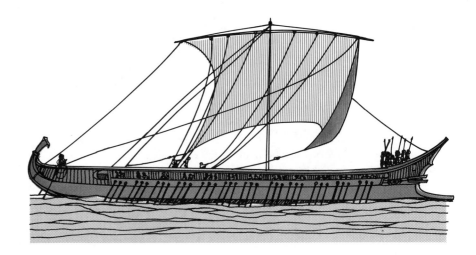

Voice of the Priestess

The Athenians sought the guidance of the god Apollo to help them defeat the Persians. They were advised to put their faith in "the wooden wall," an ambiguous phrase that was interpreted to mean the Athenian navy. Sure enough, in a decisive battle, the Persian fleet was lured into the relatively small bay off the island of Salamis where the Greek triremes outmanoeuvred them and forced them to flee.

The voice of Apollo was consulted at **Delphi**, the chief centre of prophecy for the Greeks. It was located on Mount Parnassus, far to the northwest of Athens. The Greeks believed that Delphi was the centre of the world. Apollo did not answer questions directly; he spoke through his **oracle**, a priestess who was able to go into a trance and receive his divine communication.

Delphi had been a sacred site for centuries, although the first oracles spoke for the earth goddess, Gaea. Eventually Apollo took over Delphi, killing a giant serpent named Python in the process. Only a priestess over the age of fifty could be Apollo's oracle, and she was known as the Pythia. Individuals who needed counsel visited the oracle, as did governments who wanted to know the outcome of wars and political events in advance. Delphi was showered with gifts by city-states before every major battle, and was granted the final word in all religious matters.

Each consultation with the oracle involved an elaborate ritual. The Pythia would drink from a special spring, enter the sacred temple of Apollo, and chew laurel leaves. In a trance she would speak the words of the god, which priests would then interpret and write down in verse. Usually, the predictions were vague and could be interpreted in many ways. In fact, predictions rarely changed or discouraged plans that had already been made. But participation in the ceremony of the oracle at Delphi helped to generate a common set of values throughout the Greek world.

The oracle at Delphi was eventually discredited when too many predictions in favour of Sparta were made.

The Amphitheatre and Temple of Apollo at Delphi. Here the priestess uttered the sacred oracles of the god.

The Golden Age of Athens

Under the leadership of Pericles, a great politician and public speaker, Athens consolidated the financial benefits of its empire to build a lasting monument to past victories, present peace, and the value of democracy as the Athenians understood it. The monument was to be built on the

Institutions

During the period of their dominance, the Athenians produced outstanding works of architecture, art, literature, and philosophy. Their scientific, mathematical, and political ideas have been similarly influential. The breadth of their accomplishments was partly due to their ideal of the cultured citizen as someone who would contribute to the good of the state. Every male citizen learned to read and write, but it was usually the upper-class Athenians who received a complete education in politics, public speaking, poetry, and music.

Then, between 450 and 400 B.C., wandering scholars known as **Sophists** began to stress the need for more practical training in politics, a need created by a steadily expanding empire. Sophists were especially known for their excellence in debate. Young men preparing for a career in law or politics would learn how to take any side of an argument and win it, no matter which side was "right."

Some educators, such as Socrates, were opposed to the Sophists' emphasis on worldly success. Socrates believed that education should involve the pursuit of ideals such as truth and goodness, but his ideas were eventually seen as a challenge to the Athenian social order. When an Athenian court sentenced Socrates to death, he willingly drank the poison and died calmly while talking with his students.

Acropolis of Athens, which had been the site of two temples dedicated to the goddess Athena. Both had been destroyed during the Persian occupation. Pericles wanted a new, special temple erected there for Athena, who was to be represented by an 11 m gold and ivory statue. Phidias, a sculptor and friend of Pericles, was commissioned to direct the work. The result was the **Parthenon**. Construction lasted from 447 to 438 B.C., with an additional six years needed to complete the sculpturing on the ends. The precision and skill of the planning and execution were exceptional.

Every four years a summer festival, known as the Panathenaea, was held. Celebrations consisted of athletic events, musical and oratorical contests, and the Panathenaic Procession along the Sacred Way to the Parthenon. Here Athena, represented by her magnificent statue, was presented with a new robe from her people.

The Peloponnesian War

The prosperity of the Golden Age was short-lived. When a trading rival, Corinth, appealed to Sparta, Thebes, and other allies to attack the wealthy Athenian Empire, the Greek world was thrown into a bitter struggle from which it never fully recovered. In 431 B.C., Greece was divided into two armed camps, with the city-states that supported Athens and its ideals in conflict with Sparta and other city-states that resented Athenian domination. The **Peloponnesian War**, as it was called, lasted for twenty-seven years and included atrocities by Sparta on land and by Athens at sea that betrayed the high moral standards the Greeks professed.

Inspired by Pericles's famous "Funeral Oration," which outlined the virtues of democratic life, Athens developed a war strategy of coastal raids on the Peloponnesus followed by naval blockades of food supplies. As people flooded into the city for protection against Spartan retaliation, Athens became over-crowded and a plague broke out that killed almost one-quarter of the population, Pericles among them. Athenian morale was devastated, and the war became an endurance struggle between evenly matched opponents. As Athens gradually weakened as the war dragged on, Sparta betrayed its fellow Greeks by borrowing money from Persia to build a fleet of its own. The Spartan navy overwhelmed the Athenians in a surprise attack in 405 B.C., and Athens surrendered all foreign possessions and ships to Sparta in a peace treaty the following year.

The Issue Emerges

What qualities constitute good government? Sparta, on the one hand, was known primarily for its military expertise. The Spartans' devotion to a military ideal was sufficient to hold the state together and to carry it to victory over the Athenians. Athens, on the other hand, enjoyed a rich and wide-ranging culture as well as military power. But after Sparta turned to the Persians for assistance, the Athenians were not able to withstand the Spartan

The Acropolis of Athens

The Acropolis is the rocky hill that the Athenians used as a refuge in times of danger, and on which they constructed temples, shrines, theatres, and other significant buildings and works of art. Archaeologists have discovered that the Acropolis has been settled since Neolithic times, beginning about 2800 B.C. Athena, the virgin goddess of wisdom and war, was worshipped on the Acropolis from about 1900 B.C., and the first temple was built for her somewhat later.

When the Persians occupied Athens in 479 B.C., they destroyed all the buildings on the Acropolis. The Athenians immediately began rebuilding, using the rubble from the old buildings as landfill and to make new walls.

The Parthenon, begun in 447 B.C., was the most impressive temple on the site. Although from a distance the structure of the Parthenon appeared to be absolutely straight, in reality the foundation bulged slightly toward the centre, and the columns were set at a slight angle. These adjustments were made to correct the optical illusion that makes straight lines seem crooked when viewed from afar. Every piece of marble had to be carefully shaped and fitted into place. Sculpture and coloured trim (yellow, green, and gold) provided decoration. The whiteness of the stone and the large shaded area the roof provided would have made the Parthenon a sanctuary from the scorching Mediterranean heat.

To their lasting credit, at the end of the Peloponnesian War the victorious Spartans did not destroy the Acropolis. They appreciated the exceptional artistic and architectural achievements of their long-time enemy. The buildings of the Acropolis have been used for many purposes since then. The Parthenon, for example, has been a Christian church (Orthodox and Catholic), a Muslim mosque, and a Turkish arsenal. While the Turks were defending themselves against a siege, a gunshot ignited the gunpowder stored in the Parthenon, and the resulting explosion destroyed much of the monument. Today, a partial reconstruction of the Parthenon stands amid broken stones and fragmentary buildings.

Even in its ruined state, the Parthenon displays the logic and harmony of classic Greek architecture.

Greek Architecture: the Doric Column.

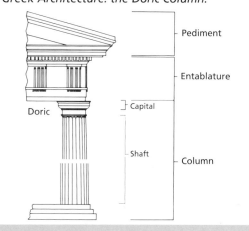

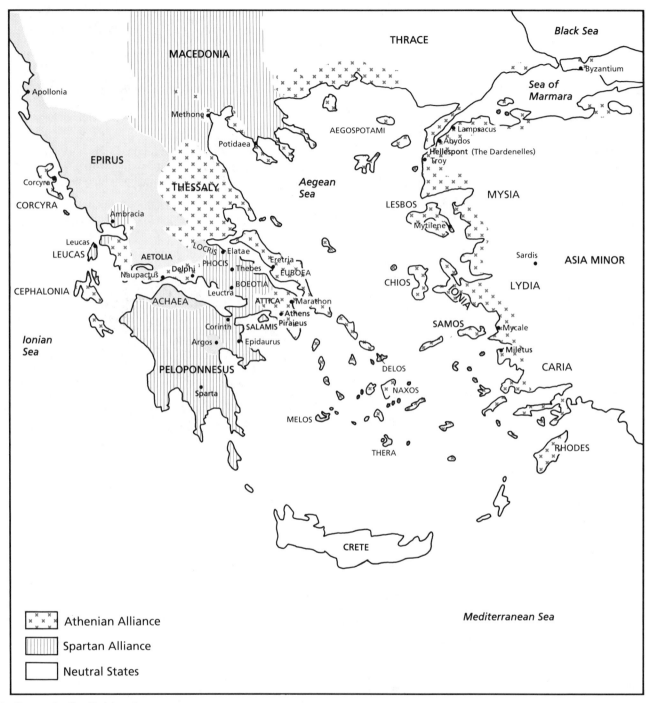

Greece in the Golden Age.

Black Sea

THRACE

Byzantium

Sea of
Marmara

MACEDONIA

Apollonia

Methone

AEGOSPOTAMI

Lampsacus

Potidaea

Abydos

Hellespont (The Dardenelles)
Troy

EPIRUS

Aegean
Sea

MYSIA

Corcyra

THESSALY

LESBOS

Mytilene

CORCYRA

Ambracia

Sardis

ASIA MINOR

Leucas

LOCRIS Elatae

LEUCAS

AETOLIA

PHOCIS

Eretria

CHIOS

LYDIA

IONIA

Delphi

Thebes

Naupactus

BOEOTIA

EUBOEA

CEPHALONIA

Leuctra

ACHAEA

ATTICA Marathon

Athens

SAMOS

Mycale

Ionian
Sea

Corinth

SALAMIS Piraieus

Argos

Epidaurus

Miletus

DELOS

CARIA

PELOPONNESUS

NAXOS

Sparta

MELOS

THERA

RHODES

CRETE

Mediterranean Sea

Athenian Alliance

Spartan Alliance

Neutral States

attacks. Was Spartan single-mindedness therefore superior to Athenian broad-mindedness?

The events that occurred after the Spartan victory make it even more difficult to weigh the merits of the two states. Sparta, like Athens, failed to find a way to unite Greek city-states in a lasting relationship. The conflict between the Spartans and the Athenians, and the final result of that conflict, raises many issues. What were the problems and weaknesses inherent in the two forms of government? Could other ways of life have brought a more fitting conclusion to the Golden Age of Greece? Was there any way in which the Greek city-states could have discovered and acted upon common interests?

PROBLEM QUESTION

Were the interests of the Greek people better served by the oligarchy of Sparta or by the democracy of Athens?

ALTERNATIVE ONE: Sparta

Based on "Greece: The Golden Age" (*Life Educational Reprint #66*, 1963)

Spartans were not always the rigid, self-denying people that they eventually became. In their Golden Age, they enjoyed pleasant pastimes such as music and dancing. Then, in 620 B.C., the enslaved Messenians rebelled. Although the Spartans crushed the revolt, it took all their strength to do so. The experience taught them a valuable lesson. If they were to control their empire and defend it against their enemies, they must sacrifice comfort and culture in order to forge themselves into a ruthless fighting machine.

Although the Spartan army was never more than eight thousand strong, their reputation for being unbeatable and their bloodcurdling war cry and disciplined attack terrified their enemies. The Spartan simplicity, straightforwardness, and fanatical dedication, which the other Greeks envied, were rooted in the Spartan constitution. The state was everything, the individual nothing. All Spartans were taught that goodness was simply strength plus bravery, and their lives were dedicated to serving this ideal. State inspectors examined newborn infants for defects and weaknesses. Those who failed to pass were left to die on Mount Taygetus.

Military training began at the age of seven. Young boys were taken from their homes and placed in schools, where they were repeatedly bullied and brutalized to toughen them for combat. They were taught that to cry out in pain was an unforgivable sin. To test their physical endurance, an annual ceremony was performed at the altar of the goddess Artemis. A few boys were whipped until the altar stones were flecked with blood. Throughout the beating, their parents urged them not to flinch or cry out. It was not unusual for a boy to die rather than show weakness. Besides physical endurance, they learned obedience and self-discipline. They also

Institutions

Pericles's "Funeral Oration" is one of many famous speeches that influenced the course of Athenian history. In fact, public speaking was an extremely important and valued skill in Athens, because the democratic government was conducted in front of all available citizens. The meetings would occur about once every nine days, and would often be attended by five or six thousand people. The crowd would listen to different speakers, each of whom would recommend a particular policy or course of action. It was essential for speakers to be persuasive, because a policy would be adopted only if a majority of citizens voted in favour of it. It took courage and self-confidence to speak out—the crowd was quite willing to heckle and shout down an orator. Although any citizen could speak, it was usually the aristocrats who did. Presumably an aristocrat had the advantage of a superior education and considerable influence.

Spartan Warrior.

learned self-sufficiency. A soldier's survival often depended on his ability to forage for food. Boys were encouraged to steal, providing they did so without being caught. Spartan courage and endurance are illustrated by the famous legend of the boy caught stealing a live fox. To conceal his theft, the boy hid the fox under his tunic. It began to claw at him and gnawed away at his internal organs, but the boy did not show his pain in any way.

The years between the ages of twenty and thirty were spent in military barracks. Life there was raw and rough, the reverse of the sophistication and grace of Athenian life. The scanty conversation was gruff and terse; the food was unappetizing. Only at age thirty, when his military service was complete, did the Spartan male become a citizen. Only then was he allowed to participate in the Assembly. His involvement, however, amounted to nothing more than listening to proposals and shouting out his vote with the others. The side receiving the loudest shout won.

The legislation put before the Assembly was prepared by a council of elders and two kings. But the real power was held by a group of five men called *ephors*. Elected annually, they had command over all. The ephors controlled education as well as both public and private moral conduct. They enforced the laws through a secret police force.

One law commanded every Spartan to breed new generations of soldiers. Spartan females were taught to be proud of their bodies, and to spend their young years in rigorous physical activity to develop them for healthy childbearing. After a certain age, those who remained single were paired off with unmarried men, a method considered just as likely to produce children as marrying for love.

Spartan women enjoyed far more freedom than any other Greek women. They had equal rights with Spartan men in everything except voting. Active military duty and the requirement that males under thirty live in military barracks gave their wives complete authority over the households. The state decreased their workload by taking care of most of the child-rearing responsibilities. The criticisms of Plutarch, the Athenian, demonstrate how other Greeks viewed Spartan women. He described them as being "bold, masculine, overbearing to their husbands ... and speaking openly on even the most important subjects."

Spartan citizens, male and female, had slaves (the Laconians and Messenians) to do much of the work. *Helots,* or serfs, farmed the land and were forced to turn over most of their yield. They were kept in check by the secret police, and, to oppress them further, the ephors declared war on them every year. In spite of these precautions, the Spartans frequently had to suppress helot revolts.

Another subjugated class, the *Perioeci,* acted as shopkeepers and tradespeople. Sparta's economy was frugal and self-sufficient, and transactions were completed with cumbersome iron bars as currency. It was extremely difficult for the *Perioeci* to gain any wealth or power.

The Spartans were a rigid, narrow-minded people. They were suspicious of anything foreign, including trade, and they resisted change of any kind. Periodically, they even deported foreigners to prevent the spread of new ideas. This attitude, which was partially responsible for Sparta's downfall, was reinforced through the educational system. Mindless obedience destroys imagination and the ability to adapt to change.

The Spartan victory over the Athenians proved their military supremacy. However, their ability to lead the other Greek city-states was not impressive. Corruption among the Spartan leaders grew rampant once gold was introduced into the country. One general, Pausanias, even offered to betray Sparta for the right price.

Perhaps the Spartans had been right to resist change, for it was change that eventually undermined their strength. New land inheritance laws meant that traditionally small lots became absorbed into large estates. Many Spartans lost their land and their citizenship, and they emigrated. The Spartan army gradually grew smaller and Sparta's power dwindled. By the fourth century B.C., Sparta was no longer a major power in Greece.

QUESTIONS

1. How did Sparta change after the Messenian rebellion in 620 B.C.?
2. a) How large was the Spartan army at its peak?
   b) Describe the reputation this army earned.
3. a) Briefly describe the training given to all Spartan men from birth to the age of thirty.
   b) In what ways do the ceremony for the goddess Artemis and the story of the boy stealing a fox reveal the self-discipline expected from all Spartans?
4. a) How did someone become a member of the Spartan Assembly?
   b) Who prepared legislation for the Assembly?
   c) How was the decision made to accept or reject the legislation?
5. a) Why were the ephors the real power in Sparta?
   b) Explain how the ephors' control over private life extended to marriage and childbirth.
6. What kind of lives did Spartan women lead?
7. a) Who were the *Perioeci*?
   b) Why were the Spartans suspicious of foreigners?
   c) Why were Spartans considered narrow-minded?
8. What was the major cause of Sparta's downfall?

ALTERNATIVE TWO: Pericles's Funeral Oration

Based on *History of the Peloponnesian War* by Thucydides, c. 410 B.C.

Our constitution is called a democracy because power is in the hands not of a minority but of the whole people. When it is a question of settling private disputes, everyone is equal before the law; when it is a question of putting one person before another in positions of public responsibility, what counts is not membership in a particular class, but the actual ability which the man possesses. No one, so long as he has it in him to be of service to the state, is kept in political obscurity because of poverty. And, just as our political life is free and open, so is our day-to-day life.... We are free and tolerant in our private lives; but in public affairs we keep to the law. This is because it commands our deep respect.

We give our obedience to those whom we put in positions of authority, and we obey the laws themselves, especially those which are for the protection of the oppressed, and those unwritten laws which it is acknowledged to break.

And here is another point. When our work is over, we are in a position to enjoy all kinds of recreation for our spirits. There are various kinds of contests and sacrifices regularly throughout the year; in our own homes we find a beauty and a good taste which delight us every day and which drive away our cares. Then the greatness of our city brings it about that all the good things from all over the world flow in to us, so that to us it seems just as natural to enjoy foreign goods as our own local products.... Our city is open to the world, and we have no periodical deportations in order to prevent people observing or finding out secrets which might be of military advantage to the enemy. This is because we rely, not on secret weapons, but on our own real courage and loyalty. There are certain advantages, I think, in our way of meeting danger voluntarily, with natural rather than with state-induced courage.

Our love of what is beautiful does not lead to extravagance; our love of the things of the mind does not make us soft. We regard wealth as something to be properly used, rather than as something to boast about. As for poverty, no one need be ashamed to admit it: the real shame is in not taking practical measures to escape from it. In our city each individual is interested not only in his own affairs but in the affairs of the state as well.... We do not say that a man who takes no interest in politics is a man who minds his own business; we say that he has no business here at all.... And this is another point where we differ from other people. We are capable at the same time of taking risks and of estimating them beforehand. Others are brave out of ignorance; and, when they stop to think, they begin to fear. But the man who can most truly be accounted brave is he who best knows the meaning of what is sweet in life and of what is terrible, and then goes out undeterred to meet what is to come.... Taking everything together then, I declare that our city is an education to Greece, and I declare that in my opinion each single one of our citizens is able to show himself the rightful lord and owner of his own person.... And to show that this is no empty boasting...you have only to consider the power which our city possesses and which has been won by those very qualities which I have mentioned.... Mighty indeed are the marks and monuments of our empire which we have left. Future ages will wonder at us, as the present age wonders at us now.

From Thucydides, *History of the Peloponnesian War*, translated by Rex Warner (Penguin Classics, 1954). Copyright © Rex Warner, 1954. Reprinted by permission of Penguin Books Ltd.

QUESTIONS

1. Pericles's speech was meant as a tribute to the Athenians who died in the first year of the Peloponnesian War with Sparta. How would you expect him to describe Athenian society in that situation? Explain your answer.

2. a) Where did the power lie in Athenian democracy, according to Pericles?
   b) How did this situation compare to Spartan society?
   c) Could a man be held back in Athenian society if he was poor or a member of a lower class? Explain your answer.

3. a) When work was completed, what kind of life could Athenians enjoy?
   b) How did this compare to life in Sparta?

4. a) When Pericles spoke of "state-induced courage," to what society was he referring?
   b) Why did Pericles feel the Athenian system was superior?

5. a) How important was politics in Athenian society?
   b) How important is politics to Canadians today? Are our present attitudes toward politics different from or similar to the attitudes described by Pericles? Explain your answer.

6. What did Pericles mean when he said, "Future ages will wonder at us, as the present age wonders at us now"?

ALTERNATIVE THREE: Athenian Democracy

Based on *What Democracy Meant to the Greeks* by W.R. Agard (1965)

Just how democratic was Athenian democracy? In *What Democracy Meant to the Greeks*, W.R. Agard examines the composition of Athenian society, its political system, and some of the advantages and disadvantages of Athenian democracy.

In 430 B.C., according to Agard, only about 10 percent of the Athenian population had political rights. These forty thousand voters were all male, over eighteen years of age, and born of Athenian parents who were citizens. The remaining 90 percent of the population comprised about twenty-four thousand aliens, or *metics*, who had settled in Athens for business purposes; one hundred thousand enslaved war captives; and the Athenian women and children. Restricting political rights was based on the belief that only those who were experienced and had a permanent stake in the city's welfare should be allowed to determine policy.

Citizenship was granted to people of every social class, which meant that both the rich and the poor had a voice in Athenian political life. According to Agard, country gentlemen and businessmen participated in government alongside farmers, day workers, and artisans who made up the majority of voters. Each policy was voted on by the entire electorate.

Participants in the Council of Five Hundred and the Jury of Six Thousand were selected annually, by lot, from a list of citizens over thirty years of age. The chair of the Council was chosen by lot every day. Only the members of the Board of Ten Generals were elected, since these positions required a knowledge of military and naval strategy not possessed by all citizens. Agard suggests that every citizen would have engaged in public service at some point in his life.

To perform their public service duties, citizens had to take time from their normal work schedule, which decreased their earning power. Since the majority of the members were already from the lower economic classes, public service threatened their ability to make a living. In compensation, council members and jurors were paid for their services. In the fourth century B.C., payment was also given for attendance at the Assembly.

This system had some disadvantages. According to Agard, there was often inconsistency between the adoption and execution of a policy. A persuasive speaker might well sway the Assembly to adopt his policy, but he had no further responsibility once it was approved. The execution was left to other men, who were not always in favour of the action.

A built-in safeguard known as *ostracism* sometimes became another disadvantage. If one man became too powerful as a speaker in the Assembly, he could be expelled from the country simply by a majority vote of the Assembly. This privilege was seldom exercised wisely. Agard tells the story of one farmer who voted for the expulsion of Aristides the Just simply because he was tired of hearing him called "the Just."

In spite of its disadvantages, Athenian democracy controlled the city-state during the century of its greatest achievements, which included the cultural, economic, and political development of approximately two hundred and fifty states within the Athenian Empire.

A democracy in which there are slaves who have no voice hardly seems like a democracy. Yet, as Agard points out, for the most part the Athenians did not have slavery as we usually think of it. He estimates that one-fifth of the slave population was confined to the mines, where life was truly hard and short. But the remaining slaves had many economic advantages, and were protected from bodily harm by legislation. Domestic slaves were often regarded with respect and affection. Others who worked as artisans or for the state were actually paid for their labours. If they saved enough money, they could eventually buy their freedom. Slaves often worked alongside citizens and *metics* in both unskilled and highly skilled jobs. Agard feels there were probably many Greek slaves who were economically secure and happy. As support, he notes that there were no serious slave revolts in Athens until 103 B.C.

Athenian democracy also excluded women, even those who were the wives of citizens. Although they were responsible for managing the households and educating the children, women had little freedom. From birth to death, men controlled their lives. Their fathers arranged their marriages, and if these ended in divorce, male guardians took control of their finances. Husbands were always given custody of the children. Xenophon, the Greek historian, said a good wife had the habits of temperance and modesty, and was easily teachable. Athenian women did not participate in public affairs, and they socialized mainly with other women. Oddly enough, *metic* women enjoyed more social freedom than Athenian women.

Controversies

While the Athenians paid homage to their goddess, Athena, they repressed their wives and daughters. One of the few women of Athens to participate in Greek culture was Aspasia (470-410 B.C.). A companion of Pericles, Aspasia was a scholar who took part in the intellectual dialogues of the day. She discussed the role of women in society and openly asserted woman's right to live as man's equal. Eventually, she was charged and tried for her outspoken behaviour.

QUESTIONS

1. a) What qualifications did a person need to participate in Athenian democracy?
    b) How many citizens did Athens have?
    c) What proportion of the total population did they represent?
    d) Is this the impression Pericles creates in his "Funeral Oration"? Give evidence to support your answer.
    e) What proportion of the total population can vote in Canada?
    f) Is Canadian democracy more democratic than the system used in ancient Athens? Explain your answer.
2. a) How were members chosen for the Council of Five Hundred, the chair of the Council, and the jury?
    b) To what extent was this procedure democratic?
    c) What advantages did this system offer?
    d) What problems did the system create?
    e) How does this system compare with the Spartan system?
3. a) What is meant by the term *ostracism*?
    b) How could the use of ostracism be abused?
4. a) Describe the rights and living conditions of slaves in Athens.

b) Do you think Athens could be called democratic despite its reliance on slaves? Give reasons for your answer.

5. a) Describe the living conditions of women in Athens.
   b) Suggest why women in Athens were treated so differently from women in Sparta.
   c) In what year did Canadian women obtain the right to vote federally?
   d) Should our view of Athenian democracy be affected by the restrictions that were placed on women at the time? Explain your viewpoint.

ANSWERING THE PROBLEM QUESTION

The problem you are being asked to consider in this chapter is fundamentally different from the problems presented earlier in the text. Previously you had to assess, and base your arguments on, various kinds of physical evidence—fossils, artifacts, monuments, ancient writings, and geological findings. This time, the issue is more abstract. You are examining how different systems of government affect people's lives. This question involves evaluating competing ideas and ideals. You should explore several key areas before you make your judgments about Sparta and Athens.

Clearly, Spartan culture was different from Athenian culture, but were there similarities as well? How did both societies hold onto their power? Other similarities are hidden beneath the surface. The Spartans thought it was humane and necessary to leave infants with identifiable defects to die on Mount Taygetus. From the strong children who remained, state-controlled education could produce the brave, dedicated soldiers needed to protect Sparta from rebellious city-states or foreign enemies. In Athens, population pressure produced similar results. Just behind the spectacular public buildings of the Acropolis and Agora, twisting alleyways enclosed some of the worst slums and unsanitary conditions of the age. Unwanted or deformed children were often placed in earthenware jars or left at isolated street corners to be picked up by slave traders, eaten by dogs, or simply to die.

You will also have to compare political and civil rights in the two societies. In both city-states, citizenship was not automatic and did not include the entire population, but the qualifications for citizenship were different in each. Although both systems had an assembly, its intended purpose and actual operation were, again, much different. Why did such a contrast exist? What was each state trying to achieve with its particular system? People of different classes were treated one way in Sparta and another way in Athens. Why was there such a contrast in the way the two states treated women, slaves, and those involved in trade?

Was the demise of Athens and Sparta a direct result of the goals they set for themselves and the systems they developed to reach their ideals? Or was it related to external forces over which they had little control? Weigh these questions and any others you feel are important, rank the answers you arrive at, and then come to some conclusion about whether the Greeks were better off under the Spartans' oligarchy, the Athenians' democracy, or neither.

THE STORY CONTINUES . . .

The Decline of the Greek City-States

The military victory finalized in 404 B.C., after the long, drawn-out Peloponnesian War, appeared to open the way for Sparta to assume Athens' former position of leadership in the Aegean and in Asia Minor. Sparta's attempts to dominate, however, resulted in thirty years of intermittent land and naval skirmishes with several city-state rivals. The Second Athenian League, which, in contrast with the Delian League, was closer to a true association of equals, crippled the Spartan fleet at Naxos in 376 B.C. Five years later, Thebes ended the legend of Sparta's invincibility on land by inflicting a crushing defeat at Leuctra. The following year, the Messenians revolted against Sparta as they had in 620 B.C., but this time they were successful.

A lack of soldiers certainly contributed to Sparta's deterioration. And, as city-state policies began to concentrate wealth in the hands of Spartan citizens at the expense of non-citizens, the high morale of city life, which had been one of Sparta's greatest assets, was weakened. New inheritance laws resulted in small lots being gradually absorbed into large estates. Many Spartans, left landless, lost their citizenship and emigrated, leaving fewer dedicated soldiers for the Spartan army. Allied briefly with Athens in 362 B.C., Sparta was again defeated by Thebes. By 340 B.C., Sparta's once-proud army numbered only about one thousand men.

It seemed that no city-state could gain control of or even exercise continuous leadership over the Greek world. The inability of individual Greek city-states to understand the advantages of political units larger than their own kept Greece divided and led to its demise. Brief loyalties for immediate gain led to alliances in one battle that were quickly abandoned in the next. This failure to overcome mutual suspicion made Greek city-states vulnerable to external forces that could *impose* unity through military force.

The Macedonian Era

Although Macedonia had already been exposed to the impressive accomplishments of Greek culture by the time Philip II came to the throne in 359 B.C., it was still an agricultural society dominated by an aristocracy of horse breeders whom the Greek city-states believed were barbarians. In Philip, however, Macedonia had a shrewd soldier and calculating diplomat able to bring order to the entire Greek world. To accomplish this goal, Philip waited patiently for the right moment and then acted decisively with an extremely efficient military organization.

These Greek pendant earrings, which feature an intricately detailed dove, are made out of gold.

This typical example of Greek pottery originated 450-350 B.C.

A cautious planner, Philip took pains to secure his northern and eastern borders from attacks by hill tribes. While the Greek city-states squabbled among themselves, Philip slowly advanced into Thrace where, by 356 B.C., he had taken control of the rich gold mines of the Pangaea Mountains. During the Third Sacred War among the Greek city-states, Philip also secured Thessaly, with its important reserves of grain and horses. He made a brief attempt to penetrate central Greece but was unsuccessful.

The Athenians, inspired by their masterful orator Demosthenes, realized that the growth of Macedonian power under Philip's leadership was a threat to their existence. Few of the other city-states were willing to commit themselves to Demosthenes's warning, and minor skirmishes between Macedonia and Athens continued until a tenuous peace between them was arranged in 346 B.C.

Philip, however, soon broke his promises of peace, and repeatedly pressed his advantage over small, isolated communities. He was unsuccessful in permanently cutting off Athens from its supply of wheat in the Black Sea or in holding Thermopylae, but he managed to gain access to northern Greece through a stroke of diplomacy. The Phocians, who had been defeated and harshly treated by Philip, gave up their capital city, Elatae, to Macedonia in return for reduced tribute. This deal alarmed the Athenians because Elatae gave Philip a route by which he could enter Greece. The danger enabled Demosthenes to seal a shaky alliance with Athens' former enemy, Thebes.

On the battlefield of Chaeronea in 338 B.C., Philip's efficient Macedonian army annihilated the combined forces of Athens and Thebes. Philip, now master of all Greece, summoned the defeated city-states and their neighbours to Corinth. He oversaw the formation of a league of Greek states, not including Sparta. The league was bound in an alliance with Macedonia, which could command Greek forces upon request in time of war.

Philip was now ready for the greatest military adventure of his career—the conquest of Persia. His dream was cut short, however, when he was assassinated at his daughter's wedding feast in 336 B.C. It would be left to his son, Alexander, to bring his dream to reality.

SUMMARY

Around 800 B.C., the many city-states of Greece began to appear. Each one consisted of an urban centre and some surrounding agricultural land that produced food for the residents. Because of Greece's mountainous topography, the city-states were isolated from one another and remained separate political units. Warfare between them was frequent.

Good farmland was scarce, so beginning about 750 B.C. different city-states established colonies beyond the Greek mainland. Most city-states had been ruled by kings, but during this period different types of government arose. Two of the most famous Greek political systems were the oligarchy of Sparta and the democracy of Athens.

In Sparta's oligarchy, most of the real power was concentrated in the hands of five men, the ephors, who introduced all the legislation. The Spartans dominated and enslaved neighbouring peoples, and, to maintain their power, dedicated themselves to military values. Boys were raised to be soldiers, and spent all their time between the ages of seven and thirty in training or service. Spartan girls were given a good education, including athletics, and, as women, enjoyed a great deal of independence, although they were expected to marry and have children. The slaves were worked very hard and had no rights; they frequently rose against the Spartans. Simplicity, discipline, and courage were the prime Spartan values. They resisted change and mistrusted outsiders.

Athens, on the other hand, was open to trade and outside influences. It was a colonial power whose military strength resided mainly in its navy. Unlike the Spartans, Athenians valued the arts and enjoyed comfort. They developed a democratic government, but voting rights were restricted to Athenian males whose parents were citizens. Women, slaves, and immigrants (90 percent of the population) had no political voice. Athenians used slave labour, but they treated their slaves better than the Spartans did. Athenian women were given few rights and little freedom.

Sparta, Athens, and other Greek city-states were forced into a military alliance under the threat of a Persian invasion. The Persian empire was expanding, and in 490 B.C. the Persians, under Darius I, attacked the Greek mainland. Although the Greeks were outnumbered, they managed to defeat their enemy. Greece was attacked ten years later by Darius's son, Xerxes, and a tremendous army and navy, but the Athenian navy proved stronger. To guard against further Persian invasions, Athens convinced other city-states to form the Delian League. Athens dominated its partners, and by 465 B.C. the League was essentially an Athenian empire.

At this time, there were military clashes between Athens and other Greek city-states, and a special rivalry developed between Athens and Sparta. Tension decreased somewhat when the two powers agreed on a truce in 445 B.C. The Athenians were at their peak during this period. Under Pericles's leadership they constructed the great public building called the Parthenon atop the Acropolis. Just as the Parthenon was being completed, the peace between the Athenians and the Spartans ended and the devastating Peloponnesian War began. The whole of Greece became involved, with some city-states siding with Sparta and others with Athens. The conflict began in 431 B.C. and ended when the Spartan navy launched a surprise attack and bested the Athenians in 404 B.C., twenty-seven years later.

For an additional thirty years, Sparta was at war intermittently with other city-states, but was not able to hold the territory the Athenians had overseen. Sparta's army deteriorated, and the city-state lost much of its power.

In 359 B.C., Philip II became king of Macedonia, a territory to the north of Greece. He built up an army, trained them in innovative battle tactics, and then moved into Greece, taking advantage of the fragmentation of the Greek city-states. By 338 B.C., the Macedonians had proved that their forces were superior. The victorious Philip forged a league of Greek states (excluding Sparta) that he could command if war occurred. His ambition was to conquer Persia, but he was assassinated before he could put his plans into action.

6

Alexander, Hannibal, and Julius Caesar

Date B.C.	Event
1200-1100	Canaanite traders (Phoenicians) settle on coast of modern Lebanon and establish independent cities
	Sea peoples destroy and sack all Mycenaean palace-states
1000	First city built by Latins on site of Rome
c. 814	Tyre founds city of Carthage in North Africa
800	Greek city-states emerge
753	Legendary founding of Rome by Romulus
616	Etruscan rule of Rome and central Italy
c. 550	Carthaginians battle Greeks in Sicily
	Magonid Dynasty established by Carthaginians; lasts 150 years
509	Romans overthrow Etruscans and Rome becomes a Republic
494-480	Phoenicians supply Persians with ships in war against Greek city-states
431	Peloponnesian War begins
338	Philip II of Macedonia defeats Athens and Thebes at Chaeronea
336-323	*Leadership of Alexander the Great*
264-241	First Punic War—Rome versus Carthage
218-202	*Second Punic War—leadership of Hannibal*
150-146	Third Punic War—Carthage is destroyed by Rome
73-71	Spartacus leads a revolt of gladiators and other slaves
61-44	*Leadership of Julius Caesar*
41	Antony and Cleopatra at Tarsus
31	Octavian defeats combined forces of Antony and Cleopatra at Actium
27	Octavian becomes Caesar Augustus, first Roman Emperor

6

Alexander, Hannibal, and Julius Caesar

BACKGROUND

Alexander

When Philip of Macedonia was assassinated in 336 B.C., his son Alexander, a young man of twenty, became king. Where Philip had been a cautious military planner and shrewd bargainer, Alexander was an impulsive man of immediate action. He regarded himself as a second Achilles, a hero described in his favourite book, Homer's *Iliad*. Like Achilles, Alexander possessed great strength, courage, and passion. He had been carefully groomed by Philip to become a military leader—at eighteen, he was given the command of the cavalry in battle. Philip also ensured that Alexander received an excellent education. He had been instilled with an interest in art, poetry, and science by his childhood tutor, Aristotle, one of the most respected Greek thinkers. But Alexander's vision of politics was quite different from Aristotle's. The teacher felt that the tiny city-state was the ultimate political unit; the student's ambition was to establish an empire.

He set about this task as soon as he became king. In the first two years of his rule, he expanded his territory to the north and west and reaffirmed Macedonia's hold on Greece. His next goal was to attack the Persians. He moved his powerful army into Persian territory in 334 B.C., and six years later he had not only defeated the Persian army, but had also usurped the Persian king and taken the throne for himself. He combined his Greek and Persian empires and helped to disperse Greek culture through all his lands. To some extent he also tolerated and even adopted Persian customs. During the next five years, Alexander extended his empire into India, but finally had to call a halt to his advance. He was planning an invasion of Arabia when he died of a fever at the age of thirty-two. Alexander's empire, which loomed so large at the time of his death in 323 B.C., quickly fell apart. His generals divided the territory among themselves:

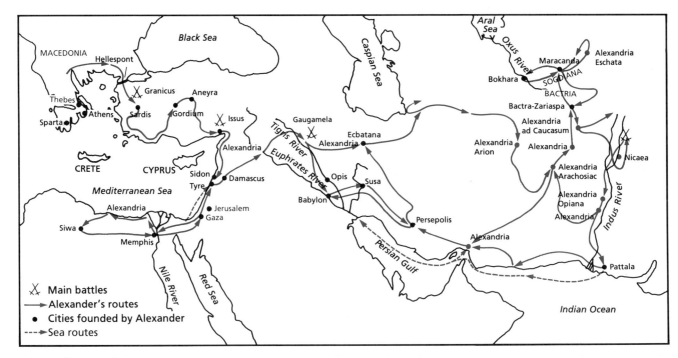

Alexander's World.

On coins and in art, Alexander was usually depicted as a beautiful youth with long, flowing hair. His clean-shaven face set a fashion in Greece and Italy that lasted centuries.

Selecus established the Seleuced Kingdom in Persia; Ptolemy established his own dynasty in Egypt; Antigonus became king of Macedonia. The cities and lands captured by Alexander in Greece and India regained their independence.

During his brief but spectacular career, Alexander never lost a battle. Tales of his exploits became legendary and spread throughout the world. From Britain to Malaysia, over eighty versions of his life's history, in twenty-four different languages, recorded his conquests. Although Greece never regained its former political power, the influence of Greek culture after Alexander was wider than it had ever been before.

Clearly Alexander was exceptional. The combination of his great ambition and his many talents changed the course of history. Not only did Alexander influence history, he also influenced the way we *think* about history. Alexander, and other individuals like him, have prompted historians to ask this question: Is history shaped and controlled by a few great leaders? According to this view, it is they who pull everyone else along with them. It is the leaders who deserve attention and study. Analysing history means assessing the achievements of these powerful few and comparing the greatness of one leader against the greatness of another. This view of history leads to many other questions. What makes a leader great? Do standards of greatness change over time? Is it right to call a leader great if his or her accomplishments include actions that are disgusting and deplorable?

Are there alternative ways of looking at history? These questions are not easily settled, and are certainly worth returning to.

Rise of the Phoenicians

Over a thousand years before Alexander, the Minoan civilization centred on Crete ruled the Aegean and the eastern Mediterranean. The rapid decline of the Minoans in the fifteenth century B.C. left a vacuum of power. Mycenaean city-states, the Egyptians, the Hittites, and the marauding "peoples of the sea" struggled for control of trade routes and colonies. No single power was able to gain the upper hand.

In this world of turmoil and change, sometime around 1200 B.C., Canaanite traders began to thrive and extend their influence. They originated in centres along the coast of modern Lebanon, and became the greatest seafarers and traders in the Mediterranean. The Greeks called them **Phoenicians**, but this term was probably never known to or used by the peoples it was applied to. They saw themselves as citizens of their individual cities—Sidon, Tyre, or Byblos—and they were jealous of one another's successes. Although they spoke the same language and worshipped the same gods, they never formed a country known as Phoenicia. As the volume and profit of their trading ventures increased, however, the Phoenicians established cities in the western Mediterranean, including the city of **Carthage**, founded by Tyre in the eighth century B.C.

With the spread of Greek colonization during the next three hundred years came several clashes between the two sea powers. Carthage launched a successful campaign against the Greeks in Sicily and created the Magonid Dynasty. It was also the Phoenicians who supplied the Persian kings, Darius and Xerxes, with ships in their costly effort to conquer Greece.

Carthage became the dominant trading city and best-fortified port in the western Mediterranean. Situated on a peninsula on the north shore of Africa, Carthage was protected by triple walls 15 m high and 10 m wide, with four-storey towers every 60 m. The sheltered harbour had anchorage for about two hundred ships. Carthaginian military strength on land and sea was supported by growing wealth through trade in grain, metals, resin, wax, honey, slaves, and wine from far-flung contacts throughout the Mediterranean.

Carthage became involved in a dispute with Syracuse, a city on the island of Sicily, who appealed to **Rome** for assistance. Rome was a new power that had just completed its conquest of the Italian peninsula. When Rome answered the call in 264 B.C., the **First Punic War** broke out and continued with heavy losses on both sides until Rome emerged victorious in 241 B.C.

Hannibal

In the two decades after the war, Carthage turned its attention to the western Mediterranean and gained territory in Spain. Fearing additional

More to Consider

Alexander could be a dangerous friend as well as a dangerous enemy. In 330 B.C., Alexander's faithful general Philotus boasted that he and his father, Parmenium, had been crucial to the Greek victory over Persia, and claimed that Alexander could not have won without them. When Alexander heard about the remark, he had both Philotus and his father executed. Two years later, at a party where everyone had drunk too much, Alexander's closest friend, Clitus, made similar remarks. He praised Alexander's dead father, Philip. He objected to Alexander's Persian clothes. And he suggested that Alexander should not take personal credit for victories that were in fact won by thousands. Alexander grabbed a spear from a guard and killed his friend—a man who had once saved his life in battle. Alexander's behaviour on a grander scale was just as cruel. There was a familiar pattern to his victories over Thebes, Tyre, Gaza, and other cities: massacring, plundering, and selling survivors into slavery. Alexander seemed to have had no concern about the harsh treatment of an already defeated foe.

Carthage

B.C.	
c. 1500	Volcanic eruption on Thera ends Minoan civilization
1450-1200	War dominates the Aegean and eastern Mediterranean Mycenaeans, Egyptians, Hittites, and "peoples of the sea" struggle for control of trade and land
1200-1100	Canaanite traders (Phoenicians) settle on coast of modern Lebanon and establish independent cities such as Sidon and Tyre
c. 814	Tyre founds the city of Carthage in North Africa
c. 550	Carthaginians battle Greeks in Sicily Carthaginians establish Magonid Dynasty; lasts 150 years
494-480	Phoenicians supply Persians with ships in war against Greek city-states
333	Byblos and Sidon fall to Alexander the Great
332	Tyre falls to Alexander
264-241	First Punic War between Carthage and Rome for control of the Mediterranean Rome wins after a long, difficult struggle
237	Hamlicar Barca of Carthage develops a base in Spain
239	Hasdrubal of Carthage founds New Carthage in Spain

Religion

The Carthaginians were resented principally for their domination of trade, but also because they preserved the Phoenician religious practice of human sacrifice. One burial ground in Carthage had thousands of clay pots with the remains of babies and children. Carthage continued this religious rite for over four hundred years after the eastern Phoenician cities had abandoned it.

Carthaginian expansion, Rome reached an agreement with Carthage to divide Spain at the Ebro River. Nonetheless, in 219 B.C., a young general named Hannibal attacked the hill fort of Saguntum, which had been placed under the protection of Rome. Hannibal knew this attack would lead to war and he was ready for the challenge.

Military leadership in Carthage was not easy. The city government retained tight control over generals in the field. One unsuccessful general was crucified on the battlefield, while another suffered the same fate at home after a defeat at sea. Hannibal, who had taken an oath as a boy of nine to dedicate his life to the destruction of Rome, had absolute confidence in his ability to command and in the quality of his troops. Although the Carthaginian army was made up largely of mercenaries, including Spanish infantry, Numidian cavalry, and Celtic warriors, each group was fiercely loyal to Hannibal. Hannibal wisely let each group fight together using familiar tactics and made no attempt to impose uniformity. He ate the same food, wore the same clothes, slept on the same ground, and suffered the same hardships as his soldiers. Hannibal was the first man in and the last man out of any battle. He felt sure he could beat the Romans if he could engage them in Italy, away from the interference of the Carthaginian government.

Like Alexander, Hannibal is remembered as a great leader, although unlike Alexander his accomplishments were exclusively military. Hannibal's attack on Saguntum resulted in the **Second Punic War**. A Carthaginian expedition, led by Hannibal, moved against Rome in 218 B.C. He took his troops through Spain, over the Alps, and into the heart of Roman territory. As Hannibal and his forces moved south through what is now Italy, they engaged with the Romans several times, winning the battles through superior, and often devious, tactics. For over two years, Hannibal moved toward

The Punic Wars.

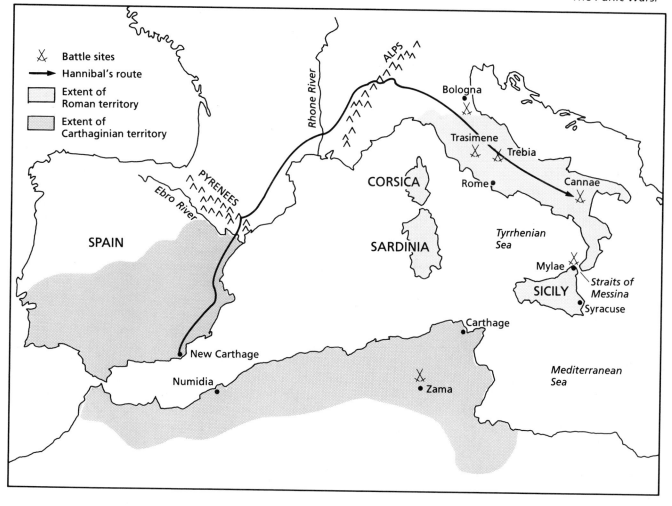

Rome, but he was unable to gain control of the territories he passed through. His army based itself in the south of Italy and continued to attack the Romans, but lacked the armaments to take Rome itself. Similarly, the Romans could not defeat Hannibal, but they could limit his range by hoarding food and burning crops in the fields.

The stand-off went on and on. Hannibal's forces remained in Italy for sixteen years. By this time, Hannibal knew that Carthage would not win the war. Scipio, a Roman general, had recaptured the Spanish territory and had moved the war to North Africa. The Numidians, once allies of Carthage, had been persuaded by promises of territory and wealth to join the Romans. In 202 B.C., Hannibal returned to defend his homeland. The Second Punic War ended when Scipio defeated Hannibal at Zama. Hannibal's forces, most of them newly recruited, simply lacked the necessary training. Hannibal was forced to flee, and lived the remainder of his life in what is now Syria.

The Birth and Development of the Roman Republic

Carthage was the most serious military threat that Rome ever faced. After Hannibal's defeat, Rome imposed heavy penalties on Carthage in an attempt to limit its rival's power. But Carthaginian influence managed to grow during the next half-century, until the Romans were finally prompted to attack the Carthaginians again in 150 B.C. By the time Rome had won the **Third Punic War** in 146 B.C., the city of Carthage was so thoroughly dismantled that Carthaginian culture virtually ceased to exist.

The rise of the Romans to this position of dominance in the Mediterranean took place over a relatively short period of time. Roman history stretches back to about the time when the Phoenician cities emerged as a distinct cultural group. The first settlement on the site of Rome was probably established by the Latins about 1000 B.C. It was only one of several small towns on the Italian peninsula. Rome, like many of the other towns, was eventually taken over by the **Etruscans**, a rather mysterious people from the north whose writing has not yet been deciphered. The invading Etruscans placed their first king on the Roman throne in 616 B.C. They possessed superior methods of farming, manufacturing, trading, and building, which enabled Rome to flourish as a city-state. In 509 B.C., the Romans rebelled and established a **republic** (a government whose leaders are elected) that lasted until 27 B.C. The Romans shook off their oppressors, but many Roman achievements can be traced back to Etruscan influence.

Initially, Rome simply hoped to survive, isolated as it was in a sea of city-states. The collapse of Etruscan power throughout the Italian peninsula, however, resulted in several subject peoples warring against each other and opened the region to invasion. In 390 B.C., warlike tribes from Gaul conquered and sacked Rome, but the city was quickly rebuilt and a new philosophy prevailed. Territorial expansion was now considered the best

The Arts

Rome, like most cities of the ancient world, had a legend explaining how it was founded. It was named after Romulus, who, according to legend, was a descendant of local rulers and possibly the son of the god Mars. As babies, Romulus and his twin brother Remus were set adrift on the Tiber River, but arrived on ground and managed to survive. A wolf nurtured them with her milk, and a shepherd's wife raised them. Romulus established the city of Rome on the site on which they had grown up. But Romulus and Remus quarrelled, and Romulus killed his brother. The image of the two boys nursing from the wolf was immortalized in sculpture in the ancient world and remains a highly visible symbol in public buildings and on tourist souvenirs in Rome today.

The Romans at War

Rome's military success was due to the development of the most disciplined and efficient infantry in ancient history—the Roman **legion**. The basic unit was a **century** of eighty soldiers. Six centuries formed a **cohort**; ten cohorts made up a full legion of forty-eight hundred men. The men in the lead century stood close together and formed a long row, sheltering themselves and those behind them with their shields. They remained motionless until given the order to throw their spears the instant before the enemy was upon them. With the enemy at close quarters, the century line moved forward for hand-to-hand combat. After twelve minutes, the period of peak efficiency, the first century fell back to be replaced by a second and then a third.

The Romans also developed huge war machines, including catapults that could hurl a 27 kg boulder 500 m, and battering rams that were so large one thousand men were needed to mobilize them for action. The ceaseless bombardment from the large weapons could be so intense that enemy commanders ordered their men to cover their ears against the noise from the whine and crash of the Roman projectiles.

After a battle or a hard day's march, every Roman soldier in the legion helped to build an overnight camp. Discipline was maintained by long hours of drill, summer and winter. Every battle tactic was practised with weapons of double weight. The drills were so intense that they have been described as "bloodless battles." In turn the battles were regarded as "bloody drills."

A legionary who failed to perform his required duties might be punished by being stoned or by some other brutal measure. If an entire unit was negligent or cowardly in battle, it was **decimated**— every tenth man was executed. The soldier who first mounted the wall during the siege on a city, however, received a crown of gold. Through this combination of harsh punishment and generous reward, Rome produced loyalty, self-sacrifice, dedication, and a high morale that resulted in continuing military success.

Roman Siege Equipment. *(Developed from Macedonian, Carthaginian, and Spanish originals.)*

The Battering Ram. The ram, protected against enemy fireballs by a roof of wet animal skins, was swung back and forth against the defending town's gate.

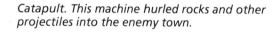
Catapult. This machine hurled rocks and other projectiles into the enemy town.

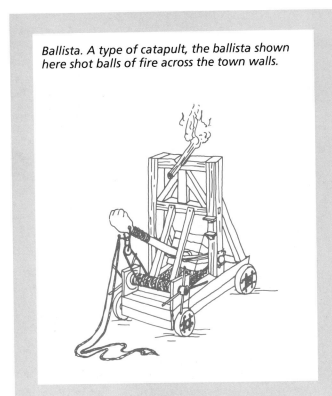

Ballista. A type of catapult, the ballista shown here shot balls of fire across the town walls.

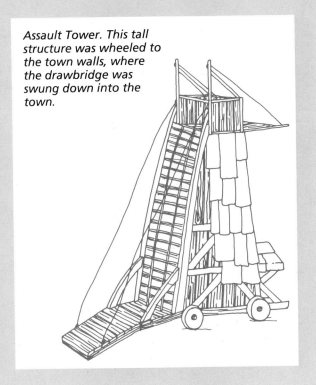

Assault Tower. This tall structure was wheeled to the town walls, where the drawbridge was swung down into the town.

defence against unfriendly neighbours. The Romans did not try to conquer large areas. Instead, they would take over the land between two potential enemies to avoid a direct conflict. At other times, Rome would temporarily befriend one enemy to defeat another. This policy of "divide and rule" greatly increased the area under Rome's control. Once a city was conquered, it was offered friendship, authority over local matters, and an alliance with Rome in return for Roman citizenship. This flexible policy allowed Rome to maintain control over subject states. The entire Italian peninsula was unified under Roman rule by 270 B.C., although the Romans had never intended to extend their authority over such a large area.

The First Punic War against Carthage marked the beginning of a period of Roman expansion throughout the Mediterranean. Again, Rome did not have a master plan, but was simply determined to defend its current position. By the end of the Punic Wars, around the first century B.C., Rome had grown from a small city-state to become the major power in the Western world, with control over the north coast of Africa, Sicily, Sardinia, Corsica, southern Gaul, Macedonia, and Asia Minor.

Rise of the Roman Republic

B.C.	
1000	First city built by Latins on site of Rome
753	Legendary founding of Rome by Romulus
616	Etruscan rule of Rome and central Italy
509	Romans overthrow Etruscans and Rome becomes a republic with a city-state government
390	Rome sacked and destroyed by Gauls but is quickly rebuilt
326	Enslavement of citizens abolished
270	Roman conquest of Italy complete
264-146	Three Punic wars against Carthage A victorious Rome now dominates the Mediterranean
135-132	Slaves revolt in Sicily
85	Intermittent civil war begins
73-71	Spartacus revolts
50	Roman control around the Mediterranean complete Extent of Republic makes it difficult for city-state to administrate outlying provinces
44	Julius Caesar uses slaves and freed men in his administration Caesar attempts to secure a hereditary monarchy Caesar is assassinated
27	End of Roman Republic City of Rome has two hundred and fifty thousand slaves

One of the signs of Roman expansion was the network of excellent roads that linked the population centres. These routes helped Roman legions move quickly, and also facilitated communication and trade. The roads were exceedingly well engineered. In most cases, a 1.5 m deep foundation underlay the paving stones. Eventually, over 310 000 km of roads were built, some of which are still used today. Roman engineering was also responsible for some superb bridges and the system of concrete and stone **aqueducts** that supplied Rome and other cities with water. As Rome grew, eleven major aqueducts, the longest of which reached 58 km into the countryside, poured water into the city. Altogether, the aqueducts brought 1100 L of water per person per day to the Roman metropolis.

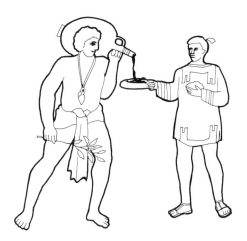

A household slave pours wine for a charioteer in this scene, originally portrayed on a Roman mosaic.

The Emergence of Slavery

Ironically, the outstanding success of Roman expansion created many problems. Grain from conquered provinces poured into Rome and sold at much cheaper prices than Italian grain. Many small farmers were forced out of business, and much of their land was purchased by a few wealthy men. These new holdings were organized into large farms called *latifundia* that required much skilled labour. The labour was provided by the conquered peoples. The success of the Roman legions was so great that Rome became a slave-based state in a very short time. The number of slaves in Rome grew from forty thousand in 325 B.C. to two hundred and fifty thousand by 27 B.C., out of a total population of 1.25 million. Wealthy Romans became so accustomed to the luxury and the status of owning a large number of slaves that even military conquest could not satisfy the demand. Pirates turned slave trading into a lucrative business. The small, independent farmer who had been the mainstay of the early Republic joined the masses of the unemployed. The government was virtually forced to provide food and entertainment to prevent the outbreak of revolution.

The idea of slavery is morally offensive today, but it was a central part of the Roman world. Wealthy Romans used slaves in almost every capacity—from cooks to tailors to chambermaids. Greek slaves were often sought to educate Roman children. Room and board and training in a profession were sometimes provided and, for years of good service, a slave might even be allowed to buy his or her freedom. Those who toiled in the mines and quarries or rowed the ships of the Roman fleet, however, clearly suffered the harshest and most hopeless existence. In general, the life of a slave depended on the time in which she or he lived and the occupation thrust upon her or him. When conditions became extreme, as they did in 135 B.C. on a *latifundia* run by wealthy Romans in Sicily, the slaves rebelled against their masters. They had only a slight chance of success, and rebellious slaves were sentenced to death by crucifixion, but slave revolts continued until the end of the Republic.

Spartacus

Often male slaves in the best physical condition were trained as **gladiators** to fight to the death in public arenas for the entertainment of the Roman masses and upper classes. For most gladiators, life was measured in months rather than years. In 73 B.C., a gladiator named Spartacus sparked a dangerous revolt. Seventy gladiators escaped with him and began a war that ravaged the Italian countryside for three years.

According to the Greek historian Appian, the rebel gladiators armed themselves with clubs and daggers taken from people on the roads and, after plundering the countryside, eventually took refuge on the slopes of Mount Vesuvius. At first, the Romans regarded such activity as little more than a raid. When the Roman army attacked the slave army, however, the

Roman general Varinius not only lost the battle but had his horse captured by a mere gladiator!

Refugee slaves and other discontented people flooded into camp, and Spartacus's army increased until it numbered about seventy thousand. Spartacus tried to leave Italy by heading north to the Alps and Gaul, but was hindered by advancing Roman armies. Spartacus turned on the pursuing soldiers and beat several Roman armies in succession, killing every prisoner in the process.

A slave successfully defying the master was a dangerous symbol. Rome was also fully aware of the military threat that Spartacus represented. At first, no one was willing to face the now well-equipped and well-trained army of gladiators. Finally Licinius Crassus, a wealthy and distinguished Roman, offered to take command of the army assigned to crush the slave revolt. Crassus hoped to use his victory over Spartacus to gain personal glory and enhance his political power within the Roman government.

With the help of ten legions, Crassus advanced on isolated groups of the slave army and weakened the overall strength of Spartacus's forces. Two additional Roman armies were summoned, one headed by Pompey and the other by Lucullus. The rebels were boxed in on three sides. Crassus hoped to fight Spartacus without assistance, eager for the glory and power a victory would bring. He got his wish, largely as a result of his own manipulations, and after a long, bloody battle, he and the Romans were victorious. Spartacus, speared in the thigh, continued to fight on one knee with shield in hand until he was killed. His body was never found. As a final reminder of the fate that a rebellious slave could expect, six thousand slaves captured from Spartacus's army were crucified along the road from Capua to Rome.

The Struggle for Power

As Rome expanded from a mere city-state to dominate Italy and the Mediterranean, it enjoyed a period of relative political stability. In theory, it had become a democracy, although participation was restricted, just as it had been in the Athenian system during the Golden Age. The **plebians**, or lower classes, achieved many political objectives. The fact that they were needed as soldiers to defend the state gave them a strong bargaining position. Nevertheless, the **patrician** upper classes enjoyed representation and power beyond their numbers.

The most prestigious political body was the **Senate**, which, although it only had the power to advise, had considerable moral authority and usually spoke and acted on behalf of the patrician class. Within the Senate, competition for power between the aristocratic families and those of the popular party, from less distinguished backgrounds, undermined Rome's stability. When Sulla, defender of the aristocratic families, became dictator in 82 B.C., he methodically slaughtered all of his political opponents in the popular party. Although the Senate's position was restored after the blood bath,

Government of the Roman Republic

Key Offices/Institutions	Description

Consuls:	-leaders of the Republic
	-two consuls elected annually
	   -each consul led the Republic in alternate months
	   -in wartime, leadership alternated daily
	-presided over Senate
	-raised and led armies in wartime
	-administered public affairs and justice
	-initiated laws
	-conducted public religious ceremonies

Pro-consul:	-leader of the Republic only during war -endorsed by Senate to lead continuously for six months

Senate:	-chief advisory council
	-three hundred members appointed for life by consuls
	   -usually chosen from a list of ex-magistrates who had
	   served in at least ten military campaigns
	   -usually members of the patrician class
	-advised public officials
	-approved proposals of other assemblies
	-supervised foreign affairs, including plans for war
	-could declare martial law during war

Centuriate Assembly:	-assembly of all land-owning male citizens -dominated by patrician class -elected senior officials, including consuls

Tribal Assembly:	-assembly of plebians
	   -representatives of thirty-nine electoral districts (tribes)
	   -aristocrats denied membership
	-elected officials not chosen by other assemblies
	-protected interests of the poor

it was becoming increasingly clear that the army was the key to power in Rome. A leader needed considerable wealth to buy the army's support. In fact, Sulla had executed many of his opponents only because he needed their money to pay his veteran soldiers a bonus.

Julius Caesar

It was in this complex world of political upheaval and intrigue that young Julius Caesar began his career. Things did not go well for him at first. Although he was an aristocrat, he took the side of the popular party, and was forced to leave Rome while Sulla was dictator. When he returned after Sulla's death, Caesar lacked the popular support needed to win even minor offices, just as he lacked the money to engage in the common practice of bribing the electorate. However, Caesar was extremely talented in many ways. He was a charming and convincing speaker. He could ride and fight with exceptional endurance. In his later years, he had enough concentration to dictate literary works and reports to two or three secretaries at a time. Like Alexander, he was subject to epileptic seizures but otherwise enjoyed good health.

Following the suppression of Spartacus's revolt in 71 B.C., Crassus and Pompey struggled for power. Shrewdly, Caesar cultivated the support of both men. For about ten years, Caesar gained power and wealth by making connections, winning political offices, and conducting successful military campaigns against the peoples of Further Spain. He returned home with a

Julius Caesar.

public **triumph** (a victory parade) in which he displayed the wealth he had acquired through war to cheering crowds of Romans. By 61 B.C., Caesar was in a position to manipulate Crassus and Pompey and to complete his careful and calculated climb to the top of the Roman political world.

The Issue Emerges

Caesar, like Hannibal and Alexander, became an important leader. Each of these individuals made decisions that affected the lives of thousands, even millions, of people. For the duration of their influence, their ambitions and their weaknesses to a large extent determined the direction of their homelands. Most people live and die without being widely recognized or remembered. But the achievements of these three are still being discussed over two thousand years later. All three occupy a prominent place in history.

Can the course of human history be regarded simply as the results of the actions of a few great individuals? And how should these actions and these individuals be assessed and judged? Is it possible to rank leaders in order of their greatness? You may be able to answer these questions by comparing the careers, the decisions, the accomplishments, and the failures of Alexander, Hannibal, and Caesar. Study the lives of these famous leaders, and try to determine whether one stands above the others.

PROBLEM QUESTION

What are the qualities of great leadership, and which individual—Alexander, Hannibal, or Caesar—fulfilled them most completely?

ALTERNATIVE ONE: Alexander the Great

Based on *Classical Greece* by C.M. Bowra (1965)

Within a year of his accession Alexander extended his dominion northward to the Danube River and westward to the Adriatic Sea. He then turned his attention to Greece, where Thebes and Athens were threatening to bolt the League. Alexander put down the insurrection in Thebes in 335 B.C. Then, to punish the city for what he regarded as treachery, he had its inhabitants slaughtered or sold into slavery and razed all of its buildings except for temples—and the house of Pindar the poet. Pindar himself was dead long since, but Alexander revered him and was eager to prove that even a Macedonian conqueror could be a Hellene [a Greek]. The savage lesson of Thebes brought results. The Athenian Assembly quickly congratulated Alexander, and the Greek states, with the continuing solitary exception of Sparta, remained Macedonian allies.

Alexander now took on a project that Philip had planned but never carried out: an invasion of Persia. Solid political reasons led him to this decision. For a century Persia had interfered increasingly in Greek affairs and had constantly oppressed the Greek cities in Asia Minor. There was always the dangerous possibility that, under a strong king, it might step up its troublemaking and once again actively take the offensive against Greece. Alexander had personal reasons for the invasion, too. Avid for glory and for identification with Greece, the young King knew no better way to win both than by attacking Greece's ancient foe.... Alexander, with his far stronger army, had good reason to believe that he could win. In 334 B.C. he crossed the Hellespont, which Xerxes had crossed in the opposite direction nearly a century and a half before. Soon afterward he defeated the Persian forces gathered to meet him on the Asian side of the River Granicus. From the spoils of this victory he sent 300 suits of Persian armour back to Athens. With them went the message, "Alexander, the son of Philip, and the Greeks, except the Spartans, have won this spoil from the barbarians of Asia," thus expressing in one brief and self-assured sentence his contempt for the Persians, his even greater contempt for the Spartans, and his conviction that he was furthering a Greek cause.

As the campaign progressed, Alexander's plan expanded. Originally his purpose had been simply to destroy the Persian army. Before long he had decided to take over the whole Persian Empire. And he went on to achieve this aim without losing a single battle. Of all the great generals of the ancient world, Alexander was surely the greatest. He possessed an almost clairvoyant insight into strategy and was a consummately resourceful tactician. Like Napoleon, he believed in swiftness of movement, but he could be patient too, as he showed in his long siege of the formidable fortress of Tyre.

He was enormously skillful at dealing with unfamiliar tactics of warfare, such as the use of chariots armed with scythes, elephants deployed in battle, and evasive, encircling movements by nomad horsemen. Sometimes he got unexpected help from the enemy. Darius, who was cruel as well as cowardly, treated prisoners with a harshness that embittered the Macedonian soldiers. In two major battles, at Issus in 333 B.C. and Gaugamela in 331 B.C., Darius fled from the field. With these two victories Alexander broke the main Persian resistance and in the autumn of 331 B.C. he entered Babylon, the winter capital of the Persian kings. In December of the same year he entered the summer capital at Susa. From Susa he went on to the ceremonial capital at Persepolis. Here he collected a treasure so vast, says Plutarch, that it took 20,000 mules and 5,000 camels to remove it. Before leaving Persepolis, Alexander burned the huge palace of the Great King for reasons that have never been clear. Possibly it was a whim, possibly he did it in a fit of drunken excitement, or possibly he did it to signify that the Persian invasion of Greece had at last been avenged.

Alexander already considered himself King of Persia, but his right to the throne was in question as long as Darius was still at large. In the summer of 330 B.C., Alexander marched north in pursuit of him. He had almost caught up with his quarry when the Persian leader was suddenly slain by his own men, finally brought to rebellion by their long resentment of his mismanagement of the Persian defense. Alexander came upon Darius' body near Hecatompylo, and ordered it sent back to Persepolis for burial in the royal cemetery of the Archaemenid kings. Now, at last, Alexander was officially the Great King of Persia. In his new role he headed east to take possession of the remaining Persian provinces. After two years he reached and subdued Bactria and Sogdiana; he now controlled all the lands that belonged to Darius.

Since his main concern was to keep the Empire functioning, Alexander tolerated many local religious and social customs. He even, to some extent, permitted each country to keep its national institutions. At the same time he introduced a number of Hellenic ideas. The most important one was that of the Greek city-state. He was liberal with his name and among cities he founded were no fewer than 16 Alexandrias. Most of them were built from the foundation up. The first and most famous one was the Egyptian city which became, a century later, the center of the Hellenistic world.

As his empire grew Alexander saw that Asia could not be administered simply as a colony of Greece. Somehow he had to bring Persians and Greeks together into a single unit. In 327 B.C., partly for political reasons, but perhaps for love, he married a Sogdian Princess, Roxane. Alexander does not seem to have cared much for women. Plutarch writes that "he was wont to say that sleep and the act of generation chiefly made him sensible that he was mortal; as much to say, that weariness and pleasure proceed from the same frailty and imbecility of human nature." Three years after his marriage to Roxane, he married the elder daughter of Darius in a purely political union. This wedding was a communal affair: at the same time, on Alexander's order, 80 of his top-ranking officers married 80 Persian girls of noble birth.

Further to consolidate his Empire Alexander drafted Persian cavalry into his own army and ordered 30,000 Persian boys to be trained in Macedonian combat techniques. He adopted Persian dress for himself and for a time even tried to get his soldiers to follow the Persian custom of prostration before the King. But his Macedonian captains were affronted by this. They felt that it implied worship, and they did not think that Alexander was a god.

Most of Alexander's ideas for consolidating the Greek and Persian peoples made little impression on his Macedonian companions. They were soldiers, not political scientists. His concept of empire did not fit their own crude ambitions and they had no sympathy for his desire to govern responsibly. They felt that he was setting himself above them, spoiling the old sense of comradeship-in-arms which had once characterized the Macedonian army. They resented his treatment of the Persians as their equals, which obliterated the age-old distinctions between Greeks and barbarians. They were dismayed when he put Greeks under the command of Persians, and made Persians governors. More than once, Alexander was faced with conspiracy. He could never be sure that forces left behind to govern occupied cities would not revolt. He could never rule out the danger of assassination. And yet he held his enormous Empire together.

After he had taken over the provinces of Bactria and Sogdiana, completing his conquest of the Persian Empire, Alexander turned south and headed into India. Nearly two centuries before, in the reign of Darius I, the Persian Empire had included part of that subcontinent. Determined to recapture it, Alexander crossed the Hindu Kush mountains, followed the Kabul River down to the Indus River and crossed overland to the Hydaspes River. At the Hydaspes, near a place now called Jhelum, he fought one of the most difficult battles of his entire career. His opponent was the Indian King, Porus, whose army was several times larger than Alexander's and superbly trained. It included war elephants, and the huge beasts reduced Alexander's striking power because his horses would not go near them. By feinting a series of attacks and finally attacking from an unexpected quarter, Alexander defeated Porus. One of the casualties of battle, however, was his own horse, Bucephalus. Alexander had earned him as a boy of 12 by riding him when no one else could. He founded a city in his memory on the site of the battle, naming it Bucephala.

From the Hydaspes Alexander advanced deeper into India. Like most men of his time he believed that the Indian continent was a small peninsula jutting eastward, and that its uttermost extremity was washed by the body of water, called simply Ocean, that encircled the world. He expected to reach Ocean and explore it as the climax of his long campaign. With this in mind he had brought with him rowers and shipwrights from Phoenicia, Cyprus, Caria and Egypt, and had even chosen his admiral, a boyhood friend named Nearchus. But his troops had other ideas. They could see the point of the Persian campaign, but not of an invasion of India. They had heard rumours of vast deserts and fierce warriors and great armies of elephants lying ahead. Besides, they were tired and yearned for home. They refused to march.

Alexander waited three days for them to change their minds. When he was convinced that they would not, he agreed to start home....

In the spring of 323 B.C. he reached Babylon, and began almost at once to regroup his army and plan an invasion of Arabia. But in June a fever struck him. The efforts and privations of the journey had undermined his hitherto magnificent health. He grew rapidly worse and soon could no longer speak. One by one his captains filed past his bed; he was unable to do more than lift his hand and make a sign with his eyes. On the 13th of June, 323 B.C., not yet 33 years old, he died.

Alexander

B.C.

338   At age eighteen, Alexander commands Philip's cavalry at Chaeronea

336   Philip is assassinated
At age twenty, Alexander becomes king of Macedonia

335   Alexander crushes revolt in Thebes
Survivors are sold into slavery

334   Alexander defeats Persia at Granicus

333   Alexander defeats Persia at Issus
Darius III of Persia flees battle site

332   Alexander occupies Egypt and plans the city of Alexandria
Alexander travels to Ammon to seek confirmation of his divine origin

330   At Arbela Alexander defeats Darius again
Darius retreats and is eventually killed by his own soldiers
Alexander marches into the Persian cities of Babylon, Susa, and Persepolis
Alexander kills Philotus and his father for daring to share credit for Alexander's victories

328   Clitus criticizes Alexander and praises Philip
In a drunken rage Alexander spears Clitus

326   Alexander expands his empire to India when he defeats King Porus in a difficult battle at the Hydaspes River

324   Alexander is forced to return to Susa when his generals will go no farther

323   Alexander dies of a fever in Babylon

311   Alexander's wife Roxane and their son are murdered
Alexander's empire is divided among his generals
India and Greece regain their independence

Adapted from **Great Ages of Man/CLASSICAL GREECE by C.M. Bowra and The Editors of Time-Life Books** © 1965 Time-Life Books Inc.

QUESTIONS

1. How did Alexander's treatment of Thebes affect Athens?
2. Why did Alexander decide to invade Persia?

3. Compare the personal qualities of Alexander and the Persian king, Darius.
4. a) How did Alexander administer his empire?
   b) What were the Hellenic ideas that he introduced?
5. a) Why did Alexander try to bring Persians and Greeks together in running the empire?
   b) How did Alexander's Macedonian followers react to this attempt?
6. a) Give examples to show that Alexander often acted for purely political reasons.
   b) Did Alexander regard himself as an equal of his followers? Explain your answer.
7. What tactical problems did Alexander overcome in his battle against the Indian king, Porus?
8. a) Why did Alexander's soldiers refuse to complete the Indian campaign?
   b) What does this incident tell you about Alexander's leadership qualities?

ALTERNATIVE TWO: Hannibal

Based on *The Enduring Past* by John H. Trueman and Dawn Cline Trueman (1982)

In April 218 B.C., a twenty-nine-year-old Carthaginian known as Hannibal set out from New Carthage in the south of Spain. His destination was Italy; his goal was to crush the Romans once and for all. Hannibal believed the Romans could only be defeated in Italy, where the people, once liberated, would ally with him against their oppressors.

Leading forty thousand infantry, eight thousand cavalry, and sixty elephants, Hannibal managed to cross the Rhone by mid-August, just three days before a Roman army arrived to intercept him. By autumn, he had reached the Alps, which were already deep in snow. This made the trek through the treacherous passes even more dangerous. It also gave the hostile mountain tribes who were accustomed to these conditions a fighting advantage. Still, Hannibal pushed on. Indeed, it is this seemingly insurmountable feat that most people associate with the name Hannibal.

The struggle across the Alps took its toll. By the end of the fifteen-day trek Hannibal had lost forty elephants and twenty-two thousand men. Considering the loss, it was a strange victory.

The Romans had missed capturing Hannibal on both sides of the Alps. Now, they hoped to catch him in northern Italy crossing the river Trebia. Hannibal, however, had his own plan. Early one bitterly cold December morning, he dispatched a small cavalry detachment across the river. It fought the Romans just long enough to be convincing, then retreated in defeat. The Romans charged after them through the icy waters. The retreating Carthaginians led them straight into an ambush. Of the forty thousand Romans, twenty thousand men were lost. The Romans retreated to the south, leaving northern Italy to Hannibal.

The Carthaginian army spent that winter in Bologna, while the Romans fervently recruited more men. In the spring Hannibal headed southward. He crossed the Apennines and made his way through the marshland of the river Arno, where he contracted an infection and lost the sight of one eye. Nonetheless, he pressed on towards Rome, ravaging the land in his path.

A Roman army of twenty-five thousand followed Hannibal's forces at a distance but they were not prepared to fight the Carthaginian force that outnumbered them. Hannibal had other ideas. He sent his men to hide in the hills surrounding Lake Trasimene. The next morning, as the Romans marched through a particularly narrow valley, the Carthaginians attacked, killing fifteen thousand in just two hours, and capturing most of the survivors.

Hannibal had now outwitted the Romans twice and their casualties had been high. He must be stopped before he reached Rome. The Roman people decided the man to defeat the Carthaginian was Quintus Fabius Maximus.

Since Hannibal's cavalry had played a decisive role in his previous victories, Fabius decided to wait until Hannibal was in a position in which he could not use his cavalry. As Hannibal continued to lay waste the countryside, Fabius was resolute in his decision not to fight until the time was right. The Romans were soon referring to Fabius as "the delayer." Eventually, Fabius's patience was rewarded. Hannibal was trapped by a mountain pass commanded by Fabius.

Yet again, Hannibal outwitted the Romans. Hannibal had his men round up two thousand head of cattle and tie bundles of twigs to their horns. Then, under the cover of darkness, they drove the cattle towards the pass, lighting the twigs on command. To the Roman guards, it looked like an advancing army bearing torches. Suddenly the paradelike ranks dissolved into a scattered arrangement. What the Romans thought was a sudden attack was in reality the cattle wildly shaking their heads as the burning twigs singed their flesh. As the fire spread through the valley, the Romans abandoned their vantage point to Hannibal and his cavalry. With this protection, the Carthaginian infantry passed through unchallenged.

Fabius's strategy had failed. Hannibal continued to ravage Italy, and the Romans were growing increasingly more impatient. When Fabius's term of office expired in 216 B.C., the consuls were ready for action. They chose a battle site near Cannae in the plains by the Adriatic, an ideal location for a cavalry engagement. Although the Romans outnumbered the Carthaginians fifty-four thousand to forty-five thousand, the Carthaginian cavalry was stronger by four thousand. Hannibal planned his strategy around this advantage. His battle formation was crescent shaped with the cavalry on each end and the infantry at the centre bulging towards the Romans. As the Roman legions pushed forward, the bulge gave way to a hollow. Still the Romans drove forward. Meanwhile the Carthaginian cavalry had routed the Roman wing and had regrouped to strike a second time. Advancing in a wide sweep around the rear of the legions, they completely surrounded the Romans. As they tightened their formation, the Romans found themselves in a slaughterpen. Once again, Hannibal was victorious.

At Cannae, the Romans lost twenty-five thousand men in battle and ten thousand as captives compared with the loss of only fifty-seven hundred Carthaginians. They also lost support from many of the towns in southern Italy, which now allied themselves with Hannibal. Nonetheless, they still had the loyalty of central and northern Italy, and Rome itself was safe for the moment. Hannibal did not have the siege weapons necessary to storm the city's high walls.

Their defeat at Cannae had taught the Romans one thing: Direct combat was not the way to conquer Hannibal. Instead, they adopted a strategy of delay tactics to wear down their enemy. Hannibal's plan, to surround Italy with enemies, meant that he must stay in Italy without reinforcements. As long as he remained in the south of Italy, Hannibal had the freedom of the countryside. It was only when he ventured northward that he encountered difficulty. There, the Romans and their allies either protected their crop harvests within the city walls or burned them to the ground rather than leave them for the Carthaginians. Once their food supply ran out, Hannibal and his men were forced to return to the south.

Neither side seemed able to defeat the other. However, the Romans had one trump card left, Publius Cornelius Scipio, a general as capable as Hannibal. Scipio had experience fighting Carthaginians. He had ended the Carthaginian Empire in Spain in 207 B.C. using a troop formation similar to the one Hannibal had used in Cannae.

In spite of Scipio's success, however, Hasdrubal, Hannibal's brother, had managed to lead thirty thousand men out of Spain and was determined to join Hannibal. The Romans, just as determined to keep them apart, dispatched one army to intercept Hasdrubal while others watched Hannibal's movements.

Hasdrubal made one critical error. He dispatched a messenger to Hannibal disclosing the rendezvous point. The Romans intercepted it, and, acting quickly, the two armies marched to the meeting place to await Hasdrubal's arrival. The battle at the Metaurus River was the first major Roman victory in eleven years. A week later, the Romans took pleasure in announcing the defeat to Hannibal by throwing his brother's head into his camp.

Scipio's next move was to convince the Senate that the only way to ensure Rome's safety was to crush Carthage itself. Towards this end, he set sail for North Africa in 204 B.C. with a force of thirty thousand Romans. It was a hard campaign, but a year later the Carthaginians were ready to discuss peace terms.

In the meantime Hannibal, who had spent sixteen years in Italy, returned to North Africa having neither won nor lost the war. His return gave the Carthaginians the courage to challenge Scipio one more time.

The two generals met at Zama. Although Hannibal's force outnumbered the Roman legions, his cavalry was slightly weaker. Once again Hannibal displayed his genius for strategy. His plan was to draw the Roman cavalry in by staging a retreat of his own cavalry and then to attack with his infantry, holding back a reserve force for the final onslaught. It appeared as though the plan was working; however, the Roman cavalry regrouped before the reserves could deliver the decisive

Hannibal

B.C.

218	Second Punic War begins when Hannibal invades Italy by crossing the Alps Hannibal defeats Rome at Trebia War elephants used for the first and only time in the Italian campaign
217	Hannibal defeats Rome at Lake Trasimene Rome elects dictator Quintus Fabius Maximus
216	Fabius's strategy is ineffective and he is removed from office as Rome grows impatient Hannibal defeats Rome through brilliant use of infantry and cavalry Ill-equipped to attack Rome itself, Hannibal's forces wander the Italian countryside winning every battle but not the war
207	Roman general Scipio ends Carthaginian Empire in Spain Rome now virtually assured of victory
202	Hannibal returns to Carthage for a last stand The Numidian cavalry switches its allegiance to Rome Hannibal defeated by Scipio at Zama
183	Hannibal commits suicide
150-146	Third Punic War—Rome destroys Carthage and creates the province of Africa Rome now dominates the Mediterranean

blow. Although Hannibal escaped, his army was cut to pieces. At last the war was over.

Rome imposed harsh penalties in the peace agreement. The Romans were not about to forget what the war had cost them, and they demanded that Carthage make reparations.

The Romans were not about to forget Hannibal's role in the war, either, and he was forced to flee to Syria. But even there, his safety was threatened by the long arm of Rome. Seeing his house surrounded by soldiers, Hannibal took the poison he always had with him. In 183 B.C., the noblest failure in antiquity died.

QUESTIONS

1. a) When he began his campaign, how did Hannibal think he would be able to defeat Rome?
   b) What hardships did he encounter in the march across the Alps?
   c) Why did this trek capture the imagination of later generations?
2. a) Describe Hannibal's military tactics at Trebia, Lake Trasimene, and Cannae.
   b) What feeling swept Rome as a result of Hannibal's success?
   c) Why was Rome itself safe from Hannibal's attack?
3. Describe the situation in Italy by 207 B.C., after Hannibal's many successes.
4. How did the Roman general Scipio undermine Hannibal's victories in Italy?
5. Why was Hannibal finally defeated at Zama?
6. Were Hannibal's military victories as impressive as those of Alexander? Explain your answer.

ALTERNATIVE THREE: Julius Caesar

Based on "The Enigma of Caesar" by Luigi Barzini (1966)

At the news of Sulla's death in 78 B.C., Caesar returned to Rome to try his hand at politics and law. Exercising his right as a citizen to sue a public official, he chose a powerful opponent ... and lost the case. The young lawyer's eloquence won many admirers; people talked about him and he began to have a following. He decided to broaden his education and set out for Rhodes.

On the way there, he was captured by pirates, whom he promptly treated as servants. When he wanted to sleep he sent orders to his noisy captors to be quiet; he joined in their games, practiced his rhetoric on them, called them illiterate barbarians to their faces and, in raillery, promised to have them crucified. They admired and obeyed him meekly, sensing the leader in him. Six weeks later, after his ransom arrived and he was freed, he hired several galleys, returned to surprise the pirates in their lair and crucified the lot as he had promised.

He returned to Rome and, to make friends, went into debt. He kept an open house; according to Plutarch, "the splendor of his life increased his political influence." His opponents did not suspect his aims. They thought he was one more frivolous young man who frittered away money on entertainment and that his growing influence would vanish when his credit gave out.

The borrowed money soon did give out and Caesar plunged further into debt which reached such an unheard-of magnitude that his political backers, men of considerable power, began to worry. Caesar must have figured out that some of these creditors would help him get an army command in hopes of being paid back. This, of course, was his great gamble....

He ran for election to a succession of minor posts, climbing steadily. In 61 B.C....when his debts were on the point of overwhelming him, he reached his first substantial and profitable position: he was appointed propraetor in charge of quelling some rebellious Spanish tribes. At the last minute an apparently insurmountable obstacle threatened to prevent his voyage and defeat his plans to find power and wealth in Spain. Some of his creditors insisted he pay a large part of the money owed them before he left and they had his baggage, carriages, and horses seized.

Caesar turned to the only man who could save him—Crassus. Crassus was the richest man in Rome ... and, like many very rich men in those times of anarchy and chaos, so nervous he had been playing every side. Crassus needed as many strong friends as he could find: ruthless, ambitious, clever, bold men, possibly in need of money but with a strong popular backing.

So Crassus paid off most of Caesar's debts and pledged himself to finance the young propraetor's expedition. On Caesar's arrival in Spain, "he not only begged for money to settle his debts, but wantonly sacked several Spanish towns," Suetonius reports, and proceeded to subdue the local tribes in a blitz campaign. "Advancing as far as the ocean, he conquered new tribes which had never been subject to the Romans," says Plutarch and which had never therefore been thoroughly plundered before. Caesar sent some of the booty to the Roman treasury, distributed more than a fair share among his soldiers and began to get rich himself. He was ready to try for bigger stakes.

The situation in Rome in 60 B.C. was extremely precarious. Once again the time was ripe for a great leader, with the means and the will, to reach for supreme power. But who? There were three candidates in sight—Crassus, Pompey, and Caesar. Crassus had his immense wealth, the backing of a large section of the population and of a fair share of the Senate and could easily find military commanders who would lend him their legions for a price. Pompey was the great military conqueror, who had destroyed the pirates infesting the Mediterranean, had defeated the Eastern rebel king Mithridates and had amassed money and men. Caesar was clearly the weakest of the three: he had neither the money of one nor the armies of the other. What should he do? The obvious course was to encourage the enmity between Crassus and Pompey and hope to come out as sole survivor of the struggle. When one of them seemed to be winning, he could rush to his aid. But it was a risky plan. Would the winner tolerate a minor rival for long? Would he not destroy Caesar, too, in the end?

Caesar's course shows the magnitude of his political genius. It took immense diplomatic ability and exceptional persuasive power. It probably would have been impossible for any other man. Afterwards, the main developments of Caesar's life fell into place, one after another, as predictably as the moves of a chess game played by a champion after the opening gambit. He simply convinced Pompey and Crassus to make peace and secretly join with him in a partnership to dominate Rome. What none of them could hope to achieve without an exhausting war, the three of them could do overnight by sealing a pact.

It was obvious that the alliance [known as the *First Triumvirate*] could dispose of the people's assemblies, all public officials, the banks; they were ... the bosses of an all-powerful political machine. With the help of his partners Caesar in 59 B.C. easily became consul and, within a year, governor of the two Gauls (Northern Italy and France). From the age of 44 to 53 he was away in Gaul (frequently coming back to North Italy, but not to Rome, to mend political fences and direct the work of his agents in the city). He consolidated his conquest and pacified the inhabitants, Plutarch says, simply by killing one million of a total of three million. Meantime, he amassed a fortune possibly larger than Crassus', and became one of the most successful generals of all ages, with a brilliant and tested staff of officers and a number of practically invincible legions, all loyal to the death.

His nature irresistibly drove him to face the greatest dangers. In his military campaigns he played for safety only when he faced an inferior and weaker enemy: he did not want to waste his own men's lives to achieve a practically certain victory. But when he found himself on unfavorable ground—with a small army worn out by marches, without supplies and far from his base, facing a superior, confident, well-entrenched enemy—he always attacked. He attacked because, at such times, the enemy least expected him to.

Many times, in those desperately uneven battles on which Caesar liked to stake his luck, he saved the day by rushing in where his men were being beaten back. During one of his early campaigns in Gaul, his troops were surprised by an overwhelming onslaught of Nervii. Caesar says in his *Commentaries* that he himself "had everything to do at one moment": raise the flag, sound the alarm, bring in the men who were digging trenches, and give orders. He then rushed over to the Twelfth Legion, which was falling back in disorder. He seized a shield from a soldier in the rear ranks, pushed his way to the front, called upon the centurions by name, then sounded the charge. The mere gesture revived his men and made them surge forward. At the end of the day, the Nervii were hacked to pieces. In the last battle he ever fought near Munda, Spain, in 45 B.C., Caesar again turned panic among his troops into victory. Feeling that this was his moment to die, Caesar charged to within 3 m of the enemy line. According to Appian, a "hailstorm of 200 arrows descended upon him; some passed without touching him, his shield protected him from the others." First the tribunes, then the entire army turned with vehemence and defeated the enemy.

In all this time the day was approaching when the ruling partnership—Caesar, Crassus and Pompey—would be reduced to two and make civil war inevitable. That moment came in 53 B.C. when Crassus, leading his privately financed army, was killed fighting the Parthians in the East. Pompey made himself the buttress of the patrician Old Guard and agitated against his former partner, Caesar, who was still in Gaul. The Senate ordered Caesar to leave his legions in Gaul (north of the River Rubicon) and return home as an unarmed private citizen. Instead, Caesar waited, weighed the risk, and finally crossed the Rubicon with a legion. It was January 11, 49 B.C., four years after the death of Crassus....

So swift and unexpected was his advance that Pompey fled first to southern Italy, then to Greece. Everybody recognized that this was not a war between the Republic and a seditious general; it was a conflict between two candidates for supreme power. Whoever was going to win, the Republic would lose. "I cannot endure the sight of what is happening," Cicero wrote, "or what is going to happen."

Caesar entered Rome (where he emptied the treasury), then went on to Spain, came back and crossed the Adriatic in pursuit of Pompey. He finally destroyed Pompey's army at Pharsalus, in Thessaly, on August 9, [48 B.C.]. Pompey, together with his wife, his son, and a small band of soldiers, escaped to Egypt, only to be murdered there by the Egyptians, who offered his embalmed head in tribute to Caesar when he landed there. Victorious Caesar refused it and wept. But he went on to wage wars against Pompey's sons and successors in command. Among them were patrician lovers of the ancient liberties, the men who, in the end, murdered him. Caesar triumphed over them all and, at 57, returned to Rome absolute master of the state.

The real problem of Caesar's generation was to find a simple method to pick supreme leaders, to govern far-flung domains with stability and establish a reasonably durable peace. The Senate was no longer able to start or stop the wars, curb the generals' ambitions, discipline the rich, keep order in the city, or defend the Roman world from invasions. The constitution, which had been good enough for a small city, for short and necessary wars, and for a few subjected peoples, was obsolete.

There was not much time to devise a new government capable of coping with the new problems, yet preserving at least the forms of the old institutions and providing a smoother way to transfer power from one leader to the next. It was with this dilemma that Caesar grappled and which he almost solved. He sometimes believed that he had been forced by circumstances to restore the legendary Roman monarchy. In the end he suspected he had introduced something new: despotic and absolute one-man rule over slavelike subjects, based on the divine worship of the ruler as god, after the example of Eastern autocracies.

Shortly before his death Caesar had assumed some of the outward forms of sovereignty: he not only installed a gilded throne in the Senate but stayed seated in the presence of standing senators, his supposed peers. He had his image stamped on coins; his birthday was celebrated by public sacrifices; the month of Quintilis was renamed July after him. Senators addressed him as Jupiter Julius and ordered a temple consecrated to him.... Caesar was delighted. Yet he had ostentatiously and publicly refused a royal diadem [crown], saying loudly: "Jupiter alone is king of the Romans"; and after a feast, when his supporters started hailing him as their king, he cried, "My name is Caesar, not Rex."

At the same time Caesar realized that he could not surrender absolute power without becoming a party to his own destruction. Forced by logic to follow one move with another in his game, he had never clearly known what he would do in the end, after final victory. He tackled legislative problems, packed the Senate with his friends (some of whom were trousered Gauls who did not know their way about the city), and carried out some reforms, but more to consolidate his power and repress possible revolutions than to reorganize the government. His most famous contribution to civilization, the reform of the calendar, seems insignificant compared to [sic] the number of battles fought, the men killed, the countries ravaged in order to bring it about.

On the day of the assassination he walked into the Senate meeting ... alone, unarmed, unescorted and apparently unperturbed. The conspirators had sworn each would plunge his blade into Caesar's body, so that all would be held equally responsible for his death. They were so awed by what they were doing that their hands trembled and, in the confusion, wounded each other at the same time.

After the first blow, Caesar did not utter another sound. But finally, when he saw Brutus—the son of his old mistress, the woman he cherished all his life—about to deliver his blow, Caesar said in Greek (as a Russian aristocrat would speak in French): "You, too, my son?" The dictator then drew himself up against the statue of Pompey, his old ally and defeated enemy—the statue he himself had generously ordered—pulled his gown over his face and allowed himself to be butchered in silence.

Julius Caesar

B.C.

82	Sulla becomes dictator Caesar flees Rome
75	Caesar captured by pirates then released for ransom Caesar returns with fleet and executes former captors
69	Caesar elected pontifex maximus with financial aid of Crassus
62	Pompey returns from the east after successful military campaigns Pompey and Crassus manoeuvre for political power
61	Caesar wins renown as governor of Further Spain
60	Pompey, Crassus, and Caesar form First Triumvirate Caesar has least power
58	Caesar becomes governor of Gaul (France) Caesar gains personal wealth and fame from military victories
53	Crassus killed in battle Pompey conspires against Caesar to get supreme control Pompey becomes virtual dictator of Rome
49	Caesar and his army cross the Rubicon River in defiance of the Senate and Pompey Civil war against Pompey begins
48	Pompey defeated at Pharsalus and murdered in Egypt Caesar arrives in Egypt and makes political and personal alliance with Cleopatra
46	Civil war ends, and Senate appoints Caesar dictator for ten years
44	Senate appoints Caesar dictator for life Caesar's attempt to secure a hereditary monarchy leads to his assassination

QUESTIONS

1. On his journey to Rhodes, Caesar was captured by pirates. Describe how Caesar treated his captors.

2. Caesar was often in debt early in his career. How did he use this to his political advantage?
3. How did Caesar acquire personal wealth during his years in Spain?
4. a) Who were the three most powerful men in the Roman world in 60 B.C.?
   b) Who was the most powerful of these three leaders?
   c) How did Caesar make this situation work to his advantage?
5. a) What event changed the balance of power in 53 B.C.?
   b) Why was crossing the Rubicon River in 49 B.C. a key event in Caesar's career?
   c) Did Caesar's gamble pay off? Explain your answer.
6. a) What was the key problem facing Rome at this time?
   b) What seems to have been Caesar's answer to this problem?
7. In your opinion, how well did Caesar handle the military and political problems he faced during his career? Explain your answer.

ANSWERING THE PROBLEM QUESTION

Evaluating the relative greatness of important historical figures is difficult. Probably the trickiest aspect of the task is defining what "greatness" is. There are many standards of greatness to consider: the standards that existed during the person's life, the standards that our own society seems to value, and your own personal standards. Many characteristics might seem desirable in a leader—decisiveness, bravery, ruthlessness, charisma, vision, mercifulness, viciousness, diplomacy ... the list goes on. Once you have formulated your own list, then you will have to put the qualities in order of importance and judge how well Alexander, Hannibal, and Caesar embodied them, or failed to embody them. You should also evaluate how effective each was. Presumably a great leader has goals for the state and for the people. Were these leaders' goals worth pursuing? To what extent did they achieve them?

As you compare Alexander, Hannibal, and Caesar, and try to establish who was the greatest, you might ponder other questions. Do you think there are great leaders living now? Would the three leaders under consideration fit into today's world? What qualities do you expect Canada's leaders to possess? What goals should Canada's leaders be pursuing?

Consider one other issue. In the ancient world, a leader was able to save his or her public comments for religious ceremonies, military victories, and other special occasions. Often, it would take weeks or months for such news to spread throughout the land. Furthermore, a leader's words and accomplishments were sparsely recorded, often by those who had an interest in presenting the leader in the best light. Perhaps writers over the centuries have romanticized the glamorous aspects of these individuals. Do you think today's leaders are similarly glamorized?

More to Consider

A famous story describes the first meeting between Cleopatra and Caesar. To gain access to him, Cleopatra had herself wrapped in a carpet, delivered by a friend to Caesar, and unrolled at his feet. Apparently Caesar was impressed by this dramatic introduction.

Controversies

The conspirators who assassinated Caesar wanted to preserve the old institutions and ways of governing Rome. Caesar seemed to have other plans. He had been granted a golden chair in the Senate chamber and the right to wear a purple toga, honours that were usually reserved for kings. His acceptance of these honours implied that he might be trying to have himself installed as monarch. After his last battle, at Munda in 45 B.C., he allowed statues of himself to be placed in temples, suggesting that he wanted to portray himself as a descendant of the gods. Through his control of the Senate, Caesar had himself appointed dictator for ten years starting in 46 B.C. By 44 B.C., the Senate had extended the term to life. During the festival of Lupercalia, one month before his assassination, Mark Antony had placed a crown on Caesar's head. At first, the crowd remained silent, but after the initial pause, Caesar removed the crown and was applauded.

THE STORY CONTINUES . . .

The Impact of Caesar's Assassination

In pursuit of Pompey in 48 B.C., Caesar arrived in Egypt to find a struggle for rule between a ten-year-old, Ptolemy XII, and his sister, Cleopatra. Caesar fell in love with Cleopatra despite the difference in their ages—he was fifty-two, she was twenty-one. Her intelligence, charm, and wit fascinated him. With Caesar's support, Cleopatra's position as queen of Egypt was secured.

It is possible that Cleopatra's influence over Caesar, and his year-long experience of the Egyptian form of government, encouraged him to see monarchy as a solution to the political troubles facing Rome. Rumours circulated that Caesar intended to shift the capital of the Roman world to Alexandria and to establish a joint monarchy with Cleopatra.

The foundation for these rumours seemed more solid when, in 47 B.C., Cleopatra had a son, presumably by Caesar. Cleopatra's spectacular entrance into Rome with her son Caesarion in 46 B.C. won the admiration of the crowd and heightened the politicians' fears that Cleopatra and Caesar would assume complete political authority. Interestingly enough, Caesar left his estate and authority to his adopted grandnephew, Octavian. Perhaps Caesar realized that Caesarion would have little chance for survival after his father's death.

Caesar believed Rome needed him alive and in command if peace was to continue. He once said:

> It is more important for Rome than for myself that I should survive. I have long been sated with power and glory; but should anything happen to me, Rome will enjoy no peace. A new Civil War will break out under far worse conditions than the last.[1]

Although Caesar was convinced that only he could give Rome the stability it desperately needed, others felt he was too ambitious. Many signs indicated that Caesar was consolidating his position and power to establish a hereditary monarchy. A number of powerful Romans, Caesar's friends Brutus and Cassius among them, wanted power to be returned to the Senate. They decided to assassinate Caesar. They chose 15 March (the Ides of March) 44 B.C. as the proper moment. Caesar had convened the Senate so that it would grant him the authority to be known as king in the lands outside of Rome. But the assassins struck before Caesar could claim the new title for himself.

Following the assassination, Mark Antony, Caesar's cavalry commander, persuaded the Roman people to condemn the assassins. Antony and his

---

1. Gaius Seutonius Tranquillus, *The Twelve Caesars*, translated by Robert Graves (London: Cassel, 1962), p. 20. Cited in Hugh Parry, *Julius Caesar: The Legend and the Man* (Toronto: Macmillan of Canada, 1976), p. 36.

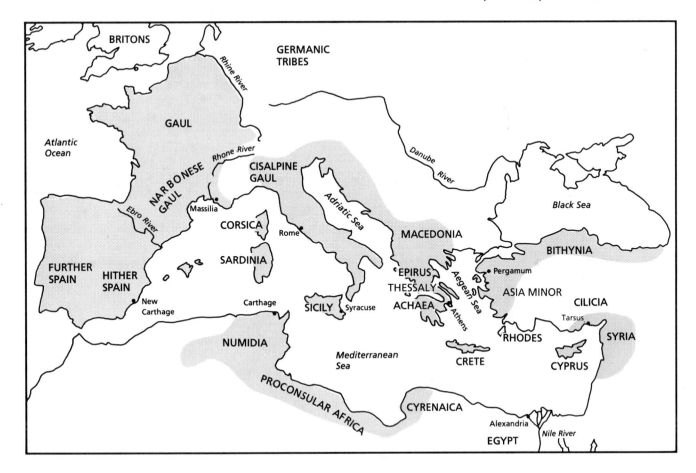

The Roman Republic, 44 B.C.

army doggedly pursued the assassins when they fled. Neither Antony nor anyone else gave much thought to Octavian, Caesar's legal heir. Although he was only eighteen, Octavian was mature, confident, and aggressive. While Antony was absent, Octavian returned to Rome, claimed his inheritance, raised an army, and, when the Senate refused to make him consul, marched on the city and secured the position anyway.

In 43 B.C., Antony, Octavian, and Lepidus, a lesser provincial governor, formed the **Second Triumvirate** to stabilize political power, just as the First Triumvirate of Crassus, Pompey, and Caesar had done in 60 B.C. The combined forces of the Second Triumvirate, led by Antony's skill and daring on the battlefield, defeated the armies of Brutus and Cassius, who both committed suicide. Caesar's inability to hold and transfer political power smoothly had indeed resulted in continued strife and conflict. The thinly veiled ambition of each member of the Second Triumvirate to achieve complete power promised more of the same.

Cleopatra and Antony, as depicted on Roman coins.

Antony and Cleopatra

Octavian was the first to consolidate his position. By 36 B.C. he had used his army and navy to take control of Corsica and Sardinia. That same year, Octavian turned on Lepidus, the weakest member of the triumvirate, winning a second triumph and the island of Sicily. Octavian was now supreme in the western Roman empire.

Meanwhile, Mark Antony, Octavian's only rival, was trying to achieve a similar position in the east. After defeating Brutus and Cassius, Antony needed money and supplies for his legions, and Egyptian wealth seemed to be the solution to his problem. He invited Cleopatra to Tarsus, a city in Asia Minor. She arrived at Tarsus by water, sailing up the Cydnus River on a magnificent barge. People lined the banks of the river to view the passage of royalty. The scent of incense emanated from the barge, filling the fresh country air. Cleopatra, who sat beneath a spangled gold canopy, was the focal point of attention. Antony, like Caesar before him, fell in love with her.

After his meeting with Cleopatra at Tarsus in 41 B.C., Antony's objectives changed drastically. He now wanted to strengthen Cleopatra's influence rather than subdue threats to Roman peace and security. He followed Cleopatra back to Alexandria while his legions suffered reverses in poorly organized military campaigns. Antony used his authority as consul of the eastern Roman world to restore to Egypt much of the territory it had lost since early Ptolemaic times. The children of Antony and Cleopatra were given Roman provinces to rule.

While Antony enjoyed a lavish life with his Egyptian queen, Octavian restored stability and order to Rome. Backed by a well-disciplined army, Octavian had himself appointed consul. He secured Antony's will and made it known that Antony had left his possessions to Cleopatra and their children. Rumours spread that Antony wished to move the capital to Alexandria, a bustling centre of commerce second only to Rome. The people and the Senate rejected this concession to a foreign city and a foreign queen, and, in 32 B.C., the Senate deposed Antony from his command in the east.

The Triumph of Octavian

Octavian's fleet confronted the combined naval forces of Cleopatra and Antony at Actium in 31 B.C. With the outcome still uncertain, Cleopatra unexpectedly withdrew sixty ships, throwing Antony's fleet into total confusion. It is possible that Cleopatra may have had an understanding with Octavian, but this has never been determined. Antony fled the battle in pursuit of Cleopatra, leaving his navy to face destruction and death. He remained with Cleopatra in Alexandria until 30 B.C., when Octavian and his legions marched on the city. Antony, who had few loyal followers left, challenged Octavian to settle the issue by personal combat. Before the fight, however, Antony was told that Cleopatra had committed suicide. He promptly stabbed himself. When he learned that he had been tricked, he asked to be taken to Cleopatra, and he died in her presence.

After Antony's death, Cleopatra met with Octavian, perhaps hoping to influence yet another Roman commander. When she realized this would not be the case, she arranged to have an asp (a species of poisonous snake) smuggled past the Roman guard in a basket of figs. She then committed suicide by letting it bite her.

By defeating Antony, Octavian had essentially seized control of Rome and all its territory. But he gave up his authority in 27 B.C., returning it to the Senate. This was a shrewd decision, because the Senate voluntarily reinstated Octavian as leader by appointing him to several key public offices. Octavian's apparently unselfish gesture had the result of making him the

Octavian

B.C.

43 Antony, Octavian, and Lepidus form the Second Triumvirate
Armies of Brutus and Cassius defeated at Philippi

41 Cleopatra's barge arrives at Tarsus; she and Antony fall in love and join political forces
Antony lives a life of luxury with Cleopatra as the dominant figures of the eastern Roman world

36 Octavian defeats Lepidus in Sicily and dominates the western Roman world
The Triumvirate is reduced to two

34 At the assembly of Alexandria, Antony and Cleopatra's children are officially given Roman lands to rule

32 Octavian has himself appointed consul by the Senate
Octavian discredits Antony by publicizing Antony's intention to leave his possessions to Cleopatra and their children, and his wish to be buried in Alexandria

31 Octavian defeats Antony in naval battle at Actium
Cleopatra flees with her ships in midst of battle
Antony follows Cleopatra, abandoning his forces to defeat

30 Cleopatra commits suicide after Antony has already done so when it becomes clear that Octavian will not become an ally

27 Octavian becomes Caesar Augustus, first Roman emperor

first Roman emperor, which of course had been his aim all along. The Senate realized that a lone ruler was the best hope for peace and stability. The civil conflict between the popular party and the patrician party, which had lasted throughout the first century B.C., during Caesar's time and before, was finally brought to an end. The power of Rome was now and would remain in Octavian's hands, and he had gained it not only through military force but because of his realistic approach to the problems facing the city and its provinces.

SUMMARY

In 336 B.C., Philip of Macedonia was assassinated and his twenty-year-old son Alexander took his place. Alexander was well-educated, decisive, and ambitious. Almost immediately, he sought to expand the empire his father had established, first by confirming his position in Greece, and then by attacking Persia. He moved into Asia Minor in 334 B.C. and won his first battle against the Persians. As his advance continued, he decided that he would take all of the Persian Empire for his own. By 331 B.C., he had defeated the main part of the Persian opposition. Darius, leader of the Persians, was murdered by his own troops the following year, and Alexander became the Great King. In order to keep his new empire functioning, Alexander allowed his new subjects to keep many of their religious and social practices. But he also brought Greek ideas to the Persians. He founded many new cities, using the Greek city-state as his model. After he confirmed his control of the outer reaches of the Persian domain, he ventured into India to enlarge the empire again. His soldiers, however, were unwilling to continue, and by 323 B.C. the force had returned to Babylon. Alexander became sick a few months later and died before he could regroup and take his army on another expedition.

Just over fifty years after Alexander's death, two other important powers were at war—the Carthaginians and the Romans. The city of Carthage was a trading centre on the north coast of Africa, founded in the eighth century B.C. by the Phoenicians. Rome was established about 1000 B.C., but rose to prominence after 509 B.C., when the Romans overthrew the Etruscans and began to expand. By 270 B.C., the Romans controlled the whole Italian peninsula. The First Punic War between Carthage and Rome lasted from 264-241 B.C. and was won by the Romans.

Carthage was ready to test its strength again by 219 B.C. Hannibal, a young Carthaginian general, led his troops into Roman territory in Spain. In 218 B.C., he pushed through Spain, southern Gaul, over the Alps, and onto the Italian peninsula; the Second Punic War had begun. Hannibal was an excellent military commander, respected by his forces for his courage and for his refusal to set himself above his troops. According to his analysis, the Romans could best be defeated on their home territory. At first, he was proved correct. Hannibal won several key victories, which intimidated the Romans and enabled him to move south toward Rome. By 216 B.C., the Romans had changed their generals and their strategy, but Hannibal continued to win. A long stand-off began. For twelve years, Hannibal's army controlled the south of Italy, but they could not take Rome or subdue the north. The war began to turn against the Carthaginians about 207 B.C. Scipio, a Roman general, defeated Carthage in Spain. He also stopped the army of Hasdrubal, Hannibal's brother, from entering Italy. Then, in 204 B.C., he took a Roman force to north Africa and battled the Carthaginians close to their home. Hannibal was forced to return, but Scipio defeated him at Zama in 202 B.C., and Hannibal fled to Syria.

The Carthaginians and Romans went to war one last time, beginning in 150 B.C. The Romans won the Third Punic War, obliterating the city of their once-mighty rival.

Rome was now the dominant power in the Mediterranean region. The Romans, like other conquerors in the ancient world, forced the peoples they defeated to become slaves. So many slaves were available that Rome developed a slave-based economy. By 27 B.C., slaves made up one-fifth of Rome's population of 1.25 million. The wealthy used slaves for almost every kind of task. Slaves were sometimes treated so badly that they rebelled. The most famous slave revolt occurred in 73 B.C., and was led by the gladiator Spartacus whose army eventually grew to about seventy thousand slaves and sympathizers. Spartacus's revolt lasted for three years and was finally put down by armies commanded by Crassus, Pompey, and Lucullus.

Although they were tentative allies against Spartacus, Crassus and Pompey were competing against one another for political control of Rome. Technically, Rome was a democracy administered by a Senate. In practice, though, political power was obtained through influence, wealth, and military strength. For ten years, from 71-61 B.C., Crassus and Pompey manoeuvred to gain an advantage over one another. Then, an apparently much less powerful man, Julius Caesar, became an important intermediary. He persuaded Crassus and Pompey that the three of them should rule Rome as a unit, and the First Triumvirate was born.

Caesar's rise to power was gradual. He began with a legal and political career, then travelled to Spain as an army commander. Through aggressive plundering, he gained wealth for himself and his soldiers. Caesar returned to Rome, forged the First Triumvirate, and then left again to continue Rome's military campaigns in Gaul. He proved to be a superior general. When Crassus was killed in battle in 53 B.C., Caesar made his move against Pompey. Against the orders of the Senate, Caesar brought his army from Gaul into Italy. A little over a year later, Caesar had defeated Pompey and his army to become the ruler of Rome.

Julius Caesar's reign was short-lived. His apparent desire to be regarded as a monarch, perhaps even a deity, antagonized powerful citizens who still believed Rome should be governed by a Senate. His alliance with Cleopatra, queen of Egypt, also worked against him, because people were afraid that Caesar's authority might pass to an heir who was not wholly Roman. Conspirators organized, and Caesar was assassinated in 44 B.C.

Several key figures emerged to fill the vacuum of power. Marc Antony, one of Caesar's generals, chased the conspirators from Rome. His army defeated theirs, and the leaders committed suicide. Octavian, Caesar's grandnephew and legal heir, used an army of his own to take control of Rome while Antony was away. By 43 B.C., Octavian, Antony, and a governor named Lepidus had agreed to form the Second Triumvirate. Seven years later, Lepidus and Octavian went to war, and Lepidus lost. Octavian now controlled the west of the empire, Marc Antony the east.

Like Caesar before him, Antony fell in love with Cleopatra. Eventually, this alliance turned the Roman people against him and gave Octavian a reason to pursue him. Octavian's navy met Antony and Cleopatra's navy at Actium in 31 B.C.; Octavian prevailed when Cleopatra withdrew her forces. Antony and Cleopatra killed themselves not long after.

Octavian, clearly the chief power in Rome, gave over his authority to the Senate in 27 B.C., and the Senate promptly appointed him to key positions. In this way, Octavian confirmed his status as the first Roman emperor.

7

The Triumph and Decline of Rome

Date B.C.	Event
27	End of Roman Republic Octavian becomes Caesar Augustus, first Roman Emperor *Pax Romana* begins
c. 3	Birth of Jesus

Date A.D.	Event
14	Tiberius becomes emperor
30	Jesus is crucified
37	Caligula becomes emperor
41	Claudius becomes emperor
54	Nero becomes emperor
64	Nero blames Christians for the burning of Rome Persecution of Christians begins
70	Revolt of Jews is crushed and they are banished from Palestine
79	Mount Vesuvius erupts burying Pompeii, Herculaneum, and other towns Dedication of the Colosseum
82	Arch of Titus, marking Titus's victory over the Jews, is built
100	Punishment for being Christian is death
118	Hadrian begins rebuilding the Pantheon in Rome
135	Hadrian suppresses the revolt of the Jews and denies them access to Jerusalem
212	*Caracalla grants Roman citizenship to all free residents of Roman provinces* Pax Romana *ends* *Decline of Western Roman Empire*
476	*The German barbarian Odoacer deposes line of Roman emperors in the West*
480-543	Saint Benedict revives the early Christian institution of the monastery
527-565	Reign of Justinian Golden age of the Byzantine Empire in the East
622	Hegira of Muhammad from Mecca to Medina
732	Charles Martel stops the Muslim advance into Europe at Tours Muslim Empire develops into a rich civilization and lasts for over 500 years
800	Charlemagne crowned by Pope Leo III
843	Treaty of Verdun divides kingdom of Charlemagne
800-1000	Muslims and Magyars threaten to expand into European lands Vikings raid coastlines from Iceland to Spain; invade France, Russia, Constantinople Old Western Roman Empire blossoms into a new civilization, Europe

7

The Triumph and Decline of Rome

BACKGROUND

Pax Romana

In 27 B.C., Julius Caesar's heir, Octavian, became the first emperor of Rome—Caesar Augustus. Beginning with his rule, Roman civilization thrived in a time of general peace and stability known as the *Pax Romana*. The Empire comprised 90 million people in forty-three provinces that stretched from the Caspian Sea to the Atlantic and from Britain to Africa. For two centuries, there was material well-being, order, and security. One government, one system of coinage, and one set of laws unified the Empire. The success of Roman government was so remarkable during this period that historians have spent a lot of effort puzzling over the eventual decline of the *Pax Romana* and the dissolution of half the Empire.

Augustus developed the administrative structure of the Roman Empire. His authority as *princeps*, or first citizen, was backed by the Roman army of almost three hundred and fifty thousand soldiers, each of whom took an oath to protect the frontiers. Within Italy, Augustus created an imperial force of nine thousand men known as the **Praetorian Guard** to protect the heart of the Empire. Although he presided at meetings of the Senate and occasionally asked its advice, Augustus himself made the decisions on appointments to major public offices. The traditional posts of the former republican government were kept, but Augustus created an imperial "household" to run the everyday business of government. This household marked the beginning of a civil service that became divided into departments controlled from a central office in Rome. It was accountable only to Augustus. Governors of provinces were chosen based on ability and, while considerable freedom was given to local communities, a careful watch was maintained on officials and tax collectors.

Augustus was a great administrator, and his system of government survived with limited changes for two hundred years. His administrative

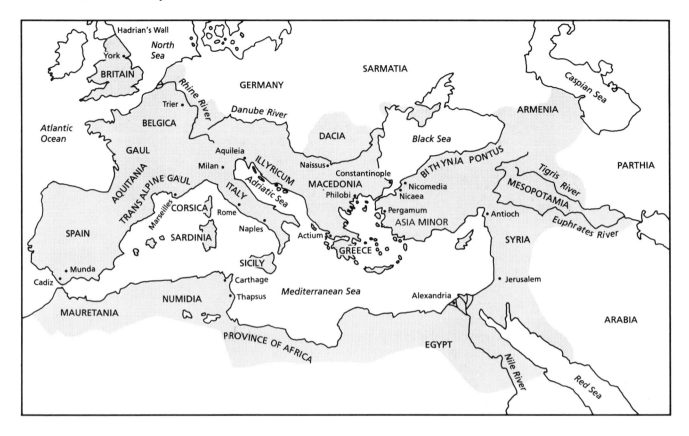

Pax Romana.

reforms, so smoothly created and enforced, endured the rule of less-able emperors such as Nero and tyrants in the worst sense of the word such as Dominitian. More talented leaders like Trajan, Hadrian, and Marcus Aurelius used the bureaucracy to keep the Empire in fairly stable operation.

Rome the Splendid City

The expansion of Rome throughout the Mediterranean produced new markets and opportunities for trade that improved the standard of living throughout the Empire. The Egyptian city of Alexandria became a centre of Hellenistic grandeur, admired for large structures such as the 120 m high Pharos lighthouse and the great library. Antioch, on the Phoenician coast, was almost as striking. The focal point and most-valued jewel of the Empire, however, was the city of Rome itself. Nowhere else were the material achievements of the Romans so lavishly displayed on such a magnificent scale.

The architecture was extraordinary. There were two circuses (racetracks), two amphitheatres, five lakes, four gladiatorial schools, eleven imperial baths, 926 private baths, 2000 fountains, eighteen squares and forums, 38 parks and public gardens, 290 warehouses, 700 public pools and basins,

The Roman Baths

As buildings and as social institutions, the Roman public baths were unique. The baths approved by Emperor Caracalla and built during the third century were fed from a one million litre cistern of water and could accommodate sixteen hundred bathers. Those of Emperor Diocletian (A.D. 285-305) were even larger, holding two thousand bathers comfortably. Beneath spacious domes, brilliant glass mosaics hung on multicoloured marble walls. Bathers could admire this extravagant interior as hot water poured along silver troughs or through the silvered mouths of statues into the sunken baths of the *calidarium*. The baths also provided lukewarm showers in the *tepidarium*, and cold water in the *frigidarium*. There were separate baths for women and men.

The baths were the only place where many Romans could get clean, but they also provided a variety of other facilities. There were lounges, art galleries, and places for reading. Recreation was encouraged in areas reserved for athletic events adopted from the Greeks, such as wrestling, discus and javelin throwing, and boxing. Furnaces were continuously stoked to provide hot air, which was trapped in underground chambers called *hypocausts* and used to heat the entire complex, including the bathing areas. Surrounding the baths were parks with manicured groves and gardens decorated with statues. At a cost of about a quarter of a cent, even the lowliest slave could gain admittance.

Bathing took place between the sixth and ninth hour after sunrise, during which time all other activity ceased. By this time, most Romans were ready for their evening meal.

Most Romans ate ordinary amounts of ordinary food, but a few of the wealthy patricians staged meals that have given the Romans a reputation for gluttony. For the wealthy, the more exotic and rare a dish was, the more desirable it became, and a multicourse dinner might include tongues of parrots that had been taught to speak, mackerel livers, pheasant and peacock brains, and lamprey milk. Lucullus, a contemporary of Caesar, seldom paid less than the modern equivalent of $5000 for a dinner party, and would send a fleet out to search the Mediterranean for the precious ingredients in such a meal. People with high status ate while reclining on couches, believing that it was not healthy to dine sitting up. Knives and spoons were used but not forks, and much of the food was picked up with the fingers. Washing as the meal progressed was common practice. It was a Roman custom to express appreciation by belching.

This Roman bath in Bath, England, is evidence of the far-reaching influence of the Romans during the time of their Empire.

The Palatine Hill, seen here across the Roman forum, was the home of the wealthiest Roman citizens.

The Arts

Greek achievements were valued long after the Greek city-states ceased to be powerful. Other peoples consciously used ancient Greece as the model for their own cultures. These new cultures, which owe so much to the Greek spirit, are given the label **"Hellenistic"** because the Greeks were also known as Hellenes. Particular works that are clearly based on a Greek original are also said to be Hellenistic.

The culture of the ancient Romans certainly owes a large debt to the Greeks. The major Roman gods were Greek gods that had been renamed. Roman artists were often content to copy Greek productions. In fact, statues and columns were stolen from Greece and used in Roman buildings. In architecture, the Romans used the columns and lintels that the Greeks and the Egyptians had developed, as well as the arches and domes first used in the Middle East.

36 marble arches, and 37 monumental gates! Statues were almost everywhere, if a fourth-century inventory list of ten thousand figures in stone and bronze is to be believed. Such splendour must have impressed residents and visitors alike. Construction in concrete was the major technological breakthrough that allowed the Romans to make the domes and vaults that were an essential part of their great buildings. Although major construction had started before and continued after Augustus's reign, the usually humble Augustus claimed to have converted Rome from a city of brick to a city of marble.

The Spectacle of Entertainment

In Rome, many days were set aside for public holidays and special events. Numerous ancient festivals were carefully observed, and new festivals were added to celebrate military victories, birthdays of important Romans, and special historical events.

During the late Republic, politicians who wanted to increase their popularity often sponsored ruthless spectacles. People filled the arenas to watch animals fight and kill each other. Frequently, bizarre combinations—a rhinoceros versus a bull, for example—would be arranged for these contests. Occasionally, humans were tied to stakes or set free in artificial landscapes of groves and brooks populated by lions and other wild beasts. Onlookers made bets as to how long the people would last, while tokens for door prizes and lunch were dispersed throughout the crowd. To celebrate the one thousandth anniversary of Romulus's legendary founding of Rome, thirty-two elephants, ten tigers, sixty lions, thirty leopards, ten hyenas, and six hippos were killed. Another festival lasted 123 days and featured combats involving eleven thousand animals and ten thousand gladiators. Emperor Hadrian so loved this kind of activity that he stepped into the arena himself and killed a lion with his bare hands. Another emperor, Commodus, boasted that he had personally defeated one thousand gladiators!

Gladiators

The Roman practice of human combat was adopted from the Etruscans, who had often forced Roman prisoners of war to fight to the death to please the spirits of the underworld. Rome, however, used the gladiatorial games to entertain the underemployed city masses. The Roman satirist Juvenal, writing around the turn of the second century A.D., described the typical Roman citizen in this way: "Only two things does he worry about or long for—bread and the big match." Presumably, out-of-work Romans would not cause social unrest as long as they had food to eat and a spectacle to distract them. The earliest official gladiatorial games staged by Rome were held in 105 B.C., and they quickly became an essential element of public celebrations.

Gladiators were recruited from the seemingly inexhaustible number of slaves and prisoners of war that accumulated as Rome expanded its Empire through military conquest. The men were taken to training grounds known as "schools," where they were treated harshly in preparation for their battles in the arenas of the Empire.

Originally, gladiators were named according to their place of origin, which was also evident from the equipment they used. The lightly armed **Thracian** had a sword, helmet, round shield, and a curved dagger; the **Gaul** had a sword and shield and was easily recognizable because of the image of a sea creature on his helmet; while the heavily armoured **Samnite** fought with a large rectangular shield and axe. These gladiators were always on the attack and were often matched against net-fighters. A net-fighter used a trident, shoulder guard, and net to capture his foe and ready him for the kill. Other gladiators were specialists: boxers, archers, horsemen, and the well-trained *bestiarii*, who fought only in the wild beast hunts.

Although gladiators usually fought to the death, a man could be spared if he distinguished himself in battle. A fallen gladiator asked for mercy by throwing away his shield and raising a finger on his left hand. If the emperor (or, in his absence, the crowd or the opponent) approved, the beaten gladiator might walk away. A down-turned thumb meant immediate execution. Gladiators who won many victories often became heroes worshipped by the adoring crowds, much as modern athletes are praised today. A top gladiator could be presented with a wooden sword, an honour that gave him freedom if he was a slave, and the opportunity for retirement if he was already free.

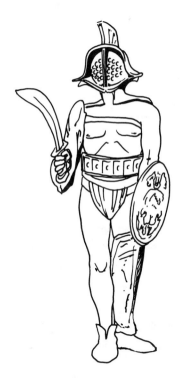

A gladiator outfitted in the Thracian style.

Religion

Six vestal virgins were selected by the Pontifex Maximus, the high priest of the Roman religion, to maintain a continuous watch over the round temple of Vesta in the Roman forum. Vesta was the goddess of the hearth and therefore of family life, and her shrine was symbolic of the safety of the city. The vestals were required to give thirty years of service; their duties included the annual renewal of the sacred flame and the preparation of the sacrifices. Any vestal who broke her vow of chastity was buried alive. The vestal virgins had a very high status and were awarded many honours.

The Colosseum

The most famous setting for the Roman spectacles was the Flavian Amphitheatre, more popularly known as the **Colosseum**. It is not known how the more popular name originated. It may have referred to the structure's gigantic size or to the 30 m statue (or colossus) of Nero that stood nearby until the fourth century A.D. The stadium was clearly built to impress all onlookers. It was elliptical in shape and four storeys in height. On the first three levels were eight arched passageways; those on the first floor were numbered so that spectators could quickly reach the seating area accorded by their social rank. The first four passageways were reserved for processions and the entrance of the emperor who, along with the senators, **vestal virgins**, and top civil servants, sat in special seats in the front rows. These seats gave them the best view of the almost-daily bloodbath of public entertainment. Each of the lower classes sat in progressively higher tiers as the importance of its rank decreased.

The arena itself had a surface of wooden boards covered with sand, measuring about 80 m long and 50 m wide. At the long ends of the arena there were two passageways, the first of which was used by the gladiators as they were paraded in front of the emperor to say, "*Caesar, Morituri te salutant!*" ("Caesar, those about to die salute you!"). Dead gladiators and wild beasts were removed through the other passage. Below the floor of the arena was a maze of cages that held the animals who were used in the show. They were raised to floor level by elevators powered by beasts of burden. It was even possible to flood the entire surface to re-enact naval battles, with gladiators in marine costumes fighting to the death on swaying decks.

The model (above) shows how the Colosseum probably looked at the height of the Empire, and the photograph (right) captures how it appears today.

This is the floor of the Colosseum as it appears today. These cages, which housed the animals destined for the arena, were hidden by the floorboards in Roman times.

To protect the crowd from the sun, a canopy called a *velarium* was raised manually using a complicated series of cables, pulleys, and winches anchored on stones that surrounded the Colosseum. About one thousand men worked in unison to complete the task. The cries of the nearly fifty thousand spectators, the roars of the wild animals, and the snapping of the velarium in the wind must have been deafening.

Much of the Colosseum was built with travertine stone (limestone) shaped into blocks that were held together with iron pins rather than mortar. Later generations dismantled and removed large portions of the amphitheatre, and earthquake damage was considerable, but it remains an impressive structure even today.

The Circus Maximus

Rivalling the Colosseum in popularity was the **Circus Maximus**, one of four major stadiums used for chariot races about two hundred and forty days a year. Under Augustus, about twelve races a day were held; under Caligula, as many as thirty-four. Emperor Domitian changed the standard seven-lap (8 km) race to five laps so that a hundred races could be run each day. Charioteers were not just able racers, they had to balance and jump from one horse to the other, stand on a horse's back, and pick up a cloth from the ground at full gallop. The risk of an accident was so great that most died at an early age. The successful drivers, like the gladiators of the arena, became idols and wealthy men. When Crescens was fatally injured at

More to Consider

The horses and the charioteers who competed against each other belonged to different stables, similar to the professional teams of today's sporting world. The most famous stables were the Reds, the Whites, the Greens, and the Blues. Each had its own trainers and its own financial supporters, who made great profits on the races. Emperor Caligula became such an avid supporter of the Greens that he once had the horses and charioteers of the Blues poisoned. Vitellius, a fan of the Blues, had people executed for shouting "Down with the Blues!" The emperor Nero wore green to the Circus and on at least one occasion had the entire floor covered with green copper-oxide dust.

the age of twenty-two, he had already won 1.5 million sesterces (about $300 000). A second-century charioteer named Diocles retired after winning almost 4500 races, earning 35 million sesterces in the process.

The Circus Maximus was of ancient origin, dating back to the early days of the Republic, and had reached a truly overwhelming size by the third century B.C. It measured 600 m long and 200 m wide, and each side had three tiers of seats, the first of which was made of stone, the others of wood. About two hundred and fifty thousand people could cheer their favourite stable to victory as chariots wheeled around the *spina*, the central dividing line of statues, obelisks, and lap counters. Sometimes the Circus Maximus was transformed into a forest filled with game—on one special occasion it was stocked with one thousand ostriches, one thousand wild boars, one thousand stags, and one thousand sheep. The spectators were allowed to capture or kill whatever they could. It took an army of game hunters working full-time to keep all the arenas of the Empire supplied with animals. They were so efficient that elephants vanished from Libya, lions from Thessaly, and hippos from the lower Nile.

Roman Theatre

The most popular nonviolent form of public entertainment was the theatre and the plays performed there. Borrowed and modified from the Greek original, the Roman theatre consisted of a D-shaped orchestra at floor level surrounded by an auditorium of seats that faced a stage and stage wall at the end. The Roman theatre at Orange, France, has a stage wall 103 m long and 38 m high. In Rome, the only remaining theatre is the twelve-thousand-seat Theatre of Marcellus; the Theatre of Pompey, which has not survived, had a capacity of forty thousand.

The tragedies and comedies were performed in the open air. Characters wore special masks and costumes and could be easily identified. Special effects were created by revolving screens of painted scenery, cranes that could raise characters from earth to heaven, and trap doors for quick exits. If the performance was dull, the audience whistled and hissed just as they might today, and, if the play was really bad, they threw apples!

Behind the Grandeur

Roman merchants were supplied with merchandise from the corners of the known world, and their shops were jammed with people. Public monuments, statues, theatres, stadiums, and racetracks were taken for granted. Politicians ran for election and catered to the masses, and the unemployed collected welfare. But alongside the continuous entertainment, great wealth, and architectural beauty were appalling slums. Almost forty-seven thousand tenements, divided into small, poorly vented cubicles, provided the cramped living space for the bulk of Rome's population. Some tenements were seven storeys high. Shoddy construction resulted in walls that

Little remains of this Roman theatre, discovered during the excavations of the city of Pompeii at the end of the sixteenth century. On 24 August, A.D. 79, Mount Vesuvius exploded, sending up a black cloud of pumice and lava fragments. The city of Pompeii was soon buried under 3 to 5 m of volcanic ash.

were too flimsy for the weight they had to support. Although aqueducts delivered water right to the apartment buildings, low water pressure meant that water had to be carried up flight after flight of stairs. Most rooms were foul-smelling, rodent-infested, and filthy. Fires broke out continually, since all cooking was done with small charcoal braziers that were a constant danger in the wood-framed structures.

The forums of Rome were all drained by an impressive network of sewers, but nothing similar was done for the slums. People either walked to public latrines or used small sewage tanks that were picked up by merchants for sale to outlying farms. It was also common for slop to be dumped into the narrow, crowded streets, which often had small sewage trenches running down the middle. The smell of the city was rivalled only by the smell of the garbage pits that ringed Rome, which were used not only for refuse but also for the disposal of animal and human carcasses from the arenas.

For many poor Romans, the streets were the only place to sleep when rent money was not available. Most streets in Rome were no more than alleyways, and few were wide enough for carts to pass each other. To reduce the never-ending traffic jams of carts and people, Julius Caesar banned vehicles from the city centre until dark unless they were needed to shore up sagging buildings. After dark, the streets echoed with the noise of wagon wheels. The absence of street lighting and the scarcity of night patrols meant that murderers and thieves threatened any who ventured out alone.

Changes in the Empire: Slavery and the Stoics

Although the Empire reached its maximum extent in the second century A.D., Rome under the emperors fought fewer wars of aggression and grew more concerned with preserving the gains that had already been made. Fewer wars reduced the all important supply of slaves, however, and as labour became scarce, it also became more valuable. The result was a more humane treatment of slaves, who were now kept working only by promises of freedom after a certain number of years of service. Many slaves did indeed earn their freedom, much to the resentment of the rest of the Roman population.

More humane attitudes towards slavery may also have been shaped by two new forces within the Empire. The first was the Greek philosophy of **Stoicism**, imported to Rome as early as the second century B.C. Stoics stressed that all events are the result of divine laws of nature and should therefore be accepted without complaint. A Stoic tried to live life calmly, unexcited by good luck and indifferent to misfortune. Stoic principles required that all people be treated with respect, since everyone possessed the spark of God.

The second force that may have influenced attitudes toward slavery was a new religion—Christianity.

Changes in the Empire: Cults, Christ, and Christianity

The gods and goddesses of Rome's state religion were almost identical to those worshipped by the Greeks, but with Roman names. After the Republic gave way to the Empire, Rome became very tolerant of foreign religions and, for largely practical reasons, willingly accepted foreign deities. Indeed, the first two centuries A.D. were dominated by the spread of oriental cults, such as those of Cybele and Bacchus, and the Egyptian cult of Isis. Perhaps the most influential was the cult of **Mithras**, which came to Rome from Persia and was spread by contact with oriental slaves in seaports and by Roman soldiers who encountered the cult at the outposts of the Empire. Even as late as the reign of Emperor Diocletian (A.D. 285-305), armies fought under the banner of Mithras (who was portrayed as an invincible sun god) because he was so popular among the soldiers. This religious toleration helped in the successful administration of the outlying provinces of the Empire. In return for religious freedom, the locals were expected to respect Roman gods in a Roman setting.

One of the many religious traditions the Romans encountered was **Judaism**. Jewish communities were found in commercial centres throughout the Roman Empire and eastern Asia. The Jews had experienced a long history of struggle and persecution dating back to the eras of Abraham (c. 2000 B.C.) and Moses (c. 1300 B.C.), recorded in the Hebrew scriptures of the Bible. Their faith in one God whose word would be revealed by enlightened prophets had helped them maintain a solidarity that brought them through oppression. The Jews looked forward to the arrival of the

Controversies

Because Christianity became the dominant religion of the Western world, the birth of Jesus was viewed in retrospect as an important watershed in history. The Western calendar regards the year of Jesus' birth as the first year. Everything before this time is dated B.C.,"Before Christ." Everything after this time is dated A.D., *Anno Domini*, "in the year of the Lord." Although this method of dating was established to set a standard for dating, it is not without serious problems. For one, the actual year of Jesus' birth was probably 3 B.C. More important, this method of dating gives prominence to Jesus and Christianity. Some non-Christian cultures favour other methods of dating. As a result, the abbreviation B.C.E (Before the Common Era) is frequently used in place of B.C., and A.D. is replaced by the abbreviation C.E. (Common Era).

Messiah, or deliverer, who would free them from hardship and establish God's rule on earth.

During the reign of Tiberius (A.D. 14-37), a Jew named Jesus of Nazareth emerged as a popular leader because of his dramatic sermons in the countryside of Judea. Jesus preached that there was one God who was the Father of all people, and that the kingdom of Heaven was open to everyone. Many of his earliest followers were Jews who felt that Jesus was the Messiah whose arrival had been predicted in the Hebrew scriptures. Most of the Jewish community, however, did not accept Jesus as the Messiah.

As Jesus travelled and preached over a three-year period, he stressed the moral obligation people had to God. He denounced personal wealth and asserted that service to God's will was the path for anyone—merchant or beggar, man or woman, black or white—who wished to enter the Kingdom of Heaven. For Jesus, there were no temples, no altars, no ceremonies; there was only the preacher spreading the word of God.

Religion

The early purpose of the Roman calendar was to list the many festivals. There were twelve lunar months in a year of 355 days. The month was divided into three parts by the **Nones** (the fifth or seventh day of the month) and the **Ides** (the thirteenth or fifteenth day). Note that some of the months were named after goddesses and gods.

Month

Martius—from Mars, god of agriculture
Aprilis—the goddess of sprouting
Maiius—Maia ("increase")
Junius—Juno ("thriving")
Quinctilis—fifth month
Sextilis—sixth month
Septembrus—seventh month
Octobrus—eighth month
Novembrus—ninth month
Decembrus—tenth month
Januarius—Janus
Februairius—("fever")

Greek and Roman Gods

Greek	Function	Roman
Zeus	king of the gods, father of the sky	Jupiter
Hera	queen of heaven, goddess of marriage	Juno
Ares	god of war and agriculture	Mars
Athena	goddess of wisdom, memory, actors, and handicrafts	Minerva
Aphrodite	goddess of love	Venus
Artemis	goddess of the moon and of hunting	Diana
Hermes	god of merchants, orators, thieves	Mercury
Heracles	god of joy	Hercules
Demeter	earth goddess	Ceres
Dionysus	god of wine and the grape	Liber
Apollo	god of health and prophecy	Apollo
Poseidon	god of the sea	Neptune
Hephaestus	god of the forge	Vulcan
Hades	god of the underworld	Pluto
Hestia	goddess of hearth and household	Vesta

Jesus' entry into Jerusalem was regarded as a danger by the Jewish leaders. They were afraid the Romans would interpret Jesus' presence as a protest against Roman authority. This fear prompted Jewish priests, with the assistance of Judas (one of Jesus' disillusioned disciples), to help the Romans arrest Jesus. He was charged with attempting to set up a new kingdom in Judea, tried, convicted, and reluctantly sentenced by the Roman procurator Pontius Pilate in A.D. 30 to be crucified. Reports of his resurrection inspired the emergence of the Christians.

One of the greatest of the early Christian teachers was Saul of Tarsus, a man who was not a disciple and had never met Jesus. Saul was a Jew who was educated in Greek and who was a Roman citizen. On the road to Damascus in A.D. 35, Saul experienced a vision and converted to Christianity. Thereafter he changed his name to Paul and travelled to the major cities in Asia, Syria, Greece, and Macedonia, and also to the capitals of Alexandria and Rome. He established Christian communities in all of these places. Of equal importance to Christianity was the disciple Peter, who also travelled the eastern Mediterranean spreading the word of God. Christianity, in the thirty years that followed the crucifixion, received little opposition in Rome.

As conditions worsened in Rome during the first century A.D., however, people became less tolerant of Christians. In contrast to the Jews the Christians possessed intense missionary zeal; and they repeatedly condemned worldly success. Christians not only refused to recognize and sacrifice to Roman gods and deified emperors, but insisted their God was the only God. Charges of cannibalism were brought against them because their Communion services, held in secret meetings at night, were misunderstood. Under Emperor Nero, Christians were used as scapegoats for the great fire that ravaged Rome, and both Paul and Peter were executed in A.D. 64, victims of the growing persecution. By A.D. 100, a confessed Christian could legally be put to death. Despite the harsh treatment and later mass executions under the Emperor Decius in A.D. 250, and then Diocletian in A.D. 303, Christianity spread throughout the Empire. Then, in A.D. 313, Emperor Constantine expanded an earlier law and granted Christianity a status equal to other religions. He was the first emperor to support the Church, and, on his deathbed, Constantine was baptized a Christian. Later in the fourth century A.D., the emperor Theodosius made Christianity the official religion of the state and declared pagan worship illegal.

Why was Christianity so successful? Ironically, the widespread distribution of Christianity was made possible by the general political and military stability of the Roman Empire, with the roads it maintained and the sea lanes it protected. The Gospels of the New Testament were written in Greek, which was used as a universal language of culture and business, particularly in the east. Christian teachings were able to be widely distributed.

The living conditions in the Roman Empire also contributed to the success of Christianity. The average Roman did not share in the wealth sug-

Religion

A **pagan** religion is any religion outside of Judaism, Christianity, or Islam. During Theodosius's time, there were many pagan religions—the worship of the Roman goddesses and gods, which had previously been the official state religion; plus the many cults and minor religions that had competed (and continued to compete) with Christianity. The word pagan usually carries a bias toward Christianity and against other religions. Here, as in most contemporary history books, it is used neutrally.

gested by the magnificent architecture of the city, and the daily hardships of life led many to seek answers in any religion that promised a better existence. It should be stressed that Christianity competed for converts with several pagan cults, and that Christians became a sizeable minority only in the third century A.D. Christianity won out because it offered a simple and clear message that benefited any slave or plebian, no matter how lowly his or her condition. The powerful saw the Christian faith in one God as a threat to their social status and control; ordinary people looked forward to life after death, where the happiness and equality denied them on earth would be theirs. Jesus had been a real person rather than a mythical figure, and, as more and more martyrs sacrificed their lives with their faith unshaken, the appeal of the Christian cause grew.

The solidification of the Church's organizational structure at a time when the political and military state of Rome was beginning to decay also contributed to Christian success. During the second and third centuries, the clerical orders of deacon, priest, and bishop were established, creating a Church administration and bureaucracy. Emperor Constantine's approval of Christianity made sense given the way the Church was evolving. Persecution had not prevented the rapid spread of the religion. It seemed possible that the Church, with its increasing strength and competent organization, might even help to preserve unity throughout the Empire. In A.D. 325, Constantine called the First Council of Nicaea, a gathering of the key religious leaders of the Christian world. The Council attempted to standardize Christian beliefs and practices and gave to history the form of the Church that is known today.

Decline of the Western Empire

The changes that occurred in the three centuries following the *Pax Romana* have been called the decline of Rome, although no specific event signalled this demise to a Roman of the time. Nor did the decline occur in all parts of the Empire. Ruling the vast Empire had become so awkward that Diocletian divided it into two sections ruled by co-emperors, an administrative change that was completed under Constantine (A.D. 312-337). The Western Empire, with Latin as its language, was administered from Rome; the Eastern Empire, with Greek as its language, was administered from Constantinople. When historians speak of the decline or fall of Rome, it is the Western Empire to which they refer; the Eastern Empire survived until the fall of Constantinople to the Turks in 1453.

The Western Empire lost control of more and more territory to tribes of Germanic people identified by Romans and known to history as **barbarians**. In the third century, the **Franks** pushed westward across the Lower Rhine to Gaul, while the **Alamanni** moved to Alsace. The Eastern Empire was threatened by the **Goths**, who moved out of southern Russia and crossed the Danube in search of plunder. Initially, these raids were checked or pushed

Religion

Many aspects of Christianity are similar to, and probably based on, aspects of other religions that flourished during the time the Christian Church was establishing itself. For example, the festival marking the birth of the sun god Sol Invictus was held on 25 December, the same date the Christians later used to celebrate the birth of Jesus. Similarly, the Christian sabbath honoured the "Sun-day" familiar to the many followers of the cult of Mithras. Indeed, the worship of Mithras involved burning candles in front of an altar, a practice that resembled ceremonies that gradually appeared in the Christian Church. The story of death and resurrection that was so important to the Christians was also a part of the worship of the Egyptian deities Isis and Osiris.

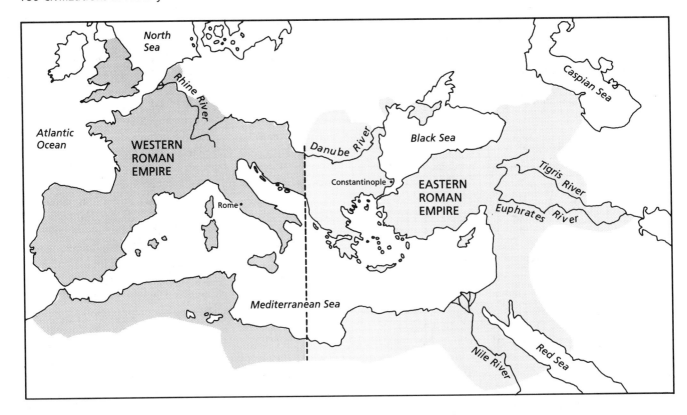

Division of the Roman Empire, Fourth Century.

back by Roman legions, but the insecurity they created was reflected in the massive walls built under the direction of Aurelian (A.D. 270-275) to fortify the open city of Rome. During the fourth century, the barbarians themselves were threatened by an even more warlike people, the **Huns**, who emerged from central Asia and subjected several Germanic tribes to their harsh rule.

To escape the Huns, Germanic people fled to and settled on Roman land in Gaul and in what is now Bulgaria. The displaced barbarians quickly tired of Roman rule and rebelled. A major victory over Rome at Adrianople in A.D. 378 opened the way for further barbarian infiltration, and eventually they dominated large parts of the Empire. King Alaric and his **Visigoths** pushed through Greece, sacked Rome in A.D. 410, and continued their march into southern Gaul and Spain. Similarly, the **Vandals** pushed outward from Hungary into central Gaul, Spain, and the north shore of Africa. Under the leadership of Clovis, the Franks established a kingdom in northern Gaul while the **Angles**, **Saxons**, and **Jutes** invaded Britain.

Perhaps the greatest military threat to Roman security came from the Huns. This powerful people had originally turned westward when their expansion into Asia was halted by the Chinese. As they swept into Europe, the Germanic barbarians were forced into increasing contact and then conflict

Decline of Rome

A.D.

270	Emperor Aurelian builds a new wall around city of Rome as protection against barbarian attack
303	Diocletian intensifies persecution of Christians Diocletian divides Empire into Eastern and Western sections
313	Constantine grants toleration to Christianity
325	First Council of Nicaea
330	Constantine makes Constantinople the new capital of the Eastern Empire
378	Barbarians defeat Rome at Adrianople
380	Christianity becomes the official religion of the Empire
395	Roman Empire permanently divided into East and West
410	Rome sacked by Visigoths Saint Augustine writes *City of God* in defence of charges that Christianity was responsible for the decline of the Empire
451	Attila the Hun defeated by a combined force of Romans and barbarians at Troyes
455	Rome sacked by Vandals
476	End of the Western Empire The German barbarian Odoacer deposes line of Roman emperors in the West

with the Roman Empire. By the middle of the fifth century, the Huns, led by Attila, had established control over several Germanic peoples, and in A.D. 451 declared war on the Western Roman Empire. The Hun threat was so severe that the Franks and Visigoths joined the Roman forces and defeated Attila's army at Troyes. Over one hundred and fifty thousand men were killed. The Huns continued to plunder southern Europe until Attila's mysterious death in A.D. 453, after which they disappeared as a distinct group.

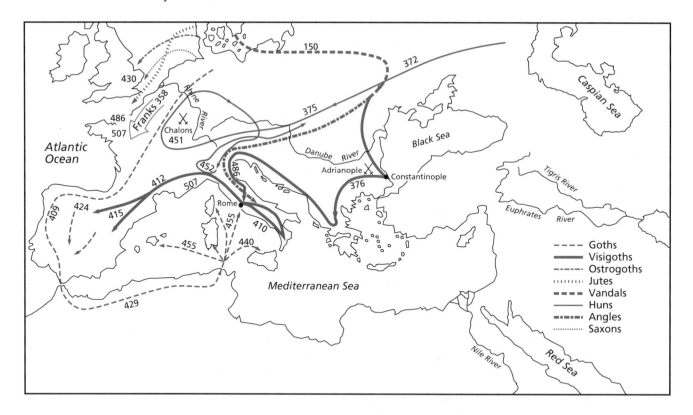

Barbarian Invasion of the Eastern and Western Empires.

The Issue Emerges

In A.D. 475-476, the Western Roman Empire was in the midst of the kind of political and military unrest that had become typical. But this time, the outcome of the upheaval was different. In A.D. 476, the German warrior Odoacer deposed the Roman emperor of the day and became the first barbarian king of the Italian peninsula. This date has become identified as the end of the Western Empire. During the two centuries of *Pax Romana*, it seemed that the Empire would last indefinitely. At their peak, the Romans possessed wealth and resources, military power, and a competent civil service and bureaucracy. What caused the Western Empire to topple from its position of dominance? The once-formidable military defences could not prevent the influx of barbarians, which suggests that the quality of the Roman army should be examined. Historians agree, though, that several factors, relating to almost every aspect of Roman life, played a part in the general decline. Any explanation must also account for the fact that the Eastern Empire outlasted its Western counterpart by almost a thousand years. Was the decline of the Western Empire inevitable, or was it due to events that could have been deflected or avoided? Could the Western Empire have been preserved?

PROBLEM QUESTION

Why did the Western Roman Empire falter after providing centuries of strong political and military leadership and a relatively stable economic and social organization?

ALTERNATIVE ONE: The Roman Army

Based on "The Roman Army and the Disintegration of the Empire" by E. Togo Salmon (1963)

In its heyday throughout the 1st and 2nd centuries A.D., the Roman army was a magnificent instrument of power. It met all the basic requirements for a first class fighting force: the soldiers were well trained and the system of command was well organized. Yet gradually the personnel composing this incomparable force ceased to be respectable elements of the Empire's population. As time went on, the army became so barbarized that, by the 5th century A.D., the defense of the Empire was quite literally in the hands of the Germans. Why and how this happened to the Roman state is an important question relating to the decline and fall of Rome.

The Roman state, under the Republic and the Empire, had the right to draft or conscript its subjects, citizens or others, for military service, and in time of war this approach was occasionally used. But short-service conscripts were not the answer for the defense of the Empire. Without the assistance of railways, the conscripts would have spent most of their time travelling to outlying trouble-spots rather than in training. Their combat efficiency would not have been very high. The Roman army became, for the most part, an army of volunteers even though the normal length of service until the 3rd century A.D. was twenty-five years! Although small by modern standards, the Roman army was enormous in size for the time: in the 1st and 2nd centuries it consisted of about 300,000 including legionaries and auxiliaries. Such an army needed an annual intake of about 30,000 new soldiers to maintain it.

The hard life of a soldier and low pay offered little reason to volunteer, moreover, those born into Roman citizenship felt it was their right to escape military service. The average Roman citizen was deliberately discouraged from taking any interest or participating in public affairs. It was the emperor who decided everything. With no universal state education and no popular press, information about imperial policies was never dispersed in a systematic fashion. A Roman citizen felt that he belonged to an invincible empire and that he was expected to leave its administration to others. If he was not needed to run the Empire, then it also seemed that he was not needed to defend it. Thus, the Roman army was not likely to be kept up to strength by volunteers amongst the Roman citizens. Citizens of the better classes enlisted only if their background encouraged confidence of promotion to a high rank.

The standing Roman army from the days of its founder, Augustus, included many non-Italians from the provinces of the Empire. By the 2nd century A.D. their numbers were overwhelming. The big inducement was Roman citizenship and the advantages it offered. Roman citizenship improved social standing and opened more doors for the soldier and his family. All provincials—those who lived outside of Italy but within a province of the Empire—were eager to acquire it and there was virtually only one way to get it: service in the Roman army. If provincials served in the legions, they obtained citizenship the moment they enlisted. But usually recruits for the legions were taken only from those living in an organized town, a setting that officials felt provided the best environment for the Roman spirit and civilization. If the volunteer served in the auxiliaries, he obtained citizenship twenty-five years later, upon his release from service. Usually, he had been a country-dweller who, in Roman eyes, was far from civilized and needed more exposure to Roman ways and outlook. Thus a highly urbanized region like Greece provided legionaries and no auxiliaries, while in the rural Gallic provinces the pattern was reversed.

Certainly the army would not have remained at full strength if it had depended on those who already possessed Roman citizenship. By A.D. 100, serious attempts to find legionaries in Italy were abandoned. Unfortunately, the more widespread Roman citizenship became, the more restricted was the area from which recruits were likely to be obtained since Roman citizens, as we have seen, were reluctant to serve. Thus, the quality of the soldier enlisting was reduced to the lowest elements in society since many in the better classes already had citizenship by the 2nd century.

A critical decision was made by Emperor Caracalla in A.D. 212 that proved disastrous for the army. In that year, Caracalla enfranchised all of the free-born inhabitants of the Empire regardless of their race, origin, creed, or mother tongue. Whatever Caracalla's motives, one effect was to eliminate what had been a prime reason for men to enlist. Thus, it eventually became necessary to go outside the Empire to search for soldiers as the number of volunteers quickly dropped off; and so did their quality.

After A.D. 212 the army was often at odds with civilians. The Roman army, like any other, had always contained a few adventurous roughnecks and even criminals in its ranks. But so long as the prospect of acquiring Roman citizenship had spurred men of a different stamp to enlist, it had not got out of hand. In the 3rd century, however, it became quite uncontrollable. It kindled an unending series of civil wars, it spawned a well-nigh inexhaustible list of pretenders, it made and unmade emperors with almost reckless abandon and greedily extorted from the civilian population whatever it could.

It would not have been easy in any case to maintain the army at full strength in the Western Empire because the population was beginning to decline. Changed conditions of warfare also made recruiting more difficult. As cavalry came to play an ever more important role, the wild cowboys of the frontier would be more in demand. But probably it was not so much the decline in population or the need for skilled riders as the universal grant of citizenship that was responsible for the deterioration in army personnel. Men of the better type no longer had any reason to volunteer.

With citizenship no longer available as a bribe, various devices were used to attract recruits: increased pay, free rations, a more frequent share of the booty from battle, and the right to legal wedlock. But it was all to no avail: none of these makeshifts improved the calibre of the troops. During the 3rd century, the men who fought for Rome knew little and cared less about Rome's mission and, when not preying upon the civilians, had not the slightest hesitation about preying upon one another.

It was the chaos caused by these unruly soldiers which provided the barbarians beyond the frontiers with their chance and they quickly seized it. The assaults of these barbarian hordes led directly to the most obvious, if not the most important, of all the causes for the decline and fall: military collapse. An Empire whose defenders were few in quantity and poor in quality must have been tempting bait to the outer barbarians. Small wonder is it that they fell upon the Empire and thereby set in motion that fateful sequence of events which resulted finally in its disintegration.

QUESTIONS

1. Describe the quality of the Roman army during the first two centuries A.D.
2. Why did the Romans usually rely on volunteers to keep a full complement of three hundred thousand men?
3. Why did the average Roman citizen *not* volunteer for military service?
4. How were people living in the provinces of the Empire encouraged to join the Roman army?
5. a) What was the critical decision that reduced the overall calibre of the Roman army?
   b) What were the effects of this decision during the third century?
6. What other factors reduced the effectiveness of the Roman army after the second century?
7. How did the barbarians react to Roman weakness?

ALTERNATIVE TWO: Decline and Fall

Based on *The Civilization of Rome* by Donald R. Dudley (1962)

Our own times understand technology, if nothing else, and there were certainly grave weaknesses in the technology of the Roman Empire. Judged by modern standards, there was little general advance in the five centuries after Rome had taken over the technology of the Hellenistic world. Large-scale exploitation, not advances in technique, was the strong point of the Romans. No doubt this stagnation can be partly explained by the influence of slavery. By providing a cheap and expendable supply of human labor, slavery discourages invention, which tends to replace human labor by the machine. In all periods of history slavery has affected enterprise and efficiency as deeply as it has morals and humanity. And yet slavery cannot be the whole answer. The number of slaves in the Roman world declined after the great wars of conquest under the Republic. There were no more slave markets on the scale of Delos in the Aegean. The early Empire is marked by the increased use of free rather than slave labor. This, and the economic boom of the period, should have provided conditions to suit the inventor. But there was no large-scale advance—certainly nothing to equal even the earliest phases of the Industrial Revolution. It is not enough to ascribe this to the Roman bent for the practical and dislike of theory. Some of the inventions that would have been of most benefit to the Roman world were precisely those which might have been expected from men of practical skill. Why did none of the thousands of Roman teamsters invent a harness that would not half-strangle a draft animal by pulling on its windpipe? Why was there no improvement in the clumsy rigging of Roman ships? Above all, why did no employee of a Roman mint ever take the easy step from stamping to printing—a discovery which would have been of incalculable importance to the spread of knowledge? There is something here as hard to explain as the failure of Peruvian civilization to invent the wheel.

Partly, no doubt, this failure in technology is bound up with the failure in education. Despite the patronage of the emperors and the eagerness of the municipalities to found and maintain schools, education under the Empire was neither sufficiently wide nor sufficiently deep. It was certainly a grave weakness that natural science and practical subjects were neglected, but it is not enough to say that the Romans were satisfied with a mere literary education. The real weakness was the undue attention paid to rhetoric and this was due to a short-sighted preference for the form of vocational training which seemed to offer the quickest way to success. Roman education produced lawyers, administrators, and teachers of rhetoric. In doing so it gave them considerable power of expression, some feeling for literature, and the rudiments of an education in morals. But it failed to stimulate intellectual curiosity, and it added nothing to knowledge.

More obvious are certain political and military weaknesses. The failure to establish a lasting and generally accepted basis for the succession of emperors stands out. Had the hereditary principle been accepted, it would no doubt have produced many weak or vicious emperors. But it would have been a principle that all could understand, and usurpers would have been seen for what they were. Had the principle of adoption been accepted for the succession of emperors, palace intrigues rather than arms of the battlefield would more likely have settled the issue. But the Romans did not consistently follow either system, and so often got the worst of both worlds. Hereditary succession produced some bad emperors in the first century. A disputed succession, especially after the time of Commodus, led to many struggles which gravely weakened the state, and not only in loss of manpower and material resources. The army became corrupted by the discovery that it was more profitable to plunder the civilized world than to defend it against the barbarians. Little more than a century separates the unruly army of Maximinus Thrace from that of Trajan, but they were poles apart in discipline, morale and fighting spirit.

In any case the system of defense against the barbarian world established by Augustus would only work so long as Rome retained a clear military advantage over her enemies. Things do not stand still on a frontier. The barbarians would become Romanized, at least in the sense that they understood Roman methods of warfare; the barbarians Arminius and Alaric both served in the Roman army. And the Roman army itself became increasingly barbarian in its personnel—even, in the fourth century, in the higher command. Under such circumstances Roman superiority could only have been maintained by greatly superior technical resources such as the use of firearms. It is true that various ballistic devices in the third and fourth centuries gave it a superiority of a kind, but not sufficiently effective to give a decisive margin over the enemy. By the middle of the fourth century an army of Goths, Vandals, or Huns could take the field against the Roman army on at least equal terms. Even at that stage the Empire must have had far superior resources of manpower, but these could not be mobilized and brought into action without increasing the already-staggering burden of taxation.

Crippling taxation was only one of the burdens which the late Empire imposed on its citizens. From the time of Diocletian on it had degenerated into a totalitarian state, controlling and directing all activities in its own interest. The agents of the state were everywhere; its regulations covered every side of life. Frozen into their hereditary occupations, struggling under the twin burdens of taxes and inflation, further harassed by incessant demands for loans, gifts, and labor, exposed to the greed of an army of corrupt officials, the citizens of the late Empire had neither the means nor the motive to better their lot. The emperors of the third and fourth century had no choice but to act as they did if the state was to survive. Their reforms did indeed make survival possible, for a time, but at the terrible price of the destruction of all enterprise and public spirit. The citizen was reduced to a helpless individual to whom the state and its agents were not responsible. The barbarians must often have seemed preferable to the officials of Rome. The excessive demands of the state were, without doubt, the chief cause of the final downfall of the West.

Since these conditions also existed in the East, the question arises as to why there was no such collapse there. It is clear that the main force of the barbarian invasions fell on the West, which had to face the worst assaults of the Goths and the Huns. There are no parallels in the East to the Frankish kingdom in Gaul, and those of the Vandals in Spain and Africa. Above all, the comparative immunity of Asia Minor meant that the East had a reserve of manpower and material resources such as Italy could not afford to the West. From this springboard in the East, Justinian, in the early sixth century, launched the great offensives which offered a brief hope of the restoration of the Empire.

QUESTIONS

1. a) Why did the Romans fail to make any major advances in technology?
   b) What inventions might have been of great benefit to the Romans if they had been made?
2. Why did the failure to find an acceptable basis for the succession of emperors cause such a problem for the Roman Empire?
3. Why did the Roman army gradually lose its military superiority over the barbarians?
4. Describe the impact on the Roman Empire of the heavy taxation begun by Diocletian.
5. Why did the Western Empire collapse in the fifth century while the Eastern Empire continued to prosper?

ALTERNATIVE THREE: The Later Roman Empire

Based on *History of the Later Roman Empire* by J.B. Bury (1923)

No general causes can be assigned that made the fall of the Western Empire inevitable. Consider depopulation [the decline in population levels]. The depopulation of Italy was an important factor and it had far-reaching consequences. But it was a process which had probably reached its limit in the time of Augustus. There is no evidence that the Empire was less populous in the fourth and fifth centuries than in the first. The "sterility of the human harvest" in Italy and Greece affected the history of the Empire from its very beginning, but does not explain the collapse in the fifth century.

There are really two distinct questions here which are often confused. It is one thing to seek the causes that *changed* the Roman state from what it was in the Republic to what it had become in the later Empire—a change which may be called a "decline". But it is another thing to ask why the Roman state could resist its enemies on many frontiers in the fourth century under Diocletian and Constantine and then give way a century later in the days of Honorius. "Depopulation" may partly answer the first question, but it is not an answer to the second.

Nor can the event which transferred the greater part of western Europe to German masters be accounted for by the number of peoples who invaded it. The notion of vast hordes of warriors, numbered by hundreds of thousands, pouring over frontiers, is perfectly untrue. The total number of one of the large East German nations probably seldom exceeded 100,000 and its army of fighting men can rarely have been more than from 20,000 to 30,000. They were not a deluge, overwhelming and irresistible, and the Empire had a well-organized military establishment, fully sufficient in capable hands to beat them back. As a matter of fact, since the defeat at Adrianople in A.D. 378 which was due to the blunders of Valens, no very important battle was won by German over Imperial Roman forces during the whole course of the invasions.

It has often been alleged that Christianity in its political effects was a disintegrating force and tended to weaken the power of Rome to resist her enemies. It is difficult to see that it had any such tendency, so long as the Church itself was united. In the political calculations of Constantine, it was probably this ideal of unity that was so appealing. As a result, he raised the Christian religion to power to offset other forces that threatened to break up the Empire. Early in the fifth century, a pagan senator posed the question whether the teaching of Christianity is not fatal to the welfare of the state because a Christian smitten on one cheek would have to turn the other cheek as indicated in the Gospel. In a skilfully written reply, Augustine, a leading Father of the Church, suggested that those who wage a just war are really acting in a spirit of mercy and kindness to their enemies, as it is to the true interests of their enemies that their vices should be corrected. Unintentionally, by stating that the Christian discipline does not condemn all wars, Augustine had argued that Christians were bound as much as pagans to defend Rome against the barbarians. All the leading Churchmen of the fifth century were devoted to the Imperial idea and when they worked for peace or compromise, as they often did, it was always when the cause of the barbarians was in the ascendant and resistance seemed hopeless.

The truth is that the gradual collapse of the Roman Empire in the West was the result of a series of unpredictable or contingent events.

The first such event was the irruption of the Huns into Europe, an event resulting from causes which were quite independent of the weakness or strength of the Roman Empire. It drove the Visigoths into the Illyrian provinces of the Empire and the difficult situation was mismanaged. Emperor Valens lost his life as a result of his own errors when Rome suffered defeat at Adrianople. That disaster, which need not have occurred, was a second unpredictable event. Valens's successor, Theodosius I, allowed the Goths to settle south of the Danube on Roman soil, which set an unfortunate precedent. Barbarians, with Roman consent, were now living within the Empire as well as pressuring Roman resistance from the outside. The premature death of Theodosius could not have been foreseen and would not have mattered if a strong emperor had succeeded to power. The government of the West, however, was inherited by a feeble-minded boy named Honorius. That was a fourth event, dependent on causes which had nothing to do with the conditions within the Empire.

In themselves, even these events need not have led to disaster. If the guardian of Honorius and director of his government had been a man of Roman birth and tradition who commanded the public confidence, all might have been tolerably well. But there was a point of weakness in the Imperial system, the practice of elevating Germans to the highest posts of command in the army. The German in whom Theodosius reposed his confidence and who assumed the control of affairs on his death was a Romanized German named Stilicho. Although Stilicho probably believed that he was serving Rome faithfully, it was a singular misfortune that at a critical moment when the Empire had to be defended not only against Germans from without but against a German nation which had penetrated inside, the responsibility should have devolved upon a German. Stilicho continued the policy of barbarian settlement on Roman land and even allowed Huns to serve as auxiliary troops in the army. Invading tribes freely roamed the countryside and when Stilicho died the Goths had Italy at their mercy while Gaul and Spain were overrun by other peoples. His Roman successors could not undo the results of events which need never have happened.

The supremacy of Stilicho was due to the fact that the defence of the Empire had come to depend on the enrolment of barbarians, in large numbers, in the army and that it was necessary to render the service attractive to them by the prospect of wealth and power. This was, of course, a consequence of the decline in military spirit, and of depopulation, in the old civilised Mediterranean countries. The Germans in high command had been useful, but the dangers of such a policy were becoming apparent. Yet this policy need not have led to the dismemberment of the Empire, and but for that series of chances its western provinces would not have been converted, as and when they were, into German kingdoms. It may be said that a German penetration of western Europe must ultimately have come about. But even if that were certain, it might have happened in another way, at a later time, more gradually, and with less violence. Rome's loss of her provinces in the fifth century was not inevitable and might not have occurred but for the sequence of unpredictable events pointed out above.

From J.B. Bury, *History of the Later Roman Empire* (London, rev. ed., 1923), vol. 1. Reprinted by permission of Macmillan & Co. Ltd.

QUESTIONS

1. a) To what extent did depopulation and Christianity affect the survival of the Western Roman Empire? Explain your answer.
   b) What two distinct questions must be considered when examining the fate of the Western Empire?
2. a) What does Bury mean by the term "contingent events"?
   b) What were the six contingent events that Bury identified in the sequence leading to the collapse of the Western Empire?
3. To what extent does Bury's view of the decline of Rome agree with the explanations given in Alternative One and Two? Explain your answer.

ANSWERING THE PROBLEM QUESTION

A **causal question** is a question about why something happened the way it did. Causal questions are a crucial part of historical study. The problem question for this chapter—Why did the Roman Empire falter?—is a particularly broad causal question. Of course, the fate of an entire civilization can rarely be reduced to a single cause. Usually a broad question such as this one involves **multiple causation**; several factors, operating in combination, best explain why things occurred in a certain way. To answer the problem question, you will have to take into account the many possible causes of the decline of Rome that were cited in the chapter and in the alternatives. The causes must be identified, related to each other, and ranked on the basis of the evidence presented.

Unfortunately, there is no magic formula that, if carefully applied, will guarantee the right answer to a causal question. It is not possible to say for certain that B was caused by A, and that if someone had only done C, then D would have happened instead. For such a formula to work, people would have to be entirely predictable, but human behaviour is not governed by a rigid set of laws. It is possible, however, to analyse a set of factors and present a meaningful explanation of why something *might* have taken place. Because such conclusions are based on certain *assumptions*, they are usually phrased tentatively rather than in absolute terms that leave no room for additional consideration.

THE STORY CONTINUES . . .

The Early Middle Ages (A.D. 476-1000)

The end of Rome's Western Empire dates from A.D. 476, when Odoacer broke the succession of Roman emperors. Between that time and the beginning of the Modern Age, which dates from about A.D. 1500, lies a time known today as the **Middle Ages**. (The term **medieval period** is also used.) The Middle Ages are further divided into three periods: the **Early Middle Ages** (A.D. 476-1000), the **High Middle Ages** (A.D. 1000-1300), and the **Late Middle Ages** (A.D. 1300-1500).

More to Consider

Until recently, the Early Middle Ages were referred to as the **Dark Ages**. There were two main reasons for the label. First, relatively little was known about the period. Second, the barbarian cultures were felt to be inferior to that of the Romans. It is true that the barbarians did not have the engineering, literary, or organizational sophistication the Romans had developed. But as historians have learned more about this period, it has become clear that the barbarians possessed a complex culture of their own. Moreover, Roman culture did not simply give way to barbarian culture; it would be more accurate to say that Roman, Christian, and barbarian cultures mixed together. This mixture provided the basis for the emergence of European civilization. As a result, the so-called Dark Ages have come to be regarded as the first half of the Middle Ages between Rome and the modern world.

Developing an Answer to a Causal Question

The following guide represents one way you can develop an answer to a causal question involving multiple causation. Of course the guide has to be adjusted to suit the specific issue being studied. A systematic approach will help you to organize the major elements of your argument.

1. List all the major events or facts that could be used to answer the question. These are the multiple causes of the phenomenon you are trying to explain.
In the case of the problem question, the events would be identified from the chapter and the three alternatives.

2. Classify the events or facts under major headings or criteria.
For this problem question, you might use these criteria: political, military, economic, and social.

Political	Military	Economic	Social
event a	event c	event b	event e
event d	event g	event f	event h
event i	event k	event j	event l
event p	event m	event n	event o
event p	event q	event r	event s
event t	event u	event v	event w

3. Now, classify the events or facts listed under each criterion by using the subheads *long term* and *short term*. Deciding whether an event or a fact is of long-term or short-term importance is a matter of judgment. Usually, long-term considerations are those conditions that existed for most of the time frame under discussion. Short-term considerations are usually those conditions that represent a specific peak or climax in a long-term trend, or events that brought an immediate, often unforeseen, change in the situation.

In the case of this problem question, the long-term causes might be measured in centuries while the short-term causes might be measured in decades. Your classification chart would then look something like this:

	Political	Military	Economic	Social
Long	event a	event c	event b	event e
Term	event i	event m	event f	event l
	event u	event s	event p	event w
Short	event d	event k	event j	event h
Term	event p	event g	event n	event o
	event t	event q	event v	event r

4. The next step is to rank each of the events or facts in the order of its importance. Assign a "one" to the most important, a "two" to the second most important, and so on. Rank the long-term group and the short-term group separately under each criterion.
Your chart might now look something like this:

		Political	Military	Economic	Social
Long	1	event a	event m	event b	event l
Term	2	event u	event c	event f	event e
	3	event i	event s	event p	event w
Short	1	event t	event k	event j	event h
Term	2	event p	event g	event v	event o
	3	event d	event q	event n	event r

5. Now, you must decide which of the major headings or criteria is most important, which is second most important, and so on. You must be able to explain your reasons for the order you have selected.

	A Military	B Political	C Economic	D Social
Long 1	event m	event a	event b	event l
Term 2	event c	event u	event f	event e
3	event s	event i	event p	event w
Short 1	event k	event t	event j	event h
Term 2	event g	event p	event v	event o
3	event q	event d	event n	event r

6. At this stage you have identified a number of events or facts that contributed to the end result you are trying to explain. For each criteria, you have established which were the most important long-term and short-term causes. You have ranked the criteria in order of importance. You have therefore achieved a *very rough* ranking of the causes. Since events and facts do not occur in isolation, you must figure out how the different causes are related to one another, and which causes are most important. There is no easy way to do this work. You must consider each cause in turn, trying to link it with the others. You might find it useful to create branching diagrams to organize your ideas.

In the case of the problem question, you might develop one or more diagrams like the one below.

Based on the interrelationships you identified, you might decide that Short-term Military event k was a principal cause of the Empire's decline.

7. In most cases, a thorough study of the interrelationships will give you a framework on which you can base a reasoned conclusion. It is possible, however, that the above process might leave some major questions unaddressed or unanswered. If you become aware of such a question, you may have to conduct further research and analysis. Then you can proceed to answer the problem question.

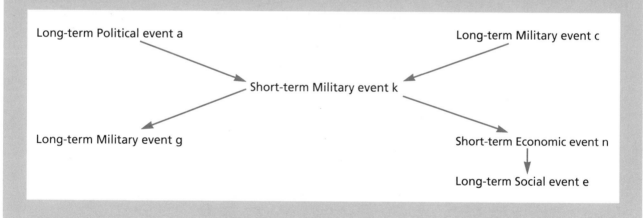

To the average Roman of the time, the date A.D. 476 had little significance. There had already been a century of chaos, conflict, and change. Of greater impact was the physical and symbolic demise of the Eternal City itself as different groups of marauders invaded throughout the sixth and seventh centuries. The Roman population was drastically reduced through war, plague, and the destruction of the aqueducts. When Totilla, a barbarian invader, entered Rome in A.D. 546, he found only five hundred people. The half-deserted city, once the centre of the civilized world, was looted of its bronze statues, artwork, and pride. Its now-roofless buildings began to crumble. Although, from the outside the Colosseum was still a showpiece of architecture, grass had begun to grow over its empty seats.

The barbarians who infiltrated the weakened Western Empire were mainly an illiterate, artistically limited, agrarian people. They brought with them their own pagan deities and religious practices. Their impact was both immediate and long lasting. They moved into what is now northern Europe, either squeezing out the inhabitants they encountered or taking possession of lands through conquest. To the south, the barbarians, though dominant in war, were less numerous and they shared the land with the original inhabitants, whose lives they had so drastically changed. This difference between north and south is reflected in Europe's population today.

The Roman roads were neglected and sometimes even deliberately destroyed for building materials, in turn eradicating the commercial patterns the Romans had developed. Towns decayed and were often reclaimed by the forest. This was a time of confusion, without central laws or administration, in which the local village became the focal point of social and economic life. Instead of having a surplus of food for trade, farmers tried desperately to produce enough food to survive.

The German barbarians were organized into war bands or tribes, each headed by a chieftain of its own choosing. When a major decision had to be made, proposals were presented to a general assembly or council of men of military age. Acceptance was signified by the clashing of spears on shields. When a chieftain planned a military action, he established a *comitatus*, a special band of warriors. They swore their personal allegiance to the chieftain,

Barbarian Gods

Germanic Gods	Symbol	Function	Day of the Week
Tieu	spear	god of the sky	Tieu's day
Wodan	black horse and wolf	god of the underworld	Wodan's day
Thor	hammer	god of thunder	Thor's day
Freya	seated goddess with fruit, bread, or horn of plenty	goddess of fertility and bounty	Freya's day

and he in return promised to share the spoils of battle. At first, each *comitatus* was a temporary arrangement, but over time they became permanent. The democratic tribal councils were thus replaced by what was, in effect, an aristocracy.

As the barbarians advanced, the system of Roman law that had prevailed throughout the Empire broke down. Justice, where it could be enforced, was administered in one of two ways, by **oath** or by **ordeal**. The swearing of oaths was allowed for a lesser offence—a person could be cleared by having friends and neighbours swear that he or she was honourable and innocent. This practice of listening to testimony before passing sentence provided the basis of the jury system of later centuries. A person accused of a more serious crime, however, would undergo trial by ordeal. The "Judgment of God" was determined by the accused's success at certain experiments using fire, water, or combat. The ordeal by fire, for example, required that the accused carry a red-hot iron for a specified distance or walk barefoot and blindfolded across red-hot ploughshares. The hand or foot was bound up for three days, then unbandaged and inspected. If the wounds were healing, the accused was pronounced innocent; if the wounds were festering, the accused was judged to be guilty. The use of ordeal was continuous in England until the middle of the thirteenth century, although it seems to have been abolished earlier throughout most of the continent.

The Emergence of Feudalism in the Early Middle Ages

In the lawless countryside of Europe, no one was safe from common thieves, barbaric chieftains, and looting invaders. For their own protection, individuals were forced to associate themselves with the most powerful man in the district. These powerful men, in turn, associated themselves with men who were even more powerful. The relationship between **lords** (higher ranking) and **vassals** (lower ranking) provided the structure of what is known as **feudalism**.

In the chains of association and obligation that developed, someone who owned a horse was more desirable than a **peasant**, who had virtually nothing to offer but physical labour. The importance of the horse in battle had increased with the successes of mounted barbarians against the rather undisciplined legions of the late Roman Empire. Now the mounted soldier, or **knight**, steadied on his steed by a stirrup, became the most sought-after military weapon. From the knight with a single horse rose a hierarchy of **barons**, **counts**, and **dukes**. The higher a man's position on the hierarchy, the larger the army of knights he could command. This army would be promised, in turn, to the person who ranked immediately above. All people of rank were vassals to the king, who could command their services in time of need.

At the heart of the feudal relationship was the **feud**, or **fief**. This feud was usually a grant of land given by a lord in return for a vassal's military service and other duties determined by local custom. The agreement

The Feudal Pyramid. The feudal order was a political and social pyramid. Feudal territories ranged in size from local estates of a few square kilometres to large kingdoms of thousands of square kilometres.

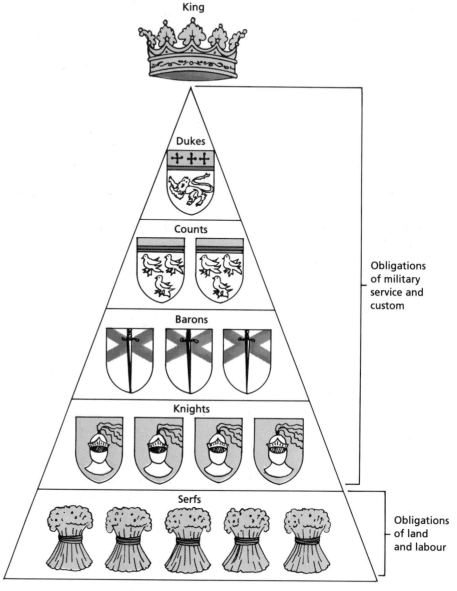

King

Dukes

Counts

Barons

Knights

Serfs

Obligations of military service and custom

Obligations of land and labour

between lord and vassal was made in a formal ceremony, during which the vassal swore that he would be personally loyal to his lord. This was the vassal's **oath of homage**. The vassal made this promise while kneeling, with his hands between his lord's hands. The lord accepted this promise of **fealty** (allegiance) with a kiss. To symbolize the bond between them, the lord gave the vassal a staff of wood or a clump of earth.

A new vassal kneels before his lord to take his oaths of homage and fealty.

The Early Middle Ages

A.D.	
480-543	Early Middle Ages begin Saint Benedict revives early Christian institution of the monastery
527-565	Reign of Justinian Golden age of Byzantine Empire in the East
622	Hegira of Muhammad from Mecca to Medina
732	Charles Martel stops Muslim advance into Europe at Tours
800	Charlemagne crowned by Pope Leo III
843	Treaty of Verdun divides kingdom of Charlemagne
800-1000	Muslims and Magyars threaten Vikings raid coasts of Europe from Ireland to Spain, and France, Russia, and Constantinople
1000	Old Western Roman Empire blossoms into a new civilization, Europe

Most vassals were men. In families without male heirs, female offspring had inheritance rights. A woman also inherited her husband's land when he died. But it was uncommon for a young woman or a widow to remain unmarried for long, especially if she held title to property. Once a woman was married, control of her lands passed to her husband.

At the lowest level of feudal society were the **serfs**, or **villeins**. These peasants worked the land on the **manors**—the estates owned by members of the nobility. A serf owed no military service to the lord. Instead, serfs were obliged to till the lord's land, use the lord's mill, fish in the lord's streams, hunt in the lord's forest, and worship in the manor church. For each opportunity, the serf paid rent, tax, or a **tithe**. (A tithe was a tax of one-tenth of the profits from the produce of a piece of land. It was paid to the Church.) The serf was also subject to the **corvée**, a term of unpaid labour occasionally required for maintaining roads and ditches on the manor. When a serf died, even a death tax (a *mortuarium*) had to be paid to the lord! A wealthy baron might own several manors, which were administered by a lesser vassal known as an **overseer**. Each manor was directed by a **bailiff**, who reported to the overseer as the overseer travelled about inspecting the manors of his domain. When disputes arose, cases were heard in the baron's court, and the serf had to pay a fee for this service as well.

Feudal society worked because people of all ranks, from the lowliest serf to the highest noble, fulfilled their promises to one another. In a world without a public legal system, society depended on mutual obligations and co-operation. These bonds were strong enough to hold together entire kingdoms. By the year 1000, feudal states, ranging in size from isolated castles to great kingdoms, such as Normandy, Burgundy, Saxony, and Bavaria, spread across Europe.

The Byzantine Empire

In contrast to the disintegration of Rome and its Western Empire, the Eastern Empire continued to flourish and survive under a succession of emperors until 1453. It was called the **Byzantine Empire** because Constantinople, the magnificent capital established by Constantine, was founded on the site of the earlier city of Byzantium. Constantinople was at the crossroads of trade routes from all directions, by land and water. As a result, the Byzantine Empire developed a blend of Hellenic and Asian culture. The golden age of the Byzantine Empire was ushered in with the reign of Justinian (527-565).

Justinian's ambition was to restore the glory of the old Roman Empire and maintain the unity of the Christian Church. In the West, North Africa, Italy, Greece, the Mediterranean islands, and part of Spain were reconquered from the barbarians. The collected treasure of generations and continued heavy taxation enabled Justinian to make Constantinople a centre of astounding wealth and opulence. Chariot races in the sixty-thousand seat

Hagia Sophia. This church was completed in five years with the labour of ten thousand workers. It is dominated by a central dome 32 m wide and 49 m high and is lighted by a base of arched windows that rests upon a second dome, which stretches to the ground. Hagia Sophia served as a basilica for 916 years and as a mosque for 477 years before being converted to a museum in 1930.

Hippodrome became the main attraction for public entertainment, but the architectural and spiritual wonder was the great church of Hagia Sophia ("Holy Wisdom"). Its walls were decorated with brilliant mosaics, gold leaf, coloured marble, silver, and ivory. Emperors were baptized, crowned, and married there.

Of perhaps even greater importance than Justinian's expansion of the Empire was his decision to establish a commission of ten jurists to study and clarify the confused mass of custom, statute, decree, and judicial ruling that made up Roman law. The product of their efforts was the **Body of Civil Law**. The Romans had determined that the principles of justice should be applied without prejudice to all cases; that the accused person had a right to defend her or himself before being sentenced; that the prosecution must prove guilt rather than the accused person prove his or her innocence; and that the spirit is more important than the letter of the law. These and other principles of Roman law were preserved in the Eastern Empire's Body of Civil Law, and eventually became the basis of legal codes in many modern societies, including France, Spain, countries in Latin America, the state of Louisiana, and the province of Québec.

The majesty of Justinian did not long survive his death. The gains in the West were completely lost by the eighth century, while pressure from Persians, Slavs, and Bulgars threatened closer to home. Nevertheless, the values of the Greek and Roman civilizations were sustained in the Byzantine Empire during the time when barbarian invasions were destroying those traditions in most of Europe.

Islam

In the seventh century, however, a force emerged from the life of a single person that changed the course of the Byzantine Empire. That person was Muhammad, an Arab born in 570 in the city of Mecca, now in Saudi Arabia. He was an orphan by the time he was six, and other members of his family took over his upbringing. Eventually he was sent to live among the Bedouins, nomadic traders who were a key part of the economic life of the Middle East. Muhammad was a shepherd first, and then became a servant and caravan agent for a wealthy woman whom he fell in love with and later married. Although he was illiterate, he was an eloquent speaker. His reputation for objectivity and honesty was captured in his nickname—Al Amin, "the trustworthy."

During his caravan journeys, he met both Jews and Christians and became greatly impressed by **monotheism**, the belief in one God. At about the age of forty, Muhammad experienced visions in which the angel Gabriel spoke to him in the name of God. At first, he shared his visions only with his wife and friends, but then he began to preach. He presented himself as a prophet of God, insisting that he was human, not divine. His teachings stated that there was only one God, creator of the world and sovereign over all peoples, no matter what their origin. Unfortunately for Muhammad,

Religion

Muslims (those who practise Islam) believe that all people who believe in God and accept Muhammad's teachings will be treated equally. There are four other religious requirements. A Muslim must pray five times daily, kneeling and facing the Holy City of Mecca. A Muslim must also give alms to the poor, fast during daylight throughout the month of Ramadan, and, where possible, make at least one pilgrimage to Mecca during her or his lifetime. Idol worship, gambling, and the consumption of alcohol and pork are prohibited.

Just as Christianity absorbed a large part of Judaism, including God and the prophets, so Islam absorbed a large part of both religions. Muslims, for example, acknowledge the authenticity of the prophets who appear in Hebrew scripture—Abraham, Jacob, Moses, and so on. In addition, they believe that Jesus was also a prophet but was not the son of God, as Christians maintain. Judaism, Christianity, and Islam all have their roots in Semitic religious experience.

Mecca was a desert city recently settled by Bedouin tribes who worshipped many gods. When Muhammad began to speak publicly, he was persecuted for his faith and in 622 was forced to leave.

Muhammad and his followers received an unexpected invitation from the religiously divided city of Medina. Muhammad sent his disciples to Medina ahead of him, then went to the city himself in triumph later in 622. The flight from Mecca to Medina is called the **Hegira**, an event so significant to those who follow the religion of **Islam** that it marks the beginning of their calendar. The teachings of Muhammad spread rapidly and, after a series of brief hostilities, he returned in honour to Mecca in 630.

Islam was the third great religion, after Judaism and Christianity, to adopt monotheism. The word *Islam* comes from an Arabic word meaning "peace." Followers of Islam achieve spiritual peace by willingly submitting their lives to God's will. God's will is known through Muhammad's teachings, which were first memorized and then written down in the **Qur'an**, Islam's holy book. (Muhammad is not regarded as the author of the Qur'an. The Qur'an is the actual word of God as revealed to Muhammad.) The success of Islam was partly a result of the clear set of beliefs it offered, a coherent alternative to the bewildering variety of religious practices and deities that dominated the region. Islam had no priests or ministers or complicated symbolism. The ethical component of Islam was equally important. Many Islamic teachings emphasized kind and considerate behaviour to all people, including the poor.

Calligraphy (elegant handwriting) is an important part of Muslim culture. These pages from the Qur'an, which originated in what is now Iran in the 10th century, show a fine example of the calligrapher's art.

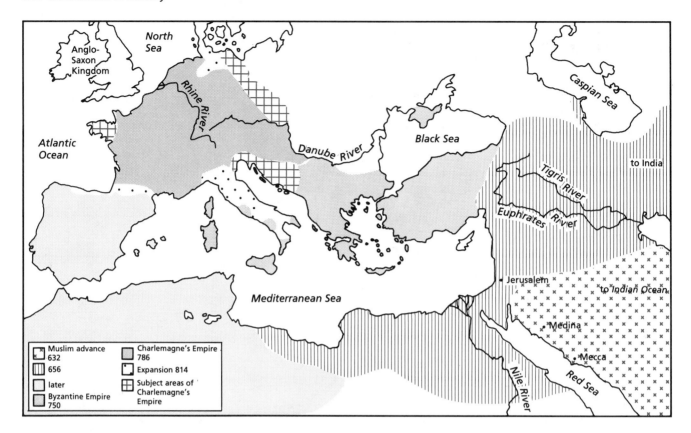

Europe in the Early Middle Ages.

Muhammad managed to gain the allegiance of most Arab tribes. After his death in 632, his successors reimposed this accord, and Islam united the Arab world. Over the next one hundred years, the Arabs used their military skill to build a Muslim Empire that stretched from the steppes of Russia to North Africa and Spain, drastically reducing the size of the Byzantine Empire. The Muslim advance, comparable in scale to that of Alexander, was stopped only by the leader of the Germanic Franks, Charles Martel, at the Battle of Tours in 732. Arab civilization left its rich cultural imprint on the lands it conquered, spreading knowledge about architecture, mathematics, astronomy, and medicine.

The Christian Church in the Early Middle Ages

Christianity went through many changes in the five centuries after the time Jesus journeyed the lands of Judea as a charismatic preacher. By the beginning of the Early Middle Ages, the institution of the Christian Church was well established. At first, those who founded and presided over Christian communities were helped in their work by respected Christians known as **bishops**. The prestige and power of the bishops increased with the size of their church congregations. As a result, the bishops working in large cities dominated those working in smaller communities. By the fourth century, five bishops who headed churches in the capital cities of the Roman provinces had become the most powerful and were known as **patriarchs**.

As Christianity spread, different religious practices developed in different regions. To keep the church from fracturing, the Roman emperor Constantine called the First Council of Nicaea in A.D. 325. Over three hundred bishops attended. Those from Rome insisted on their supremacy, because Jesus had identified Peter as his successor on earth, and Peter had become the first bishop of Rome. Each succeeding bishop of Rome had assumed the same power. Certain bishops from the Eastern Roman Empire disputed the supremacy of the Roman bishop, but the fact that Rome had been the capital of the Empire for so long and continued as the capital of the West helped support the Roman position. By the fifth century, the bishop of Rome had assumed the title of **pope**, or "father of the Church." The Church in the West became wealthy and strong.

The moral direction of Christianity from the fifth century onward was established to a large extent by Saint Augustine of Hippo in his most famous work, *The City of God*. He wrote it to defend the Church against the charge that Christianity was responsible for the decline of Rome. As part of his argument, Saint Augustine asserted that the city of Rome was unimportant. He claimed that life on earth was best seen as a preparation for life after death in heaven. This vision of Christian life provided direction to all Christians, especially to the monks.

As a formal organization, however, the Church was less unified. The regional differences that Constantine had tried to solve remained. There were long-running disputes over many key religious concepts, practices, and events. Not surprisingly, the major divisions of the Church reflected the political divisions of the crumbling Roman Empire. **Roman Catholicism**, based in Rome, dominated the faltering Western Empire, while the **Eastern Orthodox Church**, with its capital in Constantinople, dominated first the Eastern Roman Empire and then the Byzantine Empire that followed. The official split between the two Churches, known as the **East-West Schism**, did not occur until 1054, but the Church had become quite fragmented long before.

In the West, the Roman Catholic Church was the only unifying force that endured the barbarian advance and the subsequent political and economic disintegration of the Roman world. The Church survived partly because its structure mirrored the hierarchy that Imperial Rome had used. Rome had its emperor; the Catholic Church had its pope. The Roman Empire was divided into provinces administered by governors, and cities run by magistrates; the Roman Catholic world was organized into provinces, dioceses, and parishes under the respective responsibility of archbishops, bishops, and parish priests. But the Church improved on the Roman model in one important respect.

Religion

The growing wealth and worldliness of the Church was criticized by some, who felt that a meditative life organized around strict regulation of silence, obedience, labour, and religious devotion was closer to the real meaning of Christian faith. Such Christians lived in **monasteries** that contained only the necessities of life. The most influential figure in Western monasticism was Saint Benedict. He established a set of regulations called the **Rule**. His code appealed to many, encouraging the spread of monasticism throughout Europe. In fact, some isolated monasteries in France and Corfu still observe the rules laid down almost fifteen hundred years ago.

The Church for the most part solved the problem of transferring power smoothly from one leader to another. An emperor's death often resulted in chaos that only the army could resolve. In contrast, the College of Cardinals, made up of the pope's leading advisers, elected a new pope upon the death of the old, as it still does today.

The Church not only provided a unifying force in the West, it also safeguarded some aspects of Roman culture for future generations. During the Early Middle Ages, the few men who received formal education were usually trained in a monastery (by the sixth century) or in a cathedral school (by the eighth century). The Catholic Church continued to teach Latin, the language of the Western Empire, and actively studied the major works of Roman literature. In damp, cold, dimly lighted rooms, monks spent countless hours handcopying Roman manuscripts, preserving achievements that would otherwise have been lost. The Church also provided education in a more widespread, less formal way. The intimate contact of the parish priest with his parishioners, through work and prayer, made him their teacher as well as their spiritual leader.

The Church fulfilled one other unifying role in the West. It administered its own law, known as **canon law**, which was strongly influenced by Roman precedent and jurisprudence. Many of the day-to-day matters that are now settled in civil courts were handled by the Church, the influence of which touched almost every part of a person's life.

Charlemagne

Since the days of Clovis, at the turn of the sixth century, Frankish leaders in Gaul had assisted the Catholic Church and had encouraged subject peoples to convert to Christianity. At times, the Franks were the only strong Christian community to support the papacy. A series of weak, often corrupt, Frankish rulers in the seventh century—when a court official known as the "mayor of the palace" ran Frankish Gaul—resulted in even more power and prestige for the papacy in everyday affairs.

This balance of power between Church and state began to shift with the rule of Charles Martel in the eighth century. Martel was the head of the **Carolingians**, a powerful Frankish family that gradually took control of the country. He introduced the feudal concept of land grants in return for military service, and he stopped the Muslim advance into Europe at the Battle of Tours in 732. But to raise money for his military actions, Charles repossessed lands given to the Church.

His son, Pepin the Short, was more co-operative with the Church. He even protected the pope from attack by the **Lombards**, an aggressive people moving through Italy. Pepin defeated the Lombards and gave some of their land (known afterwards as the Papal States) to the Church. In return, the Church recognized him as the king of the Franks. This blending of Christian authority with the traditions of the Germanic Franks paved the way for Pepin's son, Charlemagne, to try to re-establish the old Roman Empire.

The eagles and fleur-de-lis represented on the cloak of Charlemagne became the symbols of Germany and France. Both countries claim Charlemagne as their founding father.

Charlemagne's favourite book was Saint Augustine's *City of God*, and no doubt he saw himself as the city's architect on earth. A natural leader and brilliant military strategist, Charlemagne waged at least fifty-three campaigns against the pagans, although his methods certainly contradicted the principles of his religion. For example, the troublesome Saxons, like other pagan peoples he conquered, were offered the choice between baptism and death. Their rejection of baptism led to forty-five hundred executions in a single day. Between 768 and 814, Charlemagne gained control of a territory that stretched from the Baltic to the Pyrenees and from the Balkans to the Atlantic. State and Church marched together throughout the realm in Charlemagne's scheme of operations. He shrewdly administered his lands by dividing territory into counties run by counts and bishops. Special agents were sent annually to inspect local operations.

Because the pope needed his protection against possible attacks from the Lombards and the Muslims, Charlemagne had considerable power over Church affairs. In return, Charlemagne sent money to Christians in other lands and enforced the collection of tithes for the Church. During the mass of Christmas Day in the year 800, Pope Leo III suddenly placed a crown on Charlemagne's head while the large congregation cried out, "Long life and victory to Charles Augustus, great and peace-making emperor of the Romans, crowned by God!" The chorus was repeated twice more in ancient Roman fashion. Although Charlemagne acted surprised, it is likely that he and Leo had prearranged the event.

Although the coronation recognized Charlemagne as the most powerful king in Europe, the fact that the pope handed the crown to him implied that the Church was the supreme authority, a view Charlemagne did not accept. To settle any future doubts about the relationship between state and Church, Charlemagne instructed his son to crown himself when the time came.

Charlemagne successfully embodied the traditions of the Christian Church, Germanic kings, and Roman emperors. The Byzantine emperors initially resisted his position as emperor, but in 812, after years of turmoil, they accepted Charlemagne as a co-emperor.

Muslims, Magyars, and Vikings

After Charlemagne's death in 814, the Carolingian Empire began to dissolve as his less-able grandsons fought over their inheritance. The **Treaty of Verdun**, in 843, divided the kingdom into sections from which the modern states of France and Germany eventually emerged. This division, however, came at an unfortunate time. Europe was once again under siege from almost every quarter. The Muslims threatened in southern Italy and France, while the **Magyars**—a Turkish people—moved across the Danube into Germany, but the **Vikings**, a Germanic people from Scandinavia, were the most destructive force.

Treaty of Verdun, 843.

The Vikings launched their raiding expeditions partly because of their desire for adventure, exploration, and booty. But food shortages were probably the most important factor. The Vikings were forced to expand their territory in the eighth and ninth centuries because the small amounts of arable land available in the Scandinavian countries could not feed their growing population. They built speedy, shallow-drafted ships and became expert sailors. Some went westward to Iceland, Greenland, and the coast of North America, while others struck at Europe on several fronts. Irish monasteries were obvious and easy targets, but the coastal regions of England, France, and Spain were also vulnerable to Viking raiders for nearly two hundred years. The name of the modern French province of Normandy, on the English Channel, can be traced to a land grant that the Vikings forced from a Frankish king in 911. To the east, the Vikings moved across the Baltic into Russia and then moved south as far as Constantinople.

At first, it might seem that the invasions of Europe in the ninth and tenth centuries were similar to the onslaught that had hit the Western Empire five hundred years earlier. There was, however, a crucial difference. Whereas the military and political resistance of Rome had simply faded away, the Germanic kingdoms of Europe by A.D. 1000 gradually organized their own defences and survived the storm. Feudal obligations had strengthened local kingdoms to the point where peasants were offered both protection from barbarian attacks and a system of justice in feudal courts.

As the Vikings settled in the lands they had formerly raided, many became Christians and adapted to Christian ways. In so doing, they became part of the mainstream of a new life and order that was emerging on the continent. Europe in A.D. 1000 was still violent and lawless by modern standards, but the groundwork for a new civilization had been established, a civilization stemming from the mixture of Roman, Christian, and barbarian traditions.

SUMMARY

Octavian became Caesar Augustus, first Roman emperor, in 27 B.C. To keep control over all important decisions, Augustus himself approved all key appointments, and he created a civil service accountable only to the emperor. The administrative structure he devised for the Empire helped Rome to maintain peace and prosperity throughout its lands for two centuries, an interval known as the *Pax Romana*.

Rome's magnificent architecture was a sign of the wealth flowing into the city, the result of its conquests and its encouragement of trade. There were parks, gardens, public baths, and, to keep the unemployed masses occupied, enormous facilities for games and spectacles. Most Roman entertainments featured fierce and bloody competitions. At the Colosseum, people cheered the gladiators, slaves specially trained to attack and kill one another. Romans also enjoyed watching fights between different wild animals, or between animals and humans. Chariot races and theatrical performances were popular as well.

There was great poverty as well as great wealth in ancient Rome. The poor lived in tenement slums that were dirty, infested with rodents, and susceptible to fire. Disposal of sewage, garbage, and carcasses from the games was also a civic problem.

Although the *Pax Romana* was a time of territorial stability, some interesting social changes were occurring. Slaves were treated better than they had been because, as Rome slowed its conquests of new lands, the supply decreased. New philosophical and religious ideas also influenced the way slaves and the poor were regarded. Christianity, a Middle Eastern religion inspired by the ideas of Jesus, a Jew, originated during this period. Jesus preached that there was one God and one Heaven for all people, a message that had particular appeal to the poor and oppressed. After his execution in about A.D. 30, several of his followers established Christian communities, mainly in the eastern regions of the Empire.

The *Pax Romana* ended at the beginning of the second century A.D., when the Romans began to lose some of their lands to Germanic tribes they called barbarians. For three hundred years, the Empire steadily declined. Administration became so difficult that, by the early part of the fourth century, the Romans divided their Empire in two; the Western Empire was governed from Rome, the Eastern Empire from Constantinople.

Christianity by this time had become an important force. Even though Christians had been persecuted by the state in the first century A.D., the religion continued to attract newcomers. The institution of the Church took shape with its hierarchy of deacons, priests, and bishops, and it became an undeniable part of Roman life. Constantine, early in the fourth century, was the first emperor to convert to Christianity. A few years later, Emperor Theodosius made Christianity the state religion. Probably these emperors hoped that the strength of the Church would unify the Empire. The Church continued; the Roman Empire, however, did not.

Several explanations have been offered for the decline of the Empire. The army became less capable of and less committed to keeping the barbarians out. Social and political factors contributed to the decline as well. The Roman educational system focussed on rhetoric rather than natural science and other practical areas of knowledge. Because the Romans were never able to settle on solid principles for choosing their emperors, there was uncertainty and turmoil at the centre of their government. And the government's response to the increasing demands and expense of maintaining the Empire was to raise taxes and impose state control on all aspects of life. The government was essentially totalitarian, and public spirit suffered as a result. Finally, a number of unpreventable circumstances, such as the assault of the Huns, may have made the fall of the Empire inevitable.

In A.D. 476, the German warrior Odoacer deposed the last Roman emperor, and the Western Empire was at its end. (The Eastern Roman

Empire, however, remained intact.) The Middle Ages, the period between A.D. 476-1500, was different from what had gone before in almost every respect. Unlike the Romans, the barbarians were illiterate. Their artistic productions were simple. They spoke their own languages and had their own gods. Barbarian life was rural, built around the village and agricultural production. The Western Empire broke into many regions, each ruled by a different barbarian tribe. With the loss of central government, the network of roads decayed and trade dwindled.

But, very slowly, the disintegration reversed itself. To safeguard and develop their own interests, people made agreements with one another. The weak promised to help the strong in return for protection and land. A strong lord would thus have many vassals whom he could call upon during a war, or pledge to another lord who was even stronger. Resulting from this chain of reciprocal promises was a hierarchy known as feudalism. At the top was the king; below him were the lords (dukes, counts, and barons) and their knights. At the bottom were the serfs, peasants whose obligations were agricultural, not military. Land ownership was of great importance; the term *feudalism* derives from the grant of land (feud) the lord made to his vassal. By the year 1000, some feudal hierarchies had grown in size and complexity to become great kingdoms.

The Byzantine Empire, as the Eastern Roman Empire came to be known, experienced none of these changes. It withstood the barbarians and continued to be ruled by emperors for another thousand years. In fact, under Emperor Justinian (A.D. 527-565), the Byzantines reclaimed North Africa, Italy, Greece, the Mediterranean islands, and part of Spain from the barbarians.

Justinian's gains did not last long. From the Middle East arose a Muslim Empire, forged by Arabs who were inspired by a new religion—Islam. Islam grew out of the teaching of an Arab from Mecca named Muhammad, a caravan agent who, at the age of forty, began to experience visions. He believed in one God for all people, and preached the virtues of a life devoted to the service of God's will. He was accepted as a prophet and, after a brief period of persecution, went on to found a Muslim state. The state grew into a huge empire after his death, stretching from the steppes of Russia to North Africa and Spain. Most of the gains were made at the expense of the Byzantine Empire, which by the eighth century was much reduced and under constant threat from further Muslim expansion.

With the rise of feudalism throughout the remains of the Western Roman Empire, the region now known as Europe was beginning to take shape. Some of the barbarian tribes had converted to Christianity. Charlemagne, king of the Franks, had a vision of a revived Western Empire, united by Christianity and ruled by him. Working with the Church, he managed to achieve his goal, but his empire dissolved after his death in 814. His grandsons fought among themselves before finally establishing the Treaty of Verdun, which divided the kingdom among them.

Europe at this time was under pressure from several directions—in the south were the Muslims, in the east the Magyars, and in the north and west the Vikings. The Vikings were the most dangerous. Food shortages in their Scandinavian homelands prompted them to move outward in the eighth and ninth centuries. They developed into accomplished sailors and raiders, striking at coastal settlements and moving inland along the waterways. Eventually the raiders became settlers, adapting to the culture of their new environment and even converting to Christianity. By the year 1000, barbarian, Christian, and Roman traditions were intermingled, and European civilization was on the verge of bearing fruit.

Date A.D.	Event
800-1000	Old Western Roman Empire blossoms into a new civilization, Europe
1054	East-West Schism—Christendom is divided between the Roman Catholic Church of the West and the Orthodox Church of the East
1066	Battle of Hastings—William of Normandy conquers England
1071	Seljuk Turks defeat the Byzantines and begin the conquest of the Holy Land
1076	Pope Gregory VII asserts papal authority over Henry IV of Germany
1095	Pope Urban II calls for the Crusades to win back the Holy Land for Christendom
c. 1100	Growth of towns and cities and the expansion of trade and commerce mark the rise of middle-class merchants
c. 1150	Wealthy towns and cities build impressive Gothic cathedrals
1215	Magna Carta determines the relationship between king and feudal barons in England
1271	Marco Polo begins expedition to court of Kublai Khan
1302	King Philip of France arrests the pope Babylonian Captivity—seven consecutive popes are forced to live at Avignon Church prestige declines
1337	Hundred Years' War begins between England and France
1347	Black Death devastates Europe killing between one-quarter and one-third of the population
1453	Ottoman Turks conquer Constantinople
1488	Bartolemeu Diaz rounds Cape of Good Hope
1492	*Christopher Columbus reaches San Salvador in the Bahamas* *Europeans identify this date as the "discovery" of the Americas*
1519	*Cortes begins conquest of Mesoamerica*
1531	*Pizarro begins conquest of South America*

8

Europe, Mesoamerica, and South America

BACKGROUND

The European Revival

The Western world was in a state of upheaval when the Middle Ages (476-1500) began. As law and order emerged, the population of Europe steadily increased from 35 million in the tenth century to about 80 million by the end of the thirteenth century. More intensive methods of agriculture were needed to feed this growing population. In response, much of Europe, particularly the manors of the north, adopted the **three-field system** of crop rotation: one field was planted in the fall and one in the spring, while one lay fallow for an entire year. More land was cultivated than in the older two-field system, vastly improving yields. Even the wasteland at the manor's edge and reclaimed land from drained swamps now fell under the plough.

It was the serfs' sweat and backbreaking toil from dawn to dusk that produced grain surpluses and gave the nobility its leisure time. The use of the ancient water mill, the newly invented windmill, and iron (rather than wooden) hoes and pitchforks did little to alter the dull, dreary life. About 90 percent of Europe's population laboured as serfs. Accident, injury, and illness always threatened; medical aid was virtually nonexistent; nourishment was provided by a breakfast and dinner of only black bread and ale.

An escape from this monotonous existence could be found in the towns that were developing throughout Europe. The stability of the feudal world led to the revival of trade and, with it, to the growth or rebirth of towns that had been idle since the last days of Rome. At the end of the tenth century, Europe contained only a handful of what were really local villages, none with a population of ten thousand. By the end of the eleventh century, there were dozens of towns, some with populations of over twenty thousand. An urban expansion that would continue until the fourteenth century had begun. Manor lords were hard pressed to keep their serfs tilling the soil. Many serfs simply left to seek out new lives in the nearest towns.

Science

Agricultural yields were improved not only through the switch from the two-field to the three-field system, but also as a result of several technological changes. The traditional single-pronged scratch plough, used since Roman times, required at least two passes to prepare the soil. The heavy-wheeled plough that replaced it had a mouldboard that overturned the soil in a single pass. The most revolutionary change, however, was the widespread use of the horse rather than the slower-moving ox. A series of inventions in the early tenth century made using horses possible. The introduction of the horseshoe gave the horse better traction, protected the hoof, and extended the working life of the animal; the tandem harness lined up teams behind each other and allowed a more efficient use of their pulling power; the horse collar enabled the animal to pull without the strangling effect of a yoke.

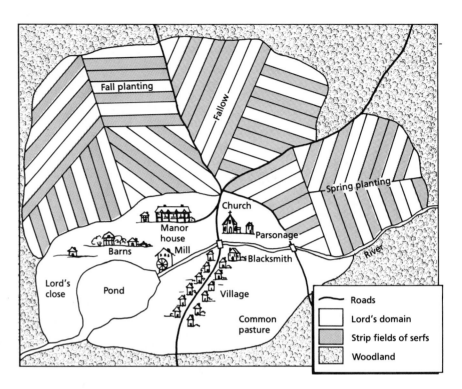

The Three-Field System of Agriculture.

Those who remained had often saved enough money to buy their freedom, which meant that they paid a fee in place of feudal obligations and then sold their produce for profit in the closest urban market.

In the north, many towns developed when wandering merchants, often in search of the trade fairs held throughout Europe, sought protection in a fortified castle or monastery. If the walls overshadowed the junction of two navigable rivers or some other transhipment point, the merchants occasionally decided to stay and set up stands for their wares. As trade expanded, people began to move to the town for commerce and work. The urban community became more than simply a religious or political centre.

The merchants would set up shop outside the castle, creating a **suburb**, which was, in turn, enclosed by a new wall. As the suburbs continued to grow, additional new walls had to be added about every fifty years or so, with each one overshadowing the older walls it encircled. The community of Carcassonne in southern France is the best surviving example of a medieval walled town.

The growth of trade in the eleventh century brought prosperity to northern towns such as Paris and Rouen in France as well as to Hamburg and Cologne in Germany. The Italian city of Venice, with its great fleet, cleared the Adriatic Sea of pirates and became a major force in the trade between the Muslim and Byzantine empires. Venice became the first com-

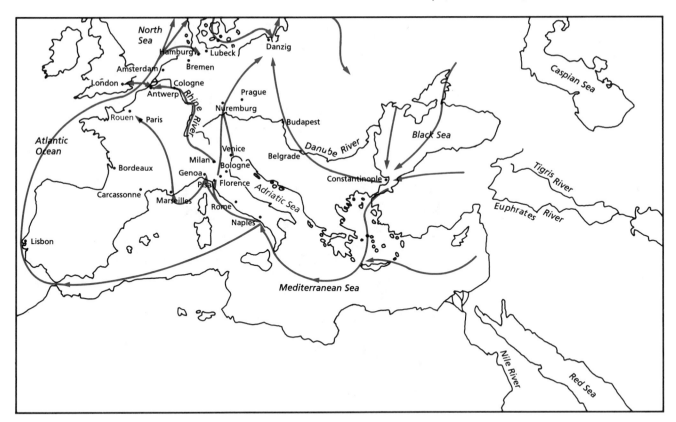

Medieval Trading Patterns.

mercially independent city of the medieval world. Genoa and Pisa entered the competition for commercial supremacy shortly afterward. Merchants from all parts of Europe met at the famous trade fair held six times a year in the French state of Champagne. Here, highly valued Flemish cloth and British wool were exchanged for spices, silks, and jewellery that funnelled through the Italian ports from the Byzantine and Muslim worlds. This renewed trade would eventually lead to European explorations of the African coast and to voyages across the Atlantic in search of new goods and markets.

Feudal life had known only two major classes, the nobility and the serf. By the end of the eleventh century, the **burgers** of Germany, the **burgesses** of England, and the **bourgeoisie** of France had emerged as a new **middle class** of merchants. The driving force of a new economic life, they organized themselves into **merchant guilds** to control prices, to maintain local monopolies, and to guarantee the quality of the items they sold. Most of the townspeople, however, were engaged in the actual production of goods and support services, and they organized into **craft guilds**. Here, a **master craftsman** would train an **apprentice** for up to seven years in a trade or

In this medieval painting, a guild master is judging the work of a carpenter and a stonemason.

business. Only when he became a **journeyman** did the apprentice receive a wage. To become a master craftsman himself, the journeyman had to complete a **masterpiece** of work that was acceptable to his superior. Then, if he had the money, he could open his own shop. Each occupation—butchers, bakers, dye and candlestick makers, and countless others—had its own guild. In times of need, guilds cared for the sick and widowed families of their members.

In the beginning, the workshops of master craftsmen were usually located in the masters' houses. Wives of the guild masters were often involved either in the actual production or in the sale of the products. Some of the early textile guilds were mixed guilds. Women and men had equal positions. As guilds expanded and most of the home workshops disappeared, however, quotas and regulations restricting women began to appear, until women were eventually excluded altogether.

Although towns were originally owned by the nobility, the close-knit ties of commerce and trade were a world apart from feudalism. To gain the independence needed to run their own affairs, the townspeople purchased a **charter** from a king or noble, usually at a terrible price and after much bargaining. This charter freed the townspeople and allowed them to set up their own government. Many nobles living in the countryside became upset when the peasants who worked their fields left for the new opportunities that a town could offer. For nobles living in the towns, however, the increased income from the rents and tolls made possible by commerce was easy to accept. Squabbles between nobles and merchants over town-council appointments, however, were frequent. Resentment of wealthy merchants, who always seemed to have more cash on hand than either the nobility or upper clergy, became commonplace. Throughout the second half of the Middle Ages, this transition from the old feudal order to the increasing prosperity and power of the new middle class was an uneasy one.

The Relationship between Church and State

By the middle of the eleventh century, Europe had not only undergone a rapid population increase, economic revival, and the growth of towns, it had also experienced near complete conversion to Christianity. As the countries of England, France, and Germany began to take shape out of the many local kingdoms, a harmony of interests developed between the individual states and the Church within their borders. This was not accidental. The Church was powerful because of its influence over the people and because of the large amount of land it controlled. The families who ruled Europe appreciated that power. For sincere and for strategic reasons, members of the ruling families joined the Church and, over time, came to occupy important positions in the Church hierarchy. Not surprisingly, the relationship between Church and state became smoother.

Pope Gregory VII upset this relationship with an assertion of papal power in 1076. The rulers of Europe were seeking the authority to appoint people of their own choosing to the Church as a way of gaining power more quickly and with greater certainty. Gregory insisted that the Church, not the kings, should control the appointment and election of archbishops, bishops, and other clergy. When Henry IV of Germany would not submit, Gregory excommunicated him and threatened to excommunicate any German clergy who did not follow his wishes.

Medieval art typically depicts religious scenes, such as Christ's ascension to heaven.

According to tradition, Queen Mathilda designed the Bayeux Tapestry and supervised its execution. The tapestry shows events relating to the Norman Conquest; only a small detail of the work is seen here. Mathilda's husband, William the Conqueror, became King of England when he won the Battle of Hastings.

Since much of Henry's army came from lands administered by the Church, he was now exposed to the ambition of the power-hungry nobles. There was a shocking collapse of royal power. All of Europe watched as Henry journeyed in haste to Italy to seek forgiveness, while Gregory, in a slower, more stately fashion, headed toward Germany to oversee the election of a new German king! Henry assured Gregory of his future obedience, and the pope forgave him his sins.

A similar struggle occurred between the Church and William, the duke of Normandy in France. William crossed the English Channel, won a decisive victory at the Battle of Hastings in 1066, and became the new king of England. The Church had hoped to profit from this victory, but William proved to be a strong king with no thought of giving in to the papacy. He feudalized the entire country (as he had Normandy), including the bishops and abbots of the Church. In contrast to the German monarch, he made every noble swear a personal oath of loyalty to him. When Gregory tried to intervene in the operation of the Anglo-Norman Church, William forbade all English clergy to go to Rome. There was little that Gregory could do.

The rivalry between Church and state continued in varying forms throughout Europe without a final resolution. There was no question, however, that Europe was united in its Christian faith. The Church presented itself as the guardian of Christian interests, and for the most part the people accepted this. They expected that the Church would respond to any threats to the faith, whether they originated inside or outside of Europe.

The Crusades

For centuries, Christian pilgrims from Europe travelled east into the Byzantine Empire, through the city of Constantinople, and into what is now called the Middle East, where they would travel south to the Holy Land. They were allowed to do so by the Muslim Arabs (or **Moors** as they were called in Spain) who held the vast territory that had once been the southern Roman Empire. By the middle of the eleventh century, thousands of pilgrims each year made the long and difficult trek to the sacred cities of Jerusalem and Bethlehem.

In 1071, however, the aggressive **Seljuk Turks**, recently converted to Islam, defeated a Byzantine army and gained control of the lands to the east of the Mediterranean. Horror stories of pilgrims slaughtered or seized for slavery or ransom filtered back to Europe. The Byzantine Empire, which had protected Europe from Asian armies since the days of ancient Rome, seemed powerless to react and appeared to be in danger of collapse in the face of Seljuk power. The East-West Schism of 1054 had divided Christendom between the Catholic Church of the West and the Orthodox Church of the East, but the Byzantine emperor, Alexius Comnenus, was so concerned that he appealed to the papacy for assistance on several occasions.

Pope Urban II finally gave Alexius the response he desired. Clearly, Urban wanted to win the Holy Land for the Cross and to oust non-Christians from Jesus' birthplace, but there were other advantages. A holy crusade would draw attention away from the dispute between Church and state that had dominated the papacy of Gregory, and, with good fortune, would unite Europe in a cause that would enhance the reputation and strength of the Catholic Church. There was even the possibility that the split between Western and Eastern Churches could be healed on terms favourable to the pope. The eleventh century had witnessed the successful start of the reconquest, or **Reconquista**, in Spain, where Spanish Christians had already regained about one-quarter of the country from the Muslims in what amounted to a holy war. Urban hoped for even more success in the East, as the Seljuk Empire began to crumble from internal squabbles after 1091.

The "call to the Cross," delivered by Urban in 1095, was a powerful speech, carefully planned for maximum emotional impact. He decided against giving the speech in England or Germany because the recent conflicts between Church and state would diminish the enthusiasm for his announcement. Instead, Urban selected Clermont in central France as his site. This choice was heartily approved by the large numbers of landless French knights who had no outlet for their energies now that the rule of feudal princes had stabilized their country. When Urban began his appeal with "Oh, race of Franks" and then went on to speak of the spoils that could be won in a land of "milk and honey," he knew he was preaching to the converted. At the conclusion of the address, the audience shouted "God wills it," and many knights cut their red cloaks into the shape of a cross, which was later sewn on their tunics.

When the main force of knights, most of them Norman or Frankish, finally set out in 1096 on the First Crusade, they ravaged the lands they crossed in Europe and the Balkans. The Crusaders finally reached Constantinople, still a city of wealth and grandeur in an otherwise decaying Byzantine Empire. A sudden and unforeseen weakening of Seljuk power,

The Call to the Cross

Christianity permeated European society, and people in every station of life—from the peasants to the nobility—responded to Urban's speech at Clermont. In fact, it was the peasants who were the first to set off for the Holy Land. Throngs of believers joined the **People's Crusade**, led by a monk called Peter the Hermit. Peter crossed Europe on a donkey, towing a cross behind him. He was accompanied by his knight, Walter the Penniless. The People's Crusade was a misguided adventure. One group so offended the Hungarians that the locals turned on them, killed many, and ended their existence as a unit. Another group slaughtered the Jews in the Rhineland. Other followers eventually made it across the Bosporus, only to be massacred by the Seljuks.

A similar religious dedication was demonstrated by a woman who, in most other ways, was Peter the Hermit's opposite. Eleanor of Aquitaine (1122-1204) was raised in a royal family in which women had considerable power, and she brought the liberal ideas of her childhood to her marriage with Louis VII of France. When her husband announced he was joining a crusade, Eleanor not only insisted on accompanying him, she also organized and led her own force of three hundred women. The Amazonian corps, as it was called, tended the wounded and fought when it could. This crusade, like the others, failed.

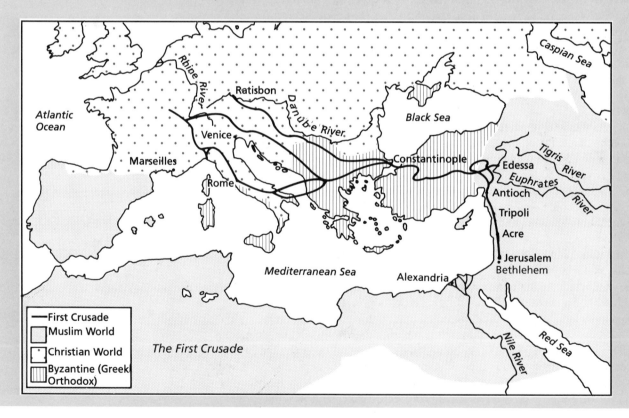

The First Crusade

- First Crusade
- Muslim World
- Christian World
- Byzantine (Greek Orthodox)

however, made the emperor Alexius less anxious to receive European assistance. The historic meeting of the Western and Eastern Christian worlds quickly dissolved into mutual suspicion and broken promises. The Byzantines withdrew from the Crusade after a few minor victories. With a total force of under ten thousand, the European knights and their infantry pushed onward with high emotion and not only took Antioch in 1098, but slaughtered tens of thousands of people in the capture of the Holy City of Jerusalem the following year.

The Holy City became the most powerful of the four Crusading States established in the subsequent conquest of Syria. To protect the gains that were made, a series of castles, among the greatest of any built in the High Middle Ages (1000-1300), were constructed overlooking strategic valley passes and communication routes. Following the First Crusade, many of these castles were either built or staffed by the two great military orders of the Holy Land, the **Templars** and **Hospitallers**. Like the monks of the monasteries, the members of the military orders took vows of poverty, chastity, and obedience. Their duty, however, was the military defence of the Holy Land. Over time, their organizations spread into England, France, Portugal, Spain, Italy, and Hungary.

Three major and several minor crusades followed the initial attempt to secure the Holy Land. Each one failed. The papacy had demonstrated moral leadership in 1095, but later invoked crusades too frequently over trivial matters to rekindle the emotion of the original effort. As the leadership of the Crusades passed to prominent rulers and as their purpose became more worldly and less spiritual, the reputation of the papacy suffered. When the pope raised taxes for a crusade, people understood. When the taxes continued as a normal part of papal revenue, people grew resentful.

What did the Crusades achieve? The direct results were extremely limited, since the Holy Land was brought under Christian control for only a short period. Clearly, the Byzantine Empire lost more than it gained from the European intervention. When the Franks of the First Crusade encountered the Byzantine world in Constantinople, they were overwhelmed by what they saw. Indeed, they were treated as, and felt themselves to be, members of an uncouth and inferior culture. The Byzantine court, however, was a mask of pomp, ceremony, and sophistication over a decaying world. The Franks, on the other hand, were the enterprising edge of a new and vigorous civilization. When the Byzantine Empire wilted during the Fourth Crusade, the way was paved for its complete overthrow by the Turks. Europe was left as the driving force of Christianty.

Most of the changes that were reshaping Europe from the eleventh to the thirteenth centuries would have taken place with or without the Crusades. Nevertheless, the Crusades certainly increased the pace and emphasis of change. The temporary conquest of Syria gave Westerners an inviting taste of Eastern luxury goods on a much bigger scale than they

The Arab Scientific Tradition

The founder of Baghdad, capital of the Arabs' Muslim Empire, was Caliph al-Mansur (754-775). Curious about the achievements of the Greeks, al-Mansur sent representatives to the Byzantine emperor to acquire books, the most famous being the *Elements* of the Greek mathematician Euclid. Subsequent caliphs sought more books, and a scientific tradition took hold among the Arabs. By 830, the **Bait al-Hikma** (House of Wisdom)—a centre of learning, a library, a museum, and an observatory—had been established by Caliph al-Ma'mun. The House of Wisdom was staffed with Christian and Muslim scholars, hired to translate Greek, Persian, Sanskrit, and Syriac texts into Arabic. But the Arabs did more than translate and preserve the learning of other peoples. They became skilled philosophers, mathematicians, and scientists themselves, correcting the errors they discovered in the works they studied.

The Arabs, like the Greeks, believed that mathematics was crucial to science. From the Hindus, they took the concept of zero, and the system of numerical notation that evolved into what are now known as Arabic numerals. They went on to make many advances, refining algebra, geometry, and trigonometry, for example.

Arabs also excelled in medicine. A hospital was built in Baghdad in the eighth century, and thirty-four more were eventually established throughout the Empire. Arabs pioneered a variety of surgical techniques and instruments. Their medical texts were influential for centuries.

In addition, the Arabs became astronomers and geographers. They created excellent clocks, calendars, navigational devices, and maps. Some uneducated Europeans thought the earth was flat even at the time of Columbus's voyage in 1492; Arab astronomers assumed that the earth was round and estimated its circumference to be 32 800 km.

Arab knowledge in these and other areas was transmitted to Europeans mainly in the twelfth and thirteenth centuries, when Arab texts were translated into Latin and Hebrew in Spain and Sicily. If it had not been for Arab enthusiasm for and expertise in science, the learning of the ancient Greeks would never have been preserved and built upon, and there would have been no basis for the Renaissance in Europe.

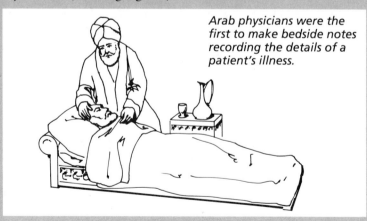

Arab physicians were the first to make bedside notes recording the details of a patient's illness.

had ever had before. Spices, valued fabrics, rugs, tapestries, glass mirrors, precious metals, and enamels found their way into the castles and manors of the rich. The trade came to Europe by way of the Italian cities of Venice, Genoa, and Pisa, which, largely as a result of their role in the Crusades, emerged as great trading republics that monopolized Mediterranean commerce. Venetian fleets had taken reinforcements to the Holy Land as early as 1100, and all crusades from the Third to the Eighth were transported by sea, usually on Italian merchant ships. The Venetians and Genoese set up trading posts in Syria and retained many of the Aegean islands taken from the Greeks until the seventeenth century. The need for cash to buy the luxury goods available from Italian traders led to the development of international banking, including loans for trade and the transfer of money by credit note throughout the Mediterranean. The commerce of Venice, in particular, slowly moved northward through the Brenner Pass into the Rhineland and up to the thriving medieval towns in Flanders and northern Germany.

Crusades to the Holy Land gave Westerners a first-hand look at the geography of the East and an interest in new lands and peoples. They gained a taste for the rewards of expansion, as well as kindling ambitions that would be active for centuries. During this time, the West also became aware of Arab scholarship and science. Most Arab learning reached Europe from the Islamic culture in Spain. There, Muslims taught Christian scholars the Greek language, virtually unknown in the West since the fall of Rome. Westerners could now study the work of Greek philosophers directly, rather than through Arab translations. In Sicily, Christians studied Arab writings on the more technical subjects of medicine, mathematics, and the natural sciences. Such co-operation was not easily achieved, since Christian warriors of the Reconquista were trying to push the Muslims out of Spain!

Cathedrals

Buildings for Christian worship were first constructed in the third and fourth centuries. The number of Christian converts was growing so rapidly that services could no longer be held in private homes. These churches were built in the style of the Roman courthouse (**basilica**). The Roman basilica had a long, high **nave**, low side aisles, and a semicircular **apse** at the end to accommodate larger numbers. When the Western Roman Empire declined, cities fell into ruin and building skills were lost. Most of the churches constructed during the Early Middle Ages were simple rectangular buildings with wooden roofs that frequently caught fire.

By the eleventh century, with the return of peace and stability, a Roman-like style of architecture emerged that became known as **Romanesque**. The old form of the basilica was again used in church construction. At one end of the long nave was a raised altar. A **transept**, which widened each side of the building in front of the apse, gave the ground plan the shape of a Latin cross. From the outside, a Romanesque church looked

Science

In the seventh century A.D., the Arabs began to use a simple and efficient system of numerals that had been developed by Hindus in Persia slightly earlier. Probably the Europeans were exposed to **Arabic numerals** in the course of their commercial relations with Eastern ports. The Venetians, for example, created a special coin featuring Arabic numerals that was used for their trade with the East. In all likelihood, European merchants quickly realized that the Arabic system was much less cumbersome than the system of **Roman numerals** that had long been used in the West. Arabic numerals gradually won out, and, of course, we use them ourselves today. This is one of the few instances in which Arabic technology passed to Europe as a result of the direct contact between the two cultures as they competed for territory in the Holy Land.

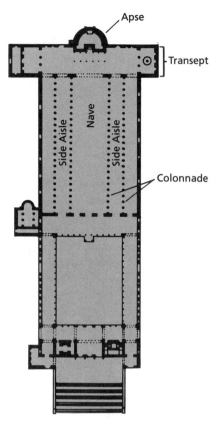

The Floorplan of a Roman Basilica.

The cathedral in Conques, France, built in the Romanesque style during the eleventh century. Its sprawling width and relatively short towers give it a solid, squat appearance.

massive and solid, with heavy, horizontal lines. The nave was covered in a fire-resistant barrel vault of stone, supported by ponderous pillars and thick walls. Little space was left for windows, which often had to be placed near the top so that the strength of the walls would not be weakened. The windows were shaped like wheels or arches, and provided little light. In an age of dim candlelight, the interior of these churches was gloomy. Sculptors and artists attempted to brighten the atmosphere with religious carvings on columns or walls and with biblical scenes painted on the ceiling.

Advances in building design, first brought together in 1140 under the guiding inspiration of Suger, Abbot of St. Denis, resulted in a dramatic new style of architecture known as **Gothic**. Gothic architects were master masons. They developed the **ribbed vault**, in which stone ribs, radiating from a slender column like the spokes of an umbrella, spread the weight of the roof from column to column toward the walls. To prevent the cathedral from collapsing outward, **flying buttresses** braced the walls from the outside. The exterior support allowed larger open spaces inside as well as larger windows. Indeed, as the **pointed arch**, which could be varied in size, replaced the more limited rounded arch, and as rose windows replaced the more simple wheel, the Gothic cathedral became a storehouse of light. Because the use of stained glass increased, the Gothic cathedrals were not necessarily brighter than Romanesque churches had been; but they were filled with rich colour and interesting lighting effects. In contrast to the spiked spires and towers of different shapes and sizes often found in Romanesque buildings, the Gothic cathedral soared toward the sky with grace and symmetry. Each arch and tower on one side had a mirror image

on the other. The effect was meant to be visually and spiritually uplifting. The building seemed higher than it really was.

Clearly, it was the religious faith of the High Middle Ages that provided the thrust for the spread of Gothic architecture from France across Europe. The Gothic cathedral is a fitting symbol of the period because it harnessed many of the new forces at work in European society. Gothic cathedrals represented the largest economic enterprise of the day, utilizing the skills of master masons, stonecutters, glass makers, metal smiths, carpenters, plumbers, and endless numbers of manual labourers.

Where did the money come from to build such grand projects? Added to the considerable resources of the Church was the commercial strength of the newly independent cities. The rise of the middle-class merchant marked a shift in medieval wealth from the land and the feudal system to the trade and commerce of the city. In a religious age, nothing could be a greater source of civic pride than to have a grand cathedral that dominated the skyline, attracting travellers and commerce. Having a magnificent cathedral meant so much that competition in building became serious. Architects and designers moved from city to city to learn the latest techniques, see the largest cathedral, and then plan one bigger than anything that had been built before.

The cathedral in Cologne, Germany. The many windows and soaring towers are typical of the Gothic style.

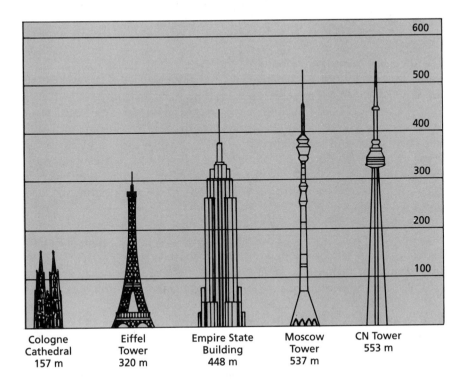

Cologne Cathedral 157 m — Eiffel Tower 320 m — Empire State Building 448 m — Moscow Tower 537 m — CN Tower 553 m

The practice of competitive building continues to this day. The Cologne Cathedral, which stands 157 m high, was begun in 1248 and completed 632 years later in 1880; the Eiffel Tower, built in Paris in 1889, stretches up to 304 m; while New York's Empire State Building, completed in 1931, stands at 448 m. The Moscow Tower and Toronto's CN Tower soar to 537 and 553 m respectively.

The first Gothic construction on record began in 1163 at Notre Dame in Paris, where the nave reached about 35 m off the floor. After careful measurement and planning, Chartres outdid Notre Dame with a nave height of 36.5 m. In 1212, the cathedral in Reims peaked at almost 38 m, while Amiens boasted a cathedral nave of 42 m within the next decade. Finally, in 1247, the apse at Beauvais soared to almost 48 m, the highest ever achieved by a Gothic cathedral. Unfortunately, it collapsed twice after 1284.

The construction of Gothic cathedrals peaked in the thirteenth century. By the middle of the fourteenth century, building enthusiasm began to lessen noticeably. Engineering know-how and technology had been pushed to the limit, so larger cathedrals were not feasible. Cathedral builders began to concentrate on decoration rather than size. Shortly after, the ornate Gothic tradition was replaced by a simpler style.

The Gothic cathedral was more than just a church. Merchants, barons, pilgrims, and travellers contributed their personal sweat and toil as they lifted blocks into place under the guidance of a master mason. In most ancient religions, the people did not have access to their religious sanctuary, but the cathedral, by design, was built to house much of the city's population and became a social centre. People often brought animals with them, talked openly, and even held town meetings in the cathedral. In some cases, towns did not build city halls because the cathedral provided such an excellent civic meeting place.

Castles

The medieval castles often found beside the cathedrals also bring to mind bold and splendid images. Whereas the church symbolized the power of the divine spirit, the castle represented the position and authority of the feudal lord. Castles were built for military reasons. They began as a **keep** (main building) surrounded by wooden barriers (**palisades**). During an attack, the lord, his family, and his knights could close the gate and withdraw to the keep. They would live off the supplies they had stored, and counterattack the enemy from the safety of the keep and the walls. The first simple castles developed into massive fortresses with thick stone walls, deep moats, and protected entrances.

Feudal society, with its reciprocal obligations from serf to lord to king, was organized for war. Castles were not only defensive strongholds commanding a dominating position over hilltop and valley, they were an aggressive extension of military operations. Mounted knights organized into cavalry, when properly used with supporting infantry, were the most effective fighting force of the day, and the castle provided a secure home base for their adventures. Ironically, the castle was also the only real defence against a strong cavalry charge.

The castle was the residence of the feudal lord, his vassal knights, and a garrison of soldiers. Although private apartments had some comforts, life in

Caerphilly Castle, South Wales. The keep (the large structure in the centre) is protected by a moat, heavy stone walls, and strategically placed towers.

the castle was hardly luxurious. Sanitation was poor, halls were drafty, and the limited heat provided by fireplaces and inefficient stoves could not warm the dampness of an earthen or stone floor. Ventilation was poor, so odours from the knights' horses and other animals were always present, and smoke-filled rooms were slow to clear. The supporting staff of artisans, cooks, and household servants made the castle a busy place. When rent had to be paid, services rendered, or lawsuits pleaded, it was to the castle that people came. Jousting tournaments that prepared the knights for the ordeal of battle were usually held in or near the castle grounds. On special occasions, serfs even ate in the great hall that was common to all castles, where they were entertained by troupes of acrobats and jugglers.

Castles were also used as prisons for men and women of political importance or high social rank. Not only were the castles secure, but they provided a more comfortable surrounding that matched the status of those detained. At this time, castle prisons were not the cold, damp, rat-infested dungeons described in storybooks. It was not until the sixteenth and seventeenth centuries that people of high rank were subjected to such inhumane conditions.

Early in the 1400s, guns and gunpowder entered European warfare, and castle walls no longer offered the protection they once had. But the new weapons could be used for defence as well, and castles remained difficult to attack. The decline of the castle in the fifteenth century was due not so much to the use of gunpowder as to the shift in power from the nobility of the countryside to the middle classes of the towns. Towns were the new centres of economic activity, wealth, and power. The castle's multiple

More to Consider

As feudalism spread outward from France, so did the presence of castles. When William conquered the Anglo-Saxons at Hastings, he transferred the feudal system to England. William initiated an ambitious program of castle building, rightly believing that castles would enable him to maintain control over uprisings within his new territory. Similarly, the Frankish knights who led the First Crusade set up feudal kingdoms in the Holy Land and left a magnificent series of fortified castles for local defence. Krak des Chevaliers in Syria, with walls over 24 m thick, immense towers, and facilities for two thousand knights, represented a crowning achievement of military architecture.

roles—military stronghold, seat of authority, courthouse, social centre, and home of the nobility—were undercut by the emergence of strong, central government in the cities. The castle became simply a stately residence.

The Power and Decline of the Medieval Church

European civilization started to flower in the High Middle Ages, around the beginning of the thirteenth century. Church reform continued in both traditional and new directions as the papacy reached the zenith of its power.

In the twelfth century, many new religious orders, including the Cistercians, Carthusians, and Carmelites, devoted themselves to a stricter Christian life in isolated monasteries, believing that the Church had become too worldly in its affairs. The prestige lost by the papacy when it called several crusades of questionable purpose was regained by Pope Innocent III (1198-1216). Like Gregory VII, Innocent believed in the supremacy of the pope, not only within the Church of Rome, but over the secular world as well. Innocent, however, proved to be a more capable leader. He successfully intervened in a feud over the German throne, settled a marriage dispute involving Philip Augustus of France, and forced King John, upon threat of invasion, to accept papal nomination within the English Church. At the same time, Innocent introduced the first of many thirteenth-century taxes on the clergy and tightened the administrative system of the Church. These reforms increased papal revenue and improved the quality of Church representatives in the eyes of the people. Under Innocent, the Church was as effective as any medieval monarchy.

The growth of towns, however, posed new problems and made it necessary for the Church to adapt to changing times. Rural monasteries were too isolated to be influential or to reach city dwellers. The answer came from the son of a wealthy merchant from the town of Assisi in central Italy. A spoiled and carefree young man, Francis experienced a sudden conversion and determined to live his life as Jesus had done, tending to the needs of the poor, the sick, the downtrodden, and even the lepers, who were quite numerous in the Italian countryside. During the Fifth Crusade, he travelled to Egypt and Palestine, where he preached the love of God. Francis's life of self-sacrifice in the service of others became a model that attracted many disciples. Their simple and emotional appeal proved so successful that Pope Innocent III recognized them as a new order of monks, the **Franciscans**, or Grey Friars. In contrast to the monks of the monasteries, who devoted their lives to contemplation and personal salvation, the Franciscan friars travelled to the towns and cities of Europe bringing their message to the people. Some of those who were unhappy with the Church but who still held sincere Christian beliefs were persuaded to remain by the work of the Franciscans.

The papacy attempted to win the minds of the educated classes by authorizing a second order of monks known as the **Dominicans**, or Black Friars, after the Spanish monk Dominic. The papacy's prime concern was the growing number of **heretics**, people who held beliefs contrary to those authorized by the Church. Many had become disillusioned with Church practices and were swayed by new ideas. As the texts of Aristotle entered Europe from the Muslim world, the Church faced a serious intellectual challenge to its teaching. Many of Aristotle's scientific views conflicted with those of the Church. The French philosopher Abelard startled his fellow Christians in the twelfth century by arguing that studying both sides of an issue could help a person achieve a deeper understanding and stronger religious faith. The Dominicans continued this study by recruiting the brightest minds available, with the intent of showing that one truth formed the foundation of both the new science and religion.

In the late thirteenth century, Thomas Aquinas, the greatest scholar of his time, joined the Dominican order and produced his famous work, *Summation of Theology*, in which he attempted to answer every possible argument that a nonbeliever could raise regarding Christian beliefs. For Thomas, there was no conflict between faith and reason. If a question could not be resolved, it meant that human reason was imperfect and that one therefore should rely on Christian faith for the answer. In this way, Thomas believed that Aristotle and Christianity were quite consistent.

The intellectual training of the Dominicans made them the natural choice to direct a special court called the **Inquisition**, established by the pope in 1233 to combat heresy. The Church demanded total obedience to its teaching. The Inquisition was an attempt to stamp out unacceptable ideas before Christians were led astray. It also represented a sincere attempt to reclaim the souls of those judged to be heretics. If a heretic admitted error and sought reconciliation with the Church, a suitable penance was administered and the trial ended. If the heretic was slow to confess, she or he was tortured. A convicted heretic was usually burned at the stake. The sight of charred bodies in the marketplaces of Europe certainly created fear, but it won little respect and few sincere converts to the Christian cause. No doubt the inquisitors felt they were performing a necessary service, but in the long run the Church could not be held together by such extreme measures.

By the early fourteenth century, papal prestige and influence began to decline rapidly. When Pope Boniface VII proclaimed papal supremacy in 1302, rather than agreeing, King Philip of France had him arrested. Philip then secured the election of the first of seven consecutive French popes. They resided not in Rome but in the French town of Avignon, where they were subjected to French pressure. Although the English and Germans were upset, popes lived at Avignon until 1378. This period is known to history as the **Babylonian Captivity** because of the corruption it produced. The Church was open to bribery, and sold its services and influence for money.

To make matters worse, rival factions of cardinals elected two claimants to the papal throne in 1378, only to be followed by a third candidate in 1409! The Church now had three popes, each with his own cardinals and bureaucracy. Although the General Church Council of Constance ended this **Great Schism** in 1418, the respect given to the papacy was at an all-time low. The Church failed to see the need for reform in the face of mounting criticism. This failure was one reason why Christian Europe divided into the Roman Catholic and Protestant faiths in the course of the next century.

Prosperity and Depression

During the High Middle Ages, cities increased in size, became more numerous, and even banded together for protection against local princes or lords. The prosperity of the middle-class merchant steadily broke the bonds of feudalism that had held medieval society together for hundreds of years.

Several trading associations developed in various regions of Europe; the most important was the collection of north German cities known as the

Some of the Major and Minor European Kingdoms, c. 1300.

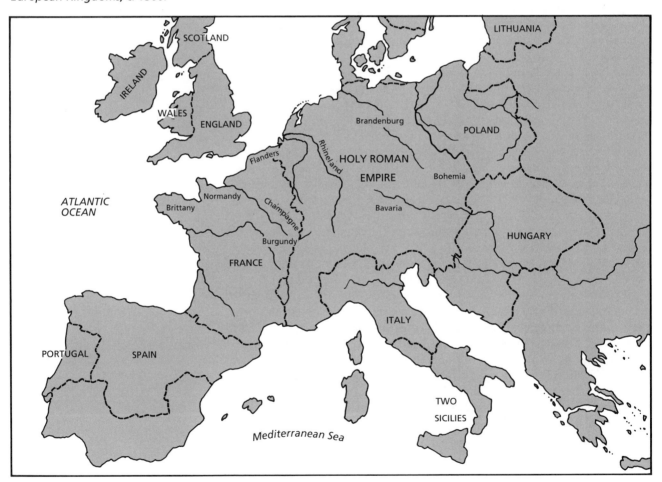

Hanseatic League. Formed to combat the revived strength of the German nobility, the Hanseatic League included the major centres of Lubeck, Bremen, Cologne, Hamburg, and Danzig, and almost one hundred smaller towns and villages. Members abided by a common set of rules for trade, enjoyed economic concessions, outfitted a navy to protect themselves from pirates, and had an army strong enough to win trading privileges from unwilling nobles and kings. By the beginning of the fourteenth century, the axis of trade moved eastward from the Champagne region of France to the German cities of northern Europe.

After three centuries of steady economic progress, however, in about 1300, the European economy began to stagnate for reasons that are not entirely understood. Agricultural production dropped, partly because there was no new land to be brought under cultivation and partly because the soil was becoming exhausted. No technological advances were developed to meet the problems of declining yields. At the same time, the climate of Europe cooled noticeably for much of the next century, and widespread famine struck hard in 1315-1317, 1333-1334, 1337-1342, and 1345-1347. Population growth not only levelled off but began to decline.

In addition, Europe's territorial expansion was halted and even reversed. The Holy Land was lost; the Scandinavians abandoned their outposts in Greenland and stopped voyaging across the Atlantic; the Moors stalled the Spanish reconquest of Spain; the break-up of the Mongol Empire in Asia ended the few ties established with the Far East; and the Ottoman Turks, a Muslim tribe from Asia, threatened the Balkans. Without new markets to compensate for a declining population, the production of goods fell, and the trade that had encouraged the growth of cities decreased. It became increasingly difficult to obtain money, and money had replaced feudal loyalty as the basis for relationships in all walks of medieval life. Vassals of the king increasingly paid fees (known as **scutage**) in place of military service, while nobles concentrated on the production of cash crops for profit. As production slowed, guild membership in the towns became more restrictive, and wages often fell behind the rapid rise in prices. Tension between journeymen and the wealthy city merchants, who had large sums of money (**capital**) to invest in trade and industry, became frequent. The peasants were usually squeezed the hardest, since their only choice was to work in the city for a low wage or return as lowly serfs to the feudal countryside. Peasant suffering became so extreme that serious peasant revolts occurred in Flanders, France, and England.

Any hope for improvement turned to despair with the arrival of the **bubonic plague**, better known as the **Black Death** because of the dark spots that appeared on the victims' skin. The disease, carried by fleas on black rats, was brought on trading ships from the Black Sea ports of Asia to the Italian city of Genoa in 1347. The narrow, winding, sewage-laden streets of medieval towns were natural breeding grounds for rats. In three

A woodcut by Hans Holbein. There were daily reminders of death during the devastation of the Black Plague. "EGO SUM," the Latin phrase on Death's banner, means "I exist."

years, the highly contagious disease spread throughout Europe, from the Mediterranean to Scandinavia, bringing horror and death to every village and town in its path. The disease was characterized by high fever, inflammation of the throat, swelling in the groin and armpits, stabbing chest pain, and the vomiting and spitting of blood. Death brought the suffering to an end within three days. Panic-stricken officials fled from their cities as the plague approached, while parents abandoned infected children, and physicians and clergy left the sick to fend for themselves.

It is hard to grasp the scale of the disaster. Between one-quarter and one-third of Europe's population, about 25 000 000 people, died from the onslaught of the Black Death. Florence had a population of 114 000 in 1338, but only 50 000 were left when the plague had passed. England had a population of 3 700 000 before the plague struck but only 2 100 000 a half-century later.

The Black Death intensified the dislocation of the medieval economy that had already been hard hit by famine and would continue to be ravaged by war. The old order seemed to collapse and it was not until the beginning of the fifteenth century that Europe began to recover.

Emergence of the Nation-State in England and France

While Germany remained divided by the power of feudal princes and Italy became dominated by rival city-states, England and France grew into national monarchies with centralized governments.

In England, strong kings such as Henry II (1154-1189) enhanced royal power considerably. Through Henry's efforts, the English king assumed more responsibility for civil law. Royal courts were given jurisdiction over appeals from local courts and questions of land tenure. The use of the jury system in royal courts slowly replaced trial by ordeal as well as the great variety of feudal legal practices. Henry thus laid the foundation for English **common law**, which would be applied equally to all individuals throughout the kingdom, and which made the people look to the king rather than to the nobles for justice.

Henry was equally concerned that the king should control the Church. He secured the appointment of his friend Thomas Becket as the Archbishop of Canterbury in 1162 to help him achieve that goal. Becket turned the tables on his sponsor, however, by insisting on special privileges for the Church in cases concerning the clergy. Not surprisingly, he clashed with Henry, and spent a six-year exile in France. Henry's pardon that followed did not conceal the fact that neither man had changed his mind. When Becket was assassinated in Canterbury Cathedral by some misguided knights who thought they were fulfilling the king's wishes, Henry was crushed and in despair. To secure his repentance, he was forced to give in to the demands of an outraged Church. Although Henry lost this dispute, he was able to dominate Church life by ensuring that bishops were elected according to the king's wishes.

Later attempts to wield royal power by less able kings contributed to England's unique political character. In a desperate effort to raise money for a war against France, King John (1199-1216) resorted to excessive taxation, weakening his support throughout the country. When defeat on the battlefield also brought the king's military leadership into question, the English barons plotted a revolt and forced John to accept the **Magna Carta** (Great Charter) of 1215. Often misquoted and misunderstood, this famous feudal document outlined the existing relationship between the king and his barons. In practice, it meant that the great council, made up of the king's leading vassals, must approve any new taxes that exceeded the king's personal or normal revenue. In theory, it established the principle that the king was subject to the law of the land and bound by its provisions.

As the thirteenth century progressed, English kings continually needed more money. The great council, which became known as **Parliament**, after the French word *parler*, "to speak," allowed the king to raise taxes in exchange for increased power. When Henry III resisted Parliament's attempt to extend its influence, a rebellion led by the king's brother-in-law, Simon de Monfort, virtually took over the state on behalf of Parliament. Membership in Parliament was granted to knights and to representatives from every borough, which meant that the people who were most likely to pay the taxes got to approve them. During the reign of Edward III, in the fourteenth century, Parliament not only approved new taxes, but signed laws debated in open parliamentary sessions. Parliament was limited by the short length of its sessions, and the king remained a powerful figure who ruled most of the time by royal decree. Nevertheless, laws were now passed by the **King-in-Parliament**, a term that accurately described the sharing of power between the king and those who were governed.

France took much longer to unite under the control of one government. When, in 987, an assembly of nobles and bishops chose Hugh Capet to become king, France was really a collection of almost independent territories that included Flanders, Normandy, Burgundy, Toulouse, Anjou, Champagne, and Aquitaine. Royal authority was limited to the Île de France in the Seine Valley and focussed on the cities of Orleans and Paris. In the territories, the members of the nobility ruled, and for two centuries their allegiance to Capetian kings was token at best. William the Conqueror, as duke of Normandy, was a vassal to the French king in this limited sense. He kept Normandy even after he conquered England. Later English kings were thus able, through a series of marriages, to claim authority over Normandy and other regions—about half of France in total.

Under the skilled military leadership of Philip II, better known as Philip Augustus (1180-1222), most of the English feudal kingdoms in France were brought under French control. This process was stalled by Richard the Lionhearted, king of England from 1189 to 1199, but Philip did much better when Richard's brother John came to the throne. After Philip won all of northern France from John and his German allies, the English king attempted to regain his former possessions but was crushed at the battle of Bouvines in 1214. At home, this defeat forced John to accept the Magna Carta that the English barons thrust upon him, while in France it weakened any English claim to French territory. Military success enabled Philip to tighten his grip over the French nobility, and his successors built on the foundation he established.

By the reign of Philip IV (1285-1314), France had become the most powerful state in Europe. Philip, known as "the Fair" because of his blond hair, called the first meeting of the **Estates General**, a council similar in appearance, but not in operation, to the English Parliament. The Estates General consisted of representatives from each of the three major classes in France—the nobles, the clergy, and the commoners—and was under direct royal control. Whereas the English Parliament and the king ran the country as partners, each of the three estates in the Estates General met and voted

At Crécy in 1346, a hail of arrows from English longbows greeted the French charge. The longbow was superior to the crossbow in terms of range and power. French horses were felled at 200 m, French armour was pierced at 50 m, and the battlefield was littered with the dead.

separately, weakening their influence. The French king could raise taxes on his own authority; as a result, the Estates General seldom met and provided little advice. As ties between the king and wealthy trading towns increased, a royal army was created that could defeat any rebellious baron. It became clear that in France the king was supreme. While England followed a path leading to parliamentary government, France was headed toward absolute rule, with the king responsible only to himself.

In 1337, Edward III of England landed in Normandy to claim the French throne, and a series of intermittent wars, known as the **Hundred Years' War**, broke out between England and France. Economic depression and the onslaught of the Black Death occurred during the same era, which meant years of hardship and exhaustion for both countries. Although more time was spent seeking out the enemy than in actual fighting, England won most of the major battles in the early part of the war, largely because their tactics were better and their smaller military forces easier to co-ordinate. The French relied on the charge of the mounted knight, not reckoning with the devastating impact of the 2 m English longbow and, later, the cannon. This introduction of heavy artillery marked the beginning of the end for the dominance of the feudal knight.

Despite its military success, England was a divided nation at home. The death of Edward's son, the Black Prince, opened the door to rival claimants to the throne. England did not have the resources to conquer a country with four times its population, and the lack of a united war effort slowly took its toll. As the French army became better organized and better supplied, the tide of the war began to turn in favour of France. In 1424, a young peasant girl, known as Joan of Arc, told the French king that angels had chosen her to save France from the English invaders. Although she had no military knowledge, she was given a minor post in the French army. Her bravery and self-sacrifice inspired enthusiasm among the French troops and fear among the English, who believed that she was responsible for many of their misfortunes in battle. When Joan of Arc was captured by the English and condemned by the Church as a heretic and a witch, she was burned at the stake and became a martyr for the French cause.

Under the peace concluded in 1453, England lost all of its territory in France except the port of Calais. The war stimulated a sense of national feeling and purpose both in France and England. In both countries, attention was focussed on the central government. The struggle for the English throne, which had weakened the country during the Hundred Years' War, continued for another three decades. The supporters of the king, Richard III, fought under the symbol of the white rose of the house of York, while their opponents wore the red rose of the house of Lancaster. When Henry Tudor, the leader of the Lancastrian forces and a claimant to the throne, won a decisive victory at the Battle of Bosworth in 1485, few people realized that a new era had begun. Henry's victory ended the instability of the

The Arts

Christine de Pisan (1362(?)-1435(?)) was the first woman in France to become a professional author. An early feminist and critic of male domination, de Pisan ardently defended women and argued for their social equality with men. Her works included *La Cité des Dames*, a tribute to the women of her time, and *La Ditié de Jeanne d'Arc*, a celebration of Joan of Arc's liberation of France.

past two hundred years and marked the beginning of prosperity for England under Tudor leadership. The wars of the fifteenth century had rendered the feudal knights less valuable in war and reduced their power as a political force; it was the central government of the nation-states of England and France that emerged as the focal points of power. Relations between the two countries remained bitter and hostile for centuries until the threat of German might drew them together before the First World War.

The Fall of Constantinople and the Ottoman Turks

The shifting tides of Western European war and politics were gradually overshadowed by the increasingly serious threat posed by the **Ottoman Turks** to the eastern borders of Europe after 1350. The Ottomans had gained their independence from the Seljuks, and in 1356 they crossed from Asia into Europe and spread through much of Greece and Bulgaria. The shrinking and decaying Byzantine Empire and its ancient capital of Constantinople were hemmed in at every turn. The city was saved from invasion only when the Mongolian warrior Tamerlane defeated the Turks at Ankara in 1402, and extended his short-lived empire from India to the Mediterranean. When the highly skilled Muhammad II came to the Ottoman throne in 1451, however, the Turks were ready for the final siege against the last great city of Christendom.

Constantinople was not the magnificent centre of former ages. The Black Death had been devastating, and by the fifteenth century only one hundred thousand people were left in a city in which over half a million had lived two centuries before. Nevertheless, Constantinople had stood for over a thousand years through peace and war as the guardian of Greek, Roman, and Byzantine culture and tradition. Of direct importance to Muhammad were the city's incredible defences, which were the most formidable in all Christendom. Set on a wedge-shaped peninsula that jutted into the Bosporus, Constantinople was protected on the landward side by a moat and triple walls over 6 km long and 10 m high that were spiked with ninety-six fortified towers. Constantinople's harbour (the Golden Horn) was sheltered from attack by 14 km of walls and a floating boom across its mouth.

Muhammad planned the siege of Constantinople very carefully. The city had survived, even in the centuries of Byzantine decline, not only because of its impregnable walls but because it could be supplied by ship from the Bosporus. In 1452, Muhammad organized and completed construction of the great Remuli fortress, which had a 3 t cannon that effectively halted any ship heading toward Constantinople from the Black Sea. The Anadolu fortress stopped any traffic from the Mediterranean. With a force of at least eight thousand soldiers, and huge guns that could shoot 500 kg cannonballs, Muhammad began his attack in April of 1453. The continuous bombardment and repeated military assaults, however, were not sufficient to take Constantinople; for six weeks, nine thousand citizens repulsed the Turkish soldiers.

Muhammad's failure to break the floating boom that blocked the entrance to the Golden Horn inspired an impressive engineering feat. A roadway of almost 2 km was laid overland from the Bosporus, across ridges 60 m high, to the shore behind the boom at the harbour entrance. Braced on wheeled cradles, seventy Turkish ships were hauled along this road by oxen and men and set afloat in the waters of the Golden Horn. Muhammad now surrounded Constantinople on all sides by land and sea. Even in this seemingly impossible situation, the Byzantines held off two Turkish assaults. With frustration rapidly mounting, Muhammad launched yet another attack during the night of 20 May 1453. He finally won a hard-fought victory when the Turks discovered a small gate that had been carelessly left open. A specially trained regiment escorted Muhammad to the city centre, and its soldiers were allowed to loot the city for three days. The great Christian church of Hagia Sophia was converted into a mosque. When minarets were added later, it became the prototype for all Islamic places of worship.

Muhammad proved to be an able ruler who consolidated the territory won from the Byzantines, and, through additional conquest, helped to make the Ottoman Turks the strongest force in the eastern Mediterranean. Under Suleiman the Magnificent (1520-1566), the **Ottoman Empire** reached its zenith, encompassing territory from North Africa, through Anatolia, over to the Persian Gulf, and up into the Balkans and even much of Hungary. The limit of its European expansion was reached only after Suleiman's force of two hundred and fifty thousand soldiers withdrew from the seige of Vienna in 1529, turned away by the local garrison. For much of the fifteenth and sixteenth centuries, however, the Ottoman Empire, as leader of the Muslim world, appeared ready to seize Eastern Europe at any time.

Travelling into the Unknown

Although European influence had extended to Jerusalem and beyond during the Crusades, the people of medieval Europe knew little about distant lands. The few Europeans who travelled brought back stories of what they had seen and experienced, and those stories were embellished and distorted as they spread. Even more dubious were the stories about things the travellers had never actually seen, but had only heard about from the peoples they encountered. There were, of course, no mass media to circulate information to all people instantaneously. There was no guarantee that knowledge gained in one part of Europe would be recorded or that it would spread to other places. Things that were known at one time could easily be forgotten. Information about the past was fragmentary, and maps of faraway places were often not reliable.

Many Europeans believed that Asia and Africa were the homes of dragons, legless birds, giant animals, and sea monsters who would sink any ship that

The Mongol Empire

Early in the thirteenth century, the mighty Genghis Khan (1206-1227) conquered the Asian tribes from China to southern Russia and created the colossal **Mongol Empire**, an empire more extensive than the territory subdued by Alexander the Great. After 1250, Christians were allowed to pass unmolested through these lands. Kublai Khan, in fact, tried to forge a connection with the Western world. He asked the "Latin" people to send one hundred teachers; their task was to convince him of Christianity's virtues. At this critical moment, when a bridge between East and West might have been built, the troubled papacy, perhaps not realizing the potential of the opportunity, sent only two Dominican friars. The friars abandoned their task when the hardships of their journey became apparent.

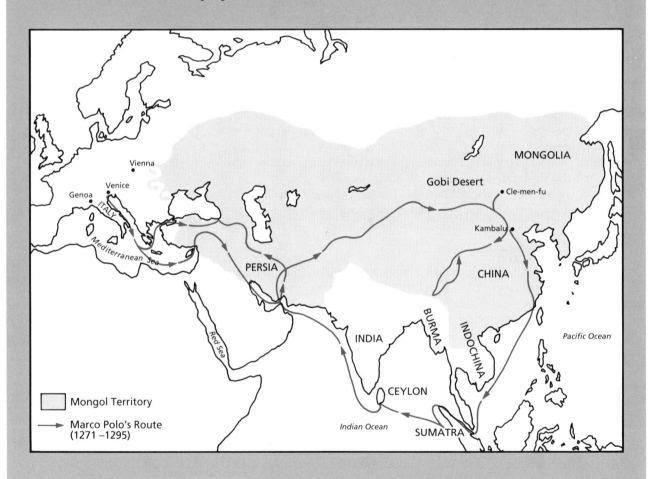

came too close. Stories said they were lands of magic, wealth, and danger, where a river of gold flowed into scorching seas too hot for any human. There was no first-hand knowledge to moderate these wondrous tales.

In 1271, however, Marco Polo, the son of a Venetian merchant who traded at Constantinople, accompanied his father on a three-and-a-half-year journey to Cathay (China), to the court of Kublai Khan (1257-1294). At the court, Marco Polo's quick wit and mastery of the Tartar language won favour with the emperor. He gave Marco an official position and sent him on numerous missions in southwestern China over a seventeen-year period. Kublai Khan wanted the Polos to stay, but they eventually made their way out of China after serving as travel guides for a Mongolian princess.

Upon the Polos' return to Europe, Marco Polo was taken prisoner by the Genoese during a naval battle with Venice in 1298. While in prison, he told his story to a writer named Rusticciano, and the resulting book, *The Travels of Marco Polo*, opened the eyes of Europe to the world of the Orient. Descriptions of untold wealth in gold, silks, and jewels, and of populations numbering in the millions, led many to conclude that Marco Polo was exaggerating, and he was ridiculed as "Marco Millions." Chinese records of the day confirm that a Polo was a member of the imperial court of 1277, which suggests that Marco Polo's story was to some extent true. In any case, Polo's tale about a powerful Christian king named Prester John, whom he had heard of but had not met, inspired hope in Europe that these distant lands could be converted to the Cross.

As the Ottoman Turks gradually ended safe Christian travel to the East, the European conception of Asia and Africa became a mixture of the old stories and the startling reports of Marco Polo. The spices, silks, perfumes, and jewels that arrived in Europe by way of overland caravan routes across Asia to Constantinople and through the ports of the eastern Mediterranean became increasingly expensive. Trade in the Mediterranean was dominated by Florence, Milan, and particularly Venice, who as intermediaries profited from the mark-up on the oriental products they funnelled into Europe. The cost of this trade caused European gold supplies to dwindle.

Improvements in navigation and shipbuilding encouraged those developing nation-states that did not profit from Mediterranean trade to search for sea routes to establish their own trade links with fabled Asian lands. They hoped not only to reduce the cost of the luxury goods, but also to conquer new lands that could provide gold and precious stones.

It was the leadership of Prince Henry the Navigator (1394-1460) that made Portugal a world leader in exploration. Although Henry did not go on any of the voyages that made him famous, he assembled geographers, map makers, and sailors who systematically collected evidence, improved charts, and extended the limits of European knowledge about open sea navigation. As the Moors were driven out of the Iberian peninsula, the Portuguese became aware of the gold, ivory, and slaves brought by Muslim

Science

Columbus had indeed greatly underestimated the distance from Europe to the fabled wealth of Cathay and Cipangu (Japan), which he had eagerly read about in *The Travels of Marco Polo*. With the assistance of the Italian physician and part-time geographer Paolo Toscanelli, Columbus had studied Ptolemy (whom he doubted), Marines of Tyre (whom be believed), and Marco Polo's first-hand calculations about the size of Asia. Columbus concluded that the distance from the Canaries to Japan was about 3900 km. The real distance by air is over 17 000 km.

caravans to the coast of Africa. Henry intended to seize these riches for Portugal, find a route around Africa, and meet the legendary Prester John, whom he hoped would join in a crusade to rid the Holy Land of Muslims once and for all. During Henry's lifetime, the coastal islands of the Madeiras, the Canaries, and the Azores were colonized, but Africa proved to be a much larger continent than anyone imagined. The work and inspiration that Henry provided, however, were responsible for the later success of Bartolemeu Diaz, who rounded the Cape of Good Hope in 1488, and for Vasco da Gama, who reached India by way of the Cape in 1498. Da Gama returned to Lisbon with a cargo valued at sixty times the cost of the voyage, but by this time another explorer, largely by luck and courage rather than systematic planning, had opened new horizons in another direction.

In 1484, a Genoese Italian named Christopher Columbus had approached King John of Portugal with a plan to reach Asia by sailing west. Columbus was turned down, probably because his estimate of the size of the earth seemed too small. Throughout history, the size and shape of the earth had been a subject of keen interest and discussion. By the fifteenth century, most informed thinkers believed that the earth was a sphere. The revived work of the ancient geographer Ptolemy was used to calculate the distance across the ocean from Europe to Asia. No one had any conception that the continents of North and South America existed. The Viking voyages of the tenth and eleventh centuries were either unknown or ignored, and, if Columbus had heard of them when he travelled to Iceland, they played no part in his quest for Asia.

Absolutely convinced of the accuracy of his calculations, Columbus went to Spain and presented his project to King Ferdinand and Queen Isabella in 1486. After six years of waiting and ridicule at the hands of those who thought he was mad, Columbus was given a chance to prove his boastful claims. He left on his voyage with the same motivations that spurred his many followers: hopes of glory and wealth, curiosity, and a sense of Christian mission that suited Spain's climate of religious zeal. In 1492, the centuries-old Reconquista was completed with the final expulsion of the Moors from Granada. The Spanish Inquisition was in place. Now Columbus's venture held out the hope of new lands for Christianity and for Spain.

The Issue Emerges

Columbus's epoch-making, thirty-five-day voyage, which reached the shores of San Salvador in the Bahamas on 12 October 1492, was long regarded as the first discovery of the Americas. The word "discovery," however, is inaccurate for two reasons. First, the native populations of the Americas were already here, had distinct identities of their own and did not feel that they were being "discovered." The indigenous civilizations and cultures that existed at the time of contact with Europeans were complex, and had roots going back thousands of years. The use of the word "discovery" in this context is an example of **Eurocentrism**, a view of the world that places Europe at the heart of all human development. The assumption behind this biased perspective is that other civilizations, histories, and cultures are important only in relation to Europe, and that European peoples are pre-eminent.

There is another reason why it is inaccurate to call Columbus's passage a "discovery." Recent archaeological evidence has revealed that the Vikings made earlier voyages across the Atlantic. Other evidence, from a variety of sources, suggests that contacts could have been made by the Egyptians and Phoenicians, or even that oriental voyagers could have crossed the Pacific Ocean long before Columbus approached America from the opposite direction. Knowledge of these crossings may have been lost, as knowledge so often was in those times. Do we really know when the first transoceanic crossing occurred? The question needs to be carefully considered. Several different theories have been proposed about pre-Columbian contact between peoples of the Americas and peoples of other continents.

PROBLEM QUESTION

Whose ideas about pre-Columbian voyages to the Americas are supported by the best archaeological evidence and the most logical speculations—Casson's, Heyerdahl's, or Hitching's?

ALTERNATIVE ONE: Who First Crossed the Oceans?

Based on "Who First Crossed the Oceans?" by Lionel Casson (1977)

Lionel Casson thinks the Vikings were probably the first to cross the Atlantic Ocean, and in his contribution to *Mysteries of the Past* he explains why.

We know that all of the Vikings, and especially the Norwegians, were expert seamen. We also know that they had robust galleys for their voyages. The first we know from epic tales. For the second, we have evidence. Between 1867 and 1903, archaeologists discovered three Viking tombs in which the dead had been buried in their boats. But why does Casson think the Vikings crossed the Atlantic first?

The same sagas that tell of the Viking skill and daring at sea also tell about their adventures. It is on these poems, written by Icelandic bards, that Casson bases his text.

The story begins around A.D. 900, when a mariner named Gunbjorn was blown off his course to Iceland and sighted the coast of Greenland. For almost a hundred years, Gunbjorn's claim was little more than the subject of a saga. Then, a Norwegian named Eric the Red, who lived in Iceland, decided to search for the site. As legend has it, Eric had committed murder and was banished from Iceland for three years. Looking for Gunbjorn's land was an adventurous way to fill the time.

With his family and some friends in tow, Eric set sail in 982, and landed on the southwest coast of Greenland. Apparently, Eric liked the country. When his exile was over, he returned to Iceland, not to stay, but to recruit settlers for his new colony near present-day Julianehab.

According to Casson, Danish archaeologists have evidence that verifies this part of the tale. The typical longhouse described in Viking legends has been found at the excavation site. The great hall, with 3 m thick walls of solid earth, measures 15 m by 5 m, and is claimed to be the home of Eric himself.

Trained as a missionary, Eric's son Leif abandoned preaching for exploring by about 1000. His father had been prompted by the tales of Gunbjorn's discovery, and Leif was lured by a similar story. Some years earlier, another mariner, who had been blown off his course to Greenland, had reported seeing land three times. With a crew of thirty-five, Leif set sail.

Poems tell of Leif's successes. He found the rocky island, the wooded areas, and the grassy island just as the mariner had described. Leif named the mainland Wineland, or Vinland, when grapes were discovered growing in the area. Leif and his crew were in for another surprise. Winter was very different from winters in Greenland or Iceland. There was no frost, the grass stayed green almost all year, and the daylight hours were longer.

Although Leif's party left in the spring, others ventured to the new land. Thorwald, another of Eric's sons, spent two years on Vinland before he was killed by an arrow during an argument with natives using skin boats. Two more expeditions followed, spent time, and returned home; there the story ends.

Just how much of the tale actually occurred and how much is poetic imagination? According to Casson, there is firm evidence of a Viking settlement in Newfoundland. Between 1961 and 1968, Danish archaeologists excavating at L'Anse-au-Meadows uncovered buildings and artifacts that were definitely Norse, dating about 1000. Could these be the remains of Leif's visit? Is northern Newfoundland Vinland? No one will say.

Casson begins his examination of the description of Vinland with the most obvious problem, the grapes. He points out that a sixteenth-century naval surgeon reported seeing "wild grapes incredible" in Newfoundland. If then, why not earlier? This could certainly be the case if there were warmer temperatures over the northern Atlantic, as many historians argue. Casson admits, however, that even warmer weather would probably not produce the abundant forests and green grass year-round as told in the sagas. Could this be the exaggeration of the bards?

If not Newfoundland, then where? According to Casson, a number of locations along the eastern seaboard as far south as Virginia have been offered at one time or another. A round tower at Newport, Rhode Island, is one example. Some scholars credit it to the Vikings, others credit it to the colonials. The evidence tends to favour the colonials.

Perhaps the most interesting claim Casson describes involved the notorious Kensington Stone, found during the last century on a farm near Kensington, Minnesota. Apparently, the stone, which bore an inscription in the Viking script, was discredited as a forgery. Later, the stone was retrieved from the farmer's yard by Hjalmar Holland, a collector of Viking artifacts, who defended its authenticity for the next fifty years. However, the validity of other objects owned by Holland was also questionable. None was found *in situ*, and the three halberds in his collection were discredited when it was discovered that they were actually tobacco cutters made for the American Tobacco Company to advertise Battle Axe Plug Tobacco.

Although the exact location of Vinland has yet to be verified, Casson is convinced that the Vikings did indeed cross the Atlantic.

Questions

1. a) What is the source of our information about Viking voyages in the North Atlantic?
   b) How do we know what Viking ships looked like?
2. a) Why did Eric the Red set out in search of Greenland?
   b) What evidence has confirmed the presence of a Viking settlement on Greenland?
3. When Eric's son Leif was carried past Greenland in a voyage about 1000, he came upon a rocky island and a coastal area he named Vinland. What were the conditions like in this new area?
4. What archaeological evidence has verified the presence of the Vikings in Newfoundland at the time of the Viking sagas?
5. a) What areas have been suggested as possible locations for Vinland?
   b) Explain how evidence has been used and misused in an attempt to locate Vinland.
6. Should the Vikings, rather than Columbus, be regarded as the first voyagers to America? Explain your answer with evidence.

ALTERNATIVE TWO: The Ra Expeditions

Based on *The Ra Expeditions* by Thor Heyerdahl (1971)

Thor Heyerdahl, adventurer and author, is convinced that the influence of Mediterranean voyagers was the source of the advanced cultures found in the Americas. To prove his theory, Heyerdahl and his crew made two journeys from Egypt in ships made of papyrus reeds—the *Ra I* and the *Ra II*. The second voyage landed in America. In *The Ra Expeditions*, Thor Heyerdahl explains the theory that prompted these adventures.

According to Heyerdahl, thousands of non-Europeans had already established great cultural centres in the Americas before Columbus's landing of 12 October 1492. For Heyerdahl, then, Columbus merely "flung open the doors of America" to his fellow Europeans.

Heyerdahl's speculations are based on a variety of evidence. For one thing, he points to the reception that the native peoples of America gave to conquistadores like Cortes and Pizarro. It was as though the conquistadores were expected. According to Heyerdahl, the Spanish were told legends of white-skinned, bearded men from across the sea who had brought with them the "secrets of civilization." Heyerdahl claims this is the reason neither the natives of Mexico nor Peru were surprised to see these new voyagers.

What is even more interesting is that these legends of early culture bearers were prevalent only in the areas of the three great kingdoms—the Aztecs, Mayans, and Incas.

After the Spanish arrived, it was only a few decades before these civilizations crumbled. Their ruin was due partly to death from war, enslavement, and disease and partly to integration. According to Heyerdahl, it was therefore easy for Europeans to take credit for the positive aspects of those cultures. Had the civilizations survived for any length of time, however, we might have learned more about their heritage.

Of course, this raises the obvious question: What really happened in Mexico and Peru before the arrival of Columbus? Heyerdahl takes this question even further. "Had descendants of barbarians from Arctic Asia received voyagers who landed in the Gulf of Mexico in the morning of time, when civilization also spread from Africa and Asia Minor up to the coasts of barbaric Europe?"

In his attempt to answer these questions, Heyerdahl examines the possibilities. If these great cultures had developed locally from ancient civilizations, then there should be archaeological evidence of this development. Yet, excavations of sites in Mexico and Peru indicate that these cultures were already mature when they arrived. The only evidence of development is later variations of the mature form.

If these cultures had arrived in fully mature form, then they must have been imported; imported from where, and how?

From his travels about the world, Heyerdahl recalls seeing papyrus-reed boats as the seagoing transportation method most frequently depicted in antiquities. In northern Peru, they were shown on ceramic pots; in Egypt, they were painted on tombs; and on Easter Island, they were part of both wall paintings and reliefs. Was this the transportation method used?

There are other intriguing parallels among these three cultures. The scenes on Peruvian pots also show a sun god or priest-king, much larger than his subjects, and surrounded by bird-headed men towing a reed boat through the water. The same elements appear on the Egyptian tombs; the imposing figure of the priest-king, or pharaoh, is surrounded by his sub-jects, with bird-headed men again towing the reed boat. There are slight variations in the Easter Island paintings. A mask represents the sun god, and the reed boats have sails, but the bird-headed men remain the same. Heyerdahl finds it fascinating that these people in the Pacific even called their sun god "Ra," just as the ancient Egyptians had done.

Another similarity is the giant monoliths that each civilization erected to pay homage to its sun god. Are the enormous statues of Easter Island and the pyramids of Peru and Egypt in some way connected, or are they coincidental?

Heyerdahl thinks there is a connection. But since ancient Egypt had ceased to exist about two thousand years before the appearance of these civilizations, the connection must have been an indirect one. Perhaps another civilization, such as Phoenicia or the island people of the Mediterranean, had been the source.

According to Heyerdahl, this is a likely prospect. The ancient Egyptians were a dynamic people who travelled about the Mediterranean and beyond, visiting Mesopotamian and other Asian ports. Certainly, they were affiliated with the people from Phoenicia, and influenced many of the civilizations on the islands.

Although little is known about the first Phoenician ships, Heyerdahl believes there is sufficient evidence from their neighbours to the south, east, and west to conclude that the Phoenicians would have used reed boats for transportation. Indeed, by the time their culture had spread beyond Gibraltar to Lixus, reed boats were definitely being used. Although numerous voyagers had ventured beyond Gibraltar, the first voyage that is documented, according to Heyerdahl, is that of Hanno, in the fifth century B.C. The event, which was recorded on an artifact in Carthage, tells of sixty ships stocked with supplies and colonists of both sexes. Hanno sailed as far as Equatoria, west Africa, stopping at Lixus on the way for navigational advice. It was the "foreigners" at Lixus who also gave Hanno advice on how to handle primitive people, who could some-times be quite hostile.

According to Heyerdahl, collaboration between different nationalities was not new. The first voyage to sail around Africa occurred about 600 B.C., and was a combined effort organized by the Egyptian pharaoh Necho and undertaken by a Phoenician crew and ships. The story was recorded by the historian Herodotus almost two hundred years later.

The idea of an expedition of mixed nationalities intrigued Heyerdahl. If such a party found themselves among primitive people in the Americas, what cultural patterns would they impose? Could such an expedition sur-vive an Atlantic crossing in a reed boat? These were the questions that prompted Thor Heyerdahl to embark on the Ra Expedition.

Questions

1. What was the reaction of the native people to the Spanish conquistadores who followed Columbus?
2. What happened to both the Aztec and Inca empires within a short time after the arrival of the Spanish?
3. What important question does Heyerdahl ask about the Americas before the arrival of Columbus?
4. a) If great civilizations had developed on their own in Mexico or Peru, what pattern should archaeologists be able to identify?
   b) Was this pattern present?
   c) What alternative thus seems worth pursuing?
5. Why did Heyerdahl make a connection among the reed boats in Egypt, Peru, and Easter Island?
6. a) How does Heyerdahl know that Egyptian and Phoenician influence spread throughout the Mediterranean?
   b) Should the voyages of Hanno and Pharaoh Necho be believed? Explain your answer.
7. To what extent does Heyerdahl's theory about the spread of culture from Egypt throughout the Mediterranean to Africa and, eventually, to Mesoamerica and Easter Island seem convincing? Explain your answer with evidence.

ALTERNATIVE THREE: Early Cartographers and the Discovery of America

Based on "Early Cartographers" and "Who Discovered America?" by Francis Hitching (1978)

In *The World Atlas of Mysteries,* Francis Hitching delves into the mystery of who first visited the Americas. The traditional account tells of migrants from Asia making their way on foot across the Bering Strait land-bridge over thirty thousand years ago. As they moved southward, small groups broke away and established societies that were influenced by local conditions. According to the conventional explanation, their physical differences are a result of adaptations that occurred through natural selection.

Are we to believe this traditional account of isolated evolution, when an analysis of ancient maps, records of seafaring voyages in small craft, and archaeological evidence suggest otherwise?

In his attempt to convince us that the Americas might well have been visited many times in the prehistoric past, Hitching examines the evidence. His first example is the map compiled by the Turkish admiral Piri Re'is in 1513. Piri Re'is himself felt that his map was unique, since it was based on earlier charts and maps prepared at the time of Alexander the Great. They were stored in the vast collection of ancient knowledge found among the million books in the Alexandrian library before its final destruction by fire in the eleventh century. Piri Re'is had only leftover fragments of the originals to work with, and today only part of the admiral's world map is left to us for study. The puzzle is that the admiral's map shows a detailed knowledge of the world's geography dating back to the time before civilization.

The state of map making in Piri Re'is's day was generally very primitive. Although latitude (the distance from the equator) was established with considerable accuracy, longitude (the vertical lines that indicate east-west positions) was only guesswork. Most of the maps in the Late Middle Ages (1300-1500) made large errors in the east-west placing of land, as did Columbus in his calculations about the location of Japan. Some ancient maps used a system of *portolans*, grids that radiate like the spokes of a wheel. These can cause locations to be tilted at the wrong angle when transferred onto a normal map. Allowing for this distortion, Piri Re'is's map is extremely accurate. The western coasts of Africa and Europe and the north Atlantic islands (with the exception of Madeira) are all in their correct longitude and are even in their proper longitudinal relationship with the coast of South America and Antarctica. The Caribbean also falls into place once the error in the use of *portolans* is corrected. The southern part of South America is drawn accurately to an average error of less than one degree, while the Falklands are at the correct latitude even though they are misplaced by five degrees on the east-west plane.

As additional support, Hitching offers a second map, drawn in 1531 by Oronteus Finnaeus, that gives even more spectacular evidence. While Piri Re'is's map shows a small portion of the Antarctic coastline known as Queen Maud Land, the map of Finnaeus shows the Antarctic coastline in detail, with rivers pouring out to sea from mountain ranges and a central ice-cap in the interior. The catch here is that Antarctica has been covered by ice since at least 4000 B.C., and it was not officially discovered until 1818! For these maps to exist, ancient travellers must have explored the coast when it was free of ice.

If ancient mariners travelled these seas in the remote past, it seems likely they also arrived on the shores of the Americas. Certainly, there was no problem in finding a suitable vessel. Today, hundreds of crossings in small boats of every description have been verified. The list includes rafts, dugout canoes, dories propelled by oars or fitted with sails, sailboats less than 2 m long, kayaks, folding boats, and even an amphibian jeep.

Hitching believes transoceanic contact took place. What he would like to know is how early, how often, and how influential were these contacts. For answers to these questions, he examines records and artifacts. One of these is a case of pottery dated to 3000 B.C. that was picked up on the coast of Ecuador. The engravings on these artifacts are identical to those on pottery from the Jamon area of Japan. Moreover, there is *no* evidence in Ecuador of earlier, more primitive pottery from which these may have evolved. Therefore, the pottery must have been imported. Were voyagers from Japan blown off course or caught in a storm that carried them almost 13 000 km to Ecuador?

Hitching points out that other transoceanic contacts have been suggested. A legend of the Hopi Indians in Arizona recalls their journey across the water by means of "stepping stones" or islands. A Chinese classic of 2250 B.C., *Shan Hai King*, contains a description of what could be the Grand Canyon. Were the civilizations that developed in Mesoamerica and Peru around 2000 B.C. influenced by the Chinese?

The currents and Gulf Stream of the Atlantic would have made crossings quite likely both in the northern areas—from Scandinavian ports to Nova Scotia—and to the south—between the Mediterranean and Central America. Such crossings may have resulted in trading partnerships, which would account for fishing gear and woodworking tools in the Great Lakes area, and slate knives in Scandinavian and the Baltic countries, all of which appeared around 2500 B.C. There were also similarities in pottery styles.

Other transatlantic contacts Hitching mentions are those interpreted from the texts of Plato and Diodorus that indicate there was trade between Phoenicians and the Americas about 1000 B.C.

Evidence suggests a variety of races visited Mesoamerica. Sculptured heads, ranging in origin from 1500 B.C. to A.D. 1500, show African Blacks, bearded Jews, and other racial types. Indeed, the similarities between Mesoamerican civilization and Egypt seem too numerous to be explained except by the influence of Mediterranean voyagers. In Hitching's view, Columbus and the Spaniards who followed were not the first but rather the last in a long line of visitors over a long period of time.

Questions

1. What is the standard explanation for historical development in the Americas?
2. a) Who was Piri Re'is?
   b) When were the earlier charts he used to construct his map produced?
   c) Why was Piri Re'is's map so puzzling?
3. What error was found on the vast majority of maps made when Piri Re'is lived?
4. a) How accurate was the map made by Piri Re'is?
   b) Why does the map made by Oronteus Finnaeus in 1531 seem so truly remarkable?
   c) What might these maps tell us about the mariners of the ancient world?
   d) Can you think of alternative explanations for the apparent accuracies of these maps?

5. Is it possible to cross the Atlantic in a small boat? Explain your answer.
6. a) Why is pottery found in Ecuador, dated to 3000 B.C., viewed as important evidence of pre-Columbian contact between the Americas and Japan?
   b) Are there other ways of explaining the pottery?
7. Hitching gives several examples of possible transoceanic crossings to the Americas. Which three examples are the most convincing?
8. Has Hitching proved that the Americas were visited before Columbus? Explain your answer.

ANSWERING THE PROBLEM QUESTION

To answer the problem question, each of the three positions must be assessed in two ways. First, what solid archaeological evidence does the author present to support his arguments? Second, how logical are the speculations he presents?

Lionel Casson is sceptical about most legends. Why does he believe that the Viking sagas contain reliable information about pre-Columbian voyages to America? Is the archaeological evidence of Viking presence in Newfoundland any more convincing than Heyerdahl's voyage across the Atlantic or the parallels between cultures that Hitching mentions?

Much of Thor Heyerdahl's work depends on the cultural parallels that exist between Egyptian and American societies. Are the similarities in buildings, pyramids, boats, and cultural practices precise enough to connect the two areas in question? Did the success of *Ra II* prove that the same trip could have been made by Phoenicians centuries before the Roman Empire existed?

Francis Hitching's position is that the maps of unusual accuracy drawn in the Late Middle Ages were based on charts dating to the pre-Christian era, and that those charts could have been produced only if the coastlines had been seen. Are his inferences from these maps sound enough to be persuasive? Are the similarities in artifacts between the Orient and the Americas, and the Americas and the Baltic, evidence of actual contact and influence?

THE STORY CONTINUES . . .

Amerindians: Mesoamerica and the Aztecs

When Columbus died in 1506, after four voyages to the Americas, he was convinced he had found the gateway to Asia. Rumours of a wealthy land to the west inspired further exploration, first by Hernandez de Cordova, then Diego Velasquez, and finally Hernan Cortes, who came not upon India but upon the empire of the Aztecs in 1519. Little did the Spanish realize that civilizations had come and gone in **Mesoamerica** (Mexico and Central America) for over two thousand years before their arrival. Indeed, even the Aztecs had only hazy recollections of the distant past, represented in the form of a series of legends.

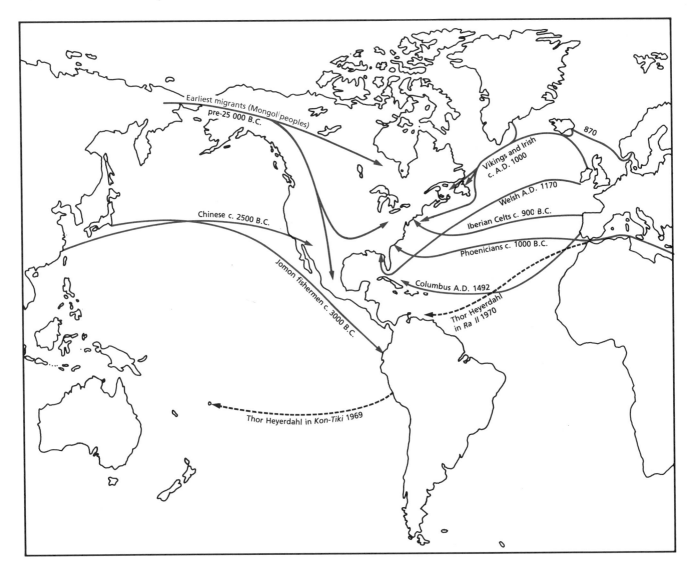

*Arrivals in the Americas
(Hypothetical and Known).*

Archaeologists are still unfolding the complicated pattern of prehistory in Mesoamerica. Although each civilization was centred in a specific region, its influence usually spread throughout a much larger area. Each civilization was thus to some extent a blend of old and new skills, lifestyles, and beliefs.

The civilization that emerged from the hunter-gatherers who first populated the region was that of the **Olmecs**, beginning about 1200 B.C. and lasting for almost one thousand years. On the Gulf Coast of what is now Mexico, the Olmecs built a series of ceremonial centres including La Venta,

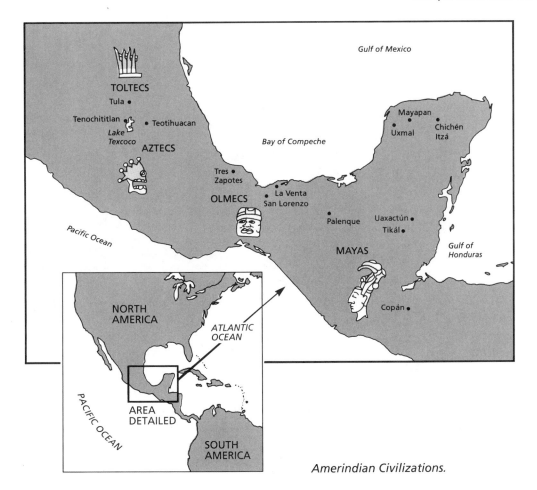

Amerindian Civilizations.

San Lorenzo, and Tres Zapotes. Each was a carefully planned community with raised platforms, courtyards, ball courts, artificial lagoons, and temples. The resident population was usually less than one thousand, but the lack of true cities did not prevent the development of distinct styles in pottery and architecture. Large and small sculptures, jade axes, and pottery vessels showed a figure that was half woman and half jaguar, the focal point of the Olmecs' religion. The Olmecs were the first Mesoamericans to move and shape large masses of stone for buildings and monumental sculptures. Large chunks of basalt, weighing upwards of 20 t, were hauled by rope and floated by raft for distances of 60 km, and were used for the colossal stone heads almost 3 m tall that stood at each of the ceremonial centres. Some of the earliest evidence of ritual cannibalism can also be found at these sites. It is likely that the Olmecs developed the carved figures known as **glyphs** and the calendar made famous by the Mayan civilization.

The structures in the Maya-Toltec centre at Chichén Itzá are noted for their massive grandeur and delicate relief. This observatory, which closely resembles its modern counterparts, reflects the Maya fascination with astronomy, time, and mathematics.

The **Maya** flourished in the lowlands of Yucatan from the third to the ninth centuries. They were fascinated by time and numbers. Used widely throughout Mesoamerica by the fourth century, the Mayan time measurement system was based on a solar calendar of 365 days and a ritual calendar of 260 days. Each moment was watched over by one of their many gods. Every fifty-two years, the two calendars coincided in a cycle known as the

One of the ceremonial pyramids built by the Maya.

The crypt of the Mayan prince of Palenque. The jade-and-jewel-covered prince was found at the end of a twisting, descending hall, 34 m below the entrance to the pyramid.

Calendar Round. This was a year of great religious importance. Like the megalithic builders of Europe, the Maya could predict the rising and setting of the sun and the eclipse cycle of the sun and moon, but Mayan accuracy was virtually to the second. Their solar calendar estimated the length of the year at 365.2422 days, which is more accurate than either the Roman Julian or later Gregorian calendars. The Mayan system of counting, like all others in Mesoamerica, was based on twenty rather than on the ten used in Western mathematics. Through the use of symbols, the Maya could count forward or backward 400 million years. In addition, they invented the concept of zero long before the Europeans borrowed it from the Arabs in the Middle Ages.

During their golden age, the Maya built extensive temple complexes with considerable skill. At Uaxactún, Tikál, Copán, and many other sites,

The Street of the Dead in Teotihuacan. The Pyramid of the Sun (left background), like other structures in the city, is situated with precise geometric planning.

temple platforms rose over 34 m off the jungle floor. Stepped pyramids, oriented toward the points of the compass, were constructed of stone cemented together with a strong lime mortar. Coloured frescoes covered the walls of many public buildings and usually showed scenes of gods, priests, and religious rituals, or wealthy merchants and nobles. Elaborate sculptures, found in every city, show that the Maya were experts at three-dimensional representation.

The Maya have left several puzzling questions. Despite their precise observation of heavenly bodies, they failed to realize that the earth revolves around the sun. They made toys with wheels, but never applied the principle of the wheel to construction, architecture, or everyday life. They built magnificent public temples, but their tools were essentially those of the Stone Age. They developed advanced systems of mathematics and time, but their writing was based on symbols rather than on a phonetic alphabet. Perhaps the greatest mystery, often explained in terms of famine and war though never settled, is the sudden decline of the entire civilization in the ninth century. During that span of one hundred years, the Maya left their traditional strongholds and moved to colonial sites such as Uxmal, Mayapan, and Chichén Itzá. Here, the Maya experienced another era of prosperity that lasted until the arrival of the Spanish.

Further north, the Mexican Plateau was dominated by the grandeur and majesty of **Teotihuacan** from 100 B.C. to A.D. 750. It was the most impressive ceremonial centre ever built in Mesoamerica, but its people left

The Pyramid of the Moon, a triumph of stepped-pyramid construction, features a complex system of interior stone piers and walls filled with earth and rubble. It is faced with trimmed stone masonry. This and other stepped pyramids resemble the mud-brick ziggurats of Mesopotamia, and served the same ceremonial purpose.

no record of their way of life. The name Teotihuacan means "place of the gods," and later peoples explained most of the buildings as tombs for kings who became deities upon their death. The central avenue, 45 m wide and 4 km long, was known as the Street of the Dead and was flanked on the north by the Pyramid of the Moon, to the east by the 66 m high Pyramid of the Sun, and to the southeast by the temple of the feathered serpent Quetzalcoatl. As the city grew, it was divided into four large quadrants subdivided into smaller squares. In A.D. 600, the city could accommodate two hundred thousand residents. This number must have swelled greatly when pilgrims arrived to celebrate religious rituals. Trade in the volcanic glass obsidian, used for making sharp tools and weapons, appeared to be a major economic activity. Brightly coloured murals of mythical beasts, animals, and birds, painted on building walls, provided a cheerful atmosphere for all passers-by. Later murals showed priests portrayed with weapons and shields, suggesting that the metropolis might have succumbed to a series of wars. The fall of Teotihuacan, however, remains one of the mysteries of civilization in Mesoamerica.

The imperialistic **Toltecs**, one of the wandering bands of Chichimec tribes, were another influential upland people. The Toltecs conquered much of civilized Mesoamerica and built their capital at Tula, which thrived from about A.D. 900 to 1200. Most of the buildings reveal a hasty construction, which suggests that their main concern was military conquest, as symbolized by the 5 m high stone warriors resting on the temple platform at Tula. The

Toltecs preserved the worship of Quetzalcoatl, the ancient Mesoamerican god who was worshipped in Teotihuacan and by the Maya as well.

As the Toltec Empire collapsed, many of its people intermarried with another Chichimec tribe, the **Aztecs** (who called themselves the Mexica). After much wandering and strife, the Aztecs settled on a rocky island in Lake Texcoco in 1325. Here, their leader witnessed a vision predicted by their tribal god: an eagle, perched on a cactus beside a rock, marked the spot of a great Aztec city that would rule all of Mexico. With their quest completed, the Aztecs began construction of Tenochititlan (Mexico City), which became a city of waterways, much like Venice. To increase the amount of arable land, islands of mud and fibre were built and joined by causeways. By 1375, as their military strength grew, the Aztecs subdued the tribes along the lakeshore, and their city became a rich commercial centre with enormous temples and palaces. The Aztec Empire was run by a chief whose successors ruled until the Spanish conquest. Although the Aztecs dominated the Valley of Mexico, many of the tribes they overran in outlying areas remained resentful and were always on the verge of revolt.

The Aztecs, like the Toltecs before them, were a religious and warlike people. According to their beliefs, four previous worlds, or "suns," had been destroyed in turn by jaguars, wind, fire, and water. After each disaster, the gods placed a new sun in the sky. The present world would be ended by an earthquake that could be prevented only if the sun was fed continually with human blood. The Aztecs borrowed this religious practice of human sacrifice from the Toltecs, whose accomplishments they admired. The military orders of the Aztecs, the Jaguars and Eagles, were constantly at war to gain the victims needed for sacrifice to the sun. In peacetime, ritual games served the same purpose.

Sacrifice to the sun was considered a glorious death. Those chosen for sacrifice were often treated to months of feasting and entertainment until the day of the ritual. When Cortes interrupted such a ceremony, the privileged youth protested that he was being denied his right to an everlasting life. The number of people sacrificed was usually low, but there were exceptions. During the opening of a new temple at Tenochititlan in 1487, at least twenty thousand victims were sacrificed in a four-day period. Women were also sacrificed, usually to the goddess of maize. Children were sacrificed to the god Tlaloc, and their tears were regarded as the rain for which the Aztecs prayed.

The Aztecs had a highly prosperous civilization that was still developing when the Spanish arrived. Their textiles were beautifully made, as was their sculpture and pottery, which featured brightly coloured floral patterns and animal designs. Although they developed no written script, they had a method of recording stories in pictures known as a **codex**. Most codices were destroyed by Spanish priests, who regarded them as evil, but, fortunately, a few have survived. The splendour of the Aztec court befitted their

Science

Some very important foods, such as beans, squash, and potatoes, originated in Mexico. But it was **maize** (corn) that was the Amerindians' main crop. Tiny cobs a few centimetres long found at several cave sites have been dated to 5000 B.C. This type of maize grew naturally. The Amerindians deliberately domesticated maize, producing bigger and better varieties. These new strains of maize were common staples by 1500 B.C. Maize could be grown in hot, steamy lowland forests, on dry upland plateaus, and in mountain valleys. Because it proved to be so adaptable, it was found throughout the Americas. Amerindians were creating new and improved varieties of maize right up to the arrival of the Spanish.

famous ruler Montezuma II, who sat alone under a feathered canopy while others entertained him and catered to his every need, and long lines of nobles gathered to pay their respects. From this court, priests and officials helped to organize a society geared for war, forcing those they conquered to pay taxes and tribute.

Aztec civilization came to an abrupt end. Hernan Cortes arrived in 1519 with eleven ships, about five hundred men, sixteen horses, and four-teen cannons. At first sight of a Spaniard riding a horse, the Mesoamericans thought they were looking at one creature. The bearded Cortes was mis-taken for the god Quetzalcoatl, who had left in disgrace from Tula in Toltec legend but had promised to return. Initial greetings were friendly, and Montezuma showered the returning "god" with gifts of gold, jade, and jewels. Relations became strained as the early weeks passed, particularly when the Spanish discovered they had been offered food soaked in blood from the human sacrifices of the Aztec religious practices that so appalled them. The Spanish captured Montezuma and, through the use of superior weaponry (cannons and guns against javelins), the assistance of tribes who resented Aztec domination, and the devastating effect of a plague (probably smallpox), conquered the Aztec Empire within two years. To the Aztecs, it seemed as if their gods had deserted them. The European exploitation of the Americas had begun.

The basaltic Sun Stone of the Aztecs was carved about 1500 and depicts the sun at its centre. The presence of the twenty-day Aztec ritual cycle on the Sun Stone led many archaeologists to conclude (wrongly) that the 26 t megalith was a calendar.

Amerindians: South America and the Inca

South American prehistory, like that of Mesoamerica, was a complex puzzle that featured the rise and decline of several civilizations long before the arrival of the Spanish. As in Mesoamerica, each culture was centred on a particular area, but extended its influence throughout much of the territory inhabited by its neighbours. Various peoples controlled the Pacific coastal region from modern-day Ecuador to Chile, an area that encompasses an incredible variety of geography, from ocean shore to the mountains of the Andes.

The **Chavin cult**, dominated by the worship of a jaguar god, was the first to unite distinct regions under a common culture. From 1000 to 300 B.C., their main ceremonial centre was Chavin de Huantar, located above an altitude of 3000 m in the eastern Andes and dominated by a temple known as the **Castillo**. Enlarged as Chavin influence expanded, the Castillo was originally a terraced platform that contained a maze of corridors, stair-ways, rooms, and even ventilator shafts. Sculptured heads projecting from the outer walls showed a snarling, jaguarlike mouth with canines bared and lips curled at the corners. Other sites have shown that Chavin pottery was decorated with designs of mythological creatures, as were the textiles they wove on their looms. Chavin motifs also appeared on gold and copper jew-ellery, belts, and even tweezers. Burial chambers containing dozens of mummies, each wrapped in layers of cloth, have also been found.

Inca Empire.

Civilization in Mesoamerica and South America

Date	Event
B.C.	
30 000	Mongol peoples cross Bering land bridge, moving south and east to populate the Americas
10 000	Bering land bridge submerged as Ice Age ends and sea level rises
1500	Maize domesticated and dispersed throughout Mesoamerica and South America
1200	Olmec civilization arises in Mesoamerica
1000	Chavin people unite several regions in the eastern Andes of South America
300	Chavin influence declines
200	Disappearance of the Olmecs Tiahuanaco established in high Andes Mochica and Nazca cultures arise
100	Construction of ceremonial centre at Teotihuacan
A.D.	
200	The Maya flourish in Yucatan Perfection of the solar calendar
750	Teotihuacan abandoned
800-900	The Maya decline and relocate their civilization Toltecs build city of Tula
1100	Chimu Kingdom dominates northwest coast of South America
1200	Toltec civilization collapses
1325	Aztecs begin construction of Tenochititlan (Mexico City)
c. 1470	Inca civilization overthrows Chimu Kingdom Inca empire reaches its peak
1514-21	Cortes arrives and subjugates the Aztecs
1531	Pizarro arrives among the Inca
1580	Inca resistance ends Mesoamerica and South America under European domination

With the decline of Chavin influence by about 300 B.C., cultural development and power became fragmented, and several nations evolved traditions of their own. At 3800 m in the high Andes near Lake Titicaca, an important centre emerged after A.D. 200 at **Tiahuanaco**. Entrance to the temple complex was made through a doorway, known as the "Gateway of the Sun," cut in a single block of stone. Atop the opening is the rigid form of the supreme god Veracocha, who, like Quetzalcoatl of the Aztecs, was thought to have white skin. Inside, a stepped pyramid, resting on a natural mound faced with stone, rises to a height of over 15 m. A lower temple platform with upright stones of 4 m may have supported a stone roof. Tiahuanaco greatly influenced the city of **Huari**, which grew into an empire that lasted until about the tenth century.

The **Mochica** culture became dominant in the north. The Mochica built several pyramid centres of adobe brick fastened with cane and wood and covered with plaster. Their temple at Huaca de Sol contained 130 million bricks and measured 228 m by 137 m at the base, which made it the largest adobe structure built in the Americas before the conquest. Irrigation systems, canals, and aqueducts turned desert into productive fields. When level clearings were not available, villages in the shadow of temple sites were built into terraced hillsides. Mochica pottery was produced in large quantities and characterized by a striking realism, whether depicting animals, humans, or gods. Metalwork in gold, silver, and copper was superior to that created by the earlier Chavin culture. Similar advances were made by the **Nazca** people of the south. They, too, built ceremonial centres, developed a distinctive pottery style showing gods and scenes from everyday life, and, like the Chavins, mummified their dead. The deformed skulls of some mummies suggest that the Nazca may have practised ritual human sacrifice.

From the eleventh to the fifteenth centuries, the coastal region from central Peru to Ecuador was dominated by the **Chimu** Kingdom, with its capital of Chan Chan. Estimates of the city's population often exceed forty thousand, which make it the largest city in South America before the conquest. Massive adobe walls, sculptured with outlines of sea creatures, gods, and decorative designs, enclosed a series of ten compounds. Each one had a labyrinth of corridors that led to the inner courtyards and burial compounds for the governing class. Connected to the coastal cities of the empire by roads, the countryside of the Chimu Kingdom was dominated by agriculture. Peasants worked on community irrigation systems, canals, and construction projects. During the 1470s, however, Chan Chan was overthrown by the Inca, who had begun to spread outward from their capital at Cuzco in the early fifteenth century.

The word **Inca** was used to identify both the people of the empire and their king, who ruled by divine right as the sun's representative. Every Incan king, assisted by a court and high priests, governed from Cuzco, where a

More to Consider

The Inca developed no formal system of writing. To transmit information over long distances, they used specially trained **chasquis** runners. A communication would be memorized by the first messenger, who would speed along one of the Incan roads and relay the message to the next runner. By such a method, a message might travel 200 km in a single day. **Quechua**, the common language of the empire, was used for verbal messages. Numerical records, also carried by the chasquis, were kept with **quipo**, which were knotted strings. The administrators at Cuzco used quipo to keep track of the yearly tribute owed by subject communities. Such tribute might take the form of a quota of goods, soldiers, or workers to maintain community fields. In return, the people received military protection and food from state storehouses in time of famine.

Fortress of Sacsahuaman. The biggest stones were placed at the bottom, and the smaller ones were aligned with the irregular-shaped sides and higher elevations. The tight lines of contact, which appear only on the outside, were probably achieved by hours of pounding with a stone hammer on the face and adjoining edges, the effects of which can still be seen on the mottled rock surfaces. Behind the outward façade, the spaces were actually quite wide and usually packed with earth.

palace was built for each successive monarch. Incan administration was efficient and tightly controlled, and almost every aspect of an individual's life was subject to laws enforced by state officials. During the reign of Topa Inca in the late fifteenth century, the Inca Empire stretched 4800 km, from Ecuador to Chile, in a belt 320 km wide, from the ocean to the jungle of Amazonia. The Inca mastered many environments—coastal lowlands, deserts, moist uplands, and the upper reaches of mountains. Their empire encompassed a greater area than was held by all of their ancestors combined. Inca engineering was exceptionally skillful. At the fortress of Sacsahuaman near Cuzco, 100 t megaliths were dragged and fitted into place within the thickness of a knife blade. The Inca combined their ability to organize large masses of labour, unique building techniques, and a logical step-by-step approach to create such massive walls.

Similar stonework can be found in the public buildings of many Incan towns, including the foundation of the lost city of **Machu Picchu**. Missed by the Spanish and unknown to the West until discovered by the American Hiram Bingham in 1911, Machu Picchu is situated at over 2700 m in the Andes and provides stunning evidence of Incan ingenuity. Rock outcrops were incorporated into the design of buildings, while natural fissures were often sealed and used as burial caves. Even though the city had been looted, 173 mummies were excavated from the caves. The steep slopes that led upward toward the city were carefully groomed with supporting walls that braced terraces used for agriculture. These slopes, along with a series of fountains and baths, were supplied with water through stone aqueducts. The layout of Machu Picchu was typically Incan; it contained a central square surrounded by temples, defensive walls, and a palace. At one temple, stone posts used by Incan priests, who were skilled astronomers, were

Machu Picchu, a tribute to Incan genius in engineering and adaptability.

aligned to predict the rising and setting of the summer sun on 21 June—the start of the Incan ceremonial year.

A marvellous system of stone and earthen roads covered the length and breadth of the Inca Empire. The Incas never developed wheeled vehicles. Domesticated llamas were used to haul loads, and the other traffic was pedestrian. The roads were constructed with typical cleverness. Where slopes were steep, switchback trails provided access to higher ground. Over deep ravines and canyons, the Inca built suspension bridges of twisted lianas (woody vines) anchored to blocks of stone on either side. When they first saw them, the Spanish were terrified of the bridges that swayed back and forth over pounding river rapids far below. But they overcame their fear, and took their armies and horses across in their conquest of the Inca.

The Inca, like the Aztecs of Mesoamerica, built an empire through political and economic organization, and skill in battle. Their slings, bolas, and swords, however, were not enough against the iron-clad Spaniards with their guns, horses, and the contagious diseases they unintentionally introduced. When Francisco Pizarro arrived in 1531 with only 62 horsemen and 102 foot soldiers, he was able to take advantage of a political struggle over the succession to the Inca throne. Pizarro seized the strongest claimant, Atahuallpa, who tried to buy his freedom with the riches of the Temple of the Sun at Cuzco. The gold was stripped from the temple and given to and melted down by the Spanish. Atahuallpa was eventually executed despite the payment, and the Spanish took control of the highly centralized political system of the Inca. Although isolated pockets of fierce resistance held out in the mountains until 1580, the sun had set on the native civilizations of South America, just as it had in Mesoamerica to the north.

SUMMARY

During the Middle Ages, Europe changed from a feudal society organized for agricultural production and war into a society driven by increasingly broad-ranging trade and commerce. As business activity increased, urban centres expanded. Serfs left the land and moved to the towns, seeking easier work and the possibility of prosperity. Europe was no longer a civilization of nobles on the one hand and serfs on the other. In between grew the middle class—merchants and tradespeople who consolidated their economic and political power by organizing themselves into guilds. Despite the development of the middle class, power resided mainly in the two institutions of Church and state; these institutions contended with one another for advantage throughout the Middle Ages.

By the middle of the eleventh century, Europe was predominantly Christian. When the Seljuk Turks took over the Holy Land and captured Christian pilgrims, Pope Urban II called for the First Crusade, which began in 1096. Other crusades followed, but Europeans gained control of the Holy Land only for a short while. During that time, however, trade networks brought the luxury goods of the East into European hands, and Europeans became aware of Eastern scholarship and science.

Two kinds of architecture are representative of the ambitions that carried Europe through the Crusades and beyond. Cathedral architecture demonstrated the central importance of the Church. Suger, Abbot of St. Denis, initiated the Gothic style of building in 1140, and the following decades saw the construction of the great Gothic cathedrals. Castles, on the other hand, were imposing symbols of the might of the state, housing the fighting forces of the day—infantry and the all-important cavalry. But as the Middle Ages passed, the power of Church and state was moderated by the financial power of the middle class. Cathedrals were built less often and less grandly by the middle of the fourteenth century, and the military value of the castle decreased at about the same time.

The second half of the Middle Ages was a time of change for both Church and state. The Church's popularity was high when the First Crusade was announced, but the greed underlying subsequent crusades tarnished its image. In the thirteenth century, Pope Innocent III created an effective Church administration and greatly enhanced the status of the papacy. He established the Franciscans, an order of friars who lived simply and travelled among the people. He also gave initial approval to the Dominicans, whose role was to monitor the religious beliefs of more educated citizens. In the fourteenth century, as a result of the Inquisition, the Babylonian Captivity, and the greed of the clergy, respect for the papacy and the Church deteriorated.

As the fortunes of the Church rose and fell, important changes in government were occurring in Europe. France and England became great nation-states, as power shifted from the feudal lords to the kings of each land. Increasingly, justice was administered by the monarchy, and taxes levied on the king's behalf. In France this transformation took longer, but the monarchy managed to hold the power it had gained, and France had become the dominant European state by the reign of Philip IV (1285-1314). The English monarchy was forced to govern alongside a council called Parliament, and never achieved the same absolute power.

English kings, tracing their lineage to William of Normandy, claimed title to portions of France. In 1337, Edward III of England went to France to assert these claims and to become king of the whole country. The two nations became embroiled in the Hundred Years War. The English forces were eventually repelled, the two nations signed a peace treaty in 1453, and England lost all its French territory except for the port of Calais. England then experienced three decades of civil war, as rival factions of nobles tried to win the crown. In 1485, Henry Tudor triumphed and became Henry VII.

Europe suffered greatly during the 1300s. The economy declined, famine struck, and the war began between England and France. The population of Europe had increased through the High Middle Ages, stabilized when the economy worsened, and then was suddenly decimated by the onset of the bubonic plague. The Black Death, as it was called, began in Genoa in 1347 and killed about 25 million people in the space of three years. All of Europe, from the Mediterranean to Scandinavia, was affected.

Also in the fourteenth century, the flow of goods from the East diminished. The Ottoman Turks challenged the Byzantine Empire, invading Greece and the Balkans by 1356. In 1453, Muhammad II took the city of Constantinople. Trade between East and West slowed at this bottleneck, and, to compensate, many European nations began to finance their own voyages to seek Eastern markets. The Portuguese sailor Bartolemeu Diaz travelled around Africa's Cape of Good Hope, and Vasco da Gama reached India by that route in 1498. But it is Christopher Columbus's voyage across the Atlantic in 1492, sponsored by Spain, that has the greatest historical fame.

For hundreds of years, the Eurocentric view has been that Columbus "discovered" the Americas. Actually, Columbus was almost certainly preceded by the Vikings, and possibly by peoples of the Mediterranean and Asia at much earlier times. More important, the Americas could not be "discovered" by Columbus because they were already inhabited by peoples who had developed their own civilizations over at least the previous two thousand years.

In Mesoamerica (Mexico and Central America), several civilizations had flourished and dispersed. The first was the Olmec civilization, which began about 1200 B.C. on the Gulf Coast of Mexico and lasted for a thousand years. Olmecs probably invented the calender made famous by another great civilization, the Maya. The Maya thrived from the third to the ninth centuries on the Yucatan peninsula. They built notable temple complexes and were expert mathematicians. The city of Teotihuacan, which was powerful from 100 B.C. to A.D. 750, was the product of yet another civilization, although little is known about the people who lived there. The Toltecs, who conquered much of Mesoamerica beginning in A.D. 900, intermarried with the peoples of another Chichimec tribe, the Aztecs, who became dominant about 1200. Both peoples established religions based on sun worship that involved ritual sacrifice of humans. The Aztecs founded Tenochititlan (Mexico City), which grew to be a remarkable city of waterways and agriculture. They had a prosperous civilization, and were skilled in the making of textiles, sculpture, and pottery. The Spaniard Hernan Cortes arrived in 1519 and disrupted the Aztecs in the midst of their development. Within two years, Cortes's guns, smallpox, and angry rival tribes had conquered the Aztec Empire.

A similar succession of civilizations and empires occurred in South America. The first unifying force seems to have been the Chavin cult, which ruled from 1000 to 300 B.C. Later, the Mochica culture dominated the north, and the Nazca people dominated the south. The Nazca also manufactured beautiful pottery. The Chimu Kingdom ruled the coast of South America from central Peru north to Ecuador from the eleventh to the fifteenth centuries. Forty thousand people lived in Chan Chan, the Chimu capital city. Chan Chan was overthrown by the Inca in the 1470s. They had begun their expansion at the beginning of the century, and about one hundred years later their territory measured 4800 km by 320 km, from Chile to Ecuador to the jungles of the Amazon. The Inca were adept engineers. Their stone and earthen roads traversed the entire Empire. The Inca maintained their rule through a combination of administrative expertise, economic organization, and military strength. Francisco Pizarro arrived in 1531 and brought the Empire down, as Cortes had finished the Aztecs. The Spanish were set to make slaves of the peoples they had conquered, and to siphon off the treasures of Mesoamerica and South America to Europe.

Date A.D.	Events
1300	Church prestige declines
1337	Hundred Years' War between England and France begins
c. 1400	The spirit of the Renaissance (c. 1400-1550) is expressed in works by Petrarch, Leonardo da Vinci, Michelangelo, Erasmus, Dürer, and others
1444	Portugal begins abducting Africans to be used as slaves
1446	Gutenburg of Mainz and Coster of Haarlem use first printing presses
1453	Ottoman Turks conquer Constantinople
1492	Christopher Columbus reaches San Salvador in the Bahamas
1517	Luther nails the Ninety-five Theses to the door of the castle church in Wittenburg
1529-1555	Catholic and Lutheran states wage intermittent wars Peace of Augsburg allows rulers to choose the state's religion
1588	English navy defeats Spanish Armada
1598	The Edict of Nantes introduces a period of religious toleration in France
1602	Dutch East India Company, with its worldwide network of trading factories, is formed
1618-1648	Thirty Years' War Religious motives give way to the interests of the nation-state
1651	English Navigation Acts reflect the mercantilist goal of self-sufficiency
1661-1715	*French civilization sets the standard for Europe during the reign of the Sun King, Louis XIV*
1713-1740	Hapsburg or Austrian Empire re-emerges under the leadership of Charles VI Frederick William, first king of Prussia, builds his kingdom into a military state Peter the Great continues the westernization of Russia, including the modernization of military forces England develops as a limited monarchy following the Glorious Revolution of 1688 France and England compete for colonial and naval supremacy European conflicts involve colonial empires

9

Europe and the Sun King

BACKGROUND

The Renaissance and Humanism

Around 1400, about the time that the Aztecs and Inca were building their cities and creating empires, medieval Europe was entering a new phase. This age (c. 1400-1550) became known as the **Renaissance,** meaning *rebirth,* because Greek and Roman knowledge and achievements were rediscovered by the West and carried forward. The label is misleading to some extent. There was no single, dramatic event that marked the beginning of the rebirth. In fact, Western Europe had maintained some awareness of **classical** writers (the writers of ancient Greece and Rome) throughout the entire medieval period, although such knowledge was limited to a small number of scholars. During the Crusades, contacts between Christians and Moors in Spain and Sicily had introduced Islamic science to the West and revived the study of Greek philosophy. Attempts were made to reconcile these bodies of knowledge with the teachings of the Church. A decline of interest in the classics during the thirteenth century was followed by a renewed enthusiasm in the fourteenth century, and it is this "rebirth" that the term *Renaissance* is meant to capture.

During the Renaissance, awareness of the Greek and Roman heritage of the West was heightened, but there was also a clear understanding that Europe was, in its own right, special. This dual recognition of past and present provided the energy for a wave of creative genius and accomplishment in writing, painting, sculpture, and architecture. The people of the Renaissance were no more or less intelligent than people of any other age. The extraordinary number of accomplishments that can only be ascribed to genius, however, strongly suggests that the environment encouraged gifted individuals to maximize their talents.

The Renaissance began in Italy. Fragmented by geography, the Italian peninsula had never been unified under a single ruler after the decline of the Western Roman Empire and the turmoil that followed. Throughout much

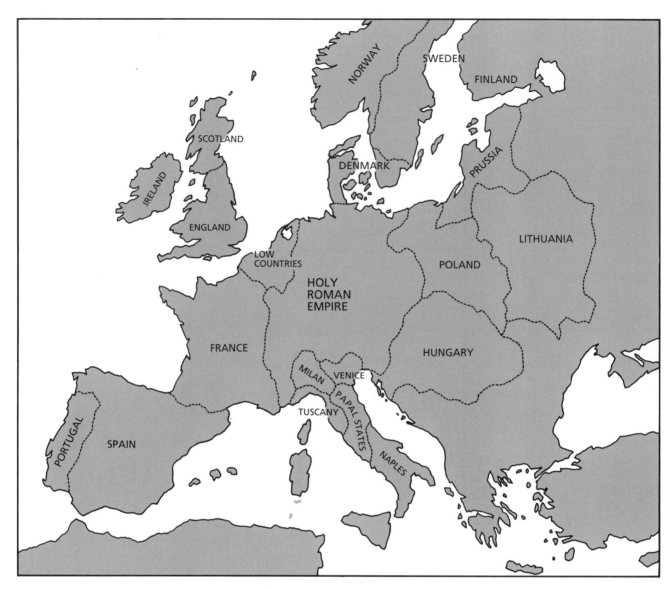

The States of Europe, 1500.

of the Middle Ages, Italy was a land of shifting loyalties, torn by the claims of the Holy Roman Empire on the one hand and the papacy on the other. The feudalism that dominated northern Europe did not develop in Italy. Instead, Italian life was organized politically around a series of independent states, including Venice, Florence, Milan, Naples, Genoa, Pisa, and Bologna. This system was similar to the arrangement of city-states in ancient Greece. There was no political unit on the scale of a nation. Instead, each city-state developed its own government and controlled its own hinterland.

Different city-states tried different methods of government. Most of the early democracies, however, gave way to governments controlled by powerful merchants, aristocratic families, and dictators who could offer protection against external threats to commercial enterprise. Landowners lived in the cities and participated in the economic, political, and social life of the day alongside prosperous middle-class merchants. Society was reorganized as a result, and wealth and power took precedence over birth.

Although friction between Italian city-states was constant, they never experienced conflict on the level of the Hundred Years' War endured by England and France. Italian cities were situated on trade routes that gave them access to luxury goods and cultures from the East, and linked them to northern markets through selected Alpine passes. Like Athens in Greece's Golden Age, they developed a cosmopolitan outlook and accumulated wealth and capital. The Italian middle class used its financial resources either to acquire valued objects or, more important, to sponsor the budding talent of young painters, sculptors, and writers. While their patrons provided food, clothing, and comfortable lodgings, those with exceptional ability were given the time and opportunity to realize their potential. In retrospect, it is not surprising that the intrigues of city life, the flourishing economy, and the contact with foreigners inspired cultural achievement.

There were splendid achievements in architecture and learning in the Middle Ages before 1400, but during the Renaissance the reasons for producing art shifted. Earlier artists made paintings, chiselled sculpture, carved wood, and stained glass to glorify God, the focal point of their creations. Living a good Christian life was regarded as necessary preparation for paradise after death. During the Renaissance, the focus moved from God and life after death to human life here and now. There was a new appreciation of the beauty of the human body, the intelligence of the human mind, and the magnificent accomplishments that humans were capable of producing. This new outlook is known as **humanism.** Though people continued to praise God and hoped to enter heaven, what mattered most was an individual's relationship to society rather than to God and the afterlife.

The wealthy Italian trading cities began an unharnessed pursuit of material goods. Individuals in every walk of life developed a heightened sense of self-awareness. Artists and composers started to sign their work, while bankers, nobles, and even popes ordered busts, portraits, and monuments created in their honour. The Church was affected by the new trend, and commissioned some of the finest works of the Renaissance. The excellence of the artwork itself, and the talent that created it, often received more attention than the purpose for which it was created. People of the Renaissance valued and celebrated their **individualism,** and their abilities in all fields of human activity.

The Italian Renaissance was also inspired, understandably, by the magnificence of ancient Rome, which, even in ruin, was impressive. The overgrown Roman forum, known locally as the "cowfield," was excavated and its treasures catalogued. As scholars sifted through long-forgotten Roman manuscripts, they discovered their ancestors and came to admire what they found. It seemed as if the ancients had reached a peak of human accomplishment in almost all of their endeavours, and that their Renaissance descendants should strive to follow their example.

Emulating the ancients led to some important changes. Medieval scholars had been associated with isolated monasteries, halls of private study and meditation, and passive acceptance of the world. Renaissance scholars, like the ancient Romans, were more apt to be public figures eager to transform the world to fit their newfound ideals. Similarly, Renaissance science concentrated on practical applications, relying heavily on Greek understandings about scientific laws and principles. But the humanistic regard for the individual was primarily a Renaissance development.

The invention of movable block type and the development of the **printing press** were further stimuli to the Renaissance. Throughout history, records of human experience had been painstakingly copied by hand: Sumerians etched clay tablets, Egyptians marked papyrus, and medieval monks inked their messages on vellum or parchment. The laboriousness of these methods limited the amount of knowledge that could be accumulated and preserved. Only a few thousand manuscripts existed in all of Europe before the printing press, and they were the cherished possessions of church libraries and the upper classes. Reading and study had been an option available only to the privileged, not to the public. With the invention of movable type, the number of books skyrocketed to at least 6 million by 1500. Although it would take a long time for the uneducated peasants to appreciate the change, the literate and wealthy middle classes, who began to stock their libraries, were quick to realize its importance. Long preserved but rarely seen mysteries were unveiled. Information, ideas, scientific knowledge, and discoveries could be recorded and distributed to the far corners of Europe, and the knowledge of one generation could be passed on to and built upon by the next.

Institutions

The citizens of Florence were intensely interested in politics and, just as they did in business, looked to the most practical solutions to political problems. After brief experiments with dictatorship in the fourteenth century, the city adopted a republican government and tried to live in the spirit of ancient Rome. In the fifteenth century, the **Medici** family, the greatest bankers in Europe, began to dominate Florentine politics. Their rule was continually controversial, and three times they were expelled from the city. Largely through Medici influence, wealth, and values, Florence gathered the great talents of the Renaissance. Cosimo de' Medici was criticized for building a private palace in 1444, but by that time his family had spent millions of dollars on public art and architecture. Lorenzo de' Medici excelled as a poet, politician, scholar, economist, and military planner. His vast personal collection of books became the first public library in Europe. During his lifetime he assisted, employed, or gave lodging to almost every talent in Florence, including Botticelli, Leonardo, and Michelangelo. But his lavish spending on behalf of the arts, which he regarded as a public duty, weakened even the Medici fortune.

Florence and the Italian Renaissance

Although Venice was Italy's wealthiest city and Rome the most prestigious, the heart of the Renaissance was Florence. Many of the most important Renaissance artists were Florentine: Boccaccio, Machiavelli, Giotto, Masaccio, da Vinci, and Michelangelo. In addition, non-Florentines such as Raphael came to the city, and what they saw greatly influenced their work.

The earliest impulse toward the Renaissance sprang from the pens of three Italian writers. Dante Alighieri (1265-1321) was the key transitional figure. Medieval writers in universities, the Church, and government wrote in Latin, and recognized Greek (which they knew little about) as the only other language worthy of cultured people. Dante, however, did some of his writing in Italian, the language of the common classes, and is known today as the father of Italian literature. Like the medieval world in which he lived, Dante was preoccupied with religion and the afterlife. His most famous work, *Divine Comedy*, however, criticizes the Church and shows an individualism that foreshadows the Renaissance.

Petrarch Francesco, better known as Petrarch (1304-1375), also wrote in Italian, but he was less concerned with religion and more with fame and fortune on earth. In his later works, his attention turned to the pagan past of Greece and Rome, and he encouraged others to locate classical manuscripts from the libraries and monasteries of Europe.

Of the three authors, Giovanni Boccaccio (1313-1375) was the most worldly and closest to the spirit of the Renaissance. His books, usually written in Italian, reflected his enjoyment of life. The short stories in his *Decameron* focus on ordinary people and ridicule the Church. This work became one of the earliest "bestsellers," and Boccaccio's approach influenced many writers throughout Europe, including the English authors Geoffrey Chaucer and William Shakespeare. On the suggestion of Petrarch, Boccaccio became interested in the Greek classics. He, like Petrarch and Dante, became an inspiration for the humanist artists who followed, not only other writers, but also painters, sculptors, and architects.

The great differences between medieval and Renaissance art can be seen clearly by comparing paintings from the two periods. Medieval figures appear stiff, flat, and unreal, devoid of muscle and emotion. This "flatness" allowed the worshipper to concentrate on the religious story being told. Although Renaissance painting retained religious themes, the emphasis was on the accurate portrayal of the human form. The goal of the Renaissance artist was to illustrate nature as he or she saw it, unhindered by conventions of the past. To achieve this end, techniques of shading, colour, and above all, perspective (which gives the illusion of depth) had to be pioneered and perfected. Giotto (1267-1336), a contemporary of Dante and, like him, a transitional figure between medieval and Renaissance styles, was the first to portray the human form in a more natural, three-dimensional way. Another Florentine artist, Masaccio (1401-1428), later achieved the realism that Giotto had attempted, particularly in his emotion-filled *Adam and Eve Expelled from Paradise*.

One of the greatest artists of the Renaissance was Leonardo da Vinci (1452-1519), whose genius in many fields of study was rivalled only by Michelangelo. As an apprentice of the most famous artist in Florence, Andrea del Verrocchio, Leonardo was allowed to paint an angel in the left-hand corner of his teacher's mural, the *Baptism of Christ*. When Verrocchio compared Leonardo's angel with his own blankly staring figures, he realized that his student, at age twenty, had surpassed him. Leonardo da Vinci became a master of proportion and perspective, but there was much more to his painting than technique. In the extensive notes he kept throughout

Controversies

Lorenzo Valla (1407-1457) of Naples and Rome was one of the many excellent humanist scholars who continued the tradition established by Petrarch and others. He focussed his expertise in Latin and history on the Donation of Constantine. This document, which supposedly originated with the Roman emperor Constantine, assigned political control of the Western Roman Empire to the papacy, thus undermining the authority of the Byzantine Empire. The Church had long used the Donation to support the pope's authority. But Valla proved that the document was created in the eighth century, not the fourth—it was a forgery that had probably been invented by the Church. Valla also wrote an unpublished criticism of Saint Jerome's translation of the New Testament (known as the Vulgate edition), pointing out mistakes and questionable phrasing in what had been an unchallenged source of Christian truth.

"It Is Far Safer to Be Feared than Loved"

Niccolo Machiavelli (1469-1527) was a Florentine diplomat and soldier who became a notorious writer. In 1502, Machiavelli met with and was greatly impressed by Cesare Borgia, son of Pope Alexander VI. By reputation, Borgia was guilty of kidnapping, torturing, and murdering his enemies. He engineered the deaths of his elder brother and the second husband of his sister Lucrezia. Because of his unscrupulous methods, however, he had a remarkable career. Machiavelli felt that Cesare was the perfect embodiment of the successful prince, and made him the model for his revealing human- ist study called *The Prince*, which was an attempt to show how politicians really thought.

According to Machiavelli, a ruler could not afford to worry about right or wrong but had to use any means to secure the safety of the state. Machiavelli envisioned a world in which govern- ment was conducted through ruthlessness, dupli- city, and the use of force. Upset by the bands of foreign mercenaries waging war in the Italian countryside, Machiavelli felt that a state must have a fully equipped army at its disposal. Surprise attacks conducted by one prince against another were justified and even desirable when they were the best means of gaining victory. One prince could never trust another, since each state would be willing to break any promise or commit any atrocity to better its own self interest. A prince should even be working to keep his own followers divided so they would not work together to over- throw him.

Machiavelli's defenders argue that he was sim- ply analysing the "mechanics of statecraft" and that he should not be condemned for the deceit and treachery of the Renaissance world. Critics suggest that his book, written a year after his dis- missal by the Medici from public service, reflected his callous and bitter attitude toward the world from which he had been excluded. As a work of writing, *The Prince* was of key importance to the Renaissance. Machiavelli had abandoned the medieval practice of writing about the ideal world, stressing instead the methods rulers actually used to ensure their survival. To this day, *The Prince* is read and argued about by those who study history and political science.

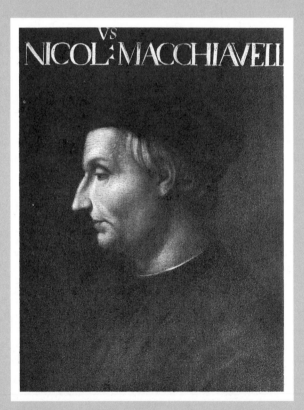

Niccolo Machiavelli.

his career, Leonardo made many references to nature, few to God, and none to the classics. The only authority he recognized was the eye of the artist, which could perceive not just the physical appearance of the subject but the emotions within. He captured the physical and emotional condition of his subject in his world-famous *Mona Lisa* and his lesser known but equally impressive *Virgin of the Rocks*. In his mural *The Last Supper*, Leonardo depicted the dramatic moment when Jesus told his disciples that one of them would betray him. The painting brings together all of Leonardo's extensive study of human psychology and practical technique. Rather than using the traditional fresco method on wet plaster, he used an experimental oil and tempera emulsion on dry plaster that allowed him to study the mural for hours as he progressed.

The later part of the Renaissance was dominated by the towering genius of Michelangelo Buonarroti (1475-1564). He was almost Leonardo's equal in versatility and influence, shared Leonardo's peak of accomplishment, and surpassed his number of completed projects. These two men make an interesting contrast. Leonardo's scientific mind and his scepticism led him to make a lifelong inquiry of nature. Michelangelo's deep faith led him to search for God in the form of the human body and in his own creativity. For Leonardo, it was the artist who created, but for Michelangelo, the artist's craft was a fulfilment of divine will.

Although Michelangelo protested that he was not a painter, in 1508 he accepted a commission from Pope Julius II to paint the ceiling of the Vatican's Sistine Chapel. The ceiling was 18 m above the floor. Working up to fourteen hours a day in dim light, Michelangelo repeatedly lay on his back in an awkward position while his legs hung loosely over the scaffolding. At day's end, he often slept on the platform, only to begin another day totally absorbed in his art. On the floor below, an impatient Pope Julius kept asking when the painting would be finished. Michelangelo, as quick-tempered and quarrelsome as he was talented, replied that it would never be done if the pope kept interrupting. After four years, Michelangelo completed the *Creation and Fall*. It seems that all the discomfort and conflict served only as an inspiration, for the ceiling fresco is overpowering in scale and impact. The biblical scenes cover 900 m^2, and contain 343 larger-than-life human figures that dazzle the eye and imagination.

Twenty-four years later, at age sixty-one, Michelangelo began another commission for another pope to paint the *Last Judgment* on the altar wall of the Sistine Chapel. Greatly weakened and less agile, Michelangelo ended many days too exhausted to hold a brush. He once fell to the floor from the scaffolding, acquiring a leg injury that left him with a permanent limp. After almost six years, he unveiled a colossal scene with over three hundred human figures. God was at the centre, surrounded by those who had been judged. At the bottom, the wicked were shown in hell, suffering their fate. Another artist later painted garments over Michelangelo's nude figures, and

After five hundred years of abuse, Leonardo da Vinci's Last Supper *is being reborn patch by patch. Dr. Pinin Brambilla Barcilon began the painstaking restoration of this masterpiece in 1977. She first examines the paint fragments through a microscope, enlarging the small area forty times. Once she has*

determined the amount of impurities to be removed, she applies a solvent, blotting quickly before the chemicals reach Leonardo's colours. It takes Dr. Brambilla a week to clean an area the size of a postage stamp.

Michelangelo's technical mastery is revealed in his Creation of Adam *from the ceiling of the Sistine Chapel. The scene shows Adam's lethargic body being animated by God.*

centuries of candle smoke have blackened the entire wall. Even so, the work remains impressive.

Two other famous Renaissance painters were Titian (1490-1576) and Raphael (1483-1520). Titian was a portrait painter for the wealthy in the prosperous city of Venice. His use of form and striking colours earned him respect and a fortune large enough to sustain a princely existence. Raphael, also a master of colour, went to Florence in 1504, where he was greatly impressed by the work of Leonardo da Vinci and Michelangelo. He developed a serene style and skill in composition that was all his own. Although, like Titian, he was primarily a painter of portraits, his best-known work is the mural-sized *School of Athens.* Considered by many to be the greatest painting of the Renaissance, it shows Greek philosophers from all periods of history, including Plato, Aristotle, Socrates, and Pythagorus, set in a circle against a backdrop of perfect classical architecture. Raphael became rich and famous, but he died before he was forty.

The vitality and movement inherent in the human form, depicted so well in Renaissance painting, was also a feature of Renaissance sculpture. Medieval sculpture had been seen as decoration for the great churches of the period, but during the Renaissance, sculpture was commissioned for its own sake, as it had been in ancient Greece and Rome. The transition to Renaissance sculpture began with the work of Lorenzo Ghiberti (1378-1455). In 1402, he won a competition to carve and cast in **bas-relief** the panels on the bronze doors of the baptistery in Florence. Ghiberti laboured

Raphael's School of Athens.

for twenty-four years. His fellow citizens were so impressed with the results that Ghiberti was rewarded with a commission for a second set of doors,

The sculpture on Ghiberti's bronze doors is done in bas-relief, which means that the sculpted forms stand out only slightly from the background. "The Story of Jacob and Esau," shown here, was part of Ghiberti's second set of doors, The Gates of Paradise.

which also took over two decades to complete! The lifelike figures in the Old Testament scenes were sculpted so well that Michelangelo claimed the gilded doors would make a fitting entrance into heaven.

Yet the greatest sculptor of the Renaissance was Michelangelo himself, who consistently achieved artistic heights that others reached only occasionally. He considered himself first and foremost a sculptor. For Michelangelo, the figure lived in the stone and he sought only to free it with his chisel. As a

Michelangelo's Moses *was originally intended for the tomb of Pope Julius II.*

relative unknown, Michelangelo had boasted that he would create the finest work in marble of his day. At age twenty-five, his ambition was realized when he finished the *Pietà*, showing Christ lying across his mother's lap after his ordeal on the cross. Michelangelo's heroic style was demonstrated in the 4.3 m statue of *David* that he carved from a huge block of marble. Equally powerful is his *Moses*, carved for the tomb of Pope Julius in 1513.

Michelangelo was not only a sculptor and painter, he was also an architect. In 1546, at the age of seventy-one, Michelangelo agreed to complete the construction of St. Peter's Basilica. The project had not gone well. It had been initiated by Pope Julius, who wanted to replace a twelve-hundred-year-old church with something grander. The original design submitted by Donato Bramante was circular in shape and was dominated by a smooth dome in the tradition of the ancient Roman Pantheon. Following Bramante's death in 1514, construction halted and several other architects recommended drastic changes. When Michelangelo took over, the building had been abandoned for so long that trees were growing out of the arches built in Bramante's day. Michelangelo had been impressed by the ribbed dome that Brunelleschi had designed for the cathedral in Florence, and his solution to the problem of St. Peter's was simply to combine Brunelleschi and Bramante's ideas. After Michelangelo's death, other architects made additional alterations, one of which was a massive facade that blocks the dome almost completely when it is approached from the front.

Upon its completion in 1626, St. Peter's became the largest church in the world, but the succession of planners and design changes and the mixture of different architectural styles diminish its success as a work of architecture.

Michelangelo simplified the design of the dome of St. Peter's Basilica by combining the vertical lines of Brunelleschi's ribbed dome with the features of Bramante's original form.

The Arts

During the Renaissance, many women achieved excellence in the arts. Isabella d'Este (1474-1539), for example, fulfilled the Renaissance ideal of the well-rounded person. She was a student of literature, theology, music, and linguistics; a creator of needle-work and art; and she became proficient in the affairs of state. She ably ruled the duchy of Mantua during her husband's frequent absences. As a patron of the arts, d'Este won lasting renown, and her private museum contained one of the best collections of its day.

Another influential woman of the Italian Renaissance was Vittoria Colonna (1490(?)-1549). Her writings dealt with religion, nature, patriotism, and the human condition. The Colonna castle was a gathering place for the greats of the Italian Renaissance, including Michelangelo.

In the seventeenth century, Artemisia Gentileschi (1590-1652) developed her artistic talent under the supervision of her father, an Italian painter. Her portraits and historical and religious paintings eventually gained her admission to the Academy of Design in Florence.

In fact, it has been argued that in general Renaissance architecture did not live up to the achievements of the medieval period. The soaring lines of Gothic architecture were largely a development of northern Europe and had only limited success in the Italian peninsula. With the humanist emphasis on ancient Greece and Rome, it is not surprising that Renaissance architects were more influenced by classical styles, and the resulting buildings are not as spectacular as their Gothic counterparts.

Michelangelo, who made outstanding contributions in several different fields, is a good example of the type of person most admired during the Renaissance. According to the Renaissance ideal, a person should strive for excellence not just in one field, but in all aspects of human life. Perhaps the best example of the ideal Renaissance individual is Leonardo da Vinci. The man who painted the *Mona Lisa* was also a gymnast who had the hand strength to bend a horseshoe. As a military engineer, he enquired into the potential of gas bombs, cannons, and exploding and conical shells, among other projects. In architecture, Leonardo's circular, central-plan schemes influenced Bramante's original plan for the rebuilding of St. Peter's Basilica. Leonardo designed water mills, aqueducts, and irrigation canals. His drawings of flying machines were aerodynamically correct, and he also worked on balloon flight and parachutes. Moved by a desire to know how the body worked so that it could be painted with greater effect, Leonardo dissected over thirty cadavers before he was denied access to the mortuary in Rome. He speculated about blood circulation, the nervous system, the operation of the eye, and drew strikingly realistic sketches of all his anatomical investigations. He described the fossils found on mountain tops and suspected that the sun did not move as ancient authorities had usually argued.

Most of Leonardo's attention, like that of Renaissance thinkers in general, was in what is now called **applied science**. He had little interest in looking at the underlying principles of the natural world or in formulating general laws and theories. The genius of the Renaissance produced visible, concrete achievements that were recognized and celebrated by an informed public eager for glory. Yet the spirit of inquiry laid the foundation for the breakthroughs in **pure science** that began in the seventeenth century.

Northern Europe and the Renaissance

North of the Alps, the feudal system had not encouraged artistic development. As feudalism declined, however, the rise of the nation-state and the commercial wealth of middle-class merchants and financiers gradually allowed change. Increasing exchanges with Italian traders, diplomats, and even tourists spread the news of Renaissance achievements. Patronage of the arts began to develop in the prosperous trading cities of northern Europe.

Italian writers had an impact on the work of many northern writers, one of whom was the civil servant Geoffrey Chaucer (1340-1400). In his famous *Canterbury Tales*, Chaucer tells the stories of thirty religious pilgrims on their way to visit the shrine of Thomas à Becket, a narrative approach used by Boccaccio in the *Decameron*. Chaucer wrote in the vernacular English of the fourteenth century, just as his Italian predecessors had popularized their own native tongue. The range of characters in the *Canterbury Tales* provides the reader with a cross section of English life.

The humanist writers of the north set their own direction and became prominent throughout Europe. Among the most respected and widely read of the classical scholars was Desiderius Erasmus (1466-1536) of Rotterdam, known as the "Prince of Humanists." In his travels to Germany, France, Switzerland, England, and Italy, Erasmus developed an international reputation for learning and reform. His influence in Italy, home of the Renaissance, led to the formation of the Oratory of Divine Love, an intellectual association that tried to upgrade the clergy through improved education. The Renaissance appreciation of good scholarship led Erasmus to publish Latin translations of the New Testament that brought into question the accuracy of the Vulgate Bible used by the Church. Erasmus felt that the Bible should be published in popular languages for all to read and interpret. Although this belief appeared to be a direct challenge to Church authority, Erasmus remained a priest and devout Catholic who believed in tolerance and education. For Erasmus, intelligent discussion raised the dignity of the individual in a way that was in harmony with the Christian spirit.

Erasmus corresponded with many of the great thinkers of Europe, including the famous English humanist Sir Thomas More (1478-1535). More gained lasting fame with his book *Utopia* ("Nowhere"), which realistically described an ideal society that shared the wealth it produced. According to More, this was the kind of world that people could build if they chose. *Utopia* was a criticism of the greed and militarism of Europe from a Christian perspective.

Several literary masters emerged in northern Europe, just as they previously had in Italy. In France, Michel de Montaigne (1533-1592), a religious sceptic who loved the classics, wrote serious essays about the need to be open-minded. William Shakespeare (1564-1616) excelled in every facet of poetry and drama. His understanding of human nature has been appreciated for centuries. Shakespeare's admiration of and debt to the classical world of Greece and Rome was evident in plays such as *Antony and Cleopatra* and *Julius Caesar*. Most important, his precise and imaginative use of words, many of them adapted to English for the first time, forever enriched the language. At about the same time, the Spanish novelist Miguel de Cervantes (1547-1616) wrote the brilliant and entertaining *Don Quixote*, which satirizes the attitudes of his own time as well as medieval attitudes.

In the realm of painting, the difference between the work of northern European and Italian artists was marked. Italian painters often showed grand religious scenes featuring an all-powerful God; the painters of the northern Renaissance preferred quieter scenes, such as Christ on the cross

Few of Leonardo's paintings were completed and fewer remain, but his reputation as an artist would have been secure even if only his sketches of humans, animals, and anatomy had survived. This chalk portrait of Judas is just one of the meticulous preliminary sketches Leonardo drew for his Last Supper.

or the Virgin Mary and child. The Italian regard for the art of classical Greece and Rome did not take hold as much in the north. Nevertheless, many excellent painters developed outside of Italy. The works of Belgian painter Jan van Eyck (1380-1441) certainly equal the achievements of the Italian painters. Van Eyck's *Man in a Red Turban* is the earliest-known example of the subject of a painting looking directly at the viewer. His famous painting *Arnolfini Wedding* provides an example of his ability to reproduce the minute details of a scene.

Albrecht Dürer (1471-1528) has often been described as Germany's answer to Leonardo da Vinci because of his achievements in a variety of fields. Dürer was the first painter to use himself repeatedly as a model in a series of portraits, and his black and white designs are excellent. Dürer was also inspired by native German tradition in his use of woodcuts and copper etchings, which were reproduced and distributed in great number. Hans Holbein (1497-1543) was also a German portrait painter of the highest order, who became famous for a series of paintings completed for his patron, King Henry VIII of England.

The remarkable artistic achievements of the Italian and northern Renaissance were driven in part by all of the new ideas that followed from humanism. These ideas provided a framework for criticism of the previous era and the creation of a new era. But this humanist desire for change was not confined to the artistic sphere. In fact, the almost perfect world envisioned by Renaissance genius was about to be exploded by the ideas of an obscure German monk.

The Protestant Reformation

The Roman Catholic Church in Europe was spiritually and economically powerful. The spiritual importance of the Church was emphasized by all its officials, from the pope to the parish priest. A person could find eternal salvation only by accepting the seven sacraments, which only the clergy could administer. In addition, the Church was among the largest landholders in Europe and played a pivotal role in education, as a patron of the arts, and as a social focal point in every community. The pope ruled outright in the Papal States and was a maker and breaker of kings and emperors.

Nevertheless, the prestige of the Church had been battered on several occasions. The financial greed that prompted some of the Crusades had been questioned and was widely resented. The Great Schism that began in 1378, during which three popes briefly ruled simultaneously, split the unity of the Church and weakened its claims to spiritual leadership. By 1500, corruption of wealth and power had filtered from the papacy to the parish. For a pope such as Alexander VI (1492-1503), human salvation seemed less important than helping his son, Cesare Borgia, gain prosperity and dominance in the provinces of Italy. Pope Julius II (1503-1513), patron of Michelangelo, was a military man with great political ambition. His successor, Leo X (1513-

1521), son of Lorenzo de' Medici, was also a patron of the arts, and was driven by a desire to build St. Peter's Basilica in Rome. In his quest to raise money, Leo was not above selling statues of the apostles, papal jewellery, plates, and furniture. He also accepted payment for the appointments of new bishops and for the annulment of marriages and other vows.

The practice of **simony**, the buying and selling of Church offices, earned Leo a bad reputation. He maintained an annual income of over a million dollars from the sale of over two thousand appointments. Many bishops who bought their positions were wealthy nobles, interested in prestige and money rather than in God's work, and their private lives were immoral. They received incomes from dioceses they had never seen, and appointed relatives and friends to local clerical positions. Many priests did not even know the Latin required for the Mass. Such abuses began to overshadow the good works performed by the dedicated members of the clergy.

The Church was also criticized for exploiting papal **letters of indulgence**. The idea of an indulgence sprang from the belief that Christ and the saints were more worthy than was necessary for their own salvation, and that the Church could shift this surplus merit to other Christians. With an indulgence, a repentant sinner would receive less punishment in the afterlife. At first, indulgences were issued to pilgrims, crusaders, and those who did "good work" at home. Eventually, a cash payment replaced the need for good work, and it became obvious that the papal motive was financial rather than religious.

Many recognized that reforms were needed to stem the Church's growing worldliness and immorality. The English theologian John Wycliff (1320-1384) argued that the low morality of the clergy could be corrected by allowing priests to marry. He criticized indulgences, the Church hierarchy, and even the pope, insisting that a person could reach heaven simply by reading the Bible and following the word of God. To give ordinary people access to the Bible, Wycliff translated it into English. John Hus (1369-1415) of Prague later translated some of Wycliff's writing into Czech. For supporting such radical ideas, however, Hus was eventually excommunicated and burned at the stake. In Italy, Girolamo Savonarola (1452-1498) of Florence attacked the lack of virtue and excess of vice in his prosperous city, was critical of the worldly ways of the pope, and argued for a simpler, stricter Christian life. Savonarola became a leading political force in Florence, but eventually he, too, was excommunicated and burned at the stake for heresy.

The spirit of inquiry that typified Renaissance humanism led to a re-examination of the practices of the Church and a desire for reform and improvement. The scholar Erasmus joined his reform-minded predecessors in condemning the greed and the power of the Church in Rome. Somehow the Church had drifted away from the simplicity of the original Christian values. The key to salvation, according to Erasmus, lay in rediscovering those values and living a humble life in the tradition of Christ. A respected scholar and faithful Catholic who personally knew the popes and kings of his day, Erasmus had unlocked the door to reform.

Unwilling or unable to listen to Erasmus and other voices of reform from within, the Church was now beset by uncontrollable pressures from the secular world. The Roman Catholic ideal of universal Christianity was threatened by the growth of nation-states and the nationalism they encouraged. Monarchs in France and England were jealous of Church wealth and resented the papal revenue that was siphoned from their domain, whether for religious purposes or war. Landless peasants longingly eyed the extensive landholdings of the Church. Middle-class merchants, who had gained economic power through private enterprise, wanted reforms that would allow them to obtain salvation for themselves through reading the scriptures.

The atmosphere was certainly right for reform, but it was a most unlikely person who initiated the changes. Martin Luther (1483-1546) came from a family of German peasants. His father's gradual success in copper mining enabled Luther to attend university, where he eventually settled on the study of law. Then, one July day in 1505, Luther was struck by lightning in a violent storm and survived. He attributed the event to the power and anger of God. Luther was so moved that he vowed to seek his own salvation and become a monk. At the local Augustinian monastery, Luther tried to gain salvation through the normal Church rituals, including rigorous fasting, prayer, and confession. Nothing seemed to help. With the hope that change might do him some good, Luther's confessor sent him to the University of Wittenburg, where he became a professor of philosophy and a priest. Luther visited Rome in 1511, only to discover that many Italians, even on the holy ground of the Christian capital, were less earnest about their religion than he was. Disillusioned, he returned to Wittenburg.

Luther remained burdened with guilt and obsessed with the need for salvation. A familiar line from the Bible—"The just shall live by faith"—led to a sudden inspiration. Not good works, not fasting, not pilgrimages nor indulgences, but *faith* in God's redemption was the road to salvation. The idea was not new, but Luther, after years of inner turmoil, gripped it single-mindedly. The entire ritual of the Church was unnecessary—faith in a loving and merciful god was the key. With this idea, Luther was about to become the focal point of a controversy much larger than he ever imagined.

Unlike England and France, Germany lacked a strong, centralized, national government. As a result, German princes often felt the heaviest weight of papal demands. In 1515, Pope Leo X proclaimed an indulgence, primarily to raise money for the construction of St. Peter's in Rome. The Dominican friar John Tetzel travelled throughout Germany, doing the actual work of raising the money. He promised his audiences that each time money hit the box, a soul jumped from purgatory into heaven. Luther objected to the fundraising for two quite different reasons. His nationalistic argument was that German money should not be used to build a Roman church. His religious argument was that salvation depended on faith alone, and that indulgences were irrelevant. Hoping to encourage public debate, Luther wrote a list of Ninety-Five Theses (statements) condemning indulgences, and nailed it to the door of the castle church in Wittenburg on

Martin Luther.

13 October 1517. This act marks the beginning of the **Reformation**, a time in which Christian practices throughout Europe would be reshaped.

Luther's statements, much to his surprise, were translated from Latin into German, printed, and circulated throughout the countryside. Although Luther had no intention of breaking with the Church, circumstances now demanded that he carefully consider the implications of his ideas. He challenged the supremacy of the pope and Church councils. Of the seven sacraments, only baptism and the Lord's Supper (the Eucharist) were necessary, because they were the only ones directly implemented by Christ. Luther argued, as others had before him, that the clergy should be allowed to marry. Moreover, he felt that the priesthood included all who believed, not just the select few whom the Church had ordained.

Luther put forward his views in a series of sermons and tracts, regarding himself as a son of the Church who was purifying Christianity, rather than as a heretic. Pope Leo X saw the issue differently, particularly as the sale of indulgences fell, and in 1520 he issued a papal bull (a decree) of excommunication. Luther was given sixty days to reconsider his position. On the final day, in front of his students and the citizens of Wittenburg, he threw the decree into a bonfire. At that moment, Luther became a national hero to many of the peasants and princes of Germany. He had defied what they regarded as the foreign authority of Rome. Although not everyone agreed with or even understood his arguments, they liked what he was trying to achieve. The German princes had been whittling away at papal authority since the fourteenth century. When Luther argued that civil authorities had a duty to reform the Church, many German princes saw a chance to control Church lands and the revenues that flowed to Rome.

Luther was excommunicated a second time, and then summoned to the Imperial Diet (the parliament of the Holy Roman Empire) in the town of Worms in 1521 with a guarantee of safe-conduct. At the **Diet of Worms**, Luther refused to admit error. He was declared a heretic and denied help of any kind; his books were not to be bought, sold, or read. Although it appeared Luther's livelihood and even his life were in danger, Frederick III, the elector of Saxony, gave him the protection he needed to continue his work. During the next decade, Luther translated the Bible into German and formulated the main elements of the **Lutheran** Church. By following a path separate from Rome, he lost the support of many humanists, including Erasmus, who desired reform but did not want to sever themselves from the Catholic Church.

Luther's heresy, however, was not the Church's most pressing problem. A number of military and political dangers loomed. The Ottoman Turks were moving toward the Danube and had advanced into parts of the western Mediterranean. France was threatening Italy, the Netherlands, and Spain. When Pope Clement VII allied the papacy with France against the Holy Roman Empire, the conflict that followed resulted in the sacking of

Rome in 1527. Meanwhile, within the German states, a rebellion of feudal knights in 1522-1523 was followed by the more serious Peasants' War in 1524-1525.

Luther, though radical in his religious thought, was essentially conservative in his attitude toward social order. He supported the German princes against the knights and the peasants. Rapid implementation of his reforms had led to violent raids on churches and the destruction of art objects, practices Luther strongly opposed. The champions of his Church, for reasons of religion and politics, were the German princes. In 1529, it was the princes who protested (hence the name **Protestant**) when the Holy Roman emperor, Charles V, proclaimed they did not have the right to determine the religion of their subjects.

Attempts by the emperor to reconcile the differences between Luther and Rome failed, and for twenty-five years an intermittent war between Lutheran and Catholic states dragged on. With the Peace of Augsburg in 1555, agreement was reached that the ruler of each state could determine its religion. By this time, northern Germany and all of Scandinavia had become Lutheran, while the southern German states remained Catholic. For the next century, Europe would be seriously divided by religion as well as politics, and a country's faith would often determine its alliances in war.

The Reformation Spreads

While Lutheran Protestantism dominated in much of Germany and Scandinavia, other forms of Protestantism emerged elsewhere in Europe. Ulrich Zwingli (1484-1531) of Switzerland, influenced by Luther, rejected the Catholic hierarchy and rituals, and accepted only two of the seven sacraments. Unlike Luther, however, Zwingli substituted a Communion service for the Mass. He argued that the body and blood of Christ were not physically present in the bread and wine, and that Communion was a symbolic representation of Christ's last supper with the disciples. Zwingli also believed in using force to convert religious adversaries, and was, in fact, killed in a religious war with Swiss Roman Catholics.

Although he established no church, Zwingli influenced the development of the **Anabaptists**. They believed that the key to salvation lay in a simple and strict morality accompanied by adult baptism. In their opposition to the worldliness of the state, the Anabaptists agreed with Zwingli, but in their total opposition to war of any kind, set a new direction.

The greatest impact on the Protestant Reformation was made by the French humanist John Calvin (1509-1564). Converted by the works of Erasmus and Luther, Calvin brought a reasoned approach and masterful organization to the Protestant cause. While in Basel, Switzerland, he wrote his famous work *The Institutes of the Christian Religion*, which gave a summary of basic beliefs that became the guideline for the faithful. Although Calvin shared some of Luther's views, he emphasized that God was all-knowing

Religion

One group of Anabaptists, the Mennonites, fled to Pennsylvania to avoid persecution. Some of their descendants, the "Pennsylvania Dutch," came to Canada during the American Revolution to start a new life in what is now Kitchener, Ontario.

and all-powerful, and that it was a person's duty to serve God. Calvin developed a doctrine known as **predestination**; each person's fate was decided by God before he or she was born, and nothing could alter it. Those who were **elected**, or saved, would lead a life of high Christian morality and faith, while those who lived a sinful existence were certainly headed for hell. It was a moral obligation to convert the wayward, an impulse that made the **Calvinists** a dynamic force in European life.

In Geneva, Calvin put his talent for organization to work and tried to create the perfect Protestant city. Calvinists regulated the economy, education, and the council that visited private homes to judge the lives of the occupants. The Calvinist interpretation of the word of God governed everything. Going to taverns, playing cards, dancing, drinking, speaking profanities, and other abuses were criticized and penalized. Simplicity was essential to all religious services, and religious images, candles, and even bells were condemned.

Visitors were often deeply impressed by the stern quality of life they saw, and they returned to their homelands filled with Calvinist ideals. As leaders were trained, Calvin established churches throughout northern Europe that echoed the philosophy of the Geneva model. In Scotland, John Knox (1505-1572), after spending time in Geneva, laid the basis for a form of Protestantism known as **Presbyterianism**, which would eventually dominate his homeland. Calvinist influence played a large part in Holland's successful revolt against Catholic Spain in 1581. French Calvinists, known as **Huguenots**, were seen as a threat to political as well as religious unity, and were subsequently persecuted by both the Catholic Church and the French government. The climax of this suppression was the St. Bartholomew Massacre of 1572, when the nobles of the Huguenot party were slaughtered while attending a royal marriage. **The Edict of Nantes**, in 1598, introduced a period of toleration, but France remained a Catholic country.

Henry VIII (1509-1547) launched the Reformation in England mainly for personal and political, rather than religious, reasons. His criticism of Luther had previously won Henry the title "Defender of the Faith" from Pope Leo X, but when a later pope would not grant Henry a divorce, Henry's priorities grew clear, and he defied the Roman Catholic Church. There were several reasons why Henry expected to get his way. The English resented the papal revenue that drained from England to Rome, and had little sympathy for the wealth and materialism of the clergy. People no longer believed the monasteries provided an essential service, and many genuinely supported the views of Luther. Opponents discovered that it was dangerous to quarrel with Henry. When Thomas More, the famed humanist, refused to support Henry's claims against the pope, he was executed. Several acts of Parliament proclaimed an end to payments to Rome, gave the king the right to appoint bishops, and finally recognized the monarch as the supreme head on earth of the **Church of England**.

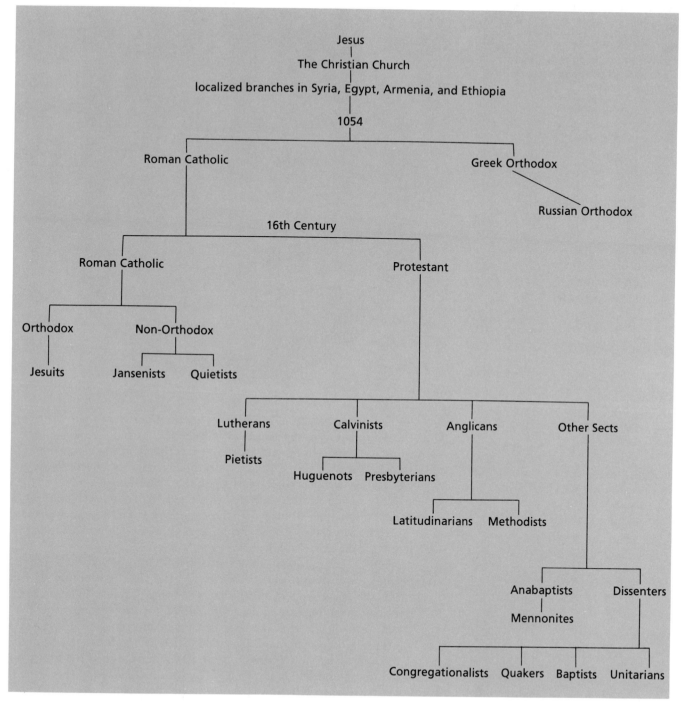

Fragmentation of the Christian Church.

Mary I, or Mary Tudor, the Roman Catholic daughter of Henry VIII by his first wife, Catherine of Aragon, became known as "Bloody Mary" because of the large number of Protestants condemned to death during her reign.

Under Edward VI (1547-1553), several changes were made to the Church of England, or the **Anglican Church**, as it came to be called. Baptism and Communion were recognized as the chief sacraments, and priests were allowed to marry. Anglican doctrine was outlined in the *Book of Common Prayer*, which most English-speaking Protestants came to own. Queen Mary (1553-1558), Edward's successor, tried to reverse these changes and re-establish Roman Catholicism in England. During her reign, about three hundred Protestants, including Archbishop Thomas Cranmer, were burned at the stake, and the nation was divided.

Elizabeth I (1558-1603), a ruler capable of effecting a badly needed compromise, came to the throne at the right moment. Working with Parliament, she established a Church that was mainly Catholic in organization and ritual but Protestant in doctrine. The Act of Supremacy, passed in 1559, reaffirmed Elizabeth as the head of Church and state, while the Act of Uniformity required all English people to adopt one form of worship based on the revised *Book of Common Prayer*. The foundation of the Church of England was summed up in the Thirty-Nine Articles. England was regarded as a Protestant country by the rest of Europe, but there were divisions

Elizabeth I, daughter of Henry VIII by his second wife, Anne Boleyn, was an extremely popular, able monarch. England's Elizabethan Age was characterized by material prosperity, confidence in the government, and high national spirit.

under the surface, and religious controversy threatened to erupt any time a weaker, less understanding sovereign than Elizabeth came to the throne.

Catholic Reorganization in the Counter-Reformation

The Church had been slow to heed the cries for reform that had begun as early as the fourteenth century, and had often ignored the recommendations of some of the finest Catholic minds. Once Luther and his followers shattered the universal Christian establishment of Europe, however, Roman Catholic response quickened to meet the challenge. This response to

Protestant reform is known as the **Counter-Reformation**. New religious orders were created whose members lived a simple, less worldly, Christian life in the service of God and the community. The Theatine order, the Capuchin monks, and the Ursuline and Carmelite nuns were among the best examples of revitalized faith.

The most successful and important attempt at reform came from the work of a young Spanish soldier named Ignatius Loyola (1491-1556). While Luther was making his stand at the Diet of Worms, Loyola was wounded fighting for the Holy Roman emperor against the French. During his recovery, he read the only books available to him—a biography of saints and a four-volume account of the life of Christ. Loyola experienced a dramatic conversion and decided to dedicate his life to Christ and the Catholic Church.

Beginning his work with only six students, Loyola received papal approval in 1540 for a "Society of Jesus," later known as the **Jesuits**. The new order was organized like a highly disciplined army, and was committed to restoring the Church to its former position of prestige and power. To become a priest, a candidate served two years as a novice, nine years in study, and two years in teaching.

As their reputation for faith and scholarship spread, the Society of Jesus came to dominate Roman Catholic education in most European countries. Missionary work became another Jesuit priority, and they actively sought converts to Catholicism throughout the world—in India, Ceylon, the East Indies, and Japan, and among the native peoples of Canada and the Americas. The Society of Jesus was the spearhead of a reformed and reinvigorated Catholic faith.

When Pope Paul III was elected to office in 1534, the Church finally had a pope who was genuinely interested in reform. He called a general council of the Church to meet in the German town of Trent to examine Catholic beliefs. The **Council of Trent** met in three sessions between 1545 and 1563. Most Catholic principles were reaffirmed and Protestant notions rejected. But, in the spirit of reform, the council eliminated the sale of indulgences and Church offices; insisted that bishops be better trained, less worldly, and live in their diocese; and that every diocese must have a seminary to train priests. Celibacy was to be strictly enforced, and every monk and priest now had to be a model of Christianity in his private as well as his public life.

With rejuvenated faith and a better-trained clergy, the Church was prepared to roll back the gains Protestantism had made throughout northern Europe. To prevent the spread of heretical ideas that might lead the faithful Catholic astray, an *Index of Prohibited Books* was published to identify those authors who were not to be read. Even the medieval institution of the Inquisition was reactivated to combat heresy. The line between Catholic and Protestant was now unmistakably drawn, with each intolerant of the other and voicing no interest in reconciliation. Europe now had to deal with the power struggle between competing religions in addition to the secular conflicts of kingdoms and nation-states that had become all too familiar.

The Golden Century of Spain

In Europe, the Late Middle Ages gave way to the cultural changes of the Renaissance and the religious changes of the Reformation and Counter-Reformation. The same period was also a time of important political changes. Two years after Columbus's historic voyage, Pope Alexander VI sanctioned the Treaty of Tordesillas, which divided the Americas between Spain and Portugal along a north-south line 1600 km west of the Azores. In practice, this treaty eventually gave Brazil—claimed in 1500 by Pedro Cabral when his ship was blown off course—to Portugal, and the rest of Mesoamerica and South America to Spain. The Christian zeal that had expelled the Muslims and supported the Inquisition propelled Spain into the exploration and exploitation of new lands once the conquistadors had cleared a path. This gave Spain an important head start in commercial development that its European rivals did not overcome for almost a century.

The firm rule of Ferdinand and Isabella gave more unity to the administration of Spain than it had ever had before. Political stability encouraged a prosperous economy, which specialized in handicrafts and the production of wool, wine, and olive oil. Upon Ferdinand's death in 1516, his grandson Charles inherited the throne.

Throughout his reign, Charles was engaged in a series of conflicts with the Turks in eastern Europe and the Mediterranean, and with France over disputed territorial claims in the Rhineland and Italy. To the Empire's rivals, such military action often appeared to be an attempt by Charles to dominate Europe, a real possibility since the Spanish soldiers the Empire hired as mercenaries were among the best soldiers on the continent. Their services were paid for by the huge quantities of silver and gold that began to arrive from the Americas, first from collections of Amerindian jewellery, and later from the mines of Mexico and Peru. Increasing amounts of silver were imported to Spain each decade after the conquest, peaking between 1591 and 1600, when 2 707 626 kg arrived. Spanish galleons also brought back almost 900 000 kg of gold before supplies were virtually exhausted. Spain restricted trade between its colonies and other countries; Spanish ships, laden with precious metals, became inviting targets for British, French, and Dutch pirates.

Spaniards had flocked to the Americas on behalf of God, hoping to find both glory and gold. Their success in securing the latter was assisted immensely by their exploitation of the Amerindian population. The Spanish policy of *encomienda* gave the colonists a "legal" right to enslave the native peoples. An *encomienda* was an estate given by the Spanish Crown as a reward to loyal colonists. Any natives living on the lands of the estate were said to be the property of the *encomendero*, the new owner. Colonists looted the homes of the natives, who had been successful farmers and

The Inheritance of Charles V

Arranged and/or strategic marriages were common among the royal families of Europe. Advantageous marriages could cement alliances, repay favours, create obligations, and expand empires. Charles of Spain was the beneficiary of a particularly rich inheritance because his maternal and paternal grandparents, through a complex network of marriages, could claim to be the rightful rulers of many of the European countries and states of the day. Upon their deaths, Charles was king of Spain; ruler of the Netherlands, Bohemia, Milan, Naples, and Sicily; and head of the Hapsburg properties, which made him king of Austria and Germany. Hapsburg rulers also generally became the Holy Roman Emperor.

The **Holy Roman Empire** was an unusually complicated and indefinite political structure. It developed after the time of Charlemagne as a confederation of German principalities. (A principality is a small state ruled by a prince.) The Empire disintegrated in 1250, only to be revived in the fourteenth century with territorial claims extending as far as Italy. The Empire's government consisted of an emperor and a diet, selected by seven electors who were German princes and archbishops.

When Charles von Hapsburg bribed the electorate in 1519 to become the Holy Roman emperor, Charles V, in theory he had control over the largest territory under a single ruler since the days of Charlemagne. But while the emperor's prestige was recognized by all, it was difficult for him to control and direct such a vast collection of semi-independent states.

Holy Roman Empire, 1526.

traders, and forced them to provide food, labour, and tribute to their conquerors. They were tortured and, in extreme cases, murdered when they did not comply. The Spanish did not intend to destroy the native population that supplied their labour. Their careless pursuit of riches, however, depopulated many of the towns scattered over the countryside of Mesoamerica and South America. Bartolome de las Casas, a former colonial who became a bishop, argued that *encomiendas* were contrary to the law of God and country. Reforms were passed, but they were easily ignored. Charles V, to his credit, did finally suspend the exploration and conquest of new territory for a decade until a more humane approach could be developed.

The fate of Spain took another turn in 1556 when Charles abdicated his throne and divided his holdings. His younger brother, Ferdinand I, became Holy Roman Emperor. His son Philip II (1556-1598) of Spain became ruler of Spain, the Netherlands, northern Italy, Naples, and a colonial empire that was the envy of Europe, making Philip the main political force behind the Catholic Counter-Reformation. Conflicts with Protestants on the mainland of Europe and in England were the eventual result.

In the Netherlands, Philip tried to centralize the authority of the Catholic Church, even though the country jealously guarded its autonomy and had a significant Protestant minority. The new administration wanted to clamp down on heresy, but Catholics and Protestants alike regarded such a measure as a threat to their freedom. When a petition of protest signed by five hundred prominent citizens was ignored, a wave of violence swept the land, led by Calvinists who destroyed statues, paintings, and manuscripts in Catholic churches throughout the country. Philip sent in the duke of Alva to quell the unrest, but his actions only led to a struggle for independence that would not end until after Philip's death.

Philip's reign was complicated by his military involvement on several fronts. Aided by the fleets of Venice and Genoa, Spain stopped the advance of the Turks in the Mediterranean with an important naval victory in 1571 at the Battle of Lepanto off the Greek coast. Philip's success in harshly suppressing heresy caused resentment in England when escaping Protestant refugees arrived from the Netherlands and told their story. English money (as well as French) helped to sustain discontent in the Netherlands, while Elizabeth secretly commissioned Francis Drake and the English "sea dogs" to pirate the Spanish treasure brought from the Americas. Philip reluctantly determined to crush England and its Protestant Church, and sent a great armada of 130 ships and thirty thousand men toward the English Channel in 1588. An additional invasion force waited in the Spanish-controlled coastal area of the Netherlands to be transported to England after the English navy had been swept from the sea. In one of history's most famous naval battles, however, the speed and manoeuvrability of the smaller English ships, the surprise arrival of fireboats at night while the Spanish anchored at Calais, and a great storm reduced the Spanish fleet to less than half its original size.

More to Consider

Originally, Philip had been England's ally, not its enemy. Philip's father, Charles V, had arranged a marriage between his son and Mary Tudor of England, in 1553. This marriage between the Spanish heir and the queen of England cemented a traditional friendship between the two countries, and marked an earnest attempt to re-establish Catholicism on the island kingdom. The marriage between eighteen-year-old Philip and thirty-nine-year-old Mary was childless. After Mary died in 1558, Philip continued his pro-English policy by offering his hand to Elizabeth. Elizabeth realized that England needed stability rather than the religious conflict of Mary's years. She initially dodged the offer from Philip and later came to ridicule it.

Spain's inability to control the sea lanes after the defeat of its armada resulted in broken supply lines, which led to additional military losses against France on the continent during the final decade of Philip's reign.

Although Spain would remain a great power until the mid-seventeenth century, the die was cast. Philip's war had been waged on a grand scale, yet Anglican England was more formidable than ever, the Dutch Protestants were in control of the northern Netherlands (Holland), and French Huguenot rights were guaranteed by the Edict of Nantes. The flow of silver and gold into Spain from the Americas left as quickly as it arrived to pay for the burdens of war and the imported goods that Spain could not produce. Spain was essentially a poor country with few natural resources and limited human resources. When the supplies of precious metals began to dwindle in the seventeenth century, Spain quickly dropped out of the mainstream of European life with little left from its time of dominance.

The Thirty Years' War and the Nation-States of Europe

Although the hegemony of Catholic Spain was halted, Europe had not seen the last of wars that freely mixed religion and politics. In 1618, with Ferdinand von Hapsburg about to be elected Holy Roman Emperor, Protestants in Bohemia (now Slovakia and the Czech Republic) feared that religious toleration would cease. They launched a revolution in Prague, stormed the palace and threw two Hapsburg ministers out of an upper window. The ministers were saved from injury by a pile of manure that graced the royal courtyard, but Europe was not to be so lucky. Ferdinand moved to crush the rebellion and to tighten control over the Protestant German states within the Holy Roman Empire. The **Thirty Years' War**, as it has become known, had begun.

Spain came to Ferdinand's assistance, but other European powers did not want to see the Holy Roman Empire grow too strong. First Denmark and then Sweden entered the conflict against the forces of Spain and the emperor. In 1635, in the face of continued Hapsburg success, Catholic France came into the war *against* its religious affiliates in Spain and the Empire. This act clearly showed that political considerations had replaced the religious issues associated with the earlier phases of the war.

The Thirty Years' War caused great devastation because the technology and tactics of war were becoming more destructive. Muzzle-loading muskets had eliminated the effectiveness of armoured knights, but a disciplined cavalry charge could reach the infantry before it had a chance to reload. Similarly, a cannon could blow a hole in a line of cavalry, but it could not prevent the bulk of the charge from coming through. Only the wall of pikes held by an experienced infantry could blunt the impact of the cavalry. More and more, the war fell into the hands of seasoned mercenaries, and the need to pay them became increasingly important as the war dragged on. Commanders on both sides resorted to plundering villages and towns to feed and equip their soldiers and to pay their wages. This looting depleted the resources of the fragmented German states where much of the war was fought. Military conflict, looting, and the dislocation of crop production and distribution reduced the population by about one-third.

The French victory at Rocroi in 1643 crippled Spanish military power, ending Spain's days as a great European nation. With Spain humbled, the Hapsburg emperor opened peace talks five weeks later. The two sides hammered out peace treaties in a five-year congress (1643-1648) in German towns of Westphalia. Since no armistice was arranged, fighting continued as negotiations proceeded, and terms changed with success or failure on the battlefield. When the **Treaties of Westphalia** were finally issued in 1648, it was clear that the medieval organization of Europe had ended and that independent sovereign states, responsible only to themselves, had become the new order. After more than a century of religious war, neither Catholic nor Protestant could claim victory. The principle that each German prince had the right to choose the religion of his state, already proclaimed in the Peace of Augsburg in 1555, was reaffirmed. That Calvinism was among the religious choices ended the medieval concept of Western European unity. Papal condemnation of the treaties reflected the fact that the pope's representative at the conference was largely ignored, and that secular rulers had accepted the fragmentation of Christendom, begun during the Reformation. The right of the princes to make treaties and alliances with any European state effectively ended the political power of the Holy Roman Empire.

By the Treaties of Westphalia, the Hapsburgs were forced to recognize the independence of the United Netherlands (Holland), the Swiss Confederation, and the small German states, including the important principality of Brandenburg-Prussia. The Hapsburgs retained control over Austria, Bohemia, and Hungary, territory that would become the basis of a future monarchy on the Danube. Spain kept the Spanish Netherlands, Franche-Comté, and its Italian territory, but remained at war with France until 1659, when the Treaty of the Pyrenees ended hostilities. France, with a foothold in the Rhineland, emerged from Westphalia as the strongest power in Europe, with opportunities for future expansion.

At Westphalia, after centuries of evolution, the sovereign nation-state became the accepted basis for political organization. Germany and Italy remained a collection of small, individual provinces until the nineteenth century, but the historical trend toward the nation-state was increasingly clear. Medieval life had been dominated by feudal lords with their military forces of armoured knights. As trade and commerce revived in the towns and cities, however, the new middle class of wealthy merchants often became civic office holders. Their interest in business usually aligned them with the king, who competed for power and prestige with the established nobility whose wealth was based on ownership of land. Through taxation of the urban middle class, the king gained a source of revenue independent of

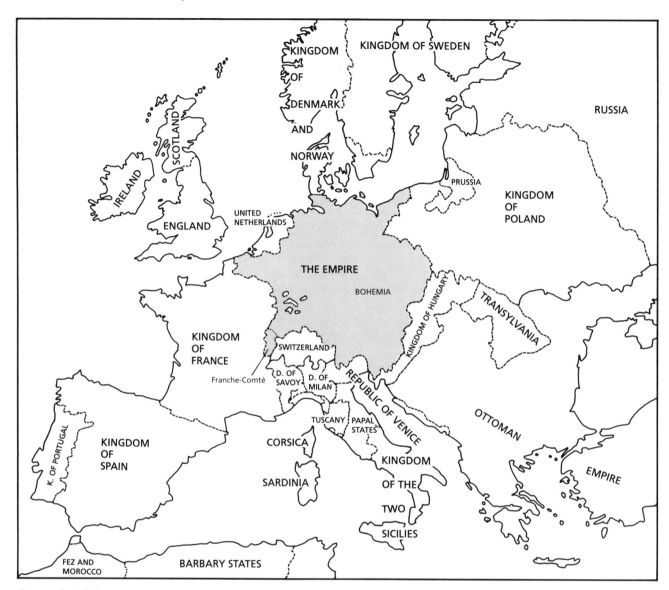

Europe in 1648.

feudal dues, and the administration of these taxes helped to **centralize** the operation of the government and the power of the king.

Centralization was a key feature of the nation-state. It appeared during the medieval period, occurring first in England in the form of the King-in-Parliament, and then in France as the monarch became more powerful. The arrangement of royal marriages for political purposes consolidated territories throughout Europe and resulted in further centralization. Changes in military technology meant that wars over disputed territories were becoming too expensive for the feudal nobility. Only a monarch had the financial resources to outfit an army with the necessary weapons.

In continental Europe, the end result of the increasing power of the various monarchs was the phenomenon of **absolutism**. Monarchs sought complete control of every aspect of life in the nations they ruled. Foreign policy and war, religious affiliation, taxation, legal reform, and economic activity were brought under the direction of the sovereign. Efforts to resist this concentration of power were regarded as threats to the national interest and were broken up and harshly punished. To maintain their authority, monarchs created extensive bureaucracies that monitored and administrated the life of the nation. Absolutism became a crucial force in Europe's development. Cultures were enriched, empires created, peoples oppressed, wars fought, and revolutions begun by those working for and against the ideal of the monarch's absolute authority.

Capitalism and the Commercial Revolution

The Renaissance and the Reformation, in combination with the development of the nation-state, affected the nature of the European economy. Humanism emphasized the value of life on earth rather than the rewards of heaven. It encouraged individual achievement and material advancement for all. Protestantism in general, and Calvinism in particular, stressed the moral value of thrift and hard work, but also gave religious approval to the collection of interest on borrowed money. For Calvin, an individual's economic success was a sign of God's favour. As strong monarchs brought increased stability and peace to their nation-states, they also encouraged individual initiative by offering assistance and special privileges to aggressive merchants and traders. With large sums of money or **capital** available, individuals could invest in large-scale commercial or manufacturing enterprises with the intent of making a profit. This form of economic activity is known as **capitalism**. Elements of capitalism were present in the ancient world and in the Italian cities of medieval Europe, but capitalism did not dominate Europe until after 1500, when the continent experienced a rapid commercial expansion that lasted until the Thirty Years' War.

The great stimulus for this **commercial revolution** came from the conquest of the Americas and the discovery of new trade routes to Asia. After the fall of Constantinople to the Turks, Venice monopolized trade with the Orient and preserved the Mediterranean as the crossroad between East and West. As the voyages of Portugal and Spain opened new horizons, however, the economic power of Europe shifted northward to the developing nation-states of the Atlantic seaboard. The careful planning and exploration of the Portuguese mariners paid off as they sailed to India, the Spice Islands, China, and even Japan. Throughout the sixteenth century, the Portuguese, along with the Spanish in Manila, controlled European trade within this vast domain and provided a steady stream of exotic spices, silks, cotton, tea, and coffee to the rest of Europe. Meanwhile, Spain gathered silver and gold bullion from mines in Mesoamerica and South America. Since Portugal and Spain manufactured few products, they had to exchange the riches of their voyages for the goods produced in other European countries. As Spain paid for imports in silver and gold, capital for commercial development (and war) greatly increased in the major commercial cities of Europe. When Spain and Portugal's supply of precious metals shrank, they fell by the wayside as major economic powers. The wealth they appropriated from the Americas, however, paved the way for Europe's economic prosperity. The population of Europe grew from 65 million in 1475 to 90 million early in the seventeenth century.

During the first seventy-five years of the sixteenth century, it was the Dutch who brought Spanish and Portuguese goods north from the Orient and distributed them throughout Europe. And it was the Belgian city Antwerp, part of the Spanish Empire after 1516, that became one of the great trading cities on the continent. Home of Europe's first stock exchange and a centre for the diamond industry, Antwerp attracted merchants and bankers from all major trading nations and states. The market in overseas products was matched by a booming inland commerce drawn along the Scheldt River. When Protestants in the Low Countries (The Netherlands, Belgium, and Luxembourg) revolted against their Catholic Spanish masters in the 1560s, however, Antwerp fell victim to the struggle. The city was sacked in 1576 and again in 1584. Eventually, at the Peace of Westphalia in 1648, Spain agreed to close the Scheldt River, and much of the commerce lost to Antwerp went to the great Dutch port of Amsterdam.

As Holland fought for independence from Spain, access to Eastern products was cut off. At first, the Dutch pirated Spanish and Portuguese fleets, but when the latter developed convoys for protection, the Dutch sailed to the East for themselves. In 1602, the Dutch East India Company was formed, and trading "factories" were established in Capetown, South Africa, where Dutch and Huguenot farmers (known as Boers) provided supplies for ships to India, Malaysia, Indonesia, China, and Japan. In the seventeenth century, the Netherlands replaced Portugal and Spain as the dominant force trading with the East, and Amsterdam became the busiest commercial centre in Europe. The Dutch were also active in the Americas through the efforts of the West India Company. Although they established colonies and bases from Brazil to New Amsterdam (later the English colony of New York), the Dutch lacked the population to maintain these territories as well as their commitments in the Far East.

The most serious rival to Dutch overseas trade was England, a country that had previously lagged behind in commercial expansion. England had little direct involvement in European affairs during the sixteenth and early to mid-seventeenth centuries, and had avoided the chaos and devastation of

The Arts

The commercial success of the Dutch during the seventeenth century was paralleled by a golden age of artistic achievement. Rembrandt Harmenszoon Van Rign (1606-1669) became famous for his portraits, which were characterized by a sensitive use of light and shadow. His work covered a wide range; he painted landscapes, nudes, studies of birds and animals, and scenes from history, mythology, and religion.

the religious and political wars on the continent. Skilled and wealthy refugees periodically fled to England to escape turmoil and persecution, and a growing business middle class began to thrive under the Tudor monarchs. Yet, England was still a small and relatively poor country compared with the other European nations engaged in exploration and trade. Indeed, the nation's commercial expansion depended on individual rather than state enterprise.

The English model for colonial development (and the forerunner of the modern corporation) was the Muscovy Company, established to trade with Russia during the reign of Henry VIII. To reduce the risk of loss, English merchants pooled their resources by purchasing shares, or stocks, in the venture. The result was a **joint-stock company** that became self-governing. Queen Elizabeth used this method of financing when she established the East India Company in 1600, which held a monopoly on all English trade with the Orient. During the first half of the seventeenth century, however, the East India Company was overwhelmed by its great Dutch competitor. Although English ships continued to harass the Dutch and would eventually enjoy success, the English were driven out of what became known as the Netherlands East Indies. With 40 warships, 150 merchant ships, and 10 000 soldiers at its disposal, the Dutch East India Company was the strongest European force on the seas.

The first permanent English settlement in the Americas was established in 1607 by a joint-stock company chartered by James I (1603-1625), first of the Stuart kings. Most of the one hundred adventurers who arrived were looking for the gold and silver that the Spanish had found so quickly in their colonies. Instead, they discovered a land better suited to the less glamorous pursuits of farming, fishing, and trade. James was also indirectly responsible for England's second colony, largely because he was a less capable administrator than his Tudor predecessors. Many people found the moderate Protestant Reformation in England unsatisfactory, and a growing movement known as **Puritanism** wanted further purification of the Church of England. James rigidly informed them that they must accept the Church as it was or they would be forced to leave. One radical group went to Holland, but remained unable to achieve its goals. With the financial support of a group of London merchants, these Puritans and some of their English friends set sail for Virginia aboard the *Mayflower*. Poor navigation and fierce Atlantic storms, however, took them to Cape Cod, where they established a settlement at nearby Plymouth in 1620.

The Tudors had developed a strong monarchy working through Parliament, but James believed in a principle known as the **divine right of kings**, which stated that the king was above the law and responsible only to God. Although this idea was popular on the continent, where it was used to support and legitimize absolutism, it led James into a struggle with the wealthy squires and merchants who dominated the English Parliament.

Charles I (1625-1649) shared his father's outlook, and made matters worse by marrying a French Catholic princess and persecuting all those who did not accept the Church of England. His attempt to establish absolute rule divided the country and resulted in the Civil War that lasted from 1642 to 1648. The success of the Puritan revolutionaries cost Charles his head in 1649. The Puritan leader Oliver Cromwell became lord protector of the republican Commonwealth, which lasted eleven years.

Despite the turmoil of Charles's reign, English settlement of North America continued to expand. By 1648, there were colonies in Virginia, Maryland, Massachusetts, Rhode Island, Connecticut, and New Hampshire, with a total population of about forty thousand. After 1630, several prosperous colonies that produced sugar, indigo, and cocoa were established in the West Indies. These colonies were considered more valuable than their counterparts in North America. Charles, despite his shortcomings in domestic affairs, did have the foresight to build an English navy strong enough to protect the commerce generated by overseas trade. England was now ready to challenge the commercial supremacy of the Dutch.

The Emergence of Bourbon France

In the seventeenth century, the ideal of absolutism found its fullest expression in the nation of France under the rule of King Louis XIV, the preeminent head of state in Europe. The monarch of France had not always enjoyed such power. When Henry IV (1589-1610) became the first Bourbon king to claim the French throne, the nation had suffered civil strife for three decades. Religious differences between Catholics and the Protestant Huguenots accounted for much of the conflict. To calm the fears of the majority, Henry, who had been raised a Protestant and had fought on their behalf, converted to Catholicism, claiming Paris was worth a Mass. In reality, he had little choice. At the same time, Henry proclaimed the Edict of Nantes to reassure his Huguenot supporters. Huguenots were given control of two hundred walled towns and were allowed to keep local revenues. They also gained the right to hold assemblies, and they even had their own soldiers. In essence, Henry had created a type of republic within the French state.

Backed tentatively by both Huguenots and Catholics, Henry tried to increase the power of the monarch at the expense of the barons by starting a program of economic recovery. He initiated canal and harbour construction, road building, and new industries. He encouraged the production of French silk. French interests in North America, left idle since Jacques Cartier entered the St. Lawrence in search of a route to Asia in 1534-1534, were revived. In 1608, Samuel de Champlain founded the first permanent settlement at Québec as part of an attempt to secure the region for France.

In 1610, at the peak of his power, Henry was assassinated by a religious fanatic. The prestige of the monarchy had not yet been fully restored.

Henry was succeeded by his nine-year-old son, Louis XIII, with his Italian mother, Maria de' Medici, as regent; in response, the nobles and Protestants again challenged the authority of the crown. The nobility did not want to rule in place of the king, but hoped to keep authority decentralized to protect their local interests. After Louis came of age, the talented Cardinal Richelieu became his most trusted adviser. Richelieu realized that the power of the Huguenots and the nobles would have to be broken if France was to become the greatest nation in Europe. He manipulated individual Huguenot towns into revolt and promptly used the royal army to defeat each in turn. The Huguenots were allowed to retain their religious privileges but not the military rights granted by the Edict of Nantes. At the same time, the nobility was relieved of its role in local affairs, while more authority was given to royal **intendants**, local administrators responsible to the king. When the nobility rebelled, as they did on five occasions, Richelieu organized the king's forces and crushed them. Louis was a more capable king than many historians admit, but it was Richelieu who engineered the foundation for the eventual triumph of royal authority.

The Sun King

Richelieu knew that his work was unfinished, and in the Italian-born Cardinal Mazarin he trained a worthy successor to fill his role as adviser and politician. When Richelieu died in 1642 and Louis in 1643, the wisdom of his foresight became clear. The king's heir was his fourteen-year-old son, Louis XIV. With the approval of the queen mother, Mazarin guided French foreign policy and safeguarded royal power through another troubled regency. Mazarin's influence in shaping the Treaties of Westphalia weakened the Holy Roman Empire and opened the door for French domination of the Rhineland. Within France, the nobles attempted yet another series of uprisings (known as the *Fronde*) in a desperate attempt to curb royal authority. Young Louis XIV was terrorized one night when plotters associated with the *Fronde* broke into his bedroom. He hid under the blankets pretending to be asleep and escaped unharmed. But by 1653 Mazarin had broken the *Fronde*, and the monarch's authority was secured.

In 1659, Mazarin concluded the Peace of the Pyrenees, six years after the end of hostilities with Spain. Spain lost territory to France, and a contract marriage was arranged between the Spanish king's daughter, Maria Theresa, and Louis XIV. Mazarin had made Richelieu's dream a reality. Hapsburg power was eclipsed, and Bourbon France became the foremost nation in Europe.

When Mazarin died in 1661, Louis assumed control of the government of France. There is no question that Louis owed a considerable debt to Mazarin and Richelieu for their skill in focussing power on the French monarchy. Yet Louis went beyond what he inherited. Louis was the dominant person of his age and he accepted the view that the king's authority

Louis XIV.

came from God. It was probable that his father uttered the famous phrase "The state, it is I," but Louis XIV embodied the spirit behind the statement and ruled accordingly. The Thirty Years' War, the English Civil War, and the *Fronde* had unsettled Europe. Absolute rule by a strong monarch responsible only to God appeared to be the best way to maintain order and stability, and Louis was determined to provide them.

Louis fully intended to be the focus of attention for his people, something his finance minister, Nicholas Fouquet, discovered the hard way. Fouquet amassed a personal fortune by questionable means and used his wealth to build a splendid chateau. The grand opening, in the presence of the king and his court, included fireworks and a specially commissioned play by Molière set against the beautifully manicured gardens and fountains of the estate. Unfortunately for Fouquet, his chateau outshone any of the royal palaces, and Louis became jealous of the glory Fouquet had drawn upon himself. Nineteen days later, Fouquet was arrested for embezzlement and imprisoned for life. All of Fouquet's property, including his chateau, was confiscated by the king.

Louis needed a stage from which the royal will would, like his chosen symbol, the sun, radiate magnificently for all to see and admire. He selected Versailles, about 15 km outside Paris, as the setting for his spectacular residence. His father had built a hunting lodge on the site, but Louis demanded a palace fit for the most powerful of kings. When Louis came to the throne, however, France was dependent upon other countries, particularly Italy, for the luxury products needed for such an enterprise. Louis and Colbert, the controller general of finance, commissioned the best foreign scientists, engineers, artisans, sculptors, and gardeners to come to France and work on Versailles. Marble quarries in the Pyrenees, left idle since the days of the Roman Empire, were reopened. The Royal Manufacturers in France were reorganized to stimulate domestic production. Within two decades, France became Europe's leading producer and exporter of luxury goods, including marble, mirrors, velvet, and lace. Versailles required the labour of tens of thousands of workers and had an estimated cost of half a billion dollars. It became the official seat of government in 1682.

The Issue Emerges

Versailles was the architectural representation of Louis's desire for absolute rule, designed to overwhelm the visitor and to proclaim the Sun King's dominance. Individuals were dwarfed by the 415 m facade of the building, the wide avenues, and the gardens carefully trimmed in geometric patterns. Fountains were everywhere, and water gushed from the mouths of statues. It was as if even nature had been made obedient to the will of the king. The numerous statues and reliefs of the Greek sun god Apollo were clear references to Louis himself. He wrote a guidebook to the palace, and on occasion personally conducted tours of the grounds to impress the aristocracy of

Louis XIV's First Meal At Versailles, 1682

four plates of soup
six hard-boiled eggs
one whole pheasant
one whole partridge
mutton dressed with garlic
ham, salad
three breads
pastry, fruit
wine cut with water

Europe with his creation. Versailles, however, was open to everyone, and it was not uncommon to find up to ten thousand people wandering its vast corridors hoping to catch a glimpse of the king and his court.

Louis kept himself at the centre of palace life. Even the smallest acts of his daily routine were part of a rigid etiquette carefully overseen by his court and over five hundred personal attendants. The *petite levée* marked the awakening of the king and was witnessed only by his closest aides and highest officials. Once Louis had washed and prayed, the *première entrée* began, and more officials entered to discuss routine business. At the end of the morning ceremony, the remaining nobility were allowed to join the *grande levée*, where they manoeuvred for the chance to give Louis a towel or help him with his coat. (Personal recognition by the king might lead to personal favour.) The king's bedchamber opened into the 72 m long Hall of Mirrors, which radiated light just as the Sun King radiated authority.

After working eight or nine hours on the affairs of state, Louis, even when exhausted, often insisted on his pleasures. In the late afternoon, he might play tennis or hunt. The evening regularly featured a lavish dinner, a concert, a masquerade ball, or a comedy. This public and hectic pace had an important purpose. Louis required that the nobility maintain themselves in luxury at Versailles, that they follow the ceremonies of his daily routine, and that they be seen at his social events. This obligation weakened the nobles financially, prevented them from developing a following in the provinces, and left them dependent on the king, who remained the focal point of all

The Hall of Mirrors at Versailles.

attention. Louis virtually eliminated the possibility of an uprising of nobles like the *Fronde* of his childhood. As additional insurance, he chose most of his advisors from the middle class to keep the nobles from power.

Versailles became the show-piece for Louis and French civilization. The best architects and artists had built and decorated the palace. Louis maintained the most impressive court of artists in Europe. Royal financial support was given to the playwrights Molière, Racine, and Corneille; the composer Jean Baptiste Lully; the poet La Fontaine; and painters such as Poussin, Lorraine, and Watteau. Foreign visitors were awed by the excellence of French manufacturers and artists. French fashion and manners were copied by the aristocratic classes of Europe, while the French language became a badge of refinement, culture, and education.

French civilization during Louis's seventy-two-year reign was often likened to the Age of Augustus in ancient Rome, and Louis was compared in greatness to Caesar and Alexander. These comparisons were exactly in keeping with Louis's belief in the divine right of kings, his desire for absolute rule, and his insistence on his own importance. The question is, were the comparisons merited or were Louis's courtiers merely echoing what the Sun King wanted to hear? Can one person take the credit for the work of thousands of labourers, artists, and administrators? On the other hand, would these achievements have been realized if Louis had not provided the right conditions?

Opinions about Louis's abilities and his competence differ. The modern historian John Wolf feels that Louis was responsible for much of what was achieved. The duke of Saint-Simon, who knew Louis well, was more critical, but he was also part of the nobility whom Louis barred from power. François Guizot, writing in the early nineteenth century, argued that the absolute government of France was indeed Louis's creation, but went on to say that it was too rigid and lacked popular support.

PROBLEM QUESTION

To what extent was Louis XIV responsible for the political, economic, military, and cultural predominance of French civilization during the Age of Absolutism?

ALTERNATIVE ONE: The Period of Brilliance

Based on *The Emergence of European Civilization* by John B. Wolf (1962)

Louis XIV had able associates, but this should not detract from his reputation as king. Cardinal Mazarin had told Louis that he could be a great king if he worked at it and Louis spent many hours each day doing just that. Although he listened to the advice of his ministers, he supervised their activities and was well aware of what they were doing.

Louis tried to bring order to the operation of his government. During the long period of warfare, lawlessness had spread throughout the countryside of France. No king could hope to gain respect if he could not keep the peace so Louis dealt with the problem directly. He sent his soldiers throughout the kingdom to catch the bandits and kidnappers who showed disrespect for the king's law and had the guilty hanged or beheaded to show that he was serious! Crime did not vanish from France but it was greatly reduced and more likely to be punished. Louis had also hoped to reorganize French law just as Justinian had done for Roman law under the Byzantine Empire. This proved to be too great a task, but the changes that Louis did make affected the administration of the treasury, the war office, the navy and other departments. Many of Louis's edicts lasted throughout the 18th century and became the basis of later French legal codes that still exist today. Certainly Louis had provided the basis for the modern bureaucratic state.

With Louis's approval, the skilful minister Colbert attempted to strengthen the French economy through close government regulation. Chartered companies were founded to trade overseas, foreign workers were imported to introduce their crafts to France, and legislation was passed to control the production of goods, including the conditions of apprenticeship. In the field of taxation, the major problem was that the two upper classes, the clergy and nobility, were largely exempted from the direct taxing power of the king. Colbert increased excise taxes on goods to share the tax burden more equitably, but little real progress was made. Nevertheless, his efficient offices collected more taxes with fewer losses than earlier governments which gave Louis an unprecedented source of wealth at his disposal.

One of the government's most successful efforts was the creation of Europe's first full-time or standing army organized by Le Tellier and Louvois. The threat of rebellion within France and Louis's ambition in Europe made such a force vital to French power and glory. Previously, European armies had been a loose collection of mercenaries whose loyalty was open to question. The new French army, a true descendant of the Roman legions, was clothed, fed, equipped and paid by the crown. Colbert equalled this achievement with the formation of the French navy, the foremost of its day. Seapower was critical to the development, protection and expansion of French commercial interests. Both the army and the navy were responsible to the king's ministers, controlled by the king's agents and completely responsive to the king's authority.

European governments of the 17th century were only tolerant of their state religion and Louis was no exception. Dissent was considered to be treason. When Louis secured power after 1661, the question of religious uniformity was raised because French Huguenots (Protestants) had been left alone in Catholic France by previous governments who were either unable or unwilling to deal with them. The Huguenots had been associated with rebellion in the past, but by Louis's reign they were loyal to the king. Louis tried to get them to change their religion at first by bribery and later through quartering of soldiers in their homes. Many Huguenots began to emigrate to England, Holland, and Germany where they could practise their religion in peace. Louis was misled by his advisers into thinking that his policy of forced conversion was more of a success than it was. Believing that it would not affect many people, Louis revoked the Edict of Nantes, which had given the Huguenots the right to practise their beliefs, and banned the "Reformed religion" in 1685.

Although this move may have appealed to Catholic sensibilities, it was a mistake. The emigration already begun continued on an even larger scale. This meant that an enterprising and skilful segment of the French population was lost to other countries who benefitted from their talents. Much like those who left after the French Revolution in 1789 and the Nazi takeover of 1933 [in Germany], the refugees ousted by Louis went abroad and agitated against the hostile policies of their homeland.

It is true that Louis had mistresses, illegitimate children, and a costly court that could be summoned at his pleasure. But Louis had a purpose in this and that was to separate and elevate himself above the nobles and princes of the land. He lived life on a grand scale to keep himself apart from the masses. Just as his love affairs were exceptional, his sumptuous palaces and formal court etiquette focussed all attention and power on himself as the 'Sun King'. Versailles was the ultimate symbol of his personal magnificence. The palace was not protected by moats which showed Louis's personal confidence in his ability to rule and keep the peace. Palace life reduced the role of the nobles, who had been his rivals in power, to mere servants who reacted with submission to the king's every whim. Being forced to leave the court, away from the presence of the king, was now seen as a major disgrace.

At first Versailles was a challenge to the nobles to match the splendor of the king who no longer feared their power. It quickly became an announcement to Europe that France had replaced Spain as the leading power in the western world. Philip II had built the Escorial as a palatial symbol of Spanish glory. Louis built Versailles with salons, gardens, fountains and reflecting pools organized on an unprecedented scale, to proclaim that France now held the hegemony of Europe. Louis chose the emblem of the sun to underline the fact that all of France, indeed all of Europe had become satellites of his grandeur. In architecture, Versailles became the supreme symbol of the baroque age in which secular buildings became more important than religious ones. Its influence would eventually be felt in such distant locations as Washington and St. Petersburg (Leningrad). Versailles cast the shadow of French civilization under which half the princes of the world would live for the next century and a half.

When Louis's armies suffered defeat and swarms of tax collectors reminded the people of the cost of the king's policies, the early years of glory seemed to be forgotten. Louis's influence on the princes of Europe, however, continued throughout the 18th century. Louis was not the first 'enlightened despot' but he was a model for those who followed him. Even Napoleon looked to Louis for inspiration in the art of government. Just as Louis had defined 'kingship', the France he did so much to build defined the nature of the bureaucratic state for those that shaped the modern world in the succeeding decades.

QUESTIONS

1. How enthusiastic was Louis XIV about being king?
2. a) What were Louis's goals for French government and French law?
   b) Did he fulfil these goals? Explain your answer.
3. What was the result of Jean Baptiste Colbert's attempt to strengthen the French economy?
4. a) Why could the new French army be compared with the legions of ancient Rome?
   b) Who controlled the new army and navy?
5. a) Did Louis oppose the French Huguenots because of their religious beliefs or because they did not bend to state authority? Give evidence to support your answer.
   b) Why was the revocation of the Edict of Nantes in 1685 a mistake?
6. a) According to Wolf, what was Louis XIV's main purpose in the formal, courtly life he lived at Versailles?
   b) What did the Escorial and Versailles represent to Europe?
7. What conclusions does Wolf draw about Louis XIV's importance in history?

ALTERNATIVE TWO: The Reign of Louis XIV

Based on *The Memoirs of the Duke of Saint-Simon,* translated by Bayle St. John in 1888

At 23 years of age he entered the great world as king under the most favourable conditions. His ministers were the most skilful in all Europe; his generals the best; his court was filled with illustrious and clever men.

Louis XIV was made for a brilliant court. In the midst of other men, his figure, his courage, his grace, his beauty, his grand manner, even the tone of his voice and the majestic and natural charm of all his person distinguished him till his death as the King Bee. He wished to reign by himself. His unceasing jealousy on this point became a weakness. The superior ability of his early ministers and his early generals soon wearied him. He liked nobody to be in any way superior to him. Thus he chose his ministers, not for their knowledge, but for their ignorance; not for their capacity, but for their want of it. His vanity, his unmeasured and unreasonable love of admiration, was his ruin. His ministers, his generals, his mistresses, his courtiers, soon perceived his weakness. They praised him with emulation and spoiled him. Praises, or to say truth, flattery, pleased him to such an extent, that the coarsest was well received, the vilest even better relished. It was the sole means by which you could approach him. Those whom he liked owed his affection for them to their untiring flatteries. This is what gave his ministers so much authority. They attributed everything to him and pretended to learn everything from him.

Though his intellect was beneath mediocrity, it was capable of being formed. God had sufficiently gifted him to enable him to be a good king; perhaps even a *tolerably great king!* His early education was neglected. He was scarcely taught how to read or write, and remained so ignorant that the most familiar historical and other facts were utterly unknown to him! He fell, accordingly, and sometimes even in public, into the grossest absurdities.

He was exceedingly jealous of the attention paid him. Not only did he notice the presence of the most distinguished courtiers, but those of inferior degree also. He looked to the right and to the left, not only in rising, but upon going to bed, at his meals, in passing through his apartments, or his gardens of Versailles, where alone the courtiers were allowed to follow him. He marked well all absentees from the court, found out the reason for their absence, and never lost an opportunity of acting towards them as the occasion might seem to justify. With the most distinguished, it was a demerit not to make the court their ordinary abode; with others 'twas a fault to come but rarely; for those who never or scarcely ever came it was certain disgrace. When their names were in any way mentioned, "I do not know them," the king would reply haughtily.

Louis XIV took great pains to be well informed of all that passed everywhere; in the public places, in the private homes, in society and familiar intercourse. His spies and telltales were infinite. He had them of all species; many who were ignorant that their information reached him; others who knew it; others who wrote to him direct, sending their letters through channels he indicated; and all these letters were seen by him alone; and always before everything else; others who sometimes spoke to him secretly in his cabinet, entering by the back stairs. These unknown means ruined an infinite number of people of all classes, who never could discover the cause; often ruined them unjustly; for the king, once prejudiced, rarely altered his opinion. He had an excellent memory; in this way, that if he saw a man who, 20 years before, perhaps, had in some way offended him, he did not forget the man, though he might forget the offense. This was enough to exclude the person from all favor. The representations of a minister, of a general, of his confessor even, could not move the king.

The most cruel means by which the king was informed of what was passing—for many years before anybody knew it—was that of opening letters. He saw extracts from all the letters in which there were passages that the chiefs of the post office, and then the minister who governed it, thought ought to go before him; entire letters, too, were sent to him, when their contents seemed to justify the sending. A word of contempt against the king or the government, a joke, a detached phrase, was enough. It is incredible how many people, justly or unjustly, were more or less ruined, always without recourse, without trial, and without knowing why. The chiefs of the post, nay, the principal clerks were in a position to suppose what they pleased and against whom they pleased.

It was his vanity, his desire for glory, that led him, soon after the death of the King of Spain, to make that event the pretext for war; in spite of the renunciations so recently made, so carefully stipulated in the marriage contract. He marched into Flanders; his conquests there were rapid; the passage of the Rhine was admirable; the triple alliance of England, Sweden, and Holland only animated him. In the midst of winter he took Franche-Comté, and then gave it back at the Peace of Aix-la-Chapelle, thus preserving his conquests in Flanders. All was flourishing then in the state. Riches everywhere. Colbert had placed the finances, the navy, commerce, manufacturers, letters even, upon the highest point; and his age, like that of Augustus, produced in abundance illustrious men of all kinds.

With the success of one war, Louis was easily persuaded by his ministers to enter that famous Dutch War in which his love for Madame de Montespan reduced his glory and that of his kingdom. Everything being conquered, everything taken and Amsterdam ready to give up her keys, the king yielded to his impatience, quit the army, flew to Versailles, and destroyed in an instant all the success of arms! He repaired his disgrace by a second conquest, in person, in Franche-Comté, which this time was preserved by France. In 1676, with more victories in Flanders, the armies of the king suddenly approached those of the Prince of Orange near Heurtebise. According even to the admission of the enemy, our forces were so superior to those of the Prince of Orange, that we must have gained the victory if we had attacked. But the king, after listening to the opinions of his generals, decided against combat and turned tail. The army was much discontented. Everybody wished for battle. The fault therefore of the king made much impression upon the troops, and excited cruel railleries against us at home and in the foreign courts. The king stopped but little longer afterwards in the army, although we were only in the month of May. He returned to his mistress.

The power of France was acutely felt throughout Europe, America, Africa, and Sicily. The peak of Louis's reign, and the fullness of glory and prosperity declined after 1688. The great captains, the great ministers, were no more, but their pupils remained. The second epoch of the reign was very different from the first; but the third was even more sadly dissimilar.

More wars followed but France gained nothing. The king was obliged to acknowledge the Prince of Orange as King of England, after having so long shown hatred and contempt for him. Our fall, too, cost us Luxembourg; and the ignorance of our negotiators gave our enemies great advantages in forming their frontier. Such was the Peace of Ryswick concluded in September, 1697.

Shortly afterwards, by one of the most surprising and unheard-of pieces of good fortune, the crown of Spain fell into the hands of the Duc d'Anjou, grandson of the king. It seemed as though golden days had come back to France. Only for a little time, however, did it seem so. Nearly all Europe banded against France to dispute the Spanish crown. The king had lost all his good ministers, all his able generals, and had taken good pains they should leave no successors. When war came, then, we were utterly unable to prosecute it with success or honor. We were driven out of Germany, of Italy, of the Low Countries. We could not sustain the war, or resolve to make peace. Every day led us nearer and nearer to the brink, to the terrible depths of which were forever staring us in the face. A misunderstanding amongst our enemies, whereby England became detached from the grand alliance; the undue contempt of Prince Eugene for our generals, out of which arose the battle of Denain; saved us from the gulf. Peace came, and a peace, too, infinitely better than that we should have accepted if our enemies had agreed amongst themselves beforehand. Nevertheless, this peace cost dear to France, and cost Spain half its territory—Spain, of which the king had said not even a windmill would he yield! But this was another piece of folly he soon repented of.

Thus we see this monarch grand, rich, conquering, the arbiter of Europe; feared and admired as long as the ministers and captains existed who really deserved the name. When they were no more, the machine kept moving. But soon afterwards we saw beneath the surface; faults and errors were multiplied, and decay came on with giant strides; without, however, opening the eyes of that despotic master, so anxious to do everything and direct everything himself.

QUESTIONS

1. a) According to Saint-Simon, what personal qualities did Louis XIV bring to the throne?
   b) How did Louis XIV's vanity affect his conduct?
2. a) Why do you think Louis XIV was so concerned about who was in attendance at court?
   b) How did Louis XIV use and misuse his network of spies?

3. According to Saint-Simon, why did Louis XIV take France into war?
4. a) How successful was France in the early wars of Louis XIV?
   b) What criticisms does Saint-Simon make of Louis XIV's conduct as the leader of the army?
5. a) According to Saint-Simon, why did the fortunes of France decline in the second half of Louis XIV's reign?
   b) Is this a valid judgment of Louis XIV's career? Explain your answer with evidence.

ALTERNATIVE THREE: Architect of France

Based on *History of Civilization in Europe* by François Guizot, translated by William Hazlitt in 1900

When we occupy ourselves with the government of Louis XIV, when we try to appreciate the causes of his power and influence in Europe, we only think of his renown, his conquests, his magnificence, and the literary glory of his time. It is to external causes that we apply ourselves and attribute the European dominance of the French government. But I believe that this dominance had deeper and more serious foundations. We must not believe that it was simply by means of victories, lavish living or even masterworks of genius, that Louis XIV and his government played the part which it is impossible to deny them.

Recall to your memory the state into which France was fallen after the government of Cardinal Richelieu, and during the minority of Louis XIV: the Spanish armies always on the frontiers, sometimes in the interior; continual danger of an invasion; internal conflicts, urged to extremity, civil war, the government weak and discredited at home and abroad. It was from this state that the government of Louis XIV saved France. His first victories secured the country and retrieved the national honor. Unlike the wars that went before it, the wars of Louis XIV were not a personal whim; they were wars of regular government, fixed in the center of its states, and laboring to make conquests around it, to extend or consolidate its territory; in a word, they were political wars. No doubt personal ambition had a share in these wars; but examine one after another, particularly those of the first part of Louis's reign, and you will find that they had truly political motives; and that they were conceived for the interest of France, for obtaining power, and for the country's safety.

The results are proofs of the fact. France of the present day is still, in many respects, what the wars of Louis XIV had made it. The provinces which he conquered, French-Comté, Flanders and Alsace, remain yet incorporated with France. These were not senseless conquests, as others were up to Louis's time; a skilful, if not always just and wise policy, motivated Louis's expansionist ambition.

Leaving the wars of Louis XIV and turning to diplomacy, the results were similar. Diplomatic relations between countries had not been systematic prior to the 17th century. There had been no long alliances, or great and durable combinations, directed according to fixed principles, toward a constant aim, with that spirit of continuity which is the true character of established governments. During the course of the religious revolution, the external relations of states were almost completely under the power of the religious interest; the Protestant and Catholic leagues divided Europe. It was in the 17th century, after the Treaties of Westphalia, and under the influence of the government of Louis XIV, that diplomacy changed its character. It then escaped from the exclusive influences of the religious principle; alliances and political combinations were formed upon other considerations. It became systematic, with certain aims and principles. The regular origin of this system of balance in Europe belongs to this period. It was under the government of Louis XIV that the system, together with all the considerations attached to it, truly took possession of European policy.

It has often been said that the spread of absolute power was the main principle of the diplomacy of Louis XIV; but I do not believe it. This consideration played no very great part in his policy, until latterly, in his old age. The power of France, its dominance in Europe, the humbling of rival powers, in a word, the political interest and strength of the state, was the aim which Louis XIV constantly pursued, whether in fighting against Spain, the Emperor of Germany, or England; he acted far less with a view to the spread of absolute power than from a desire for the power and aggrandizement of France and of its government. For example, Louis tried to keep royal power in England weak—a move that would keep France in a strong position—by working to revive the republican party against Charles II. During the embassy of Barillon in England the same fact constantly appears. Whenever the authority of Charles seemed to obtain the advantage and the national party seemed on the point of being crushed, the French ambassador directed his influence to this side, gave money to the chiefs of the opposition, and fought, in a word, against absolute power, when that became the means of weakening a rival to France.

You will also be struck with the capacity and skill of French diplomacy at this period. The names of MM. de Torcy, d'Avaux, de Bonrepos, are known to all well-informed persons. When we compare the dispatches, the memoirs, the skill and conduct of these counsellors of Louis XIV with those of Spanish, Portuguese, and German negotiators, we must be struck with the superiority of the French ministers; not only as regards their earnest activity and the application to affairs, but also regards their liberty of spirit. There was no diplomacy in Europe in the 17th century which appears equal to the French, except the Dutch.

You see, then, that whether we consider the wars of Louis XIV, or his diplomatic relations, we arrive at the same results. We can easily conceive that a government, which conducted its wars and negotiations in this manner, should have assumed a high standing in Europe, and presented itself therein, not only as dreadworthy, but as skilful and imposing.

Let us now consider the administration and legislation of Louis XIV. Administration is the total means to propel the will of the central power through all parts of society, and to make the force of society, whether consisting of men or money, return again, under the same conditions, to the central power. It is the chief means of providing unity; and this was the work of the administration of Louis XIV. Up to this time there had been nothing so difficult, in France as in the rest of Europe, as to effect the penetration of the action of the central power into all parts of society. To this end Louis XIV labored, and succeeded, up to a certain point; incomparably better, at least, than preceding governments had done. Just run over, in thought, all kinds of public services, taxes, roads, industry, military administration, and others. There is scarcely one of which you do not find either the origin, development, or great improvement under Louis XIV. It was as administrators that the greatest men of his time, Colbert and Louvois, displayed their genius and exercised their ministry. It was by the excellence of its administration that his government acquired a generality, decision, and consistency which were wanting to all the European governments around him.

The legislative point of view gives the same fact. The great ordinances he issued, the criminal ordinances, the ordinances of procedure, commerce, the marine, waters, and woods are true codes that recast the laws just as our codes do today. Many of Louis XIV's laws were full of vices, but they were conceived in the interest of public order and for giving regularity and firmness to the laws. But even that was a great progress; and we cannot doubt that the ordinances of Louis XIV, so very superior to anything preceding them, powerfully contributed to advance French society in the career of civilization.

And now we inquire how it happened that a power, thus brilliant, thus well established, so rapidly fell into decline? How, after having played such a part in Europe, it became in the next century, so inconsistent, weak and inconsiderable? The fact is incontestable. In the 17th century the French government was at the head of European civilization; in the 18th century it disappeared; and it was French society, separated from its government, often even opposed to it, that now preceded and guided the European world in its progress.

Here we discover the evil and the infallible effect of absolute power. I will speak not of the faults of the government of Louis XIV; of the War of the Spanish Succession, of the Revocation of the Edict of Nantes, or of excessive expenses and other measures that compromised his fortunes. But, by the very fact that the government had no other principle than absolute power, its decline became sudden and well merited. The ancient

French institutions, if they merited the name, no longer existed: Louis completed their ruin. He did not try to replace them. The absolute government of Louis XIV was a great fact, a fact powerful and splendid, but without roots.

It was not Louis XIV alone who was becoming aged and weak at the end of his reign: it was the whole absolute power. Pure monarchy was as much worn out in 1712 as was the monarch himself. This, then, is the state in which Louis XIV left France and power: a society in full development of riches, power and all kinds of intellectual activity; and side by side with this progressive society, a government that was stationary, having no means of renewing itself, of adapting itself to the movement of its people; devoted, after half a century of the greatest splendor, to immobility and weakness, and already, during the life of its founder, fallen into a decline which seemed like dissolution.

QUESTIONS

1. a) According to Guizot, how did the government of Louis XIV change France?
    b) What evidence regarding war and diplomacy does Guizot offer to support his claim?
2. Why does Guizot rule out the possibility that Louis XIV was trying to spread absolute power?
3. How talented were the French ministers of state compared with those in the rest of Europe?
4. Why does Guizot feel that the administration and legislation of Louis XIV was more successful than that of other French governments?
5. Why did Louis XIV's government decline in the second half of his reign?
6. Considering the views of Wolf, Saint-Simon, and Guizot, can it be said that Louis XIV was a great leader? Explain your answer with evidence.

ANSWERING THE PROBLEM QUESTION

When you compared the achievements of Alexander, Hannibal, and Julius Caesar, you developed criteria for greatness, measured each leader against these criteria, and then decided which of the three leaders was greatest. The problem question for this chapter goes much further. Louis XIV dreamed of a French hegemony in every field of human endeavour; midway through his reign, it seemed as if his ambition was realized. The question is, was Louis's goal achieved because he *controlled* the course of history? Can any individual exert that much control?

There are many issues you should consider as you try to answer the problem question. Could Louis have completed the organization of the

French bureaucracy without the groundwork laid by Richelieu and Mazarin? Colbert, Le Tellier, and Louvois were perhaps the most talented advisers in Europe. Does their success in improving economic efficiency, assembling artists at court, and creating a standing army detract from Louis's role? Or should the Sun King be given credit for their appointments in the first place? It was Louis's architects and artists who created the great works France became famous for; can Louis take the credit because he provided the driving force behind them? The court life at Versailles was more clearly Louis's personal creation. How important was this aspect of French society? Imitation has been called the highest form of flattery and, during Louis's reign, French architecture and custom were copied throughout the aristocratic corners of the continent. Was this popularity the result of Louis's style, or would France have produced this quality of life without his guidance?

It has been said that Louis would have been a much greater king if he had died halfway through his reign. The glory of his early years was offset by a series of unsuccessful wars, climaxed by the disastrous War of the Spanish Succession. His ministers of state during the early years had died by the 1680s, and their successors were much less able. Were the French military failures their responsibility? Was Louis simply unable to rule well without his key people? Or was the elderly king simply not the leader he once was? His record is uneven. At his death, France was deeply in debt, and the burden of taxation still fell on the peasant class, which was less and less able to pay. French military domination had been checked, but not surpassed on the continent. French culture continued to be admired.

What is your conclusion about Louis XIV's career? Was he responsible for the political, economic, military, and cultural predominance of French civilization during the Age of Absolutism?

THE STORY CONTINUES . . .

Absolutism in Europe after Westphalia

Louis XIV's attempt to bring order to France through absolute rule was mirrored in other European states. The Thirty Years' War redefined the nations of Europe. Out of the ashes of the Holy Roman Empire, which had been politically neutralized, emerged two new powers—the **Hapsburg Empire**, still centred in Vienna, but smaller than it had been; and the state of **Brandenburg-Prussia**.

In 1683 the Hapsburg Empire was greatly endangered when the Turkish army besieged Vienna. The city held out until Polish and German armies, and the military brilliance of Prince Eugene of Savoy, forced the Turks to retreat. Prince Eugene continued the campaign with a series of successful battles that eventually drove the Turks out of Hungary. He then played a major role in limiting the expansionist policies of Louis XIV with victories in the War of the Spanish Succession. The Hapsburg Empire

The Sun King's Wars

Date	Initial Action	Opponents	Results
1667	Louis advanced questionable claims to the Franche-Comté and Spanish Netherlands.	France *versus* England, Holland, and Sweden	Treaty of Aix-la-Chapelle in 1668 was a compromise. Louis gave up his claims but kept a few towns in Flanders.
1672	Louis marched through the Spanish Netherlands to attack the Dutch.	France *versus* Holland, Denmark, Brandenburg, Austrian and Spanish Hapsburgs	Louis's forces were worn down. Peace was made at Nijmegen in 1678. Holland survived intact. Louis kept the Franche-Comté.
1681	Louis seized the independent republican city of Strasbourg.		
1683	Louis seized Luxembourg and financed a rebellion in Hungary.		The problems in Hungary encouraged the Turks to lay siege to Vienna. **Louis was now at the peak of his power.**
1688	Louis seized the Palatinate, a small German territory on the Rhine.	France *versus* the League of Augsburg: Holy Roman Empire, Spain, Sweden, Bavaria, Saxony, Palatinate, Holland, and England	English and Dutch fleets defeated the French. Louis won several battles but could not subdue the Dutch. A tired Louis was forced to accept the Peace of Ryswick in 1697. He lost all he had gained in the east but kept Strasbourg.
1700	Louis seized fortresses in the Spanish Netherlands thereby challenging Europe and beginning the War of the Spanish Succession.	France, Bavaria, and Spain *versus* the Grand Alliance: England, Holland, Brandenburg-Prussia, Holy Roman Empire, Duchy of Savoy	Treaties of Utrecht, 1713-1714 France remained a great nation but its threat to the balance of power had been checked. England emerged as a great colonial power.

gained strength, and by 1713 the family territories in Austria, Bohemia, and Hungary became indivisible under the leadership of Emperor Charles VI (1711-1740).

Although the Hapsburg, or **Austrian**, Empire had opposed Louis XIV in battle, it chose to emulate his style of kingship. The Hapsburg nobility built several impressive works of **baroque** architecture, similar to Louis's Versailles, to express the power and grandeur of their state. Just beyond the gates of Vienna, Prince Eugene built the splendid palaces of Upper and Lower Belvedere as summer residences used by royalty for state occasions.

Schönbrunn, one of the three royal residences of the Hapsburgs.

Even more striking was Schönbrunn, rebuilt under Joseph I after its destruction by the Turks, and given its modern form by Maria Theresa in 1743. The main chateau almost matched the scale and glory of Versailles and even boasted the same type of carefully patterned French gardens and beautiful fountains. Within the city of Vienna, the twenty-six-hundred-room Imperial Palace, even larger than Schönbrunn, was the winter residence of the royal family and the main seat of government.

Frederick William (1640-1688), the "Great Elector" of Brandenburg, was less concerned with pomp and ceremony and more concerned with power. He brought together the scattered family possessions of the Hohenzollerns under one government to form, for the first time, the state of Brandenburg-Prussia. Like Louis XIV, Frederick William believed in absolutism, and since Brandenburg-Prussia was created as an act of state with no natural boundaries, centralized control was essential. Frederick William forged a strong monarchy that demanded discipline. The Thirty Years' War had weakened most of the feudal nobility, known as the Junkers, and they were glad to serve in the new army or as high-ranking government officials responsible to the state. As in France, Frederick William appointed royal supervisors to manage the provinces. Because he encouraged immigration, twenty thousand skilled and industrious Huguenots arrived from France. With a standing army of thirty thousand, and the strong civil service that grew out of the need to maintain it, Frederick William made Brandenburg-Prussia the strongest state in Germany.

After the War of the Spanish Succession, the ruler of Prussia was given the title of king rather than Great Elector. Frederick William I (1713-1740) built upon the foundation of his grandfather (Frederick William, the Great Elector) by strengthening the economy, filling the treasury, and increasing the size of the army to eighty thousand. Indeed, about 70 percent of the national income was spent directly or indirectly on the army. Frederick William I made Prussia a military nation that stressed absolute obedience, duty, and personal sacrifice to the will of the state. A Frenchman of the day aptly claimed that Prussia was not a state with an army but an army that possessed a state. Prussia had gradually increased its possessions on the Baltic and in Europe since the time of the Great Elector and it now possessed one of the largest and most efficient armies on the continent. There was no doubt that Frederick William I had completed the moulding of Prussia into a major European power.

Absolutism was also a feature of the Russian state. Russia had been largely untouched by the civilizations of ancient Greece and Rome. Founded as a small state by the Vikings in the ninth century, Russia was later converted by missionaries to Eastern Orthodox Christianity and adopted elements of Byzantine culture. Vast regions of open plains left Russia exposed to invasion by the Huns and the Mongols of Genghis Khan, but Ivan the Great (1462-1505), the grand duke of Muscovy, ended foreign rule and established the foundations of imperial Russia. When the Muslims occupied Constantinople, Ivan took up the cause of the Byzantine world and became the protector of the Greek Orthodox Church in the tradition of the Roman Caesars. Ivan IV (1533-1585), better known as "the Terrible," eventually took the title of tsar (from Caesar) and consolidated his absolute power by executing thousands of nobles and taking their land. The tsars gradually extended their control over more and more territory until, by the establishment of the Romanov dynasty in 1613, the Russian state ruled much of modern Russia absolutely.

Russia was geographically isolated, and was more Eastern than Western. The Renaissance and the discoveries and advances of the sixteenth and seventeenth centuries hardly touched Russia. Peter the Great (1694-1725) became concerned that the quality of government service and the efficiency of the Russian army were inferior to their Western European counterparts. He directed his considerable energy toward "opening windows to the West" in order to westernize and modernize Russia. To achieve this goal, Peter travelled incognito, mainly to Holland and England but also to the German states, France, Switzerland, Austria, and Prussia. He visited mills, shipyards, museums, hospitals, and the shops of artisans, trying to absorb all aspects of Western life. Architecture, printing, dentistry and, of course, the preparations for war on land and sea were among his interests. Peter arranged for five hundred European artisans to visit Russia to introduce new methods and for a few Russian youths to study in the West to learn as much as they could.

Institutions

Peter the Great's form of absolutism was more extensive than that of any nation in Western Europe. As part of his policy of Westernization, Peter taxed men who wore long, oriental-style beards, and stationed barbers at the entrances to towns to trim beards to the required length. He encouraged the use of tobacco, which was a Western habit, and forced nobles and town officials to wear clothes cut in a French or German style. Women were encouraged to take part in social events, and the Eastern custom of the harem was abolished.

As a result of Peter's travels, Russia adopted Western methods of administration, and created an imperial bureaucracy to carry out his policies. Opposition was not tolerated. When the nobility and Imperial Guard challenged his authority, Peter not only crushed the revolt but personally beheaded some of the rebels and ensured that his own son was put to death.

Peter's modernization of Russia's military forces was a key element in his imitation of the West. Western officers trained and reorganized the army. A shipbuilding industry was begun to support the creation of a new navy. To end Russia's landlocked isolation, Peter wanted to secure ports on the Black Sea and the Baltic. Although he was only partially successful in his campaign against the Turks in the south, the Northern War (1700-1721) against Sweden gave him his chance. Victory over Sweden brought the Baltic states under Russian control and enabled Peter to choose a site for a new capital, named St. Petersburg. Just as Louis XIV had created a new seat of government at Versailles away from Paris, Peter compelled the members of the nobility to build residences in his new city away from the conservative influences of Moscow. The Treaty of Nystad, in 1721, confirmed Russia's position as the dominant force in northern Europe and marked the beginning of a new period of expansion. Peter had given Russia a new direction by introducing elements of Western culture. The impact of these changes and the continuing adjustments they made necessary are still being felt today.

England: The Success of Limited Monarchy

Absolutism, the cornerstone of order in the nation-states on the continent, was not the answer to the troubled politics of England. Despite the best of intentions, Cromwell could not secure a workable Parliament following the execution of Charles I, and the real power of the state rested with the army and Cromwell himself. His strict, Puritan rule became increasingly unpopular, and after his death a freely elected Parliament invited the exiled Charles II in 1660 to become king. The **Restoration**, as it is known, was marked by the growing power of Parliament at the expense of the Crown. Charles was not allowed to raise money by taxing his subjects. He was given less income than he needed, and was forced to accept the return of the Anglican Church as the official Church, replacing the Puritanism of Cromwell. Both Puritans and Roman Catholics were excluded from politics. His willingness to accept these terms and to deal with Parliament enabled Charles to live out his reign in his homeland, rather than in exile.

In 1685, Charles was succeeded by his brother James, who managed to bring the Stuart monarchy to an end in three short years. James II believed in a more extreme form of absolutism than that which had cost Charles I his head only thirty-six years earlier. He ignored the laws of Parliament and appointed Roman Catholics to public office as magistrates and army officers, and to positions in the universities. In trying to impose Roman Catholicism on a country already drained by a religious civil war, James alienated much of the political and public support usually given to the Crown. The birth of an heir to the throne raised the possibility of yet another Roman Catholic monarch. Opposition groups united to eliminate this possibility. In 1688, a parliamentary committee ruled that James had violated his oath to the people and the laws of the land, and that the throne was now vacant.

The king's daughter, Mary, raised as a Protestant before her father's conversion to Catholicism, and her husband, William of Orange, were asked to accept the throne of England. Abandoned by his generals, James fled to France. The flight of the king became known as the Glorious Revolution. It proved that the authority of Parliament was equal to the authority of the king. In 1689, the Bill of Rights outlined the limits of royal power; among other restrictions, it declared that the monarch could not levy taxes or raise an army without the approval of Parliament. At the very moment that absolutism reached its zenith under Louis XIV in France, England had become a limited monarchy bent in a direction that allowed the power of Parliament to grow at the expense of the Crown.

The Emergence of Mercantilism

The sudden influx of gold and silver from the Spanish colonies in the sixteenth century brought a new source of wealth to Europe, but it also dramatically increased prices. Governments, dependent on relatively stable incomes, often fell into debt because of the expense of wars and the confusion and destruction they brought. At the same time, there were no breakthroughs in industry or agriculture to increase production. The new nation-states of Europe came to believe that real wealth depended on a large domestic supply of gold and silver.

As a practical method of controlling their supply of bullion, European nations introduced a set of policies that have become known as **mercantilism**. The goal was economic self-sufficiency. Since exports brought money (gold) into the nation, they were encouraged. Since imports had to be paid for in money that left the nation, they were kept to a minimum. If a nation could maintain a favourable balance of more exports than imports, in other words, if it could sell more and buy less, the national income would be high and the supply of bullion would increase.

Colonies were considered valuable if they contained gold or silver, or if they provided raw materials and goods that could be traded for precious metals. In addition, they served as protected markets for the mother country's manufactured goods. Only the mother country could trade with its colonies, and only the mother country's ships could transport goods back and forth from the colony, a precaution designed to prevent competitors from making a profit. In an age of frequent warfare, a healthy treasury enabled a government to hire large numbers of mercenaries, who fought for pay rather than for love of country.

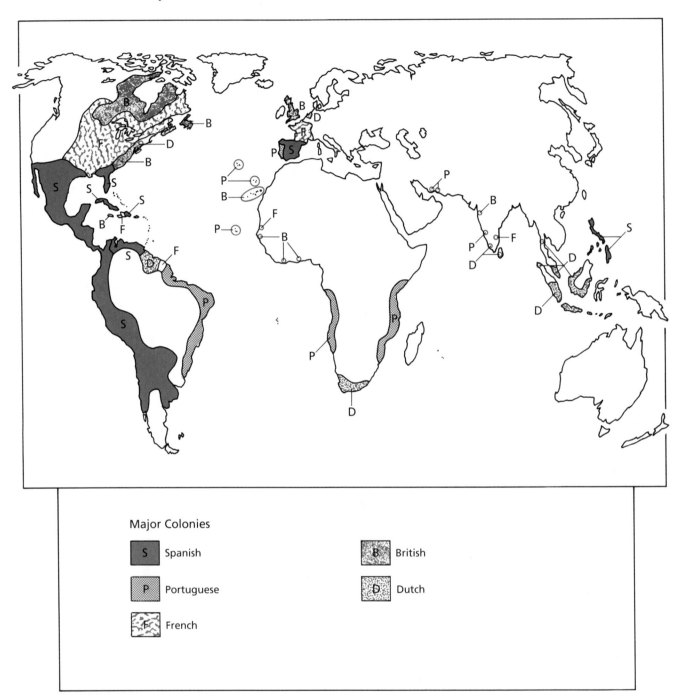

Major Colonies

S Spanish

P Portuguese

F French

B British

D Dutch

Colonialism c. 1650.

In 1651, England passed the first of a series of Navigation Acts in an attempt to limit Dutch trade. Collectively, the Navigation Acts and their supporting legislation required that all trade to and from the English colonies must be carried in ships built, owned, and crewed by English subjects. They also declared that European goods imported into the colonies must go through England, so that English merchants would benefit from the increased trade or perhaps undersell the competition with their own manufactured goods. Since the Dutch were the great carriers of European trade, such legislation threatened their commercial supremacy. Soon after the first Navigation Act was passed, England and Holland became embroiled in the first of three naval and commercial wars that broke out in just over two decades. Holland had the larger navy, but its command was divided among provincial admiralties. The English fleet was administered through the more centralized agency of the lord admiral. Overall, the naval battles were fairly even, though the Dutch colony of New Amsterdam became the English colony of New York as a result of the conflict of 1665-1667. Slowly, however, England regained control of its own trade from the Dutch, and London eclipsed Amsterdam as the leading port in Europe.

London's growth semed to be at an end when a plague struck the city in 1665, killing over seventy thousand. Within a year, the Great Fire erupted, burning for three days and levelling half the city. The fire had the unforeseen benefit, however, of wiping out the last remnants of the epidemic. London was quickly rebuilt as a city of stone and brick rather than of wood and, by 1680, it had become Europe's largest city with a population of almost seven hundred thousand. By the end of the seventeenth century, with England in a dominant commercial position, England and Holland joined forces to face Louis XIV, whose attempt to subdue Europe threatened both countries.

The greatest proponent of mercantilism in the seventeenth century was Jean Baptiste Colbert. Colbert was not only Louis XIV's controller general of finance, responsible for increasing revenues and reducing the debt, but also the minister of the marine, in charge of colonial administration. Just as absolute government had regulated domestic life in France, Colbert saw to it that the government directed commercial development in overseas trade. His critics later argued that the French bureaucratic state was too authoritarian and that its methods stifled initiative, but Colbert had inherited a difficult situation that required action. Development of Canada by land grants and chartered companies had stagnated, while progress in the more valued sugar islands of the Antilles had been somewhat haphazard.

Under Colbert, a common administration was established in each colony. It included a French governor who was the highest-ranking official, an intendant who was the governor's assistant, and a sovereign council who dispensed local justice. French commercial aims were greatly expanded when charters were given to the French Senegal Company to exploit the resources of Africa and to the French East India Company to challenge the monopoly of the Dutch and the English in the Orient. In true mercantilist spirit, Colbert supported any cause that might strengthen the French economy and national self-sufficiency. To improve the quality of the French navy, a necessity for a worldwide empire, Colbert rebuilt harbours and dockyards, established training schools, and even published an atlas that became the accepted manual for shipbuilding in France. The navy grew from fewer than two dozen vessels of various kinds in 1661, to 270 warships in 1677. Tariffs protected French industries. Roads, canals, and ports were built to improve internal transportation. The Académie des Sciences, a scholarly society, was commissioned to develop and use science for the benefit of humankind in general, but also for the benefit of France in particular. Efficiency increased in almost every venture Colbert organized, but the outbreak of wars and the late start by France in the race for colonial development initially limited the degree of success. After Colbert, much of the enthusiasm for administrative improvement and increased production declined, and control fell into less capable hands.

Anglo-French Rivalry for Empire (1661-1740)

The goal of mercantilism was a self-contained economy for the mother country and its colonies. The competition that developed between rival colonial empires almost inevitably led to conflict. The nations of Europe were the focal point of power, but, because the all-important resources and markets were located in the colonies, the conflicts of Europe were carried throughout the world. England and eventually France, with their superior domestic resources, outdistanced their Spanish, Portuguese, and Dutch rivals. They became the great colonial powers.

Much of France's exploration in the Americas had been motivated by a quest for riches, a desire to convert the native peoples to Christianity, and a hope of finding a passage through North America to the East. Colbert's plan, known as the Compact Colony policy, was designed to make New France a thriving enterprise with a diversified economy concentrated on the banks of the St. Lawrence River. With the development of agriculture, industries, and fisheries, Colbert hoped the colony would become an important part of the mercantilist economy of France. The St. Lawrence, however, is linked to the Great Lakes, a natural system of waterways that stretches over 3200 km into the heart of the continent. Despite Colbert's plan and the opposition of colonial officials, French colonists were enticed into the interior by the profits of the fur trade, a sense of adventure, and the need to contain the English. By 1673, Louis Jolliet and Father Jacques Marquette had explored the upper 900 km of the Ohio and Mississippi rivers and, in 1682, Robert Cavelier de La Salle travelled the Mississippi to the Gulf of Mexico. Over the next half century, the French built a series of strategic posts along the Great Lakes-Ohio-Mississippi system to consolidate the frontier they had pioneered.

Meanwhile, on the eastern seaboard, hemmed in by the Appalachian Mountains, the English colonies had grown and prospered, and boasted a population ten times that of New France. French-English rivalry had been evident in numerous coastal skirmishes early in the seventeenth century, but, as the fur trade grew in importance, clashes became more frequent. The French, the Dutch, and the English allied themselves with various native peoples and armed them in an attempt to secure an increasingly larger hinterland to supply the furs. With France at the peak of its power, Louis XIV provoked the War of the League of Augsburg, intensifying the situation in North America. The war in Europe was paralleled by several minor scuffles among the colonists. These skirmishes were called King William's War, after the newly crowned King William of England. The Treaty of Ryswick that ended the European war in 1697 addressed the situation in the colonies as well. All territories in North America were restored to their original holders, except that France retained the trading posts it had won on Hudson Bay.

When the War of the Spanish Succession broke out in 1702, the conflict again spilled over into the colonies. The fighting in Queen Anne's War (as it was known in North America) was more extensive than it had been in King William's War. The results were also more advantageous for the British. In the Treaties of Utrecht (1713-1714), France gave up Acadia and Newfoundland and returned the posts on Hudson Bay.

During the peace that followed, France strengthened its position worldwide. Although the combined might of Europe had frustrated Louis XIV's foreign policy of expansion, France remained the strongest military power. The merchant marine was enlarged to eighteen hundred ships as France assumed control of much of the trade that flowed back and forth from the Middle East to Turkey to Western Europe. In India, the decaying rule of the Mogul Empire allowed the French East India Company and its English counterpart to manoeuvre and compete for economic and political advantage. For the first time, France became a serious competitive threat to England's commerce in the East.

In the Americas, a triangle of trade was prosperous for both England and France. The manufactured products of the mother country were traded mainly for the sugar and molasses of the Antilles, which were converted into rum. Rum was then traded for what most Europeans regarded as commodities—people from the Gold Coast of Africa who were abducted into slavery. These people, valued for their labour on the plantations, were then traded for additional sugar and molasses.

Between 1713 and 1740, the trade of France doubled, reflecting the new prosperity that spread throughout Europe. Protection of trade and commerce and the colonies that made them possible was seen as a necessary function of the state. With the establishment of New Orleans at the mouth

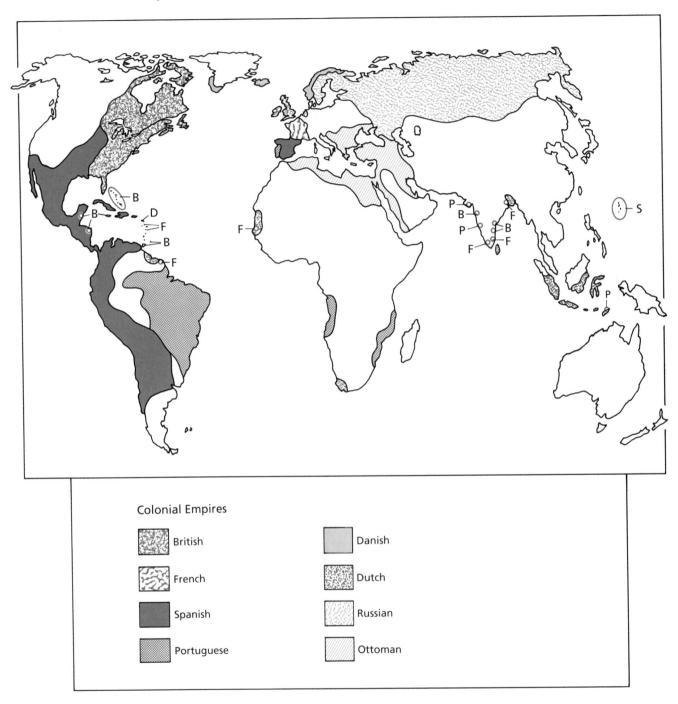

Colonialism c. 1740.

of the Mississippi as the capital of French Louisiana in 1718, and the construction of the great fortress of Louisbourg on Cape Breton Island after 1720, France staked out the perimeter of the North American empire that it fully intended to defend. When Maria Theresa inherited the Hapsburg throne in 1740, the stage was set for another European war that would again have repercussions throughout the world.

Slavery and Empire

Slavery probably originated in prehistoric times, when conflicts between agricultural societies led to conquest for the victor and servitude for the loser. It is also possible that people sold themselves to pay their debts, or became enslaved as punishment for breaking local customs or laws. Slavery has played an uncomfortably prominent role in the development of many civilizations. As the European nations became colonial empires, much of their food, drink, and material prosperity came from the involuntary servitude of non-European peoples. Modern Europe did not invent slavery, but it all too easily channelled many of the societies it encountered into directions that satisfied European rather than local interests.

The Portuguese exploration of Africa in the fifteenth century set the tone for the more than three centuries of slave trading that followed. Faced with a shortage of labour at home, the Portuguese began to import Africans in 1444 at a rate that reached seven hundred to eight hundred per year by 1640. While the Portuguese exploited the west coast of Africa, Arab traders were sending people from central Africa to the slave markets of the Middle East and the Orient. Both Christians and Muslims believed they were bringing the benefits of civilization and religion to the people they enslaved. Slavery was a common practice among African peoples and native dealers were willing to trade captive warriors for manufactured goods, simplifying the task for foreign buyers and lessening any moral burden they might have felt.

When the conquistadors arrived in the Americas in the sixteenth century, they quickly realized that the Aztecs, Maya, and Inca used slave labour for agriculture and war. The Spanish in turn imposed the "civilizing influence" of the *encomienda* on those they conquered. Mesoamericans and South Americans were not only deprived of their freedom but also of their lives, as they succumbed to disease and hard labour. To replace the rapidly dwindling number of natives available for exploitation, the Spanish joined the Portuguese in the quest for African slaves. During the seventeenth century, as the Dutch, French, and English colonized Caribbean islands, they also eagerly entered the slave trade that spread along the African coast. The extreme working conditions usually killed an African slave after about six or eight years in the field, which meant the supply of slaves had to be constantly renewed. The slave trade flourished.

African slaves were first brought to the English colonies of North America when a Dutch trading ship arrived at Jamestown, Virginia, in

1619. Throughout the first half of the seventeenth century, their legal status remained vague, since no provisions in English law allowed them to be treated differently from European servants. Almost half of the immigrants to the English colonies came **in bond**. They signed a written contract to pay for the cost of the voyage with two to seven years of labour for their sponsor. These **indentured servants** often worked and socialized with black Africans, although the European prejudice against blacks was always present. African slaves, however, did not have the benefit of a written contract that defined their rights. They were made to work not for a few years but for life. The children of black servants who were held for life became the property of their masters.

As the profits of the plantation economy of the South grew during the second half of the seventeenth century, legal codes were gradually changed to clearly establish the relationship between master and slave. The English colonies granted religious freedom to European whites, but, by the early eighteenth century, the black African slave was viewed as an exploitable resource with no right to freedom.

SUMMARY

The beginning of the Modern Age dates from about 1500. At that time, the Western world was undergoing a number of important changes. Almost every area of life was being transformed—culture, religion, politics, and economics.

The cultural flowering of the West began at the end of the Middle Ages and is known as the Renaissance (c. 1400-1550). It was stimulated by Western Europe's growing familiarity with and interest in the achievements of the ancient Greeks and Romans. The Italian peninsula, which was divided into a number of independent city-states, was the birthplace of the Renaissance. As these states profited from trade between East and West, their increasingly prosperous middle classes used their wealth to sponsor the arts. Throughout the Middle Ages, culture had primarily served religious purposes, but the art of the Renaissance glorified the potential of the human body and mind. This new outlook is known as humanism.

The centre of the Renaissance was the Italian city of Florence. Many famous artists were born in Florence or moved there to do their work: the writers Dante, Petrarch, Boccaccio, and Machievelli; the painters Titian and Raphael; and the sculptor Ghiberti. But Leonardo da Vinci and Michelangelo Buonarroti, both of whom were talented in many fields, gained the most renown. In his portraits, Leonardo captured the emotions as well as the physical appearance of his subjects. He demonstrated his interest in invention, design, and engineering in drawings and sketches that are still admired for their excellence. Like Leonardo, Michelangelo was a great painter, and he was also the foremost sculptor of his day.

It took longer for the Renaissance to become established north of the Alps, but great writers and artists arose in that region of Europe as well. Among the writers of note were Cervantes of Spain, Montaigne of France, and Shakespeare of England. The Belgian van Eyck and the Germans Dürer and Holbein were outstanding painters. The north also produced humanist scholars, such as Sir Thomas More of England and Desiderius Erasmus of the Netherlands, whose work was influential throughout Europe. Erasmus, a Catholic priest, embraced the principles of humanism and argued that the Church must reform itself to be in harmony with new ideas and the growing respect for scientific knowledge.

The Church was indeed in need of reform. Europeans remained Christians, but questioned the Church as an institution. It was the economic power of the Church, and the means by which it maintained that power, that gave rise to most of the dissatisfaction. The Church was wealthy because of the enormous amount of land it owned and because of the money it raised through tithes, simony, and the selling of indulgences. In fact, wealth and power seemed to be more important to Church leaders than spiritual concerns. Under the force of the swelling criticism, the Church finally fractured, and the revolutionary events of the Reformation occurred.

Martin Luther, a Catholic monk from Germany, was the key figure. In 1517, he opposed the Church's practice of selling indulgences, nailing his objections (the Ninety-five Theses) to the door of a church in Wittenburg. Threatened by this public act of rebellion, the Church tried to intimidate Luther. But the monk went on to found his own church (the Lutheran Church), as did other religious reformers throughout Europe. The ideas of Zwingli, a Swiss reformer, influenced the development of the Anabaptists. Calvinism, a religious philosophy named after the French humanist John Calvin, gave rise to the French Huguenots and the Scottish Presbyterians. King Henry VIII created the Church of England, although his motives were as much personal and political as they were religious.

The founding of the various Protestant Churches was not simply a matter of academic debate. From 1529 to 1555, wars flared up between Lutheran and Catholic states in the Holy Roman Empire and elsewhere. English Protestants were persecuted and killed until 1558, when Elizabeth replaced the Catholic Queen Mary. In France, Catholics and Huguenots clashed with one another until 1598, when the Edict of Nantes recognized the Huguenots and gave them many important rights. For about one hundred years after Luther launched the Reformation, all European wars had a strong religious component to them.

Although the religious divisions and differences of the Reformation have affected European history down to the present, they were the primary factors for only a relatively short period. Political and economic factors, which were closely linked, proved to be more important. Spain's colonization of Mesoamerica and South America had profound implications for

Europe. The Spanish enslaved the indigenous peoples and carried away their wealth. Shiploads of gold and silver enriched Spain and made it powerful. When Charles V inherited the Spanish throne in 1516, he was in an excellent position to dominate Europe. Through his family's intermarriages, he was the ruler of many states—an area equalling Charlemagne's empire. Spain's precious metals were used to employ Spanish mercenaries, the best soldiers on the continent. Charles, however, was unable to expand his empire, and in 1556 he abdicated and divided the empire between his grandson Philip and his brother Ferdinand. Philip II ruled Spain, the Netherlands, and several other states; Ferdinand I, who was head of the Hapsburg family, became the Holy Roman Emperor.

When Philip II tried to impose Catholicism on the Protestants of the Netherlands, he engendered a rebellion that drew in other European powers intent on limiting Spain's influence. Conflict arose between Spain and England, which under Elizabeth was predominantly Protestant. In 1588, the English defeated the Spanish Armada; because of the resulting loss of supplies, Spain's military endeavours on the continent were unsuccessful. The newly acquired gold and silver drained out of Spanish hands to pay for imported goods and wars. This transfer of wealth finished Spain as a great power and strengthened the other states of Europe. Colonial empires were acquired by the Netherlands, England, and France, who would eventually turn on one another in competition and war.

Elsewhere in Europe, control of the Holy Roman Empire had passed indirectly from Ferdinand I to his grandson Ferdinand II, who worked ardently on behalf of the Catholic Counter-Reformation. His attempts to stifle German Protestantism led to rebellion within the Empire, which became the Thirty Years' War (1618-1648). Spain fought beside the Empire, but France, the other powerful Catholic state on the continent, took the side of the Protestants. The reason was simple. France was more interested in curbing the influence of the Hapsburgs than in supporting Catholicism, demonstrating that state interests had become more important than religious interests. When the war ended and the Treaties of Westphalia were issued, Spain and the Holy Roman Empire had been checked and France was now the strongest force in Europe.

Throughout Europe, goods from the colonies and increased trade gave several nation-states resources they used to consolidate their positions. Two phenomena appeared, one political (absolutism) and the other economic (mercantilism). Monarchs such as Louis XIV (1661-1715) of France took steps to gain absolute control over the operations of the nations they ruled. Louis, building on the work of previous heads of state, created a bureaucracy through which he could manage domestic affairs. He also built a standing army and extensive navy that gave him the military strength to extend France's territory. Versailles, the grand palace Louis commissioned, was the symbol of the king's unmatchable authority. Its grounds were extensive and carefully landscaped, and its interior was decorated with magnificent art. Louis virtually forced France's nobility to reside at Versailles. Through this requirement, Louis controlled the nobility's ambition for power; they were kept from their bases of power, and their money was consumed by the expenses of court life.

Absolutism was the guiding principle of several other European monarchs. By the early eighteenth century, Emperor Charles VI (Hapsburg Empire), King Frederick William I (Prussia), and Peter the Great (Russia) had established absolute rule. Earlier, a combination of Catholicism and absolutism had caused extreme division and civil war in England. In 1649, Charles I, who like his father, James I, believed in the divine right of kings, was dethroned by a Puritan revolution and then beheaded. The revolution floundered, and in 1660 the Restoration brought back the monarchy and England had a king again, Charles II. Unfortunately, Charles was succeeded by his brother James II, an extreme absolutist who was quickly driven from the country. Throughout the turmoil, England's Parliament had grown stronger and, by 1688, when James II's daughter Mary and her husband William were installed on the throne, additional legislation ensured that Parliament and the monarch would share power.

Just as the monarchs of Europe tried to dominate the powerful people within their own countries, so different nations tried to gain advantage over one another. Mercantilism was the means by which they contended for economic superiority. A commercial revolution had occurred as a result of colonial expansion. There seemed to be more of everything after 1500—more land to explore and claim, more goods to trade, more manufacturing and industry, more Europeans (prosperity led to population growth), and more money. These large sums of money, or capital, were invested and the growth continued. Nations wanted to maximize their own growth and minimize their competitors'. A nation could achieve this aim through mercantilism—importing goods only from its own colonies and trying to export its products as widely as possible. The goal of nations was to be almost self-sufficient, to have lots of money coming in and very little going out.

Colonial empires were the key to mercantilism, because they provided both goods and markets. Wars in Europe were often echoed by wars in the colonies. In the mid-seventeenth century, for example, the English and the Dutch fought three wars over trade. England bested Holland, then went on to confront France in Europe and also in the Americas. Allied with other European nations, England managed to keep Louis XIV from gaining ground in Europe. France had not done well in its colonial wars against England, but negotiated well in the peace treaties signed at the end of the seventeenth century, and maintained its power abroad. France was the most powerful nation in Europe, and its colonial empire rivalled England's.

Cheap labour in the colonies was necessary to produce the goods that fed the cycle of trade, and much of the labour was obtained through the slave trade. People from Africa were captured, sold as slaves, and shipped to colonies in the West Indies and elsewhere in the Americas. Working and living conditions were appalling; many slaves died after only a few horrible years of toil. Europeans viewed colonization in terms of exploration, adventure, opportunity, and profit. Few were concerned about the exploitation or domination of the peoples who inhabited the lands they invaded.

10

Europe and the French Revolution

Date A.D.	Event
1517	Luther nails the Ninety-five Theses to the door of Castle church in Wittenburg
1540	*The Age of Genius* (c. 1540-1690) The rise of science: new ideas about the nature of the physical world
1700	*The Enlightenment* (c. 1690-1790) Course of human development is explained through reason Philosophers identify natural rights and natural laws governing human behaviour
	Enlightened Despotism Monarchs such as Catherine the Great of Russia, Frederick the Great of Prussia, and Joseph II of Austria claim to implement progressive ideas
1715	Louis XV becomes king of France
1740-1748	War of the Austrian Succession
1756-1763	The Seven Years' War—Britain emerges as world's greatest colonial power, France loses its North American empire, and Prussia becomes a great power
1769	James Watt improves efficiency of the steam engine
1771	Richard Awkright organizes first cotton mill in Britain
1774	Louis XVI becomes king of France
1776	American Revolution—thirteen British colonies declare their independence
1778	France allies with United States against Britain and war pushes French deep into debt
1784	Peter Onions and Henry Cort develop puddling process in iron production
1787	France's attempt at financial reform fails
1788	France experiences crop failure, drought, and economic depression
1789	*The Estates General meets in France on 4 May* *The National Assembly forms on 17 June* *French Revolution—Moderate Phase*
1792	*French Revolution—Radical Phase*
1795	*The Directory*
1799	*Napoleon's coup d'état*
1815	Napoleon defeated at Waterloo; Congress of Vienna
1830-1848	Revolution and radical change fail

10

Europe and the French Revolution

BACKGROUND

The Idea of Progress in History

The Greeks and Romans assumed that history ran in cycles of brief periods of success followed by decline and disaster. Other civilizations have had different views of human history. In the West, one commonly held view is that society is constantly improving, but this conviction goes back only about three hundred years. Europeans of the sixteenth and seventeenth centuries, thanks to the humanists of the Renaissance, had become aware of the achievements of the ancient Greeks and Romans and were starting to measure their own civilization against those standards of greatness. Could the "Moderns," as they called themselves, ever hope to equal or surpass the glories of the "Ancients"? Was there progress in history?

The debate about the merits of the "Ancients" and the "Moderns" began tentatively with questions about the structure of the universe. The second-century Greek astronomer Ptolemy had assumed that the earth was the centre of the universe, and his ideas were accepted with surprisingly few modifications throughout the medieval period. In 1543, however, Nicholas Copernicus (1473-1543) published his book, *On the Revolution of Heavenly Bodies,* in which he set forth the revolutionary theory that the sun, rather than the earth, was the centre of the solar system. There was no way to prove or disprove Copernicus's idea, but it posed some challenging problems for astronomers. How could the motion of the planets and other heavenly bodies be explained? What kept the planets from simply drifting off into endless space?

A half century later, William Gilbert (1540-1603) proposed that the planets were held in place by a magnetic attraction, a suggestion that foreshadowed subsequent discoveries. But it was the German scientist Johann Kepler (1571-1630) who made the next important contribution. Kepler demonstrated that the planets moved in elliptical orbits rather than in circles,

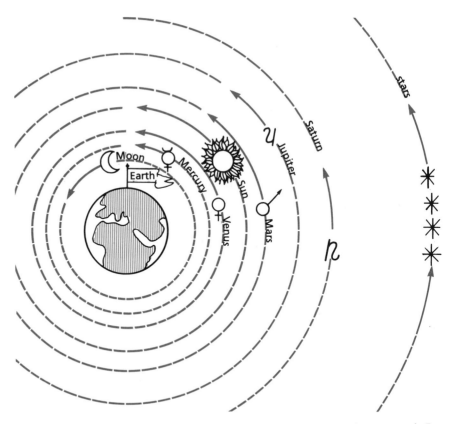

The Universe According to Ptolemy. The sun, moon, and planets circle the earth, which is positioned at the centre of the universe.

the "perfect" figures of God's work that had been previously accepted. In addition, Kepler showed that mathematical laws applied to the speed, motion, and distance of a planet from the sun.

In 1609, Galileo Galilei (1564-1642) made the next major breakthrough, when he built a telescope and studied the solar system. He discovered that the moon's "perfect surface" was rough with mountains and plains, that other planets had their own systems of moons, and that none of his discoveries made any sense unless the earth and the other planets revolved around the sun. The evidence that Galileo produced to confirm Copernicus's theory shook the foundation of the Church, since all philosophy and theology were based on the Ptolemaic assumption that the position of the earth was fixed. Galileo was brought before the Inquisition in 1633 and forced to deny his work, but he knew that time and the evidence would prove his case. What was of key importance was that ancient learning had been questioned and, as a result of the publication (in lucid Italian) of Galileo's research, that scientists continued their inquiry into the operation of the universe.

Science's crowning achievement came in the seventeenth century, when Isaac Newton (1642-1727) refuted Ptolemy's conception of the universe.

Newton's work synthesized Copernicus's theory, Gilbert's ideas about magnetism, Kepler's laws, and Galileo's study of movement. The key to his discovery was Newton's realization that the force of gravity always worked the same way and that it was present everywhere. He convincingly demonstrated that gravity explained the falling of an apple as well as the motion of the planets and the moon. The law of gravity he discovered could be expressed in a simple mathematical formula. This was exactly in keeping with Descartes's ideas about a well-ordered universe held together by a set of natural laws that humans could understand through the application of rational thought.

In 1687, Newton published his *Mathematical Principles of Natural Philosophy*. His synthesis convinced the educated world and was soon translated from the original Latin into the popular languages of Western Europe. Newton did more than anyone of his time to show that natural laws were universal, and he was one of the few geniuses to receive due recognition for his accomplishments in his own lifetime. Even the Catholic Church eventually accepted Newton's conclusions, although it took more than a century for it to do so. Newton was a devout man who did not intend that his explanation of a rational universe de-emphasize the central role of God in human lives. Nevertheless, his work became a kind of wedge between two views of the world; there was God's truth revealed through the Church, and there was scientific truth revealed through the exercise of reason and the application of the scientific method.

The idea of progress, which seemed clearer with each scientific achievement, weighted the debate about the Ancients and the Moderns in favour of the latter. Among the first and most eloquent to express this view was Bernard le Bouvier de Fontenelle (1657-1757), secretary of the French Académie des Sciences, who interpreted and popularized the new learning. In his short but important pamphlet, *Digression on the Ancients and Moderns*, published in 1688, Fontenelle argued that human knowledge progresses through the build-up of experience, as if the educated mind of the present contains the minds of preceding ages. Fontenelle did not accept the full implications of the idea of progress. While he believed that the progress of knowledge was inevitable, he also thought that, since humans had not changed physically, their behaviour and moral character had remained largely the same over time. It was left to others to expand the idea of progress in knowledge to a theory of progress in human society.

The Idea of Progress in the Enlightenment

The intellectual leaders of the eighteenth century felt that the breakthroughs of science had uncovered a layer of ignorance and superstition, and that Europe was now entering a more advanced period they termed the **Enlightenment**. In sharp contrast to the pessimism of the past, there was optimism about the course of human development. The use of reason had

Science

Along with the scientific breakthroughs that were occurring, there was a desire to establish a **scientific method**—sound principles for conducting scientific inquiry. Francis Bacon (1561-1626), lord chancellor under James I of England as well as a scientist and essayist, proposed a method based on close observation and careful analysis. In any study, each fact should be examined, then fitted with other facts. The inquiry would thus proceed from the specific to the general, a process known as **inductive reasoning**. This method, according to Bacon, would prevent people from jumping to conclusions that were not supported by observation and fact.

The French philosopher René Descartes (1596-1650) took a different approach in his landmark study, *A Discourse on Method*, published in 1637. He felt that the universe operated mechanically according to universal laws of nature that could be expressed mathematically. The search for truth should, therefore, begin with a statement of a general principle and through mathematical reasoning arrive at logical conclusions about specific instances. This method of working from the general to the specific is called **deductive reasoning**.

Close observation and logic are fundamental to modern science, and induction and deduction are both used in the quest for scientific understanding.

answered fundamental questions about the universe, and there was unrestrained confidence that reason applied to human problems would produce universal human happiness. Humanity was indeed perfectible. If natural laws explained the operation of the universe, there must be natural laws of human behaviour that could be applied to economic, social, and political institutions.

For the great thinkers of the **Age of Reason** (a term often used for the Enlightenment), rationality rather than religion was the measuring stick of

John Locke, born in 1632, was the son of a strict but genial Puritan. His views about education, which have been very influential, developed partly as a result of his warm relationship with his father. According to Locke, a good education takes into account a person's physical and mental needs. He recommended that learning be accompanied by exercise, play, and plentiful sleep, "the great cordial of nature."

usefulness and progress. The Church was often seen as the source of superstition that had to be overcome. Although religion remained important, Europe was, for the first time since the early Roman Empire, under the control of secular rather than religious forces. Architects and artists now accepted royal palaces rather than churches as their major commissions. Many intellectuals were intrigued by the power of the secular nation states to achieve reform based on reason and logic. Ironically, they often pursued their beliefs with the enthusiasm of religious converts. Their faith in reason and their optimism about controlled change eventually inspired political and social upheaval on a scale that few could have imagined.

The impulse toward the Enlightenment in the late seventeenth century came from Newton's work in mathematics and physics. It was magnified by the studies of politics and human nature done by his fellow Englishman John Locke (1632-1704). He attacked two established principles: the Christian belief that all people are born evil, and the popular notion of the divine right of kings. Locke believed that at birth a person's mind is a "blank sheet" (*tabula rasa*), void of all knowledge. A person acquires knowledge through observation and the experiences of the senses. As information is gathered, the mind, through the use of reason, shapes it into ideas. This theory implied that problems in the human environment cause society's faults, rather than fundamental flaws in human nature. If the human environment was reformed, society would progress and there would be greater happiness. Locke went on to argue that all individuals possess universal natural rights that cannot be taken away by a king or state. Should a king or state break this "contract" with the people and violate their natural rights, the people have a right to change the government, by force if necessary.

Locke's arguments were published in *Two Treatises on Civil Government*, written in 1688 to justify the removal of King James II, and in *An Essay Concerning Human Understanding*, completed two years later. Locke was of critical importance to the French *philosophes*, a group of writers whose concern about a wide range of social, moral, religious, and political issues made them the heart of the Enlightenment. Among the most famous of the *philosophe* writers were Montesquieu, Voltaire, and Diderot, whose books spread Locke's ideas as well as their own throughout the upper and middle classes of European society. (The importance of books had increased with every generation since the invention of the printing press.) It became quite fashionable among French intellectual circles to discuss the new ideas of the Enlightenment in local coffee houses and in the salons of socialites such as Madame de Lambert and Madame Dupin.

The French aristocrat and *philosophe* Baron de Montesquieu (1689-1755) was influenced by the works of Locke and Newton, but developed considerable insight into political theory from his own travels and study. In his political classic, *The Spirit of Laws*, published in 1748, Montesquieu argued that geographical, social, and historical circumstances determined

Institutions

Locke's ideas about using force to overturn an unjust government were eventually translated into revolution when the Americans turned against the British. That Thomas Jefferson owed an intellectual debt to Locke when he wrote the Declaration of Independence is clear:

We hold these truths to be self-evident, that all men are created equal, that they are endowed by their Creator with certain unalienable rights, that among these are life, liberty, and the pursuit of happiness...That to secure these rights, governments are instituted among men, deriving their just powers from the consent of the governed...That whenever any form of government becomes destructive of these ends, it is the right of the people to alter or to abolish it, and to institute new government, laying its foundation on such principles and organizing its powers in such form, as to them shall seem most likely to effect their safety and happiness.

political institutions. People developed different kinds of government because they lived under different conditions. The English constitution provided Montesquieu with the model of government he most admired. He believed that Parliament, the monarch, and judges worked separately, each acting to limit the power of the others, to preserve individual liberty. Although Montesquieu actually misrepresented how the English system operates, his idea of checks and balances through the separation of powers greatly influenced the political leaders who drafted the American Constitution of 1789.

The guiding spirit and ultimate expression of the Enlightenment was found in the works of François-Maurice Arouet (1684-1778), better known

Voltaire—A Man of Wit and Wisdom

I have never made but one prayer to God, a very short one: "O Lord, make my enemies ridiculous." And God granted it.

In general, the art of government consists in taking as much money as possible from one class of citizens to give it to the other.

by his pen name, Voltaire. He was born into the upper middle class, but desired to improve his wealth and social standing. Voltaire's mistrust of authority and contempt for mindless obedience became evident early in his career. He rejected both the Catholicism of his Jesuit teachers and opportunities for a business career, intending instead to win fame as a writer. With the success of his classical tragedy *Henriade* in 1723, Voltaire gained access to the small but influential literary élite of France, which included the bourgeoisie as well as liberal-minded members of the clergy and aristocracy. Among this group, the ideas of the Enlightenment flourished, ideas that convinced Voltaire that reason could solve most, if not all, of society's problems. Voltaire's principal skill lay in the devastating satire he hurled at the Church, the nobility, and the government. His pen became an intellectual sword that caused him to be feared and admired by the very classes he mocked.

The criticism Voltaire levelled against the existing political and social structure of France in his *Lettres philosophiques*, published in 1733, only enhanced his reputation. Voltaire's sharp wit and self-righteous manner often got him into trouble, and he was twice sent to the Bastille, the famous and dreaded prison in Paris. Fortunately, as his fame increased so did his wealth, and the four estates Voltaire purchased in the countryside of France and Switzerland provided sanctuary from offended critics. He became personally involved in trying to help a number of people who were victims of injustice. Voltaire also advocated religious toleration and, like other *philosophes*, endorsed the reasoned approach of **deism**. Deism accepted the Newtonian idea that God created the universe and that the universe operated according to natural laws. Since God could not alter these laws once God had set them in motion, there was little need to pray or follow the rituals of organized religion. What was important was to identify the natural laws and to live by their code. Recognizing his skill and popularity, royalty and aristocracy sought Voltaire's attention, but the Catholic Church never forgave his "betrayal"—his constant criticism of Christian attitudes and positions. For Voltaire, the Catholic Church (and intolerance of any kind) represented an obstacle to progress, which he and other *philosophes* believed was the key to a better society. The Church denied Voltaire a Christian burial when he died in 1778, but, during the French Revolution, his body was returned to Paris and paraded through the streets in triumph.

Although Voltaire exposed the weaknesses and injustices of French society, he had no great love for the masses, and he stopped well short of endorsing democracy. In fact, he believed that society's welfare could only be entrusted to **enlightened despots**, monarchs who would act according to progressive ideas to improve the condition of their subjects.

Several rulers in Voltaire's time became interested in the idea of enlightened despotism. Catherine the Great (1762-1796) of Russia recognized that the French *philosophes* shaped the direction of European thought. She was genuinely interested in their ideas, and corresponded with Voltaire and his fellow *philosophes* Diderot and d'Alembert. In her letters, she deliberately cultivated her image as an enlightened despot, described her policies in the most favourable manner, and became a public-relations success. As Catherine probably calculated, the *philosophes* discussed her ideas in the salons of French society and her reputation grew accordingly.

The reality of Russia was much different. Although administrative reforms were made during her reign, their purpose and impact were to strengthen central authority. When an illiterate Cossack named Pugachev led an ill-fated peasant rebellion in 1773, the Russian army overwhelmed his disorganized forces, and he was caged, drawn, and quartered. After this, Catherine entertained no thoughts of reform to improve life for the peasants. Catherine's efforts in industry, business, and education benefited the upper classes whose privileges were confirmed in the Great Charter of the Nobility in 1785. As the strength of the nobles increased, the living conditions of the Russian serfs reached an unprecedented low.

Catherine pursued an expansionist policy to the south that resulted in the defeat of Turkey, the annexation of the Crimea and, eventually, control over the north shore of the Black Sea. In the east, Russia, Prussia, and Austria totally absorbed Poland after the last of three partitions in 1795. Poland ceased to exist as a country until it was resurrected after the First World War in 1919. Catherine's approach was much more in the despotic, tsarist tradition than it was enlightened. Her intention was to improve the image and strength of Russia. Her success in achieving these goals earned Catherine a reputation as a "great" monarch.

Frederick the Great (1740-1786) was somewhat closer to the ideal of an enlightened despot. Frederick was famed for his intellect and was interested in music, art, literature, and philosophy. Recognizing Voltaire's contribution to the mainstream of the Enlightenment, Frederick initiated a correspondence with the French scholar and invited him to Potsdam to live, work, and help him with his own writing. Although Voltaire's stay was short-lived, the parties, plays, and philosophical discussions at court did much to advance Frederick's reputation as an enlightened monarch.

Frederick made himself the sole creator of Prussian policy. He spent long hours issuing his instructions through hand-written letters, and rarely consulted his ministers. A network of spies was employed to weed out corruption in the bureaucracy, while a system of civil service examinations allowed promotion for talented administrators based on merit. In the spirit of the Enlightenment, Frederick pursued a policy of religious toleration, prevented landlords from expropriating peasant landholdings, and introduced practices that improved agricultural production. Legal reforms gave Prussia a deserved reputation for honesty throughout Europe.

Frederick's major goal was the efficient operation of the Prussian state. He clearly sided with the Junker nobility and supported their privileged position at the expense of the serfs. Frederick believed that only the nobility

JOSEPH II.
EMPEROR of GERMANY.

Enlightened Despots. Some European rulers were attracted by the ideas of the philosophes *and considered themselves to be enlightened despots. Most were less "enlightened" than they liked to believe. From left to right, Joseph II of Austria, Catherine the Great of Russia, and Frederick the Great of Prussia.*

possessed the natural leadership ability required to improve the Prussian economy, and he did not interfere with the nobles' administration of their estates. Mercantilist principles governed the economy as a whole, with subsidies, monopolies, and tariffs applied where needed to encourage the growth of domestic industry. The result was a diversified economy that strengthened the Prussian state but did little to improve the living conditions of the people. Like his predecessors, Frederick drained the wealth of the state to support the army, which had grown in size to about two hundred thousand soldiers. The victories Frederick won with the best-trained fighting force in Europe, rather than any of his enlightened reforms, established his reputation for greatness.

Perhaps the most sincere of the enlightened despots was Joseph II (1765-1790) of Austria, who not only tried to rule according to the ideas of the *philosophes*, but cared about his people. Like Frederick, Joseph felt it was his duty to provide good government for his people—without their participation. Joseph shared power as co-regent with his mother, Maria Theresa, for the first fifteen years of his reign, and her conservatism restrained his more extreme ideas. After her death in 1780, Joseph began a major overhaul of the Hapsburg lands without recognizing that the collection of states in Hungary, Italy, the Netherlands, Bohemia, and Austria represented five different cultural traditions. With only minor exceptions, German was made the official language of every regional administration. As in Prussia, a secret police watched over the operation of the bureaucracy. Joseph passed laws that recognized the legal equality of all classes, supported religious toleration, placed education and marriage under civil authority, and virtually abolished serfdom. He even revised some of the mercantilist practices in favour of the new ideas of economic freedom.

Unfortunately, Joseph moved too quickly with his reforms and often succeeded in offending those who were required to change while failing to gain the support of public opinion. When his agrarian reforms pushed the nobility to the brink of revolt in 1789, Joseph halted their implementation. This flip-flop served only to alienate the very peasants he was trying to help and did not win the confidence of the nobles he had challenged. Joseph died a frustrated and disillusioned man in 1790, amid the woes of social turmoil and economic depression. His brother and successor, Leopold II (1790-1792), repealed most of Joseph's enlightened and revolutionary legislation. The nobles remained in control of their great estates and serfdom continued until 1848. Nevertheless, some of the peasants' new legal rights were preserved. Although Joseph's attempts to institute reform from above were largely a failure, they set an important example. In keeping with *philosophe* ideas about social progress, the Austrian state had assumed responsibility for the welfare of its citizens.

The *philosophes*, however, were not politicians or rulers, but thinkers and writers, and the grandest project they undertook was the famous *Encyclopedia* (1751-1772), which eventually filled seventeen large volumes. Even though their *Encyclopedia* was not the first ever, its scope was the most comprehensive and it became the model for those that followed. It was edited by Diderot and d'Alembert, and Montesquieu and Voltaire were among the 130 contributors who attempted to summarize human knowledge. It was conceived as a work of reason and contained descriptions of the scientific breakthroughs of the seventeenth century, explanations of how rational thought could solve the social problems of the eighteenth century, and any other information that might advance the cause of civilization. The implicit assumptions were that progress could be made through enlightened education, and that an understanding of social and historical forces could lead to improvements in the conduct of human affairs.

The idea of progress through rational reform was also applied to the field of economics. Mercantilism dominated the economic theory and practice of the seventeenth and eighteenth centuries. According to mercantilism, a government could achieve wealth and national self-sufficiency by actively using its power to pass legislation and impose tarriffs and taxes. In 1776, Adam Smith (1723-1790), professor of moral philosophy at the University of Glasgow, published his pioneering work, *An Inquiry into the Nature and Causes of the Wealth of Nations*. It proposed a theory of economics in tune with the ideas of the Enlightenment. Newton's natural law of gravity was paralleled by Locke's natural political rights. Smith argued that there was a natural law of economics—the law of **supply and demand**. He promoted economic freedom for individuals and free trade among nations. Restrictive government intervention in the economy in the form of tarriffs, taxes, and

The Arts

As work on the *Encyclopedia* advanced, it became increasingly evident that any summary of existing knowledge, particularly when written from the *philosophe* moral perspective, illustrated the unfairness of living conditions in France. The importance of the picture the *Encyclopedia* presented was not lost on the intellectual bourgeoisie who compiled it or on those who were ready to fight for change in 1789. Nor was it lost on those whose power was implicitly threatened. Diderot was imprisoned frequently, and the Encylopedia was suppressed. Nevertheless, it managed to reach a wide audience.

related measures should be eliminated so that the natural law of economics could function without interference. *Philosophes* such as François Quesnay (1694-1774), who wrote articles for Diderot's *Encyclopedia*, had anticipated Smith's **laissez faire** ideas of free trade. It was Smith, however, who laid out the theory in full. It was widely discussed and became Great Britain's supreme economic policy during the nineteenth century.

The most significant critic of the Enlightenment ideal of rationality was the philosopher Jean-Jacques Rousseau (1712-1778), whose ideas greatly influenced later generations. Rousseau had had an unhappy childhood that left him with feelings of insecurity and alienation from society throughout his troubled and unconventional life. He agreed with Locke that humans

Jean-Jacques Rousseau, born in Geneva in 1712, set out on his own at the age of sixteen, wandering first to Italy, then to France. Rousseau gained sudden fame in 1750, when the Academy of Dijon awarded him a prize for his essay Discourse on the Arts and Sciences.

originally lived in a state of nature and that they possessed certain natural rights. Rousseau set himself apart from the *philosophes*, however, by arguing that the good qualities of human nature sprang from emotion rather than reason. It was civilization and the growth of private property that produced evil, conflict, and bad government. He recognized, however, that humans could not abandon civilization or recapture this primitive state of nature.

In his most important and famous work, *The Social Contract*, published in 1762, Rousseau suggested how a government might secure natural equality for all. According to Rousseau, when people first left the state of nature, they made a contract with each other to be governed by the **general will**. In its simplest form, the general will represents the real, unselfish desire of each individual and is, therefore, the purest wish of the people. Since the goal of the general will is the well-being of all members of society, freedom consists of total obedience to it. Any individual following a different path must be "forced to be free" or, in other words, compelled to accept the general will.

The faith in rational thought that characterized the Enlightenment suited the interests of the educated élite in the bourgeois and aristocratic classes. Enlightenment intellectuals often overlooked or underestimated other interests; as a result, some of their judgements about the course of human progress proved to be inaccurate. For example, Voltaire and other deists speculated that the Christian Church would come to an end in the next generation. They failed to see that the vast majority of people continued to be impressed by the good works performed by both Protestant and Catholic clergy, and by the emotional comfort they provided. Indeed, a series of movements to free the churches from state control greatly appealed to the local shopkeeper, peasant, and artisan. Similarly, the *philosophe* faith in enlightened despotism proved to be over-optimistic; more often than not, the so-called enlightened despots preserved the existing structure of privilege in their society rather than acting as agents for change.

Nevertheless, the Enlightenment inspired a lasting faith that reason and progress would ultimately prevail. While the *philosophes* were essentially reformers, their ideas played a significant political role in the American and French revolutions. Their work fostered a wider acceptance of religious toleration and individual freedom, and communicated the need to combat superstition with education. Moving from the humanism of the Renaissance, which glorified artistic achievement, the *philosophes* developed a humanitarian concern for individual well-being that has become an entrenched feature of Western tradition. Through the *philosophes*, the individual gained a status that found full expression in nineteenth-century liberalism.

Anglo-French Rivalry and the War of Europe 1740-1763

When Emperor Charles VI (1711-1740) died, he believed that his daughter Maria Theresa would succeed him on the Austrian throne. Within weeks, however, the newly crowned Frederick II ("the Great") of Prussia extended a questionable family claim to Austrian territory in Silesia, and Maria Theresa was immediately faced with the prospect of invasion. So began the **War of the Austrian Succession** (1740-1748), which soon engulfed most of the major European states.

The continental struggle spilled over into the competition between England and France for colonies and economic supremacy. Most European nations agreed that there was only a fixed amount of trade and commerce and that every country should take steps to maximize its share of the market. Through mercantilist policies, countries tried to monopolize trade within their own colonies and to become part of the trading systems of their rivals' colonies. Economic expansion through increased trade became so important that war on behalf of commerce was justified as a responsibility of the state. England and France confronted each other in the West Indies, the Mediterranean, India, and the heart of North America. European and colonial conflicts became so intertwined that victory in one part of the world could be offset by defeat in another.

The War of the Austrian Succession ended in 1748, and the Treaty of Aix-la-Chapelle marked Prussia's arrival as a major European power. Under Frederick's skillful leadership, the army secured Silesia from Austria, doubling Prussia's population and greatly increasing its resources. The treaty forced Maria Theresa to formally accept the loss of this territory. In the colonies, the British capture of the great French fortress of Louisbourg humbled French naval power in North American waters, while, in India, France captured the British city of Madras. Overall, the war in Europe and in the colonies was indecisive, and the peacemakers were forced to return almost exactly to the unsatisfactory situation of 1713; the Prussian acquisition of Silesia was the only significant exception. Louisbourg was exchanged for Madras, but the major issues in Europe and the colonies were not resolved, and further conflict was probable.

The breathing space that the peace of Aix-la-Chapelle provided encouraged another spurt of English and French commercial activity, and the volume of overseas trade continued to increase throughout the eighteenth century. The European desire for coffee and tea, oriental art objects, fur hats, and tobacco for snuff and smoking could not be satisfied. To secure territory and increase trade at the expense of the competition, English and French colonies throughout the world engaged in intermittent conflict without formal declarations of war. In India, the British and French East India Companies used existing rivalries among the colonized peoples as an excuse to fight each other after 1750. French and English slave traders had several skirmishes off the coast of west Africa, while smuggling in the West Indies led to further confrontations. The most serious situation developed in North America, where the French built a chain of small forts to prevent the movement of Virginian land speculators and to stop native traders from

European Warfare in the Eighteenth Century

Between 1618 and 1648, most European states had been drawn into the Thirty Years' War. The immense devastation was felt not only by soldiers but by people from all walks of life. Towns were plundered, and whole regions were stripped of their agricultural produce, which went to feed the troops. By the eighteenth century, however, wars were fought less passionately and on a smaller scale. There were several reasons for this change. For one, absolute monarchs, despite their considerable power, had difficulty increasing tax revenue, and money limited the size of the armies that they could raise. In addition, there were never enough trained officers to meet military needs. By tradition, officers were recruited from the "respectable" elements of society, but these groups were often exempt from duty. Those who were regarded as society's "natural leaders" were not quick to enlist, partly because officers had the job of disciplining the mercenaries, vagabonds, and prisoners who were either hired or kidnapped into service. The poorly kept roads were another important factor in the size of wars. They slowed mobility to a snail's pace, impeded supply lines, and further restricted war to those trained to fight it.

But it was also through choice that military conflicts between states remained relatively small.

No one wanted to experience the turmoil of the Thirty Years' War again. Nobles and subjects alike recognized clearly that soldiers fought wars and that the lives of ordinary people should not be threatened or overly disrupted. It was not uncommon for a battle to rage in the countryside while the civilian population pursued its daily chores with little interest in the outcome. As for the soldiers, each side understood the rules of conduct, followed precise military drills, and satisfied itself with victory on the battlefield rather than total destruction of the enemy.

Absolute monarchs supposedly acted in the best interests of the state, but the indifference of the public to the wars presumably fought on their behalf suggests that they may have had other motives for the fighting. In fact, many of the wars of the eighteenth century were almost private, dynastic conflicts organized by monarchs and nobles interested in preserving or extending their own power and privilege. Ironically, the nobility's flagrant pursuit of its own interests eventually engendered the hatred of the masses and the incredible violence that flared up in the revolutions and wars of the late eighteenth and early nineteenth centuries.

securing more territory once they crossed the Appalachians. At Fort Duquesne (now Pittsburgh), the French badly defeated the Virginian militia, led by Colonel George Washington, in 1754, and began the French and Indian War two years before hostilities broke out in Europe.

European wars were fought to maintain a balance of power, preventing any one state from dominating the continent. Before the Thirty Years' War, several states opposed attempts by the Austrian and Spanish Hapsburgs to consolidate their domains. During the reign of Louis XIV, the powers of Europe united to limit French hegemony. With the success of Prussia in the War of the Austrian Succession, new alignments were needed to prevent the expansion of yet another major state. In the so-called "Diplomatic Revolution" of 1756, countries formed alliances to match the new circumstances. France allied itself with Austria, its traditional enemy, as well as with Russia, Saxony, and Sweden in opposition to Prussia, Great Britain, and the British kingdom of Hanover. Frederick felt that bold action was needed to save Prussia, surrounded on several fronts with no natural frontiers, from its precarious position. The Prussian army marched into Saxony in August, 1756, and Europe was again plunged into a war that quickly became linked with the Anglo-French struggle over colonial empires.

Prussia looked as if it would be overwhelmed throughout much of what came to be known as the **Seven Years' War**. With 4 million people, Prussia's population was only one-third that of Austria and one-fifth that of France and Russia, but Frederick's military genius and perseverance prevented collapse. The enemy forces were usually divided and Prussia could defeat them individually. When Prussia lost a battle, the coalition against Frederick did not know how to exploit its opportunity. France was successful at the start of the war, but soldiers and resources had to be diverted from its colonies, giving Britain a major advantage in the struggle for empire. Under the leadership of William Pitt in 1757, the supremacy of the British navy ensured that colonial forces were well supplied. Britain was able to subsidize Frederick's war effort on the continent while winning a series of victories against France overseas. In 1758, the British captured the French fortress of Louisbourg for the second time. The climax of the colonial struggle came the next year, when General James Wolfe led a British army against the French forces of General Louis Joseph de Montcalm and won a decisive victory on the Plains of Abraham outside Québec City. The door was opened to the St. Lawrence and British control of North America. In India, the British navy and the military skill of Robert Clive overcame the superior forces of France and won the province of Bengal. Total victory in India was assured when the British captured the French post of Pondicherry in 1761. Meanwhile, the British navy swept France from all but one of its island colonies in the West Indies.

By 1763, Russia and Sweden had already withdrawn from the war and the remaining participants were eager to make peace. The war in Europe

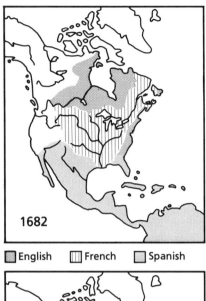

1682

English French Spanish

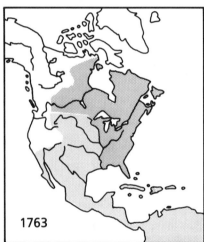

1763

Rivalry for the Expansion of Empire.

had been a stalemate, and the Treaty of Hubertusburg reflected this result. It returned conditions to those that had existed before the conflict. Prussia gave up Saxony but received confirmation of its ownership of Silesia. The Treaty of Paris ended the imperial struggle between Britain and France in the colonies. Due to the skill of French negotiators, France did better at the bargaining table than it had in the battlefield. All of North America was lost except for the two small islands of St. Pierre and Miquelon in the fishing grounds off Newfoundland, but Martinique, Guadeloupe, and San Domingo were retained in the West Indies. The British took control of the major slaving stations in Africa and, while France did maintain trading rights in a few towns, its power in India was crushed.

The treaties of 1763 stabilized the balance of power in Europe for a generation. Prussia was firmly established as a great power. Indeed, the centre of power had shifted toward the military states of central and eastern Europe. France, though still formidable, was badly shaken by the costs of the war and the loss of prestige when Britain triumphed as the principal colonial power. Little did anyone realize that the removal of the French threat in North America would stimulate a move toward independence that would separate Britain from a large part of its empire.

France and the Ancien Régime: Framework for Revolution

Ancien régime (old regime) is the term used to describe the French state and the people who controlled it from the time of Louis XIV to the French Revolution. During his reign, Louis XIV made several important changes. He elevated members of the bourgeois class to positions of favour as advisers. At the same time, he weakened the traditional power of the nobility by requiring their presence at the court of Versailles. They had no opportunity to build power bases in the provinces, and the expenses of court sapped their wealth. But Louis's wars of expansion and the extravagance of his lifestyle affected the nation's financial health. The labour of the lower classes, whose taxes rose higher and higher, paid these enormous debts. Louis's successors faced the daunting task of finding a way to moderate the extreme inequities.

The long reign of Louis XV (1715-1774), the Sun King's great-grandson and successor, was disastrous for his country. Louis came to the throne at the age of five, and by the end of his regency had developed a lazy and carefree attitude toward his responsibilities as king. Initially, he left the administration of the country to his officials. Under the able direction of his tutor, Cardinal Fleury, French prestige increased, the economy improved, and France began to recover from the human and material losses of Louis XIV's time. When Fleury died in 1743, however, Louis decided to rule by himself, although he had little understanding of government. His leadership was characterized by secrecy and intrigue; ministers came and went in rapid succession according to his whims.

Louis XV's apathetic and confused leadership weakened the central government and encouraged the nobles to reassert their power at the local level. Louis tried to impose a universal 5 percent tax to finance the War of the Austrian Succession. The nobles were able to use the *parlements* to pressure the king and government to reverse this tax policy. When the *Parlement* of Paris engaged the support of the Church to oppose the 5 percent tax, the king and his ministers gave in to their demands.

With the Seven Years' War, the burden of the national debt continued to increase, but Louis became indifferent to the daily routines of kingship. Again, he abandoned the operations of state to ministers willing to tackle any problem except financial reform. Throughout his life, Louis preferred the diversion of the royal hunt or the company of his favourite mistress, Madame de Pompadour. Though Louis did, at times, have good intentions, he lacked the ability and inclination to translate them into policy. His often-quoted words, "after me, the deluge," provide a fitting comment on the condition of France at the conclusion of his reign.

Louis XVI (1774-1794) was no more suited to be king than his grandfather had been. He shared the Bourbon enthusiasm for the hunt, and was so interested in construction and physical labour that he often helped workers move paving blocks and girders. It has been said that he would have been much happier as a locksmith or carpenter than as a monarch at court. Louis was a simple, shy, and moral man who never seemed certain about what to do next. He prided himself on being honest and frugal and the people of France seemed to respond to his humble dignity. No matter how much criticism was levelled at the government and the system of entrenched privilege, Louis himself was popular with his people until the end.

Louis's marriage to Marie Antoinette (one of Maria Theresa's sixteen children) was arranged to consolidate the alliance between France and Austria. Yet it only served as a reminder of a greatly resented foreign influence at court. Marie Antoinette was irresponsible and frivolous, enjoyed parties, and lived an extravagant life. She was accused of buying a diamond necklace valued at 1.6 million livres and, although the accusation proved to be false, she could not shake her reputation as "Madame Deficit." As a result, she came to represent all the excesses of the ancien régime and was disliked by both the peasants and middle classes.

Louis began his reign intent on doing the best for his people by ruling as an enlightened despot. His choice of Anne-Robert-Jacques Turgot as controller of the treasury seemed like a good start. In keeping with the enlightened economic attitudes of the era, Turgot tried to reduce the chaotic restrictions on trade and to substitute a mild tax on all landowners in place of the traditional corvée (maintenance of roads). By this time, however, the nobles had regained much of their formal political power and, along with the clergy, were in no mood to give up their exemption from taxation. Turgot lost his job after only two years in office. Although Marie

Elizabeth Vigée-Lebrun (1755-1842) became a popular artist among the aristocracy; eventually she was appointed court painter to Marie Antoinette. Vigée-Lebrun's portrait of Marie Antoinette with her children, shown here, was the Queen's favourite. On the eve of the Revolution, the artist fled with her father and spent twelve years in exile, where she continued to be prolific and was awarded many honours. She returned to France during the Napoleonic regime, painting more than eight hundred portraits and landscapes over the next twenty-two years.

Antoinette wanted Turgot sent to the Bastille, Louis settled for dismissing him instead. Turgot left with his famous warning, "Never forget sire, that it was weakness that brought the head of Charles I to the block."

Louis's weakness, or at least his poor judgment, was clearly apparent when he could not resist the urging of Marie Antoinette and his advisers to enter the American Revolution on the side of the United States. France was still bitter about the losses suffered at British hands in the Seven Years' War. When the thirteen colonies proclaimed the Declaration of Independence in 1776, the opportunity for revenge was open. War supplies were sent almost immediately and, when success seemed possible after two years of struggle, France and the United States were formally allied. The price of British defeat, however, was 1 billion livres to a French economy already strained to the breaking point. Moreover, a democratic spirit spread among the French soldiers who fought with the Americans and brought back their ideas to France. If the English colonies were willing to revolt because tax *could* be applied, it seemed obvious that the French lower classes, who were *already* oppressively taxed, had a much stronger case for reforming or rebelling against their central government. Enlightened ideas about the natural rights of humans were no longer just the pleasant fodder of discussion in a Paris salon. They were the rationale for a successful revolution.

The financial condition of France was approaching the crisis point. To the people, the visible symbol of wealth and waste was the court at Versailles. Two hundred carriages and two thousand horses had to be maintained, as well as the expense of over five hundred personal servants for Marie Antoinette. In actuality, the people's anger was somewhat misplaced. The court of Louis XVI had been trimmed down from those of his predecessors and consumed only 6 to 8 percent of government revenues. The major cause of the financial woes was the century of wars that had pushed the total national debt to over 4 billion livres. Over half the revenues collected each year was used to pay just the interest on the amount owing. It was clear that France was a rich nation with a poor government, and that those who could least afford it shouldered the greatest weight of taxation. The nobility entertained no thought of relieving the lower classes from the burden of paying off the national debt. After 1783, the skillful Charles Calonne became controller general. He approached the issue of financial reform with enlightened ideas similar to those of Turgot—the nobility and the clergy would have to pay taxes if France was to avoid repudiation of its debt and a loss of confidence among foreign moneylenders. Louis took Calonne's proposals to a special Assembly of Notables, made up of the privileged classes whom Calonne wanted to tax. When the assembly rejected Calonne's plan, Louis dismissed him. The king then personally tried to ensure the acceptance of a uniform tax on land, but the *Parlement* of Paris, followed quickly by the *parlements* of the provinces dominated by the nobles, took up a common refrain. They demanded that Louis call the Estates General.

The Estates General and the Political Crisis

The nobles believed they would control the proceedings of the Estates General and preserve their traditional privileges. This assumption seemed safe. The **Estates General** consisted of three houses—the **First Estate** (the clergy), the **Second Estate** (the nobility), and the **Third Estate** (the rest of the population). According to the rules drawn up in 1614, each estate had a single vote, and each met separately to decide what the vote would be. As long as the clergy and the nobility voted together, they would win a two-to-one majority and could block any action proposed by the Third Estate. Neither the First nor Second Estate gave any serious thought to the fact that the Third Estate represented 98 percent of the people, and that some might see the system of voting by estate as unfair and unacceptable. The Estates General had not been called since 1614, largely because the king had been so dominant. The nobles did not realize that their attempt to dominate a weak king would become the first important step on the road to the French Revolution.

There was an uproar in 1788 when Louis XVI announced that the Estates General would indeed meet the following year according to the old rules. The Third Estate knew its position was weak, despite its strength as the majority of the population. The most famous of the many pamphlets written in protest came from the hand of the philosopher and priest Abbé Sieyes, who crystalized the feeling of the masses in the following words:

1. What is the Third Estate? Everything.
2. What has it been in the political order up to the present? Nothing.
3. What does it demand? To become something ...

The Third Estate ... includes everything that belongs to the nation; and everything that is not the Third Estate cannot be regarded as being the nation. What is the Third Estate? Everything.

In the spring of 1789, forty thousand local meetings were held, and the government instructed each to elect deputies to the Estates General and to draw up a list of grievances known as *cahiers*. By the time the deputies were elected, the Third Estate had won the right to seat as many representatives as the combined total of the clergy and nobles. The elections produced 300 deputies from each of the First and Second Estates and 648 deputies, mostly from the bourgeoisie, to speak for the Third Estate. At the same time, the *cahiers* produced a host of demands that included a more equitable system of taxation, the abolition of feudal dues and customs, and a constitution. The Third Estate, in an attempt to increase its influence and to eliminate the privileges of the clergy and nobles, wanted the three orders to sit together and vote by head. The clergy and the nobles, understandably, wanted to continue to sit separately to maintain their two-to-one majority over the Third Estate and the privileges they had long enjoyed. All of the *cahiers* expressed what was probably a genuine feeling of loyalty to the king, but they were equally opposed to the exercise of his absolute power. At this point, no one in any class was thinking of revolution, but everyone in the Third Estate was expecting change of some kind.

An economic depression that paralleled the political crisis only stimulated the anticipation for reform. In 1788, hail, wind, and drought led to widespread crop failure and a shortage of bread. The coldest winter of the century froze the Seine River and prevented the proper distribution of what grain there was to Paris and the countryside. These events doubled and sometimes quadrupled the price of bread and meant that the poor had to spend up to 80 percent of their income on food. On several occasions, hunger drove the destitute to food riots in Paris and other communities. At

A Closer Look at the Estates General

A general description of the Estates General gives the impression that each Estate was a solid block of like-minded and similar people. In reality considerable division and diversity existed within each one. The First Estate was made up of about one hundred and thirty-five thousand members (.5 percent of the population) of the Church hierarchy. Archbishops, bishops, and leaders of monastic orders, who often had ties to the nobility, were regarded as the **upper clergy**. They had a vested interest in protecting the resources of the Church, which, as the largest landowner in France, obtained its wealth from tithes and endowments. The Church retained this revenue because of its exemption from taxation. The **lower clergy** included monks, friars, and parish priests, who were often sympathetic to the people even though they were tied to the interests of their superiors.

There were at least nine major distinctions of wealth and status within the nobility of the Second Estate, which numbered about four hundred thousand (1.5 percent of the population) in 1789. They, too, were exempt from taxation, even though, of all the people in France, the nobles of the higher orders were the most able to pay. Most, but not all, of the nobles and the clergy wanted to maintain the laws that sustained their wealth and social prestige. As the pressure for reform grew during 1789, the divisions within the First and Second Estates began to show.

The most diverse of the social orders in France was the Third Estate—24.5 million people involved in an infinite number of occupations. Among its ranks were the peasants, who made up about 90 percent of the population, the urban workers and, most important, the bourgeoisie. Throughout the eighteenth century, the economic situation of the peasant had gradually improved, although pockets of extreme poverty could be found in the countryside, but life for city workers was often appalling. Conditions generally took a turn for the worse in the 1780s. Despite bad harvests and higher prices, the nobility used its increased influence to reaffirm forgotten privileges, and they collected their feudal dues with greater efficiency. The Church was equally vigorous in collecting tithes. This meant that customary dues *and* government taxation were increasing at the same time. The downtrodden members of the Third Estate came to resent the social superiority of the nobles and the political power they arrogantly exercised through local *parlements*.

Perhaps the most significant element of the Third Estate was the bourgeoisie, a loosely associated group of merchants, lawyers, writers, doctors, and manufacturers. The nobles slowly removed them from the favoured positions they had held under Louis XIV. Although most members of the bourgeoisie enjoyed a comfortable life, they did not enjoy the social status or political influence they believed they deserved. Among this group, the Enlightenment, with its stress on knowledge, natural rights, and humanitarianism, took firm hold. The application of reason showed the ancien régime to be inequitable, callous, and ripe for reform. The Revolution proved, however, that the bourgeoisie's ideas about reform were different from those held by the workers and peasants who made up the bulk of the Third Estate.

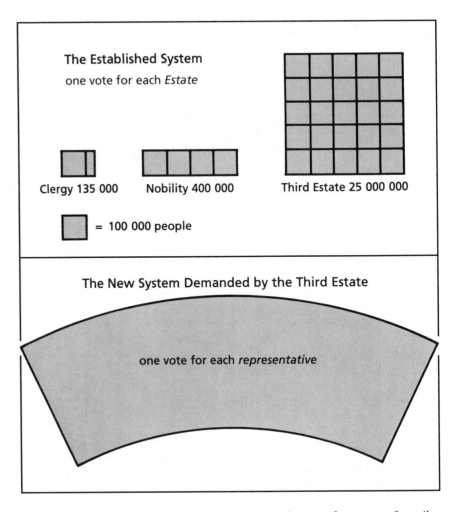

Make-up of the Estates General.

the very moment that agriculture failed, French manufacturers of textiles and hardware were faced with a flood of imports from England, the result of government policies that lowered tariffs. Unemployment increased to dangerous levels and made the common people receptive to any kind of reform that might decrease the suffering. In towns throughout France, pamphlets and letters containing ideas about reform were circulated by clubs that had developed from bourgeois literary societies, and by groups specially created to meet the present crisis. A network of these political "cells" moulded public opinion in favour of the Third Estate at the moment elections for the Estates General were being held. These clubs became the very fibre of the demand for change.

The Estates General had no meeting place. Finally, a series of lesser rooms and salons at Versailles was chosen so that the king and queen could maintain their social routine. Would the First, Second, and Third Estates meet and vote separately, or would they sit as a single body, with each deputy's vote counting equally? This question was crucial. When the controller general, Jacques Necker, failed to deliver reform in the direction of the already popular slogan "equality and liberty" in his opening address to the Third Estate on 4 May 1789, the issue was hotly debated by the deputies for over five weeks.

The nobles now perceived the widespread expectation of reform as the greatest threat to their influence and status. They formed an alliance with Louis, their former adversary, to oppose the efforts of the Third Estate to create a single body of voting deputies. Some of the minor clergy and a few liberal nobles sympathetic to reform supported the Third Estate, which went ahead and proclaimed itself the **National Assembly** on 17 June 1789, declaring that it was the true representative of the nation. In response, Louis ordered the meeting hall used by the Third Estate closed for repairs. Under the leadership of the Comte de Mirabeau, the National Assembly reconvened in an indoor tennis court at Versailles on 20 June and, after distress and division, swore the famous "Tennis Court Oath." They vowed never to separate until a constitution had been established for the nation. By this time, the entire clergy had been won over to the National Assembly and more nobles were wavering. Louis initially tried to veto the Third Estate's decision and commanded the estates to meet separately as originally instructed. On 27 June, the irresolute Louis reversed his stand and officially

The National Assembly, 1789.

National Assembly 1789

merged the three estates to form a National Assembly of twelve hundred deputies.

It seemed that moderate reform had been achieved, and that France could become a limited monarchy which operated in accordance with a written constitution. The political crisis had apparently been resolved in favour of the Third Estate, led by the oratory of the bourgeoisie who made up the majority of its deputies. The first two weeks of July, however, would bring a decisive change to the direction of France and unleash forces that would eventually alter the fabric of Western civilization.

The French Revolution: Moderate Phase (1789-1792)

The joy that surrounded Louis's reluctant acceptance of the National Assembly proved short-lived, when Louis summoned troops from the provinces around Paris and Versailles. This move has often been interpreted as his preparation to force the submission of the Third Estate. Certainly, rumours to that effect quickly spread among the crowds of the city, but it is not clear that this was Louis's intention. The hungry Paris masses, still angry with the nobility, were stirred by a flood of revolutionary pamphlets and by the rousing oratory of people such as the duke of Orleans and Camille Desmoulins. Violence erupted almost daily during the first half of July, usually because people needed food. In their desperation, they were easily persuaded by the inflammatory words of any speaker.

One of the key elements in this charged atmosphere was the royal army. The foreign troops, mostly Swiss, under the king's command, could be relied upon to carry out their orders. The French troops, however, could not be shielded from the political pamphlets that voiced the need for reform. Many soldiers mutinied and their aristocratic officers could do little.

The bourgeois leaders of the National Assembly needed the support of the army to impose their ideas for reform upon the king. When the arrival of royal troops in Paris was followed by the dismissal of the popular controller, Necker, it seemed as if Louis was immediately going to roll back the gains the National Assembly had made. This indiscreet action united together the divided elements of protest, and the newly unified resistance to arbitrary royal authority quickly gained the upper hand in Paris. On 14 July 1789, rioters in Paris seized some weapons and stormed the Bastille, the prison that symbolized royal absolutism and the oppression of dissent. Although the old feudal fortress was surrendered without violence on the promise of safety for its guards, the crowd went wild. Only after several hours of fury, two hundred deaths, and the mutilation of several corpses did the riot subside. Surprisingly, only four forgers, two deranged inmates, and a common criminal were actually found in the prison, but the storming of the Bastille was hailed as the symbolic triumph of freedom over tyranny throughout France and Europe. The French still celebrate their national holiday on 14 July.

With the rebels in control of Paris, a new government, the **Commune**, was established at the hôtel de ville (the city hall), and a new citizen army created. Known as the **National Guard**, it was commanded by the liberal noble the Marquis de Lafayette, veteran of the American Revolution and a friend of George Washington. After some hesitation, Louis returned to Paris on 17 July 1789 with the National Guard. Standing in front of a large crowd, Louis accepted a blue and red ribbon (the colours of Paris) to which Lafayette added the white of the king. The *tricolore* became the emblem of the French Revolution, and Louis wore this badge on his hat when he visited the National Assembly at Versailles to demonstrate his acceptance of the new order.

Just as the stones of the Bastille were eventually scattered over the French countryside, the Revolution spread to the provinces. Paris was used as a model for the creation of thousands of local republics that overthrew the nobility in their towns. Real and imagined threats of royal troops and hired bands of thugs created the "Great Fear" of late July, in which peasants, armed with pitchforks and scythes, ransacked country houses, seized food, destroyed records of their feudal dues, and brought government to a standstill. News of violence in the provinces quickly reached Versailles, and the National Assembly realized that the grievances of the peasants had to be redressed quickly if order were to be restored. On 4 August 1789, amid frenzied enthusiasm, the privileged classes rose and renounced their traditional rights with such thoroughness that feudalism and the ancien régime were abolished. There were no longer lords and serfs but only French citizens and the nation of France. As a statement of intent about the proposed constitution, the Assembly issued the Declaration of the Rights of Man and the Citizen on 26 August 1789. Based on English and American precedents, this bourgeois document captured the ideals of the Enlightenment with the stirring words, "Men are born, and always continue, free and equal in respect of their rights." Among these natural rights were "Liberty, Property, Security, and Resistance of Oppression." Law was defined as "the expression of the will of the community," while the nation, more than any individual, was "the source of all sovereignty." The rights they proclaimed—equality of taxation, equality before the law, freedom of speech and the press, and religious toleration—were the moderate reformers' highest aspirations.

The August decrees catered to two different interests in French society. To the peasants, the abolition of feudalism was sacred. They were willing to support any group that could claim their rights in the new order. The Declaration of Rights also reflected the idealistic, even naive, hopes of the bourgeoisie, who seemed to believe that proclamations alone could solve the problems of France. Such high expectations were raised that disappointment was bound to follow.

By September, order had been restored to the countryside, but Louis fumbled his way into another upsurge of violence before the year was out.

The French Revolution–Moderate Phase (1789–1792)

1788	August 8	Louis XVI summons a meeting of the Estates General
1789	January	Abbé Sieyes leads demand for reform of voting procedure of the Estates General
	February-March	Lists of grievances known as *cahiers* are drawn up by the three estates
	May 5	Estates General assembles at Versailles
	June 17	The Third Estate proclaims itself the National Assembly
	June 20	The National Assembly takes the Tennis Court Oath
	July 14	Paris mob storms the Bastille
	July 17	Louis XVI returns to Paris with the National Guard and accepts a cockade of red, white, and blue–the tricolour of the Revolution
	July–August	Peasants experience the "Great Fear"
	August 4	National Assembly abolishes feudalism
	August 26	The Assembly passes the Declaration of the Rights of Man and Citizen
	October 5	Women march on Versailles
	October 6	Louis XVI agrees to move the royal family to the Tuileries Palace in Paris
	October 20	National Assembly moves to Paris
	November 2	National Assembly confiscates Church lands
1790	June 19	National Assembly abolishes the practice of hereditary nobility and respective titles
	July 12	Civil Constitution of the Clergy is proclaimed
1791	June 20	Royal family's flight to Varennes fails
	August 27	Emperor of Austria and the king of Prussia issue the Declaration of Pillnitz
	September 3	The National Constituent Assembly proclaims the Constitution of 1791
	October 1	Legislative Assembly holds first meeting under the new constitution
1792	April 20	Legislative Assembly declares war on Austria; Prussia joins Austria against France
	July 25	Manifesto of the duke of Brunswick is issued
	August 10	Paris Commune seizes power by killing the king's Swiss guards at the Tuileries
	September 2–7	The "September Massacres" occur
	September 21	The National Convention abolishes the monarchy; France is declared a Republic

Characteristically, he hesitated in accepting the abolition of feudal privilege and the Declaration of Rights. He also held a royal military banquet at Versailles at the very moment when food shortages in Paris were again critical. On 5 October, Parisians organized a **March of Women** so that their cries of hunger could be heard at Versailles, but it turned into an undisciplined mob of men, women, and children by the time it reached the palace. Lafayette and the National Guard followed them in an attempt to maintain order, but the following day the protesters broke their promises and rushed into the palace. Peace was restored only when Louis agreed to move from Versailles to the Palace of the Tuileries in Paris. The National Assembly returned to Paris ten days later. Lafayette and the National Guard could not control the protests that now erupted into violence. The National Assembly was now under the critical eye of the Parisian crowds who regularly attended the public sessions, cheering when revolutionary ideas were introduced and jeering anything that smacked of moderation.

During the next two years of relative calm, the National Assembly hammered out a new constitution. At the same time, it had to deal with the pressing financial problems, which became even worse when the direct and indirect taxes of the ancien régime were swept aside. The single tax on land and income issued by the Assembly fell well short of the required revenue. Under the direction of Mirabeau, the Assembly nationalized the extensive landholdings of the Church and used them to back the printing of paper money known as **assignats**. Though this measure was successful in the short term, the government eventually printed more money than its collateral warranted, and the value of the assignats fell sharply.

Of even greater consequence was the Assembly's passage of the Civil Constitution of the Clergy in July, 1790. Church lands had already been confiscated. Now the Civil Constitution brought the Church under state control and provided public funds to pay the clergy. Bishops and priests were to be elected by the people rather than appointed by Rome, and all clergy would be required to pledge an oath to uphold the imminent constitution and the Civil Constitution of the Clergy. Most bishops and priests refused to swear loyalty to the new order, and Pope Pius VI condemned the overturning of papal authority. Many citizens were also displeased with the Assembly because they did not believe that the Church should be linked to and subordinate to the state. With grave misgivings, Louis accepted the Civil Constitution.

Beginning in July of 1789, many nobles, known as **émigrés**, had left France to seek aid from foreign rulers to work against the Revolution. Louis resolved to do the same. On 20 June 1791, he and Marie Antoinette slipped by the guards at the Tuileries and, disguised as a valet and governess, fled by stagecoach. At Varennes, almost within sight of his goal, Louis was recognized and brought back as a prisoner to Paris. Unfortunately for Louis, he had left a letter proclaiming his belief in absolute rule and his intention of leading a royal army of émigrés back to France to destroy the Revolution and re-establish the ancien régime. The flight to Varennes discredited Louis in the eyes of the people, but the majority still believed that a constitutional monarchy was the only acceptable form of government.

Meanwhile, the National Assembly was still working on the new constitution; it had become known as the **Constituent Assembly** in honour of this purpose. Most proposed reforms reflected the bourgeois interests of the deputies. To replace the Estates General, a new elected body known as the **Legislative Assembly** was to be created. Although equality for all had been proclaimed in the Declaration of Rights, the right to vote would be restricted to those who paid a certain amount of tax. The bourgeois deputies wanted only those changes that would ensure their own political power. They were blocking the aspirations of the lower classes of society they originally claimed to represent. The minimum tax qualification limited the vote to about fifty thousand men—equality failed to recognize women—which meant that wealth rather than ancestry became the measure of political power. To offset the centralization absolutism had established, France was divided into eighty-three departments, which in turn were subdivided into communes and cantons run by elected officials. In fact, the amount of power local government held hindered the operation of the entire political system.

The new constitution was issued in September of 1791. With its task complete, the Constituent Assembly dissolved itself. In an unselfish gesture, the members of the Assembly made themselves ineligible for re-election. Unfortunately, this decision meant that the most experienced politicians were no longer available to run the Legislative Assembly. In effect, the Assembly was thrown into the shifting and difficult tides of the Revolution. Although Louis vowed to uphold the new constitution, his attempt to flee the country showed clearly that he could not be trusted. France now had a constitutional monarchy with a monarch who did not believe in its principles, greatly reducing its chances of success.

During the emotion of 1789, hundreds of political clubs had been organized throughout France. The most famous, as well as the most important, was the Friends of the Constitution, later changed to Friends of Equality and Liberty, and better known as the **Jacobin Club**, after the former Jacobin monastery where it met in Paris. Initially it represented the opinions of a wide spectrum of the Parisian middle classes. But in 1792 the Jacobin Club became even more diverse when membership widened to include the poorer classes. Over four hundred branches sprang up in the provinces.

Within the National Assembly, a faction of the Jacobin Club known as the **Girondins** (after the department of Gironde near Bordeaux) became a powerful voice. The Girondins wanted to preserve the progress of the

Revolution and became convinced that only a successful war that exposed the enemies of their cause could unite the country. Following Louis's attempted escape, Emperor Leopold II of Austria (the brother of Marie Antoinette) and the king of Prussia jointly issued the Declaration of Pillnitz, which threatened intervention against the Revolution by the powers of Europe. This action and related agitation by the émigré nobles drove the Girondins to argue that the Revolution in France was not safe until similar ideas had triumphed across Europe. Less honourably, the bourgeois Girondins were supported by wealthy business and shipping interests who believed that such a war would yield increased production, commerce, and profit. When Leopold's sudden death placed his more conservative brother, Francis, on the Austrian throne, the Girondins won the day. In April, 1792, the Assembly declared war against Austria and proclaimed it a "war against kings, peace with all peoples." Prussia joined the fight against France soon afterward.

A Parisian Sans-culotte.

The inadequately prepared French army, weakened by the loss of its émigré officers, suffered a series of defeats in the early going. It appeared that Louis might be saved by his foreign friends, as enemy troops were soon on French soil heading toward the capital. Pandemonium ruled in Paris. Gripped by an upsurge of nationalism and marching to the stirring words of the "Marseillaise"—later to become the national anthem—French patriots pushed on against the foreign invaders and turned against their king. They believed that monarchists were plotting to overthrow the Revolution. A crowd broke into the Tuileries on 20 June, ridiculed Louis, and forced him to wear the red cap of liberty. Hearing of the insult, the Austrian duke of Brunswick issued a manifesto warning that, if the king and his family were harmed, the people of Paris would suffer a terrible punishment. Instead of helping the royal cause, the Brunswick Manifesto led directly to the fall of constitutional monarchy.

The anger of Parisians, which had been quiet since Lafayette and the National Guard had fired on a mass demonstration the previous year, reached a new peak as patriotic feelings swelled and food prices again became extremely high. Crowds of angry **sans-culottes** ("without knee breeches"), so-called because they wore the long, loose pants of the Parisian worker, poured through the streets around the palace on the night of 9 August 1792. Convinced that Louis had given the army's battle plans to the enemy, the extremists, led by Georges-Jacques Danton, engineered a military coup the following morning. The king's Swiss guards were all killed. Louis and the royal family sought refuge in the Legislative Assembly, but arrived only to be taken prisoner. With constitutional monarchy at an end, the Assembly, in desperation, declared an election for a **National Convention** to draw up another constitution. As the Prussian army neared Paris, chaos and fear guided the mob. For six days in September, the **September Massacres**, Jean-Paul Marat led the extremists in a raid of prisons and jails. Upward of two thousand people, including nobles, priests, prostitutes, and criminals, were accused of counter-revolutionary activity and murdered. On 20 September 1792, the same day the Prussians were halted at Valmy, the National Convention held its first meeting. The following day France was declared a Republic.

The French Revolution: Radical Phase (1792-1794)

The summer chaos of 1792 moved the Revolution from its path of moderate change toward a constitutional monarchy to the radical ambition of the new Republic. Genoa, Venice, the Dutch Republic, and the Swiss Confederation were the only other republics in Europe, and they were in a state of decline or stagnation. The American experiment, though inspirational, was far away and beset with problems. But France was the greatest nation in Europe. It transformed the word "republic" into a cry for revolution against other absolute monarchies. French victories in the fall of 1792, due more to its enemies' mistrust of each other than French military genius, provided the basis for ambitions to spread the Revolution.

The Jacobin Club, which controlled the hastily elected National Convention, had become divided. Although the Girondins had pushed for war, they were horrified by the senseless killings of the September Massacres. Their efforts to place the Revolution on a more moderate course resulted in their expulsion from the Jacobin Club and left the radical elements of the Jacobins as the most powerful block in the National Convention.

Louis's fate was in the hands of the Convention. There was no doubt of Louis's treason, but there were different ideas about how to deal with it. The Girondins wanted to delay his trial and avoid an execution that might stir additional foreign hostility against France. The more radical Jacobins, known as "the Mountain" because they sat in the highest seats of the National Convention's amphitheatre, demanded the king's head. Following months of debate, the Convention held the trial. The final vote in favour of execution was 387 to 344. The Mountain had won. On 21 January 1793, at what is now the Place de la Concorde, "Citizen Louis Capet," as the king came to be called, stepped up to the guillotine. "I die innocent of all crimes imputed to me," he proclaimed. "I pardon the authors of my death, and pray God that the blood you are about to shed will never fall upon France." His head was raised to the cries of a cheering crowd seconds later.

With Louis's death, the tide temporarily turned against the young Republic. Eager to extend earlier victories, the National Convention declared war against Holland and England in February 1793; Spain joined the coalition against France soon after. France was not ready to take on the combined powers of Europe, and the military situation was made worse by a monarchical rebellion in La Vendée and food riots in Paris, the result of yet another round of high prices and low supply. At this difficult moment,

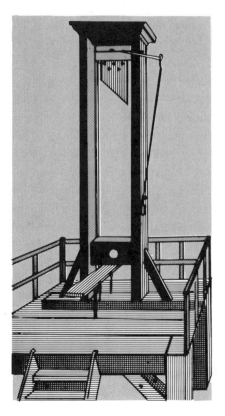

"Madame Guillotine."

the politicians of Paris turned the crowds that engulfed the Convention hall in favour of the Jacobin Mountain. Any Girondin leaders who could be found were arrested and guillotined in what amounted to a continuation of the September Massacres. To deal with political dissent and civil disorder, the Convention authorized a twelve-member Committee of Public Safety to rule with almost dictatorial power until the emergency passed. The democratic constitution that the Mountain had drafted was never put into practice. Policing powers were given to the Committee of General Security, while the Revolutionary Tribunal tried counter-revolutionaries according to the "law of suspects" with little regard for due process.

The committees and the Tribunal were the administration and instruments of what came to be known as the **Reign of Terror**. From June 1793 to July 1794 hundreds of thousands of people were imprisoned and upward of forty thousand guillotined to save the Revolution from supposed traitors. Although the victims ranged from Marie Antoinette to peasants and workers, only 15 percent came from the nobility and clergy. The leading spirit of the Terror was Maximilien Robespierre, a member of the Committee of Public Safety who had led the Mountain in its attack on the Girondins. For Robespierre, the purpose of the Terror was clear and desperate:

> ... To establish and consolidate democracy, to achieve the peaceful rule of constitutional laws, we must finish the war of liberty against tyranny ... We must annihilate the enemies of the Republic at home and abroad or else we shall perish ....

The justice of the Terror, in Robespierre's view, was "swift, severe, and inflexible." Its methods were despotic, but Robespierre believed that the "government of the Revolution is the despotism of liberty against tyranny." Moreover, he believed that the Terror was essential to the expression of what Rousseau called the "general will," the wishes of the people. But Rousseau had never explained how the general will could be determined. Robespierre and a few key advisers on the Committee of Public Safety became the self-appointed interpreters of the people's will. The public executions organized for the crowds of Paris were meant to convey that the government was serious about its revolutionary ideals.

But the real threat to the Revolution came from the armies massing on the borders of France. To deal with the military situation, the Committee of Public Safety took decisive action that had a lasting impact on the nature of modern warfare. The entire nation of France was mobilized behind the war effort in the *Levée en Masse* of 23 August 1793. Able-bodied, single men between eighteen and twenty-five years of age had to serve in combat; married men had to "forge arms and transport provisions"; women had to "make tents and clothing and ... serve in hospitals"; while children had to "turn old linen into lint." The elderly were ordered to go to public places and preach the virtues of the Republic to encourage enthusiasm for the war. The ranks of the army swelled to eight hundred and fifty thousand by the

Controversies

Mary Wollstonecraft (1759-1797), a British novelist and feminist, was outraged at the French Revolution's failure to emancipate women. In her book, *A Vindication of the Rights of Woman*, she argued that the progress of human knowledge and virtue would be halted until women were given equal status with men, and that both sexes should receive an identical education.

In France, Olympe de Gouges (1745-1793) expressed similar views. The Declaration of the Rights of Man and the Citizen, issued by the National Assembly in 1789, had ignored the rights of women and children. In response, de Gouges wrote the *Declaration of the Rights of Woman*, in which she demanded equal rights for all people in public and private life and before the law. For her condemnation of the revolutionaries and their new government, she was sentenced to death by Robespierre and guillotined.

The French Revolution–Radical Phase (1792–1794)

1792	September 21	The National Convention abolishes the monarchy; France is declared a Republic
1793	January 21	Louis XVI is executed
	February 23	Food riots break out in Paris
	March 10	Revolutionary Tribunal is established to try enemies of the Revolution
	April 6	Committee of Public Safety is established
	May 21	Jacobins begin attack on the National Convention
	June 2	Jacobins demand expulsion of Girondins at the Convention
	June	The Reign of Terror begins
	July 27	Robespierre joins the Committee of Public Safety
	August 23	Conscription is introduced in an effort to mobilize the people to defend the Republic and the Revolution; the *Levée en Masse* is called
	September 17	The Law of Suspects is introduced
	September 29	The Law of General Maximum is introduced
	October 16	Marie Antoinette is executed
	October 31	Girondins are executed
1794	April 5	Danton and his supporters are executed
	July 28–29	Robespierre and his followers are executed; the Republic of Virtue ends

spring of 1794, making it the largest in European history. A young soldier and supporter of the Jacobins, Napoleon Bonaparte, displayed his talent for organization and rose to the rank of brigadier-general by the age of twenty-four, but it was the older commanders who led the attack against the divided European coalition. By late 1793, France had pushed back the enemy and was on the march to its "natural frontiers" of the Rhine, the Alps, and the Pyrenees, a territory that exceeded the conquests of the Sun King, Louis XIV.

The success of the *Levée en Masse* meant that other European nations would eventually be forced to imitate it or suffer defeat on the battlefield. As nation mobilized against nation, the scale of warfare greatly expanded. The tidy conflicts of the eighteenth century, where soldiers fought soldiers while civilians went about their business, were gone. Although it served the Revolution, the *Levée en Masse* was the first step toward the horrible, total war of the twentieth century.

With the guillotine greatly reducing the number of outspoken opponents of the Revolution, and the success of French armies on the battlefield, Robespierre attempted to establish the **Republic of Virtue**. This was a sincere but misguided attempt to reshape life in France. In a formal ceremony in June of 1794, Robespierre asked the French to abandon Christianity, which was seen as counter-revolutionary, and worship the "Supreme Being of Nature" instead. He tried to introduce a number of other "virtuous" social practices.

The Reign of Terror eventually overtook its creator. The execution of Marie Antoinette could be easily justified as a symbol of the end of the ancien régime. When the same fate befell first the Girondin leaders, then the radical sans-culotte Jacques Herbert and his Commune followers, and finally the more conservative Jacobin Georges-Jacques Danton, it became clear that no one was safe. Yet Robespierre was not overthrown by popular protest. His attempt to control food prices and the ruthless approach used by commissioners to requisition supplies from the countryside were resented, but most people remained silent for fear that they too would become the victims of "Madame Guillotine." The turning point came when the other members of the Committee of Public Safety became convinced that *they* were soon to be executed. In a carefully designed plot on the ninth of Thermidor (27 July 1794), Robespierre was denounced at a meeting of the National Convention and, in the next two days, the "tyrant" and ninety-two of his followers were beheaded. So ended the Republic of Virtue.

Thermidorian Reaction and the Directory (1794-1799)

With the death of Robespierre, the year of bloodshed ended. Former revolutionary zealots now denied any connection with the Republic of Virtue, but many Jacobins were murdered by those who had been made to suffer in the name of the Revolution. In what has been called the **Thermidorian Reaction**, the machinery of the Terror, including the Committee of Public Safety, the Tribunal, and the Jacobin clubs, was dismantled. The French press and French artists welcomed the return of freedom of expression. Several Catholic churches were reopened. Many of those imprisoned by the Jacobins were released, and émigrés came home by the thousands. The withdrawal of price controls, however, increased prices and precipitated a march by the sans-culottes on the National Convention in May, 1795. Their protests, now out of favour, were muted by the Convention. The Paris Commune, so much a part of the unpredictable nature of the Revolution, was finally dissolved.

The National Convention drew up another constitution, proclaimed on 22 August 1795. It reflected the interests of the bourgeois middle class by making property qualifications so high that only twenty thousand men—less than half the number allowed in the 1791 constitution—were enfranchised.

Institutions

Robespierre's Republic of Virtue showed that his vision of reform went far beyond government. The terms *Citoyen* and *Citoyenne* (citizen) replaced *Monsieur* and *Madame* as terms of social address. The conventional images of nobility were removed from packs of cards; figures of the sans-culottes, soldiers, Rousseau, and famous individuals from Republican Rome were substituted for kings, queens, and jacks. Of more lasting impact was the introduction of the metric system of weights and measures, based on the rational organization of the decimal system and worked out by a commission headed by Joseph Lagrange. Another creative twist was the adoption of a revolutionary calendar that changed the names of the months, eliminated saints' days and Sundays, and declared national holidays to commemorate events of the Revolution: 14 July (1789)— the storming of the Bastille; 10 August (1792)—the overthrow of the monarchy; 21 January (1793)—the execution of Louis; and 21 May (1793)—the seizing of control of the National Convention by the Jacobins and Paris Commune.

Maximilien Robespierre.

Clearly, democracy and the will of the people were now viewed with suspicion. Legislative power was given to a Council of Ancients and a Council of Five Hundred, who appointed an executive **Directory** of five men to serve for five years.

Royalists as well as city workers opposed this plan because the bourgeois leaders decreed that two-thirds of the new councils had to come from members of the existing Convention. Plans among royalist sympathizers in the provinces to place Louis XVI's son on the throne ended with the boy's premature death at the age of ten in June of 1795. Then Louis XVI's brother, exiled in Italy, declared his intention to regain the throne and re-establish the ancien régime. The Directory, buoyed by popular opinion, resolved to prevent the return of the monarchy at all costs. In October of 1795, royalist riots in Paris that involved twenty-five thousand protesters were broken up when they were fired upon by four thousand troops led by the former Jacobin, Napoleon Bonaparte. His famous "whiff of grapeshot," which killed or injured over five hundred people in the crowd, showed that the army was now the key to political power.

With the royalist "right" in temporary abeyance, the Directory was now faced with a challenge from the working class "left." In 1796, François Babeuf, known as "Gracchus" after the populist leaders of ancient Rome, organized a "Conspiracy of Equals" on behalf of the labourers and poor artisans of Paris. Often regarded as the first class-conscious socialist, Babeuf wanted to abolish private property and introduce a planned economy. When he was betrayed and guillotined, the uprising he had desired was easily defeated and the Paris crowds were finally disarmed. Nevertheless, the riots of 1795-1796 clearly showed the precarious position of the Directory, with its narrow base of support among the propertied middle class.

With France's finances in chaos and its political position unstable, the fate of the Directory became increasingly involved with the career of Napoleon. Without question, the people of France wanted peace as part of a return to normal life after the Terror. The war to liberate freedom-loving peoples from oppression had become a more traditional conflict to advance the prospects of the French nation. Peace was made with Spain, Prussia, three other German states, and Holland during 1795, on terms generally favourable to France. Only England and Austria remained at war. In 1796, Napoleon was given command of the French army in Italy as a reward for saving the Directory from the rioters the previous year. His famous words at the start of the campaign stirred his troops:

> You are badly fed and nearly naked—I am going to take you to the most fertile plains in the world. You will find there great cities and rich provinces. You will find there honour, glory, and wealth.

Though his army was ill-equipped and usually outnumbered, Napoleon's brilliant military tactics led to a series of victories over Austria and its Sardinian allies. In the harsh Treaty of Campio Formio of 1797,

Austria was compelled to recognize the French annexations of Belgium, the left bank of the Rhine, and Lombardy. Northern Italy was reorganized into the Cisalpine Republic, essentially a French satellite territory. In return, Austria was allowed to annex Venice, a republic that had been independent for over a thousand years. Tribute in cash and art poured over the Alps into France, and Napoleon became a national hero.

As Napoleon's popularity soared, the Directory ran aground. The elections of 1797 had returned a majority of royalists to the councils, threatening the political power of the middle-class directors. Only by annulling the elections, with the support of a military force commanded by an aide of Napoleon, did the Directory hang on. Partly as another reward and partly to keep him away from the centre of power, Napoleon was given command of an army that was to invade England. England was the one country that stood between France and peace, or, perhaps more important, between Napoleon and his dream of additional conquest and glory. Recognizing that England's strength depended on overseas commerce, Napoleon decided to cripple English trade in the Mediterranean by invading Egypt and then campaigning overland as far as India. At the Battle of the Pyramids in July, 1798, the French forces massacred the Turks and easily took control of Egypt. The following week, however, the British fleet, under Admiral Horatio Nelson, destroyed the French navy near the mouth of the Nile River. Napoleon had suffered his first defeat and was now stranded with his army in Egypt.

Trapped by the British navy, although in control of Egypt, Napoleon decided to advance upon Syria. Recognizing the danger of French expansion in the Mediterranean, in 1799, Europe formed a Second Coalition against France that included England, Austria, Russia, Turkey, Naples, Portugal, and the papacy. As these powers began to challenge the European territories recently occupied by France, the Directory became increasingly unpopular. Another election returned an overwhelming majority for the opposition, and rumours of royalist plots to overthrow the government abounded. Amid this confusion, Napoleon saw his chance. Forced to return to Egypt to subdue a Turkish attempt to retake it, Napoleon abandoned his troops to certain surrender, slipped through the British fleet, and returned to France. He immediately allied himself with a plot organized by one of the directors and executed a successful coup d'état to end the Directory. A new government of three consuls was established, with Napoleon as first consul. Shortly afterward, Napoleon and his fellow consuls made an announcement: "Citizens, the Revolution is established on the principles upon which it was founded: it is over."

The Issue Emerges

The specifics of the French Revolution—the grievances and rallies, the riots and executions, the succession of governments—were unique to the time

Thermidorian Reaction and the Directory (1794-1799)

1794	August	Machinery of the Terror is dismantled; the Convention follows a middle path between radicals and moderates
1795	April-July	Peace is made with Prussia, Holland, and Spain
	May	Sans-culottes march on the National Convention demanding "bread and the Constitution of 1793"
	August 22	Constitution of 1795 is proclaimed
	October 6	Napoleon suppresses royalist riots in Paris by firing on the demonstrators The Directory governs France until 1799
1799	November 9	Napoleon overthrows French government in coup d'état

and place. The underlying questions of principle, however, are as relevant today as they were then. The relationship between individual freedom and the authority by which individuals are governed is central to civilized life. Just what this relationship should be was a major theme of the Enlightenment and a practical matter for the leaders of the French Revolution.

Before and during the Revolution, the French people had to resolve some extremely pressing questions. Who should lead them? How much power should the leader have? How could the voice of the people be heard and acted upon? How could change be allowed and accommodated? Some of the questions were practical. Who should pay for national expenses? What should those expenses be? Which members of the French public should make such decisions? Or, to put it another way, who should be allowed to vote? Abstract ideas about government proliferated during the Enlightenment. These ideas were heatedly discussed and sometimes even put into practice. A historian might ask, in retrospect, whether one of these ideas might have been especially beneficial to the French state and the French people.

When the English writer Thomas Hobbes (1588-1679) published his *Leviathan* in 1651, he anticipated the discussion of principles examined later by the French *philosophes*. Hobbes was thoroughly critical of the chaos caused by religious disputes and the English Civil War, which had ended with the execution of Charles I. He proposed that a supreme authority with absolute power to preserve peace and order could achieve the best government. Hobbes believed that humans in their natural, ungoverned state would fall into a "war of each against all." They would destroy themselves, much as the English had done in the civil war in his own time. In Hobbes's view, the only reasonable choice was for people to give up their individual freedom to create a sovereign state that no self-interested individual could challenge. This would ensure the safety of all. Although the sovereign state would have unlimited power, which was all the justification it would need, its goal would be to satisfy the needs of its subjects so that it, too, could survive. The ancien régime had many of the elements of the sovereign state imagined by Hobbes, despite the weaknesses of Louis XVI. What was better for the French people—the absolute rule of Louis XVI or the chaos and bloodshed of the Revolution?

John Locke, another prominent English thinker, believed that human beings possessed natural rights to life, liberty, and property, and that they formed societies to protect these rights. In contrast to Hobbes, Locke argued that citizens were justified in changing or overthrowing their government if their natural rights were violated. Locke used this argument to explain and defend the Glorious Revolution of 1688 in England. Locke's concept of natural rights can be associated with the moderate phase of the French Revolution. Were the people of France better off as a result of their pursuit of their natural rights?

Jean-Jacques Rousseau agreed that humans first lived in a state of nature and that they have certain fundamental rights. Unlike Hobbes, who argued that humans in the state of nature could not be trusted, Rousseau believed that they were basically good and that the general will of the communities they formed represented the best intentions of the people. Since the general will was always right, any opposition must be wrong and had to be defeated for the benefit of the community. Rousseau's ideas are often associated with the radical phase of the Revolution, and there is no doubt that, under Robespierre, his ideas were taken to a bloody extreme. There were, however, some positive accomplishments during the radical phase; in addition, forces were unleashed that greatly affected the subsequent history of France and Europe. Was France a better place in which to live as a result of these changes? Would the French have benefitted by adhering to one of these abstract ideas? If so, which one?

PROBLEM QUESTION

Given the events of the French Revolution, were the political, economic, and social interests of the French people best represented by Hobbes's theory of absolute rule, Locke's concept of natural rights, or Rousseau's theory of Social Contract?

ALTERNATIVE ONE: Leviathan

Based on *Leviathan* by Thomas Hobbes (1651)

Origin of the State

The final cause, end, or design of men, who naturally love liberty, and dominion over others, in the introduction of that restraint upon themselves, in which we see them live in commonwealths, is the foresight of their own preservation, and of a more contented life thereby; that is to say, of getting themselves out from that miserable condition of war, which is necessarily consequent, to the natural passions of men, when there is no visible power to keep them in awe, and tie them by fear of punishment to the performance of their covenants, and observation of the laws of nature.

For the laws of nature, as "justice," "modesty," "mercy," and, in sum, "doing to others as we would be done to," of themselves, without the terror of some power to cause them to be observed, are contrary to our natural passions, that carry us to partiality, pride, revenge, and the like. And covenants, without the sword, are but words, and of no strength to secure a man at all. Therefore notwithstanding the laws of nature, which everyone hath then kept, when he has the will to keep them, when he can do it safely, if there be no power erected, or not great enough for our security, every man will and may lawfully rely on his own strength and art, for caution against all other men.

The only way to erect such a common power as may be able to defend them from the invasion of foreigners and the injuries of one another, and thereby to secure them in such sort as that by their own industry, and by the fruits of the earth, they may nourish themselves and live contentedly, is to confer all their power and strength upon one man, or upon one assembly of men, to bear their person; and everyone to own and acknowledge himself to be the author of whatsoever he that so beareth their person shall act, or cause to be acted, in those things which concern the common peace and safety: and therein to submit their wills, every one to his will, and their judgements to his judgement. This is more than consent, or concord; it is a real unity of them all in one and the same person, made by covenant of every man with every man, in such manner as if every man should say to every man, "I authorize and give up my right of governing myself, to this man or to this assembly of men, on this condition, that thou give up thy right to him and authorize all his actions in like manner." This done, the multitude so united in one person is called a "commonwealth," in Latin *civitas*. This is the generation of that great leviathan, or rather, to speak more reverently, of that mortal god, to which we owe under the immortal God, our peace and defense. For by this authority, given him by every particular man in the commonwealth, he hath the use of so much power and strength conferred on him, that by terror thereof, he is enabled to perform the wills of them all, to peace at home, and mutual aid against their enemies abroad. And in him consisteth the essence of the commonwealth; which, to define it, is "one person, of whose acts a great multitude, by mutual covenants one with another, have made themselves every one the author, to the end he may use the strength and means of them all, as he shall think expedient, for their places and common defense."

And he that carrieth this person is called sovereign, and said to have sovereign power; and everyone besides, his subject.

The attaining to this sovereign power is by two ways. One by natural force; as when a man maketh his children to submit to themselves, and their children, to his government, as being able to destroy them if they refuse; or by war subdueth his enemies to his will, giving them their lives on that condition. The other is when men agree among themselves to submit to some man, or assembly of men, voluntarily, on confidence to be protected by him against all others. This latter may be called a political commonwealth, or commonwealth by institution; and the former, a commonwealth by acquisition. Now, I shall speak of a commonwealth by institution.

The Nature of Sovereignty

A commonwealth is said to be instituted when a multitude of men do agree and covenant, everyone with everyone, that to whatsoever man or assembly of men shall be given by the major part the right to present the person of them all, that is to say to be their representative; everyone, as well he that voted for it as he that voted against it, shall authorize all the actions and judgements of that man or assembly of men in the same manner as if they were his own, to the end to live peaceably among themselves and be protected against other men.

From this institution of a commonwealth are derived all the rights and faculties of him, or them, on whom sovereign power is conferred by the consent of the people assembled.

And as the power, so also the honour of the sovereign, ought to be greater than that of any or all the subjects. For in the sovereignty is the fountain of honour. The dignities of lord, earl, duke, and prince are his creatures. As in the presence of the master the servants are equal, and without any honour at all; so are the subjects in the presence of the sovereign. And though they shine some more, some less, when they are out of his sight; yet in his presence, they shine no more than the stars in the presence of the sun.

QUESTIONS

1. a) According to Hobbes, why do people willingly live in a commonwealth?
   b) Did the ancien régime serve this purpose? Explain your answer.
2. a) What are the laws of nature as presented by Hobbes?
   b) Did Hobbes believe that people would follow these laws of their own accord? Explain your answer.
3. a) How much authority does the commonwealth possess?
   b) Did Louis XVI and the government of France have this much power? Explain your answer with evidence.

4. Describe the formation and characteristics of a "commonwealth by institution."
5. a) What degree of honour is given to the sovereign power?
   b) Did Louis XVI receive this kind of honour as the absolute monarch of France?
6. To what extent was the ancien régime the "Leviathan" described by Hobbes?

ALTERNATIVE TWO: Civil Government

Based on *Second Treatise on Government* by John Locke (1690)

Chapter II: Of the State of Nature

To understand political power, we must consider the natural condition of all men, and that is a state of perfect freedom to do as they please and dispose of their possessions and persons as they think fit, within the bounds of the law of nature, without asking leave or depending upon the will of any other man.

A state also of equality, wherein no one has more power or authority than another ....

The state of nature, which has the law of reason to govern it, teaches all mankind who will but consult it, that being equal and independent, no one ought to harm another in his life, health, liberty or possessions; for men being all the workmanship of one omnipotent and infinitely wise Maker; all the servant of one sovereign Master, sent into the world by His order and about His business; they are His property, whose workmanship they are, made to last during His, not one another's, pleasure. Such is the natural condition of all men, until they consent to become a member of a political society.

Chapter VIII: Of the Beginning of Political Society

When any number of men have, by the consent of every individual, made a community, they have thereby made that community one body, with a power to act as one body, which is only by the will and determination of the majority ....

Chapter IX: Of the Ends of Political Society and Government

If man in the state of nature is free, why will he part with his freedom and subject himself to the dominion and control of any other power? To which it is obvious to answer, that though in the state of nature he had such a right, the enjoyment of it is uncertain and constantly exposed to the invasion of others. This makes him willing to quit this condition which, however free, is full of fears and continued dangers; and it is not without reason that he seeks out and is willing to join in society with others who are already united, or have a mind to unite for the mutual preservation of their lives, liberties and estates, which I will call by the general name—property.

The great and chief end, therefore of men uniting into commonwealths, and putting themselves under government, is the preservation of their property; to which in the state of nature there are many things wanting ....

And so, whosoever has the legislative or supreme power of any commonwealth, is bound to govern by established standing laws, issued to the people; and to employ the force of the community at home only in the execution of such laws, or abroad to prevent or redress foreign injuries and secure the community from inroads and invasions. And all this to be directed to no other end but the peace, safety and public good of the people.

Chapter XVIII: Of Tyranny

Where law ends, tyranny begins, if the law be transgressed to another's harm; and whosoever in authority exceeds the power given him by the law, and makes use of the force he has under his command to break the law, ceases in that to be a magistrate, and may be opposed as any other man who by force invades the right of another. Exceeding the bounds of authority is no more right in a greater than a petty officer, no more justifiable in a king than a constable. But so much the worse in him, since he has more trust put in him, is supposed, from the advantage of education and counsellors, to have better knowledge and less reason to do it, having already a greater share than the rest of his brethren.

Chapter XIX: Of the Dissolution of Government

When legislatures and rulers break the trust given to them, and either by ambition, fear, folly, or corruption try to grasp for themselves, or put into the hands of others, an absolute power over the lives, liberties and estates of the people, by this breach of trust they forfeit the power the people had put into their hands for quite contrary ends. The people now have a right to resume their original liberty, and by the establishment of a new legislature (such as they shall think fit), provide for their own safety and security.

QUESTIONS

1. a) Compare Locke's view of the state of nature with the Hobbes's ideas.
   b) What role does the "law of reason" serve in the state of nature according to Locke?
2. a) Why does an individual surrender personal freedom to become part of a community?
   b) In Locke's view, what is the main objective of government?
3. How must the supreme power of a community try to govern?

4. a) What condition results when the laws of a community are broken?
   b) What can be done when government breaks the trust the people have given to it?
5. a) When the Estates General met in 1789, what classes of French society felt that Louis XVI had violated the trust given to him?
   b) What motivated the attempt to reform France into a constitutional monarchy during the moderate phase of the Revolution?
   c) Were living conditions in France better during the moderate phase of the Revolution than they were during the ancien régime? Explain your answer.

ALTERNATIVE THREE: The Social Contract

Based on *The Social Contract* by Jean-Jacques Rousseau (1762)

Man is born free, and everywhere he is in chains. Many a man believes himself to be master of others who is, no less than they, a slave. How did this change take place? I do not know. What can make it legitimate? To this question I hope to be able to furnish an answer.

I assume that mankind reached a point when there were more disadvantages than advantages in remaining in a state of nature. The original state of nature could not last under such conditions and the human race would have perished unless it changed.

Men cannot create new powers, but they can unite and control those they already possess. Only by coming together and pooling their strength could men meet the challenges exerted upon them. They had to develop a central direction and work together. Such a focus of power can happen only when agreement is reached among several individuals. But the self-preservation of each individual comes from his own strength and freedom. How can he limit these without harming himself and neglecting his duty to his own concerns?

Some form of association had to be found in which the strength of the whole community will be enlisted for the protection of the person and property of every citizen in such a way that, when united to his fellows, he renders obedience to his own will, and remains as free as he was before. This is the basic problem solved by the Social Contract.

The clauses of this Contract are determined by the Act of Association in such a way that the least modification will render them null and void. Although the terms of the association may never have been formally accepted, they must be the same everywhere and universally recognized. Should the Social Contract be broken, each associated individual would regain the rights that were his in a state of nature.

In the Social Contract, each individual voluntarily gives up all his rights to the community. Since each man has made the same sacrifice without reservation, the conditions are equal for everyone. And because conditions are equal, it is in everyone's interest to make life pleasant for all.

Moreover, since all rights have been surrendered to the community, the union is as perfect as it can be and no one has any claim against the community. If individuals retained certain rights, with no superior authority to choose between them and the public good, then each would attempt to expand his personal rights. A state of nature would still exist. And the association would become ineffective or despotic.

The Social Contract can be reduced to the following terms: "Each of us puts his person and all his power in common under the supreme direction of the general will, and we receive into the body politic, each individual as an indivisible part of the whole...."

For the Social Contract to work, everyone must realize that any individual who does not obey the general will must be forced to do so. Thus, a man must be forced to be free since freedom is now defined as obedience to the will of all.

QUESTIONS

1. What did Rousseau mean when he said, "Man is born free, and everywhere he is in chains"?
2. What basic problem does the Social Contract solve?
3. Why did Rousseau feel that people have no right to revolt?
4. a) What is the "general will"?
   b) Rousseau did not explain how the general will was to be determined. Why could this omission become a problem in practice?
5. a) Robespierre admired Rousseau's philosophy. Did the Reign of Terror accurately reflect Rousseau's ideas? Explain your answer.
   b) Did the Republic of Virtue contribute anything positive to France that could be attributed to Rousseau's philosophy? Explain your answer.

ANSWERING THE PROBLEM QUESTION

The problem question asks you to study three social theories formulated in three historical contexts, then to evaluate which might have given the French people the best answers to the many crises faced by the ancien régime and the reformers. As it turns out, elements of each theory can be found in the different phases of the Revolution, which allows you to measure the correspondences and discrepancies between theory and practice. Of course, it is difficult to apply theories to actual events. France changed rapidly during the Revolution, and at times no one seemed to be in control. Masses of desperate and angry people carried out acts of destruction and violence virtually without restraint.

Hindsight allows us to know the results of the French Revolution and Napoleon's quest for power. As you answer the problem question, however, it is important to remember that at each moment of change France had several options, each of which would have meant something different for the future. Historians often try to identify crucial decisions and then explore the different options that were available by framing questions for consideration. For example, when the nobles forced Louis to call a sitting of the Estates General, they hoped to solidify their position within society and enhance their existing political power and privilege. Would French society as a whole have benefited if the nobles had achieved their objectives? Would the reforms the Third Estate sought have helped anyone other than the bourgeoisie? Would the lower classes have been better off under legislation passed by Louis XVI, or was a whole new form of government necessary?

You should not only assess the possible outcomes of some of the most important options, but you should also attempt to weigh the positive and negative aspects of the events that actually did occur. The Reign of Terror, administered by Robespierre and the Committee of Public Safety, led to tens of thousands of executions and changed almost every aspect of French life. Were these authoritarian actions necessary to bring order to the country? Robespierre equated the policies of the Committee of Public Safety with the general will described by Rousseau. But these policies, which caused widespread carnage, particularly among the lower classes, can also be seen as an attempt to establish and maintain power at any cost rather than as an attempt to uphold revolutionary ideas in a "Republic of Virtue." The Committee went on to rally the emotions and resources of the nation with the *Levée en Masse*. The result was the largest army that Europe had ever seen, and its success in expanding the frontiers of France fuelled French pride and nationalism. In saving France from foreign invasion, did the new army justify the tactics of the Terror?

Obviously, the problem question has no right or wrong answer. The persuasiveness of your argument will depend on how successfully you use the events of the Revolution as evidence. Interestingly enough, the answers you arrive at may give you some insight into the decisions and dangers nations face in our own time by seeking to change the way they are governed.

THE STORY CONTINUES . . .

From First Consul to Emperor

Abbé Sieyes, famous for his inspirational document in support of the Third Estate in 1789, had one of the most intriguing careers of the revolutionary era. With considerable skill, Sieyes adapted to each major shift in political power and emerged as one of the five directors in 1795. In fact, Sieyes was the director who decided to "use" Napoleon to carry out the coup of 1799, without realizing how quickly the young general would consolidate the situation in his own favour.

After his return from Egypt and his participation in the coup, Napoleon arranged four assemblies of state, carefully preserving the illusion that France was a democracy. But there was no doubt he intended to centralize

Napoleon Bonaparte

By 1800, Napoleon had demonstrated many of the qualities that made him so extraordinary. He had come a long way since his birth on the rugged island of Corsica in 1769. His childhood, contained few hints of the remarkable career to come, although there is a story that Napoleon painted the walls of a bare room with rows of soldiers in battle formation. His father, a poor lawyer, was able to secure a scholarship for Napoleon, and sent him to a French military college in 1779. Napoleon was on his own from the age of ten, and his Corsican accent, unrefined clothes, temper tantrums, and intense seriousness set him apart from his classmates. Napoleon was only an average student, but if something interested him, he could easily absorb vast amounts of material.

In 1784, Napoleon obtained an appointment to the École Militaire in Paris and earned a commission as a second lieutenant in southern France the following year. Assigned to a regiment in Louis XVI's army, Napoleon received practical training as an artillery officer. During this period, he became deeply impressed with the writings of Rousseau. The outbreak of the Revolution in 1789 and the emigration of many nobles from the officer corps, created undreamed-of opportunities for ambitious young officers who stayed in France. Napoleon embraced the Revolution with enthusiasm, spending much of the first four hectic years organizing revolutionary political clubs in Corsica. Forced to leave his homeland when his attempt to seize power went awry, Napoleon, now a captain, joined a military detachment of the Revolution. His direction of the artillery led to the French recapture of the port of Toulon from the British in late 1793, after months of limited success. Napoleon emerged as a brigadier-general for his efforts.

His affiliation with the Jacobins worked against him after the execution of Robespierre. He was briefly jailed as a terrorist, and his rapid progress was sidetracked. Even after his release, it appeared that Napoleon's military career was finished until Director Barras appointed him to end the threat to the Republic in 1795. He ordered his soldiers to fire on the royalist demonstrators in Paris, killing hundreds on the steps of the Church of St. Roch.

Just before he took command of the Italian expedition, Napoleon fell in love with and married Josephine Beauharnais, a woman whose aristocratic connections elevated his social status to that of his military rank. Josephine, though alarmed by Napoleon's impetuous courtship, believed he could repay her debts. Napoleon returned from Italy as a triumphant general, later revealing that his victory at Lodi, near Milan, first stirred his tremendous ambition: "From that moment, I foresaw what I might be. Already I felt the earth flee

A portrait of Napoleon as a student at the École Militaire.

from beneath me, as if I were being carried into the sky."

Napoleon's Egyptian campaign followed. He carefully crafted his image as a military hero, exaggerating details of his most famous encounter, which he called the "Battle of the Pyramids." (The European study of Egyptology dates from Napoleon's campaign and was stimulated by the stories of ancient grandeur that followed him home.) His self-promotion drew attention away from his defeats in Egypt, and from the ruthless slaughter of almost three thousand Turkish prisoners who had surrendered at Jaffa on the promise that their lives would be saved.

Napoleon's unique combination of charisma, ego, and intensity enabled him to dominate people. He inspired loyalty and devotion among his generals, support staff, and soldiers, even in times of defeat. His military genius was admired by all and feared by his enemies. The duke of Wellington claimed that Napoleon's presence on the battlefield was worth forty thousand troops. Yet this natural leader, who claimed to be devoted to his men, would remorselessly sacrifice thousands of soldiers for a limited gain if the situation demanded it. His achievements, for which he is still held in awe, came at the cost of hundreds of thousands of lives.

power in his own hands as first consul. *After* the three consuls implemented a new constitution and Napoleon's position as first consul was secure, Napoleon went to the people for approval in a popular vote known as a **plebiscite**. This was a shrewd move. First, it was in tune with the idea that sovereignty rested with the people, the basic principle of the French Revolution. At the same time, the plebiscite by-passed the elected representatives of government. Napoleon judged the mood of the people correctly: on 7 February 1800, the vote for the constitution showed a staggering 3 011 007 in favour and only 1562 opposed! Napoleon also perceived that the French people were tired of the turmoil caused by the quest for freedom, and that they would prefer peace and order. Within France, Napoleon moved quickly to crush the royalist rebellion in La Vendée that had been waged intermittently since 1793, terrorizing the countryside. In foreign affairs, France was confronted by the Second Coalition. Overtures from Napoleon helped to persuade Russia to withdraw from the coalition and from active participation in the war. At the same time, Napoleon proposed peace to Austria and England, knowing that the offers would be rejected as long as France dominated Belgium and the Rhine and knocked on the doorstep of Italy. Napoleon was then victorious in a two-pronged attack against Austria. The Treaty of Luneville, in 1801, slightly enlarged the concessions Austria had made four years earlier at Campio Formio.

Once again, only Britain was left to oppose France. The war between the two great powers was becoming stalemated—Britain was supreme at sea while France dominated the continent. The Treaty of Amiens, signed in 1802, though generally favourable to France, reflected this situation.

Napoleon took full credit for the peace and the victories that preceded it. Although the British public was disappointed by the treaty, the French greeted it with joyous enthusiasm. Napoleon used the euphoria of the moment to hold another plebiscite to amend the constitution and make himself consul for life. Again, the vote was overwhelming, with 3 568 885 in favour and only 8374 against. Napoleon realized however, that the break in hostilities was only a truce and that the war would soon resume.

As a domestic reformer during the Consulate, Napoleon was at his creative and energetic peak. He gave France many institutions that have endured in one form or another to the present. The task of centralizing the administration, begun by Richelieu and interrupted by the Revolution, was completed. France was divided into departments, *arrondissements*, and communes (towns), with a corresponding set of officials (prefects, subprefects, and mayors) appointed directly or indirectly by the central government. Napoleon recruited able ministers and officials to ensure that his intended reforms were implemented properly, and France was better off for the choices he made. He also introduced an effective system to collect and audit taxes, a reform that reduced corruption and distributed the tax burden more equitably. The Bank of France, created to stabilize currency, became an important agent of the government in controlling national finance and, in 1803, acquired a monopoly on the right to issue banknotes.

Legal reforms were also needed. The task of making sense of the tangle of Roman, feudal, national, and local customs had already begun under Louis XIV, but it was Napoleon who completed it. Napoleon knew little about legal technicalities and, despite keen interest, his presence at meetings often hindered rather than helped the proceedings. Yet the end result of the effort, the **Code Napoléon**, gave French civilization a solid legal foundation that became the hallmark of domestic peace. The code was issued in five parts as each was completed, and it combined all areas of law into one unified legal system. The bourgeoisie applauded the protection given to property, the declaration that all men were equal before the law (women continued to be treated differently from men), the supremacy of the state, and the freedom of conscience. It has since been amended and added to, but it remains in force to this day.

Napoleon probably lacked even a trace of religious conviction, but he understood the emotional importance of religion in society. The Revolution had been at odds with the Roman Catholic Church, which only served to divide the nation in crisis after crisis. Napoleon intended to mend this division. He also wanted to be seen as a good Catholic in Italy, because Church opposition could be a major obstacle to French rule in the states he planned to conquer. The Concordat of 1801, which Napoleon forced through over the objections of his non-Catholic advisers, was an agreement with the Roman Catholic Church on terms favourable to France. France agreed to maintain churches and pay the clergy, while the pope gave up all claims to

Controversies

Legislation protects the rights of the citizen, but it also defines what those rights are. The Code Napoléon was eventually criticized for the rights it defined and failed to define. For example, legislation in the Code gave a husband control over the property of his wife. Women seeking equality protested the unfairness of such a law. The Code was also biased in favour of the bourgeoisie, because it outlawed collective action on the part of labourers. The Code had the benefit of stabilizing France, but its rigidity also stood in the way of important social changes that were occurring at the time.

Church land sold during the revolutionary decade. The French government was given the right to nominate bishops, but the pope retained the right to install them. Although Roman Catholicism was recognized as the religion of the majority, other religions were tolerated. The Church agreed to the Concordat but was uncomfortable with it, especially after the late addition of the "Organic Articles," which proclaimed the supremacy of the state over the Church.

Of equal concern to the Church were the educational reforms that Napoleon initiated. Revolutionary governments had been too preoccupied to implement changes in education, and so education had remained the preserve of the Church. In 1802, however, Napoleon introduced a national system of education that featured select secondary schools known as lycées that would be run by the government. They emphasized state indoctrination, military training, science, and mathematics. In 1808, the process of centralizing education was completed with the establishment of the University of France to supervise higher education in regional centres throughout the nation. From this system, Napoleon expected to groom the skilled personnel needed to run the country. Elementary education, however, was largely neglected. Napoleon saw no reason to educate the common people. His attitude toward the education of women, which would be considered outrageous today, was a major step backward even for the time:

> I do not think that we need trouble ourselves with any plan of instruction for young females; they cannot be better brought up than by their mothers. Public education is not suitable for them, because they are never called upon to act in public. Manners are all in all to them, and marriage is all they look to.

To reward exceptional individuals, Napoleon created another institution that has survived to the present—the Legion of Honour. Those who applauded the abolition of all noble titles in 1790 were concerned about the apparent return of distinctions. For Napoleon, such honours, given at his own discretion to achievers regardless of their social class, were another means of encouraging loyalty and harnessing the service of the capable. Though membership was initially limited to six thousand and was usually given to military personnel, those who demonstrated talent in any field were eligible. The League soon became an "army" in size, but the honour remained highly valued.

The reforms introduced by Napoleon were a mixture of original ideas and the completion of projects begun or conceived by earlier governments. Although he certainly deserved praise for instituting so many important changes, he also took credit even when he had not earned it. Napoleon's desire for personal recognition was in keeping with his grand idea of his own role. He believed that a strong, enlightened, absolute ruler was best for France. The reforms he accomplished were one result of his belief. Another result of his quest for power was more ominous. The police arrested his

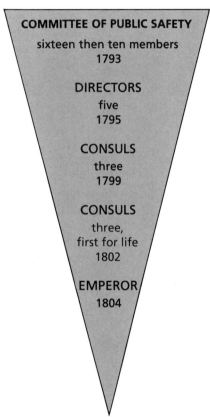

COMMITTEE OF PUBLIC SAFETY
sixteen then ten members
1793

DIRECTORS
five
1795

CONSULS
three
1799

CONSULS
three,
first for life
1802

EMPEROR
1804

The Government of France, 1793–1804. Note how power becomes concentrated in fewer and fewer hands until it is finally held by one person—Napoleon.

political opponents, and newspapers critical of the Consulate were closed.

Following the plebiscite that confirmed his appointment as consul for life, Napoleon allowed himself some of the privileges of royalty. His image appeared on coins, and only his first name was used on official documents. Long inspired by the power of the Caesars, Napoleon added a series of classical arches and columns to the public works plans for a modern network of canals and roads. Paris was to be beautified with a Roman flavour. But, despite his eminence, Napoleon had to wait for the right occasion to consolidate absolute power. A royalist conspiracy engineered by envious generals gave him his chance to act. The conspirators implicated an unknown member of the Bourbon family as the central figure, but no one could identify him. Napoleon's first move was to arrest the generals. He then decided, without evidence, that the missing Bourbon was the young duke d'Enghien. The unfortunate duke, who knew nothing of the scheme, was arrested in his hunting clothes, tried after Napoleon had instructed the judges to render a guilty verdict, and shot. Although some observers were highly suspicious and abhorred the incident, the press printed what it was told and the public believed the story. In the tense atmosphere of the trials of the generals, most of whom were also executed, the legislative bodies of the Consulate gave Napoleon the title of hereditary emperor in May of 1804. Napoleon again appealed to the people by holding a plebiscite. The results were similar to the others: 3 572 329 in favour with only 2579 opposed.

Napoleon arranged an extravagant coronation worthy of Roman pageantry. It was held in the Cathedral of Notre Dame in Paris in December, 1804. Napoleon invited the pope to consecrate the empire and the crowning of the new Charlemagne. In the prearranged ceremony, the pope lifted the crown—a duplicate of Charlemagne's original—and Napoleon took it and crowned himself. Perhaps the concentration of absolute power in the hands of one person was the logical conclusion to the Revolution. The twelve members of the Committee of Public Safety had been replaced by five directors, who were themselves replaced by three consuls. The three consuls were eclipsed by a consul for life, who then became hereditary emperor. Napoleon dearly wanted to leave his empire to his offspring, but he never lost sight of the fact that power alone was the justification for his throne. Napoleon's rise to the pinnacle of France in five years was remarkable, but it only whet his appetite for greater worlds to conquer.

War and Empire

The peace that had been established between Britain and France in the Treaty of Amiens lasted little more than a year. In 1803, anticipating the outbreak of hostilities, Napoleon sold the Louisiana territory, recently acquired from Spain, to the United States, doubling the size of the American republic and strengthening an overseas rival to Britain. Already

The Arts

When Napoleon came to power, Ludwig van Beethoven's reputation as a composer and performer had already spread beyond the musical élite of Vienna. He was an enthusiastic supporter of the French Revolution, and his opposition to tyranny was symbolized by the bust of Brutus that sat on his desk. Beethoven had dedicated his third symphony, the *Eroica*, to Napoleon, but he was so provoked by Napoleon's decision to be crowned emperor that he withdrew the dedication.

The Coronation of Napoleon *(detail) by Jacques Louis David. The painting shows Napoleon crowning his wife, Josephine, as empress. Napoleon's mother is shown seated in the gallery (top left). In fact, she did not attend the ceremony.*

upset with the continued French occupation of the Austrian Netherlands (Belgium) and with French trade restrictions, Britain declared war on France three weeks later.

In response, Napoleon planned to invade Britain with a flotilla of fifteen hundred barges and boats. Over the next two years, he assembled his Grand Army of one hundred thousand at Boulogne, opposite Dover, and another eighty thousand between Brest and Antwerp. The plan's success depended on temporary control of the English Channel. To achieve this, Napoleon devised a trap in which the French admiral Villeneuve would decoy the British fleet to the West Indies, leaving the English Channel unprotected. Napoleon was so confident of victory that a column was raised at Boulogne to celebrate the occasion. Meanwhile, he used the terms of the Treaty of Luneville to reorganize the territories of the German states, making drastic changes geared to suit his own interests. This manoeuvring caused alarm in several states. Prussia decided to remain neutral, but, by April 1805, Austria and Russia had joined Britain in a Third Coalition against Napoleon.

Napoleon hastened to implement his deception against Britain, and Villeneuve successfully lured away the British fleet. The British quickly uncovered the plan, however, and Napoleon only discovered his admiral's return to Europe by reading a British newspaper almost two weeks after Villeneuve had reached Spain! With the invasion foiled, Napoleon marched the Grand Army across the continent and overwhelmed a surprised Austrian force at Ulm on 20 October 1805. The following day, French and Spanish fleets encountered the British navy at the Battle of Trafalgar. The British admiral Horatio Nelson split the French and Spanish line of thirty-three ships and engaged each half on his own terms. After five hours of fighting, twenty of the French and Spanish vessels were disabled, while Nelson's fleet of twenty-seven survived without a loss. Nelson was fatally wounded by a French sailor but died aboard his flagship, H.M.S. *Victory*, knowing the day was won.

Trafalgar crushed Napoleon's dream of invading England and marked the beginning of a century of British naval supremacy. On hearing the shattering news of England's success, Napoleon tried to open peace negotiations with Austria and Russia, but was refused. The emperor then marched his army from Vienna to the town of Austerlitz, where, on 2 December 1805, he destroyed an Austro-Russian force in what he later described as his most brilliant military victory.

Humiliated for the third time by Napoleon, Francis II of Austria left the coalition and agreed to negotiate with France. The resulting Treaty of Pressburg saw most central European states become satellites of France. Napoleon officially dissolved the Holy Roman Empire in 1806. At the same time, he reorganized French client states in Germany to form the Confederation of the Rhine. In so doing, however, Napoleon ignored the interests of Prussia, whose continued neutrality had been bought with the gift of Hanover after Austria's defeat. Concerned by expanding French influence, isolated Prussia declared war on France, only to be humbled by Napoleon.

After occupying Berlin, Napoleon marched his army eastward to face the Russians, who had entered the war too late to alter the outcome. Following the bloody but indecisive battle at Eylau, Napoleon won a major victory over the Russians in June, 1807, at Friedland in east Prussia. Tsar Alexander I met Napoleon aboard a raft in the Niemen River to discuss peace terms, while the Prussian king, Frederick William III, paced anxiously along the river bank waiting for the results. Alexander was spellbound by Napoleon who, in the Treaty of Tilsit, took half of Prussia's territory, demanded an indemnity (payment for war expenses), limited the size of the Prussian army, and imposed a French army of occupation. Napoleon agreed to help Alexander against the Turks, but in return Alexander had to recognize all French conquests in Europe and to assist France against Britain if the war continued.

The Treaty of Tilsit represented the apex of Napoleon's power. His Grand Empire and satellite kingdoms extended from Belgium and Holland in the north to Spain in the west, Naples in the south, and the Grand Duchy of Warsaw in the east. With the Austrians, Prussians, and Russians forced into military alliance, Napoleon's Grand Empire exceeded the realm of Charlemagne and the Rome of the Caesars. As Napoleon rolled over Europe, he always presented himself as a "liberator," freeing the people he conquered from their oppressors while his troops spread the ideals and accomplishments of the revolutionary era.

The Continental System and Nationalist Backlash

Officially, Napoleon said that Trafalgar was an unwise skirmish followed by a storm that cost France some ships. Unofficially, he recognized that Britain was now safe from invasion. He decided to conquer his most stubborn adversary through economic warfare. If Britain was master of the sea, Napoleon ruled much of the land, and he determined to use his military power to cut off Britain's export trade with Europe. Napoleon reasoned that with a severely reduced export market, British manufacturing would rapidly decline, unemployment would skyrocket and the social havoc would force Britain to beg for peace. At the same time, the continent would co-ordinate its own production and trade, with France at the centre, and attain a high degree of economic independence. Britain would be allowed to buy certain French goods, which would drain British gold reserves and hasten economic collapse.

From Berlin, following the defeat of the Prussians, Napoleon issued a decree in 1806 that launched the **Continental System**. It forbade all states controlled by or allied with France to trade with Britain. But because Napoleon lacked the navy to enforce a blockade, neutral countries could continue to trade with Britain. The British responded in 1807 with the

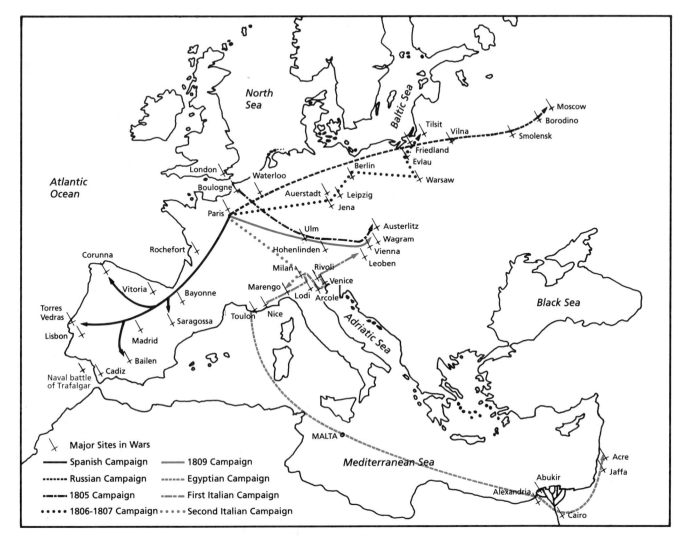

The Campaigns of Napoleon.

Orders in Council, which required ships from neutral countries to harbour in Britain before proceeding to any country participating in the Continental System. Since Britain did have a strong navy, its blockade was more effective than the emperor's paper proclamations. Napoleon claimed that the British were violating the rights of neutral countries and, in December, 1807, he decreed that neutral ships that complied with the British Orders in Council would be treated as enemy ships. To subdue Britain, Napoleon was willing to manipulate all of Europe.

The Continental System became the focal point of the Napoleonic Empire, but its effects differed from what Napoleon intended. The British economy was inconvenienced rather than threatened. French manufacturers did enjoy increased prosperity in continental markets, but the neutral countries and French allies suffered badly. Britain's control of the sea lanes not only limited the continent's selection of goods, but forced Europe to use overland transport, which greatly increased prices. At the same time as they were coping with the cost of supplies, the allies also had to provide troops for Napoleon's army. Natural resentment of the conqueror was paralleled by ideas about liberty that the emperor and French troops had originally planted. Unwittingly, Napoleon's attempt to cripple Britain served mainly to stimulate nationalist opposition to the Grand Empire.

Rebellion began in the Iberian Peninsula (Spain and Portugal). Portuguese resistance was quickly smothered, but Spain proved to be Napoleon's undoing. Although allied with France since 1796, Spain was a country led by clergy and aristocrats who had little sympathy for the French Revolution. When Napoleon occupied the country to enforce his economic warfare against Britain, he forced the king to abdicate and placed his brother Joseph on the throne. The aristocrats and clergy led a mass insurrection against the French.

Napoleon's military success in Europe had been facilitated by his use of **forced marches**. Troops were commanded to keep an exhausting pace, and supplies were kept to a minimum so that the armies were not hauling "unnecessary" materials. This tactic enabled Napoleon to strike with surprise. The army would then live off the agricultural produce of whatever community it was occupying. But the mountainous and barren terrain of Spain had little agriculture and was more suited to the hit-and-run tactics of the Spanish guerillas. Although the emperor might win an encounter he personally directed, the poorly armed Spanish guerilla force was able to tie up an enormous French army at great expense to the French treasury. The pope's excommunication of Napoleon in 1808, after he had overrun the Papal States to force Italy to align with the Continental System, motivated the pious Spanish to fight even harder. The future duke of Wellington landed a British force in support of the Spanish cause, and the six-year **Peninsula War** gradually eroded the military and psychological hold Napoleon had exercised over the Grand Empire.

It did not take long for news of the Spanish rebellion to spread across Europe. With France in difficulty, Austria declared war in 1809, intent on breaking free from the French yoke. Napoleon realized that the Grand Empire and the Continental System depended on the use as well as the threat of force. He hastily returned from Spain to take command of another French army, this one relatively inexperienced. In central Europe, where Napoleon's tactics were ideal, he overcame the Austrian forces. The victory was much less decisive than the one at Austerlitz in 1805, but it was clear that Austria could not defeat France by itself. The Treaty of Schönbrunn compelled Austria to cede territory, enter another alliance with France, and submit to the Continental System. Following the treaty, Napoleon tried to soothe Austrian feelings. He secured an annulment of his marriage to Josephine, who had failed to provide an heir, and married Marie Louise, daughter of Francis II of Austria and niece of Marie Antoinette. The arrangement did not abate Austrian hatred of Napoleon or make for a warm marriage, but Marie Louise and Napoleon did have a son together.

By 1810, the Grand Empire again seemed secure, particularly after Sweden was forced to accept the Continental System and Holland, which had offered stubborn resistance, was incorporated into France. But the bitter struggle in Spain, characterized by savage atrocities on both sides, and the improved showing of the Austrian army, encouraged growing opposition from Tsar Alexander. No longer awed by Napoleon, Alexander was upset by the lack of French assistance against the Turks, Napoleon's choice of an Austrian rather than a Russian bride, expansion of the Grand Duchy of Warsaw, and the loss of British manufactured goods. Alexander knew that anti-French sentiment was widespread at the Russian court and to ignore it was to invite assassination. He broke from the restrictive Continental System by opening Russian ports to British ships, and prepared for war.

This was a difficult moment for Napoleon, although its importance seemed to escape him. His physical deterioration was obvious and was accompanied by disturbing periods of drowsiness, an inability to concentrate, and a refusal to accept advice. Growing opposition to the Continental System in Europe was paralleled by the opposition of the French business community which, despite previous prosperity, began to feel that more profits could be made with a different economic approach. The emperor ignored the problem. Though burdened with a ruinous war in Spain, Napoleon hoped to make the Grand Empire "the metropolis of all sovereigns" and to personally become "something fabulous, something colossal and unprecedented." After his coronation as emperor, the wars of France had become Napoleon's wars, and his will, he believed, was that of the people of France. Napoleon felt that one more victory would fulfill his dream and, aware of the difficulties involved, organized a military force of over six hundred thousand soldiers to invade Russia in June of 1812.

Although the Grand Army was made up of reluctant conscripts from seven states of the empire, Napoleon was supremely confident that he could squash Alexander's resistance once and for all. Alexander, however, withdrew into the vastness of Russia, at first out of confusion and then by design. Alexander avoided major conflict, destroyed supplies, and burned the countryside in a "scorched earth" policy of retreat. As Napoleon pursued, he overextended his supply lines and, as in Spain, found nothing to replace them in the Russian wasteland. Napoleon pushed on, against his own better judgement, in the hope of fighting a decisive battle, but the reality of starvation led to the death or desertion of almost half a million soldiers.

The Russians finally dug in at Borodino, 110 km from Moscow. Napoleon's depleted army won a narrow victory in a bloody battle—fifty

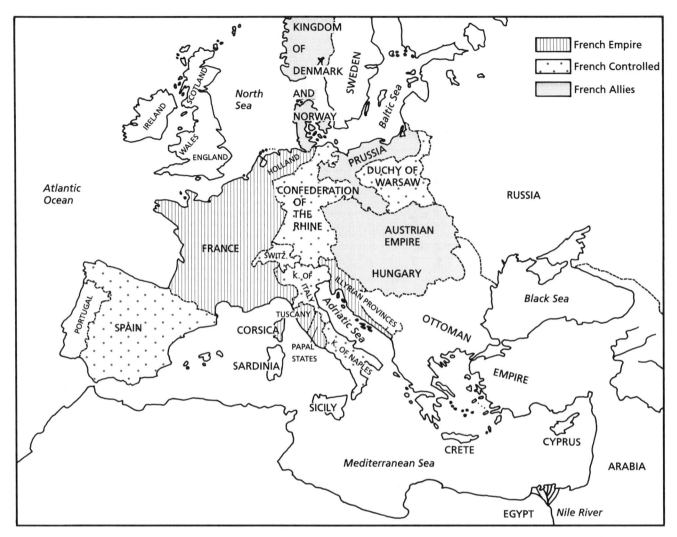

Key:
- French Empire
- French Controlled
- French Allies

Napoleonic Empire at Its Peak, 1812.

thousand died and twenty thousand were wounded. Anxious to reach Moscow to witness its legendary grandeur and to obtain fresh supplies, Napoleon trudged onward. Much to his surprise and frustration, he found Moscow practically deserted and in flames when he entered it in September. Forced to retreat within a month, Napoleon's weakened army straggled home in subzero temperatures, contending with almost daily attacks from the well-supplied Russian army that now advanced in its wake. Fewer than thirty thousand men crossed the Niemen River. The Grand Empire appeared to be finished.

The decimation of the French forces in the disastrous retreat from Moscow provided clear evidence that Napoleon was not invincible. In

Prussia, the emancipation of the serfs created an atmosphere of optimism, and coincided with the spread of patriotic literature and a surge of nationalist sentiment. A revised system of military service created a reserve army of one hundred and twenty thousand men and signalled Prussia's arrival as a modern state. The Napoleonic policies that had brought civil equality and domestic improvement to the Italian states now served to inspire riots aimed at ending French domination. Wellington pushed French armies across the Pyrenees from Spain into southern France at the very moment that the Confederation of the Rhine began to crumble. Out of this backlash against the Grand Empire arose the Fourth Coalition of Prussia, Russia, Austria, and Britain, which embarked on a "War of Liberation" to remove the French yoke from Europe. Even the northern power, Sweden, agreed to send troops to assist the cause.

Napoleon rushed back from the Moscow campaign to deal with the spread of opposition. It was a tribute to his organizational genius and personal magnetism that he was able to raise an army of two hundred and fifty thousand men in four months, but, like the Grand Army of the previous year, it was inexperienced. Napoleon's tactical skill secured three minor victories in the early going, but he failed to pursue the defeated Prussian forces.

At the Battle of the Nations near Leipzig in 1813, the combined forces of Prussia, Austria, Russia, and Sweden overwhelmed Napoleon. On the run at the very moment that Wellington penetrated southern France, Napoleon rejected generous peace terms and recruited another army of about one hundred thousand largely untrained youths. Though greatly outnumbered, Napoleon staged a brilliant defence until the coalition armies abandoned him and marched on Paris. With the capital in foreign hands, Napoleon's own marshals forced him to abdicate. By the Treaty of Fontainebleau in 1814, Napoleon relinquished the throne, but remained the emperor of the tiny Mediterranean island-kingdom of Elba, to which he had already been exiled. France had experienced almost a quarter century of war, paid for by the blood of the common people.

From his confinement in Elba, Napoleon watched and waited as the victorious nations gathered first at Versailles, then at Vienna, to thrash out a general peace agreement for Europe. The Bourbon Louis XVIII returned to rule France alongside a parliament in accordance with a written constitution. Many of the émigré nobles also returned and immediately demanded reforms that would return them to political office, military rank, and their old social privileges. By comparison, Napoleon's régime suddenly seemed much more appealing.

The Hundred Days

Napoleon escaped from Elba and landed in France on 1 March 1815 with a few hundred soldiers, beginning "the Hundred Days" between the end of his first exile and his final banishment. His charisma and bravery quickly

FIRST COALITION (1792–1793)

France *versus* Austria
Prussia
French émigrés
Spain
England
the United Netherlands
Sardinia
Naples
Sicily
Portugal

SECOND COALITION (1799)

France *versus* England
Austria
Russia
Turkey
Naples
Portugal
the papacy

THIRD COALITION (1805–1806)

France *versus* England
Spain Russia
and Austria
Napoleonic Sweden
satellite Naples
states Prussia

FOURTH COALITION (1813)

France *versus* England
and Russia
Napoleonic Austria
satellite Prussia
states Sweden

won over the troops sent to arrest him. The general discontent with the Bourbon government enabled Napoleon to regain Paris in three weeks without firing a shot. The crowds cheered wildly upon his return, and Napoleon proclaimed his intention to establish a liberal régime.

The allies at Vienna promptly stopped squabbling, condemned Napoleon, and prepared for war. At Waterloo in Belgium, the better equipped armies of Prussia, Holland, and Britain greatly outnumbered the French force that was, on this critical occasion, not so skillfully handled by Napoleon. The Austrian and Russian armies waited in the wings to finish off any French survivors. On 18 June 1815, after a three-day battle, combined forces of Europe again defeated Napoleon decisively, and he was compelled to abdicate for a second time. He was sent to the distant British island of St. Helena, over 7200 km away in the South Atlantic. There, Napoleon spent the last six years of his life writing his memoirs.

Napoleon's career cannot be crystalized in a single passage, but these words by Alfred de Musset suggest the contradictions inherent in his achievements:

> The life of Europe was centred on one man; all were trying to fill their lungs with the air he breathed.... Never had there been so many sleepless nights as in the time of that man; never had there been seen ... such a nation of desolate mothers; never was there such a silence about those who spoke of death. And yet there was never such joy, such life, such fanfares of war in all hearts. Never was there such pure sunlight as that which dried all this blood.

The Emergence of Industrialism to 1850

The Enlightenment prepared the way not only for political revolution but also for the **Industrial Revolution**. This term, with its connotations of sudden and extreme change, is somewhat misleading. The Industrial Revolution had no precise beginning, and much of its impact was gradual. The changes continue to affect our lives today, and the process continues to spread to the developing nations of the Americas, Africa, and Asia. The essence of the Industrial Revolution was the substitution of machinery and mechanical power for manual and animal labour in the production of materials and goods.

For many reasons, such machinery appeared first in England, around 1760. Britain was the world's leading commercial nation, provided with an excellent location for overseas trade. The need for finished goods to export to the colonies and the Orient stimulated domestic production. Institutions such as the Bank of England, which originally provided credit for trade and commerce, were also available to back larger industrial enterprises and government financial needs as they arose. Provincial banks, which numbered four hundred in 1790, provided local credit to merchants and manufacturers. In addition, Britain had long been free from foreign invasion, and there had been no internal strife since the Glorious Revolution of 1688. The country escaped the dislocation and damage of war that plagued the continent during the eighteenth century. The British government was able to pursue policies favourable to commerce and industry that were not possible in the divided German states or amid the web of tariffs and tolls that fragmented the French economy.

Britain was small and relatively flat, with many natural harbours, an abundance of navigable streams, and a good system of roads. Communication was easy and transportation was cheap. Overland transportation on the unimproved roads of the continent was more expensive and much less efficient. As industry grew in the later eighteenth and early nineteenth centuries, hundreds of miles of canals and turnpikes were built, giving Britain better transportation than any other country in Europe. Britain was also fortunate enough to have large reserves of coal and iron, essential for the new technologies.

Changes in agricultural production greatly assisted industrial development, and again Britain had a major advantage over the continent. Village farmlands had traditionally looked like patchwork quilts of rectangular furlong fields, subdivided into half-hectare strips. Farmers employed the three-field system, always leaving one field fallow. Ploughing was done co-operatively and, since farmers usually owned a strip in each furlong, every farmer had at least some land under cultivation. Farmers also had the right to pasture grazing animals on the common land of the village. From the sixteenth century onward, however, English landlords began the **enclosure movement**. Fields were sectioned off with fences, and farmers received single lots equal to the total area of the strips they had owned. Common pasture disappeared. Large farms could be operated more efficiently than small ones; farmers who had less land were squeezed out because they could not compete and because they could not survive without access to common pasture. As owners of large farms gobbled up the smaller, less productive lots, Britain developed a class of wealthy landlords who owned huge estates that they rented to tenant farmers in holdings of 40 to 200 ha. During the same period, French farms averaged only 5 ha in size, while German farms, except for the estates of the Junker class, were even smaller. Higher production on British farms led to surpluses that could be sold, and to the increased commercialization of agriculture. By the eighteenth century, less labour was required to produce more food. Many peasant farmers who could not find work on large farms began to emigrate to the cities and even to America to find jobs and a new way of life.

During the early eighteenth century a new interest in scientific experiment and innovation produced techniques as revolutionary as the "enlightened" ideas about social progress. Improved methods of agriculture helped to increase yields, and new breeding practices resulted in more productive livestock. Lord Townshend introduced the turnip, a crop that could be grown on marginal land and that could be used with clover to provide forage

Science

Due to technological developments in the seventeenth century, muskets and artillery permanently replaced the sword and pike on the battlefield. Bigger, bulkier, and more efficient weapons also became a part of naval warfare. To increase their military strength, the British invested heavily in these new armaments. In 1632, England's Royal Navy listed only 81 brass and 147 iron pieces in its arsenal. By 1683, English warships were armed with 8396 cannons and over 350 000 cannon balls. As a result of their pursuit of superior weaponry, the British increased their knowledge about the combustion of gunpowder and the construction of gun chambers, barrels, and carriages. The resulting technologies and skills had many non-military applications, and probably helped to lay the foundation for the Industrial Revolution, which had its beginnings in the British Isles.

for livestock and to add nitrogen (a fertilizer) to the soil. A fallow field planted with turnips and clover would produce significantly more wheat and barley the next growing season. After watching vineyard workers in France maximize yields by hoeing and aerating the soil, Jethro Tull developed animal-drawn machinery, including his famous drill-plough, to plant seeds in rows, break the ground, and keep weeds under control. Robert Bakewell was equally successful in developing new selective breeding methods. His work paved the way for the introduction of new breeds, including Hereford cattle, Berkshire hogs, and Leicester sheep. As a result of these breeding advances and the increased availability of animal feed, the number of sheep and cattle in Britain doubled by the end of the century. The animals were twice as heavy and had a higher proportion of meat.

With meat now a regular part of people's diet, and with improved sanitation and medicine, the death rate declined. Population growth skyrocketed because more children reached adulthood and adults lived longer and had larger families. The number of people in Britain increased by less than .5 million between 1700 and 1750, but between 1750 and 1800 it jumped by 4 million, and between 1800 and 1850 by an astounding 10 million people. As the population rose, many people chose or were forced to go into the cities. London grew from 959 000 in 1800 to 2 681 000 by 1850. This increase was typical of England's five largest cities. By 1850, more people lived in the city than in the country, and it was the urban population that provided most of the cheap labour demanded by the new technologies of the industrial age.

The dynamic thrust that produced the industrial age came from innovations in three key areas, the first of which was textile production. Indeed, it was the rapid progress made in the British textile industry that gave rise to the term *Industrial Revolution*. At the turn of the eighteenth century, most manufacturing was done in the **domestic system**. Merchants or capitalists would buy material and distribute it to people who produced the finished products by hand in their own homes. The cotton textile industry depended on imports of cotton fibre that were turned into cloth by thousands of spinners and weavers across the country. Textile manufacturers had successfully lobbied the government to pass the Calico Acts of 1700 and 1720, which prohibited the importation of finished cotton cloth from India. This legislation gave the domestic industry in Britain a chance to develop.

A series of inventions, each related to the other, resulted in spectacular growth in the textile industry during the last half of the eighteenth century. The first step came in 1733, when John Kay invented the **flying shuttle**, which allowed one weaver to do the work of two and increased the demand for yarn. This demand was met in 1765, when James Hargreaves developed his **spinning jenny**, which turned four spindles at the same time and produced a fine cotton thread. Four years later, Richard Awkright built (although Thomas Highs invented) the **water frame**, which produced a

much stronger thread at even cheaper prices. In 1771, Awkright organized the first cotton mill. He brought together a large number of spinning machines and employed workers from the local villages to run them so that cotton could be produced on a large scale. The idea caught on and, by 1788, there were 119 cotton mills in Britain. Perhaps the most significant breakthrough, perfected in 1779, was Samuel Compton's **mule**, which combined elements of the spinning jenny and the water frame. The mule produced a fine *and* strong thread, and by 1812, 80 percent of Britain's cotton was produced on this machine. Mechanical weaving began when Edmund Cartwright secured a patent for a **power loom** in 1785. The savings from power spinning and weaving were such that cotton cloth could now be exported to India, where it undersold the local market! The demand for cotton cloth could not be satisfied. Following Eli Whitney's invention of the **cotton gin** in 1793, which cheaply separated the seeds from American short-staple cotton fibres, the United States became the major supplier of raw cotton to British mills. British imports of cotton fibre rose from about 2 000 000 kg annually in the 1770s to over 400 000 000 kg in 1860. The methods that enabled cotton to replace wool as Britain's leading industry were soon adapted to sugar refineries, rope factories, distilleries, and a host of other industries whose owners appreciated the value of **mechanization** and the **factory system**.

The second major impetus toward industrial development came from the iron industry, which had existed since the medieval period. Wood, in the form of charcoal, had traditionally been used to heat the iron ore, but wood was now in short supply. Forests were depleted to satisfy the demands for ships, houses, furniture, and heat. British coal was abundant, but it added impurities that reduced the quality of iron. In 1709, Abraham Darby discovered how to make an improved grade of iron by using burnt coal (**coke**) with limestone to smelt iron ore. Even so, British iron was still inferior to the iron produced in other countries. In 1760, Britain imported over twice the amount of iron it produced, mostly from Sweden and Russia. During the 1770s, the application of steam to operate bellows and hammers improved the quality of British iron. The turning point in iron production came in 1783 and 1784, when Peter Onions and Henry Cort independently perfected the **puddling** process, in which molten iron was stirred in puddles to cleanse the iron of impurities. Cort, who was intent on making better guns for the British navy, also developed the **rolling mill**. White-hot iron was sandwiched between massive rollers and shaped into sheets, rods, beams, and rails. British iron production took off, just as the textile industry had. Britain's iron output rose from 18 288 t in 1757 to about 127 000 t in 1796 to 2 286 000 t by 1850. In the same period, Britain moved from being a net importer to being the world's leading producer and exporter of iron and its associated products.

The third critical advance was the improvement of the **steam engine**. Like the Egyptians at the dawn of history, eighteenth-century industrialists had to rely on wind, water, and human and animal labour for power. Better windmills and water wheels were built, but they were dependent on the seasons and the whim of the weather. In 1709, Thomas Newcomen built a cumbersome steam engine with a low efficiency that could only be used to pump water out of a mine. In 1769, after years of experimentation, James Watt, an instrument maker at the University of Glasgow, developed an external condenser that solved the problem of removing the steam from the cylinder. Watt teamed up with a successful entrepreneur named Matthew Boulton, and they built an engine that could change the vertical movement of the piston into a rotary action capable of driving industrial machinery. Watt and Boulton received a twenty-five-year patent for their steam engine in 1775 and agreed to install their engine in return for a rental fee. All 481 steam engines operating in Britain in 1800 came from the Boulton-Watt factory. The engine was first employed as an efficient water pump, but was soon used in many industries.

The benefits of all these inventions were quickly apparent, and industrial development became self-perpetuating. In factories, workers concentrated on one particular task in the manufacturing process, so several people, rather than just one, would make a product. This **division of labour** greatly increased production, and was gradually applied to industry after industry. Demands for high-quality iron created a corresponding demand for coal to produce the iron. Iron and coal had to be transported, and the solution was the railroad. British coal carts had run on wooden rails since the sixteenth century. These were steadily replaced by iron rails, but gravity, humans, and horses did the work of moving the carts. In 1804, Richard Trevithick built a rather inefficient **steam locomotive** to ease the task. It was not until 1825, however, that George Stephenson's locomotive, the *Rocket*, made a successful run and demonstrated new possibilities. The railroad era was launched in 1830, when Stephenson's engine opened the Liverpool and Manchester line, the first railroad line specifically built for steam locomotives. The railroad not only became essential for transportation, but increased the demand for iron and coal. By 1850, Britain had built 10 560 km of track, far more than any country in Europe and second only to the United States, where distances were much greater.

The short-term and long-term benefits derived from higher production were offset by the misery of those who endured the living and working conditions of the early industrial city. People flocked into urban areas that were ill-equipped to provide the necessities of life for so many. Tenement buildings and rows of decrepit cottages housed up to twelve people per room, and the streets were strewn with rotting refuse that produced foul odours and disease. Sanitation facilities were virtually nonexistent. Construction was so shoddy that entire blocks were known to crumble. The squalor often equalled the worst conditions of the pre-industrial era. Over the cities hung the black smoke that left grit on every brick. Although the death rate for Britain dropped dramatically, it actually increased significantly in the five largest cities during the 1830s and 1840s when industrialism became firmly entrenched. Death always came earlier to the labouring classes, and in the industrial cities, a labourer's average age at death could be twenty-one years or less. With the congestion increasing the danger of crime, and few outlets in the form of parks or recreation, the industrial city was a place to which people were driven when they had nowhere else to go.

Working conditions were a product of the rapid pace of industrial development and a reflection of employers' attitudes. The new middle class of capitalists owned the banks, factories, businesses, and railroads. They grew up believing in a laissez faire business environment, in which the government placed no restrictions on economic development. Their economic strength was translated into political power when the **First Reform Bill** of 1832 began to concentrate parliamentary representation in the cities and enfranchised the middle class by introducing new voting regulations. From this time onward, the influence of the landed aristocracy—unless they took advantage of the new opportunities—began to give way to the influence of those who made their money in industrial development.

Equally new and far more numerous were the industrial workers, a loosely knit class that included a wide range of occupations and interests. It was this group that had to suffer its employers' attempts to keep costs down and production up in order to compete successfully with other manufacturers. Women

Gustave Doré's Over London by Rail *shows English city life during the Industrial Revolution. Construction of row and tenement housing was often so shoddy that walls simply collapsed.*

were treated with less respect than men, but children were treated the worst of all. Because they had little power, children were docile and accepted the lowest wages and appalling working conditions. Employers willingly exploited hundreds of thousands of children in an effort to pay for the costs of the new machinery and other overheads. In the textile industry, the employers lengthened the working day from twelve to fourteen to sixteen hours, with few stops for meals or rest. Children were awakened at five o'clock in the morning to begin a long day and were often whipped so they would not fall asleep. The luckiest ones were simply pale, sickly, and poorly clothed. Many others were deformed through injury and overwork, attesting to their employers' lack of concern for safety standards and the dangers of the new machinery. For example, to keep humidity high and prevent thread from breaking, the windows of the cotton mills were kept closed. The workers breathed hot, dusty air filled with cotton fibres throughout their working lives. They were stunted and enfeebled after spending years in such adverse conditions.

The situation was no better in the mines that supplied industries with raw materials. All workers faced the rock slides, cave-ins, and flooding common to the industry. Women and children crawled on hands and bare knees pulling and pushing loaded carts in dimly lit, poorly ventilated, narrow tunnels. Miners were often tied to the company through the "truck system." They were paid in goods, services, and company money that was redeemable only at the company store. Conversion of company money into real money was difficult and was often discouraged by the company.

And yet the age was not without conscience. As humanitarian reformers from all political parties tried to catch up to the abuses imposed by rapid change, legislation began to reverse the damage that was done. The specifics of reform bills suggest how extreme the problems were. The **Factory Act** of 1833 prohibited children under the age of nine from working in textile factories; children between nine and thirteen were limited to nine working hours a day and forty-eight hours in a week; while children from thirteen to eighteen could work only twelve hours a day and sixty-nine hours in a week. The **Mines Act** of 1842 prohibited boys under the age of ten and all women from working in the mines. In 1847, the twelve-hour day was introduced for men in most industries, while children under eighteen and women were restricted to ten hours a day.

Other attempts to improve the lot of workers were less successful. Robert Owen, the humanitarian owner of England's largest cotton mill, did what he could to provide decent conditions for his own workers. Owen's efforts to organize workers into one big union in 1834, however, failed as a result of government repression and division within the ranks. Workers then tried another approach. With only one man in eight eligible to vote after the First Reform Bill, an attempt was made to extend democracy to industrial working-class men. The **People's Charter**, drawn up in 1838, called for universal male **suffrage** (the right to vote), the annual election of Parliament, the secret ballot, and equal electoral districts. To allow working-class men to run for office, the Charter advocated that members of Parliament be paid, and that property requirements be abolished. Parliament, controlled by the middle class, turned down the petitions presented on behalf of the **Chartists** in 1839 and 1842. In the strikes and riots that followed, the government jailed many Chartist leaders and even sent some to the penal colony in Australia. A final petition of over 2 million signatures, many of which were falsified, was prepared. Workers throughout Britain participated in strikes and rallies in support of the petition and the Charter. There were plans for a great demonstration in London, to be mounted by five hundred thousand supporters. The Chartists' intention was to present the petition to Parliament; the show of force presumably would guarantee government action. But, alarmed by the possibility of revolution, the government hired one hundred and seventy-six thousand constables to disperse the crowd and again rejected the petition. Significant reform was left to succeeding generations of the working classes.

The demand for British products after 1815 stimulated continued industrialization and between 1830 and 1850 the process was completed. Britain was the world's financial, commercial, and industrial leader. With the repeal of the Corn Laws (which had taxed imported grain) in 1846 and the Navigation Acts in 1849, Britain virtually abandoned the mercantilist

Controversies

The workers who paid the price of industrial development did not always try to solve their problems through legal reforms. For some, violent protest seemed to be the only answer to the many injustices they were forced to bear. The rapidity of technological change not only created the factories with their appalling working conditions, but also made certain occupations suddenly obsolete. Jobs disappeared by the thousands. With the introduction of the power loom, for example, weavers skilled with the hand loom lost their livelihood. For almost twenty years (1811-1830), the weavers organized to try to stop what was happening to them. They called themselves **Luddites** in honour of Ned Ludd, who had protested against the use of stocking-knitting machines during the 1780s. They held secret meetings, practised military drills, and circulated notices calling on factory workers and communities to destroy the new machinery until its use was banned by Parliament. Riots and protests in several cities resulted in hundreds of deaths and injuries, but the power of the middle-class factory owners and their local militias was not to be denied.

For the Luddites, technological "progress" meant misery, not advancement. Technological change continues, and the problems the weavers faced are being faced by today's workers as well. Is it desirable, or possible, to delay or stop such change?

system and turned to free trade. British products could compete favourably with the products of any nation. Since most other European countries were only in the earliest stages of industrialization, they continued to follow policies of protection to encourage the development of their domestic industries.

In the decade after the Napoleonic wars, British methods spread to Belgium, which had the advantages of newly won independence, proximity to Britain, and large reserves of coal. By 1830, Belgium's coal production was triple that of France, steam power began to change Belgium's textile industry and, as in France, coal began to replace charcoal in iron production. In 1835, Belgium inaugurated an efficient railroad system that won the carrying trade of northwestern Europe. French trade and production had declined with the collapse of Napoleon's Continental System, but by the 1830s France ranked second on the continent to Belgium in industrialization. In the rest of Europe, industrialization was not completed until the second half of the nineteenth century.

Suppression and Control

During the first half of the nineteenth century, Europeans who held power tried to maintain control over the revolutionary political, social, and economic forces that had gained momentum in the eighteenth century. At the **Congress of Vienna**, assembled between September of 1814 and June of 1815, the countries that had defeated Napoleon ironed out a general settlement for Europe. They had two main objectives. The first was to prevent French domination of the continent. This they accomplished in the Second Treaty of Paris in November, 1815. France was reduced to its boundaries of 1790, subjected to an army of occupation for five years, and forced to pay an indemnity of 700 million francs and to return its stolen art treasures. The Congress's second objective was to prevent the catastrophe of endless war in Europe, which it sought to do by re-establishing a balance of power among European nations. The chief architect and manipulator of the settlement was Austria's chancellor, Clemens Wenceslas Lothar von Metternich (1773-1859). Lord Castlereagh of Britain, though not an admirer of Metternich, was also influential. Disagreements, squabbling, and even diplomatic confrontations resulted as negotiators manoeuvred for advantage before achieving a final settlement. The Congress, imbued with a conservative philosophy, wanted as much as possible to restore the old order that had existed before the French Revolution. They attempted to replace the governments that Napoleon had left behind with "legitimate" governments headed by absolute monarchs and supportive nobilities.

The Congress of Vienna did manage to achieve a relatively long-lasting balance of power. Although isolated struggles occurred, there was no war in which all of the great powers were involved until after 1850, largely because the terms of 1815 gave no reason for conflict. When the congress had finished

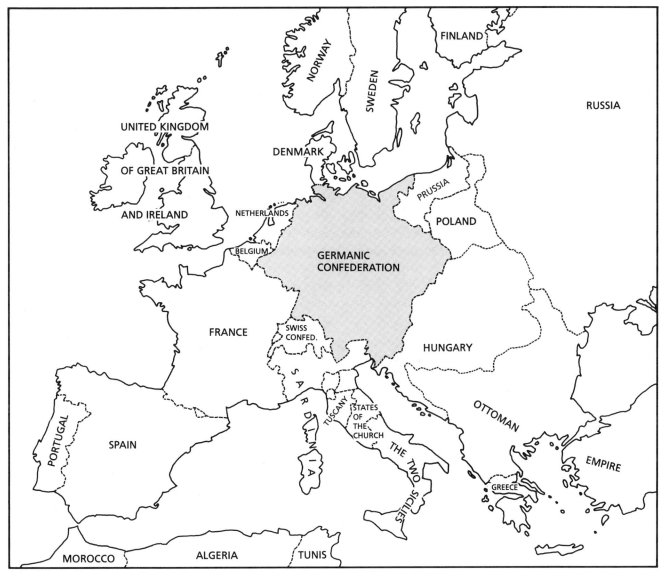

FINLAND

NORWAY

SWEDEN

RUSSIA

UNITED KINGDOM

OF GREAT BRITAIN

AND IRELAND

DENMARK

PRUSSIA

NETHERLANDS

POLAND

BELGIUM

**GERMANIC
CONFEDERATION**

FRANCE

SWISS
CONFED.

HUNGARY

S A R D I N I A

TUSCANY

STATES
OF
THE
CHURCH

OTTOMAN

PORTUGAL

SPAIN

THE TWO SICILIES

EMPIRE

GREECE

MOROCCO

ALGERIA

TUNIS

*Europe after the Congress of
Vienna (1815–1839).*

redrawing the map of Europe, Holland received the Austrian Netherlands
(Belgium and Luxembourg), while Austria was compensated with Venice
and Lombardy in Italy. Prussia received territory from Saxony (an ally
of Napoleon) and the left bank of the Rhine, thereby becoming the
protector of German interests. No one wanted the reinstatement of the
Holy Roman Empire with its three hundred states, so the loose German
Confederation of thirty-nine states (including Prussia), under Austria's leadership, replaced Napoleon's Confederation of the Rhine. Denmark, another

supporter of Napoleon, was penalized by losing Norway to Sweden, a nation that had sent troops to ensure the emperor's defeat. Russia retained its conquests of Finland and Bessarabia, but Tsar Alexander had to abandon his dream of an expanded kingdom of Poland. Britain, which had financed much of the war with generous subsidies to the allies, retained strategic posts which the navy had taken for the British Empire, including Heligoland, Malta, the Cape of Good Hope, Singapore, Ceylon, Trinidad, and Tobago.

The **Quadruple Alliance** of Russia, Austria, Prussia, and Britain was concluded the same day as the Second Treaty of Paris. The great powers agreed to defend the Vienna agreement, by force if necessary, and to hold conferences to discuss ways in which peace in Europe might be preserved. This unity, however, lasted only until 1828.

For a while, the nations of Europe had reached an agreement with one another, and the influence of the Bourbons, the Hapsburgs, and other royal families had been resurrected. But this new arrangement was not secure. With the redefinition of national borders, people of different ethnic backgrounds were placed under governments they disliked and had no voice in choosing. The force of **nationalism**, which had been spawned by the French Revolution and carried to the corners of Europe by Napoleon, was potentially dangerous to a state such as Austria, which comprised many distinct peoples. The Poles, Czechs, Croats, Slovaks, Ruthenes, Magyars, Serbs, and Italians under Austrian rule dreamed of the day they might achieve independence. Nationalism often became aligned with **liberalism**, an ideology that advocated freedom and equality for all individuals. Liberalism and democracy were also closely allied, since in a democracy, each individual had a say in choosing the government. (In the nineteenth century, however, few men accepted the idea that women should also be allowed to vote.) Government by democracy threatened the nobles and kings whom the Congress of Vienna had arbitrarily put in place. Metternich equated democracy with revolution and believed that the French Revolution was the "hydra with jaws open to swallow up the social order."

A series of revolutions, initiated on behalf of nationalism, liberalism, and/or democracy, broke out after 1819. Uprisings in Italy and Spain gave Metternich his chance to invoke European solidarity, and most of the allied powers agreed to intervene militarily. The revolutions were successfully subdued. Nationalism was also a factor in the Greek rebellion against the Ottoman Empire, which began in 1820. In 1828, Britain, France and Russia used their navies to help the Greeks achieve independence, while Prussia and Austria took the opposite side. The alliance of European nations that Metternich had tried to forge was at an end.

Conservative elements in each nation turned to the task of flattening dissension within their own borders. In Germany, nationalist agitation was centred in the universities. When a university student assassinated an unpopular reactionary journalist in 1819, Metternich secured the passage of the repressive **Carlsbad Decrees**. The Decrees set up strict censorship of the press, prohibited meetings, and established a special inquiry to investigate student activity. Metternich's victory was so complete that there were few nationalist disturbances for almost three decades.

The year the Carlsbad Decrees were passed in Germany, a British crowd assembled in St. Peter's Field, Manchester, to listen to a speech advocating government reform. The gathering was peaceful, but local authorities panicked and arrested the speaker. They ordered first the local militia and then a group of Waterloo veterans to disperse the crowd. In the confusion that followed, known as the **Peterloo Massacre**, eleven people were killed while over four hundred were injured. The government responded with the **Six Acts** of 1819, which restricted the press, public meetings, and the right to bear arms.

It became increasingly difficult to suppress change as commerce expanded and Europe began to industrialize after 1815. The number and influence of middle-class capitalists, industrialists, merchants, bankers, teachers, and lawyers grew significantly. They wanted the last vestiges of feudalism removed and political power equivalent to their economic strength. Usually, they demanded reforms that would increase their representation in government. In the early stages of this process, they asked for and received support from the **working class**, which had become the largest class as factories multiplied in the cities. Once the middle class was entrenched in power, however, its members began to oppose further reform that might shift control in the direction of the workers. In Britain, where the political and social structure bent in accordance with the liberal trend, the middle classes secured their political goals without violence in the First Reform Bill of 1832. Across the English Channel, the rising ambition of the French middle class came into conflict with the interests of the aristocracy and turned to revolution.

The Bourbon Restoration in France had not turned back the clock to 1789, thanks to the good sense and realistic attitude of Louis XVIII (1815-1824). The Constitutional Charter had guaranteed the basic equality and freedom of all French citizens, and an elected Chamber of Deputies had been instituted, although the electorate was limited to one hundred thousand of the wealthiest citizens from a population of 29 million. Despite the political turmoil of its early years, Louis's government paid the war indemnity and passed some liberal reforms.

Upon Louis's death in 1824, his brother became Charles X (1824-1830), and he immediately and unwisely determined to reverse the Revolution. Through financial manipulation of the national debt, Charles saved 1 billion francs and then gave the money to the nobility to pay for losses suffered after 1789. This gesture alienated the middle-class holders of government bonds, who now had to accept lower interest rates to make the savings possible. An attempt by Charles to reintroduce elements of feudalism was stopped in the legislature. When elections in 1830 gave strong representation to the middle class, Charles dissolved the government, called another election, and found himself faced with more middle-class opposition than before. On 26 July 1830, Charles issued the **Ordinances of St. Cloud**, which suspended the freedom of the press, dissolved the Chamber of Deputies, and reduced the size of the electorate to weaken the voting strength of the opposition. Two days later, "La Marseillaise" could be heard in Paris and the streets were barricaded with paving stones, furniture, wagons, and any other available material to heights of 20 m. A revolution had begun, and Charles, who had left for a brief hunting trip, now fled the country for Scotland. The **July Revolution**, although supported by radical students and workers, quickly came under the control of more moderate, middle-class reformers. Louis Phillippe (1830-1848), the duke of Orleans, was invited to be the king.

When Tsar Nicholas I (1825-1855) heard about the July Revolution, he exclaimed, "Saddle your horses, gentlemen, France is in revolution again." And France did ignite a series of revolts across Europe. Uprisings in Germany and Italy enjoyed initial success but were then firmly quelled by Austria. Belgium won its independence from Holland, while Britain, to avoid revolution, was spurred to parliamentary reform. Tsar Nicholas squashed a plot organized by Polish aristocrats and university students by imprisoning and executing thousands, while as many more Russian intellectuals fled to the safety of London and Paris. In essence, the forces of change had succeeded in Britain, France, and Belgium, where industrialism was most advanced and the middle class was large and determined. Revolutions in Germany, Italy, and Poland failed because industrialism was less developed, and conservative governments could overpower the fledgling middle class.

After 1830, nationalism and liberalism intensified throughout Europe. Radical intellectuals began to prepare new ground with theories of **socialism**. Proponents of socialism argued that governments, not individual capitalists, should control the production and distribution of goods. The "Utopian socialist" Henri de Saint Simon dreamed of a society governed by intelligent leaders who would ensure that people worked according to their talents and were rewarded according to their contributions. Louis Blanc, who originated the phrase, "From each according to his abilities, to each according to his needs," believed that governments should build national workshops, which he said would become so efficient that they would run the capitalists out of business.

In January of 1848, the *Communist Manifesto*, written by Frederick Engels and twenty-eight-year-old Karl Marx, was published in German. It had no effect on the events of that year and remained a little-known work until later activities made the authors famous. What set the framework for the revolutions of 1848 were the economic slump in England, high unemployment throughout the continent, and the failure of the potato and grain crops in 1845 and 1846, which forced up food prices. Starvation threatened.

Again, the spark that set the continent ablaze with revolution came from Paris. A shot fired to intimidate some demonstrators had the opposite effect, and the streets were barricaded again. As in 1830, government troops lacked the will to fight. Louis Phillippe abdicated to Britain. When workers and students in Vienna heard about the revolution in France, they stormed the palace and forced Metternich into exile. First the Hungarians, then the Czechs proclaimed the existence of autonomous parliaments within the Austrian empire, and Austrian troops were driven from Milan and Venice. In Berlin, Prussian troops, untrained in back-alley warfare, were humiliated when bricks, boiling water, and chimney pots were dropped on their heads from the rooftops. Frederick William IV gave in and summoned a parliament.

But in little more than a year, conservative forces had regrouped, rolled back the wave of revolution, and reasserted their control. When the new government in France held elections, Louis Napoleon Bonaparte, nephew of the emperor, became the president of the Second French Republic. He soon took steps to rule in the same fashion as his namesake had. Within the Austrian Empire, the imperial army crushed resistance in Venice, Milan, and Prague, and, with the assistance of one hundred and forty thousand Russian troops, subdued the Hungarians. In Prussia, the army remained loyal to Frederick William IV, who retook Berlin, recovered his crown, and implemented a new conservative constitution that gave limited voting rights to the wealthiest classes.

By 1850, conservatism appeared triumphant. The Hapsburgs in Austria, the Romanovs in Russia, and the Bourbons in Naples had power and prestige. British workers had not succeeded in their attempts to gain political power. But nationalism was an active and growing force. For Austria, it had the potential to break up an empire. For Italy and Germany, it had the potential to build nations. Liberalism and socialism had been temporarily discredited, but they remained very much alive. Though the revolutions of 1848 had failed, they had made an impact. The demands of the masses could no longer be ignored.

SUMMARY

Revolutionary changes exploded in Europe in the eighteenth century. The desire for change was expressed in the writings of the French *philosophes*, the most famous of whom was Voltaire. He satirized the Church, the nobility, and the government, revealing their flaws and proposing new ways of acting. Like other *philosophes*, Voltaire believed that a rational analysis of human problems could solve all problems. This optimistic outlook was fully expressed in the masterwork of the *philosophes*, the *Encyclopedia*, which was completed in 1772. It was meant to be a thorough, rational description of the world, and also a blueprint for rational social change.

The Enlightenment (1690-1790), or the Age of Reason as it is also known, is characterized by this faith in human goodness that might be achieved through rational thought. To some extent, the Enlightenment was made possible because of scientific breakthroughs. In 1543, Nicholas Copernicus had published a treatise claiming that the sun, and not the earth, was the centre of the universe. Copernicus's ideas were rejected because they threatened the view of the world promoted by the Church. But Isaac Newton's work, published in 1687, drew on the work of many great scientists and confirmed Copernicus's theories. Newton, relying on rational thought and a clear methodology, had discovered a universal law—the law of gravity. Other thinkers, such as the Englishman John Locke, became convinced that the same approach could be applied to problems in other fields—education, social relationships, and government, for example. The *philosophes* were influenced by and then extended Locke's work.

One important French writer of the time questioned the *philosophes'* faith in rational thought. Jean-Jacques Rousseau believed human goodness sprang from the emotions, not from reason. He also argued that people in society must conform to the "general will," the natural human impulse toward the greatest good. People who, out of self-interest, went against the general will should, according to Rousseau, be forced into conformity.

Ideas about change that arose during the Enlightenment were not only written about and discussed, they led to action. For example, Voltaire suggested that states should be led by enlightened despots, all-powerful monarchs whose benevolent decisions would improve the lives of the people they ruled. Several monarchs claimed to fulfil this ideal. Catherine the Great of Russia (1762-1796), Frederick the Great of Prussia (1740-1786), and Joseph II of Austria (1765-1790) each implemented policies that were presented as reforms to benefit the people. Catherine and Frederick's changes, however, tended to favour those who were already affluent and powerful, while Joseph's efforts resulted in strong counter-measures and were mostly reversed. All too often, "enlightened despots" were more despotic than they were enlightened.

European rulers, whatever the ideals or principles they professed, continued to compete with one another for territory and economic advantage. The War of the Austrian Succession (1740-1748) began when Frederick the Great claimed part of Austria. Eventually, most European states were dragged into the battle. England and France, who fought on opposite sides, used the war as an excuse to continue their colonial antagonisms that had begun in the seventeenth century. Prussia's eventual success altered the balance of power in Europe. Once new alliances had been established, Prussia launched the Seven Years' War (1756-1763). England, Prussia's ally, helped to finance the war in Europe and, at the same time, fought France in the colonies. The war in Europe settled little, but in 1759 England won the battle on the Plains of Abraham at Québec City, greatly reducing France's overseas empire. In 1776, less than twenty years later, France had a chance for revenge. It supported the Thirteen Colonies in their War of Independence against England, assisting in the birth of the United States and indirectly striking back at its enemy's empire.

Unfortunately for the French king, Louis XVI, his decision to finance the war in North America cost France an additional 1 billion livres. This debt presented an unmanageable problem for the ancien régime, as Louis's administration was known. The only way to reduce the debt was to increase taxes, but essentially there was no one from whom taxes could be collected. The Church (the First Estate) and the nobles (the Second Estate) had considerable resources, but French legislation exempted them from being taxed. As a result, the middle classes and the poor (the Third Estate) had shouldered an increasing share of the burden; they had little money left to be taken.

At this time, *philosophe* ideas were put into practice again, with cataclysmic effects on the history of France and the rest of Europe. As part of his efforts to alter the tax structure and to raise money, Louis called for a session of the Estates General in 1788. The Third Estate called for Enlightenment ideas and demanded reforms, including a more equitable distribution of taxes, the final dismantling of feudalism, and a constitution. The First and Second Estates opposed these changes. An economic depression, food shortages, and high unemployment increased the anger and desperation of the Third Estate. Crisis followed crisis in the power struggle that ensued. Finally, on 17 June 1789, the Third Estate redefined its role and called itself the National Assembly. The Moderate Phase of the French Revolution had begun.

Soon after, the Revolution turned violent. Louis summoned troops to Paris, precipitating the riots of 14 July 1789 and the storming of the Bastille. The rebels took control of Paris and by late July the Revolution had spread to the countryside. During the Great Fear, peasants attacked the strongholds of the nobility throughout France, at which point the nobility relented and gave up their privileges.

For almost two years France enjoyed a measure of calm and peace, as the new government tried to draft a constitution and to put its principles into effect. But in 1791, a number of factors combined to take the Revolution in a new direction. Parisians were hungry again, and the government appeared to be blocking changes demanded by the lower classes. Louis XVI's attempted escape from France seemed to confirm the threat of a monarchist counter-revolution. In addition, people feared that other European states would move against France. France took the initiative, declaring war against Austria in April 1792. The early success of Austria and Prussia against France provoked the Radical Phase of the Revolution. There was a military coup in August 1792, followed by the September Massacres; thousands of so-called counter-revolutionaries were murdered. By 20 September 1792, the French army had halted the invaders and France declared itself a Republic. Louis XVI was executed at the beginning of 1793.

Over the next two years, France remained at war with the other nations of Europe and also with itself. The Jacobins were the most powerful group within the government. A particularly radical faction of the Jacobins, known as the Mountain, executed the leaders of other factions and instituted what came to be known as the Reign of Terror. Maximilien Robespierre was the Jacobin who presided over the imprisonment and execution of tens of thousands of French citizens. He believed he was acting in accordance with the general will that Rousseau had described. Robespierre tried to create a Republic of Virtue, a state where all would be equal and where religion and superstition would not exist. To combat the armies and monarchies of the other nations of Europe, he organized the *Levée en Masse*, a mass draft that essentially threw all of the French people into the war. But Robespierre's extremism provoked yet another coup—the Thermidorian Reaction. In July 1794, he and his followers were sentenced to death.

France was now governed by a Directory of five men. The war against the rest of Europe was no longer being fought to spread the Revolution but to enhance French interests. A young army officer named Napoleon Buonaparte conducted several military campaigns, and finally arrived in Paris to help the Directory maintain its control. Ironically, the saviour of the Directory was interested in control himself and by February, 1800, had attained the position of first consul. In war, he defeated Austria and stalemated Britain. Napoleon then began to implement measures to improve France's domestic condition. He centralized the administration, created an effective system of taxation, instituted a new legal code, the Code Napoléon, and undertook educational and religious reforms. In 1804, when a plot against him appeared to surface, he not only broke it up, but used the occasion to have himself declared emperor of France.

By this time, France was at war again. Napoleon defeated Austria, but the naval battle at Trafalgar against the British went against the French, and England continued to dominate the seas. Knowing that England could not be invaded, Napoleon tried to subdue his rival through economic warfare. In 1806, he devised the Continental System to keep British goods out of the rest of Europe. He hoped that the British economy would collapse and the government would fall to revolution. In the meantime, Napoleon put down another Austrian attempt at war, and went on to humiliate the Prussians as well. When the Treaty of Tilsit was settled in 1807, Napoleon's Grand Empire covered much of Europe.

Unfortunately for Napoleon, the actual result of his Continental System was quite different from his plans. England organized its own trade blockade in 1807. France continued to prosper, but its allies and neutral countries had to pay more money for fewer goods. Dissatisfaction within the Grand Empire was expressed through nationalist rebellion, first in Spain

(1808), Austria (1809), and finally Russia (1812). Napoleon's efforts to subdue Russia proved to be a disaster. He took over six hundred thousand troops toward Moscow, but over half a million of them were killed or deserted. The Russians increased his losses when he retreated. Prussia, Russia, Austria, and Britain formed the Fourth Coalition to take advantage of Napoleon's weakness. By 1814, the emperor had been defeated and exiled to the island of Elba. He returned and managed to raise an army, but was defeated for the final time on 18 June 1815.

Economic and commercial relations played a crucial role in the European wars of the late eighteenth and early nineteenth centuries. Manufacturing and production were undergoing momentous changes, which have become known as the Industrial Revolution. The foundation of the Industrial Revolution was the spirit of scientific inquiry that had become established in the sixteenth century. Knowledge increased, and so did practical applications of that knowledge. For many reasons, most of the applications first appeared in England. New agricultural techniques resulted in better crops and livestock. But most advances took the form of machinery. Indeed, the replacement of human and animal labour by machinery is the essence of the Industrial Revolution.

First, the textile industry was transformed by a series of inventions—the flying shuttle (1733), the spinning jenny (1765), the water frame (1769), the mule (1779), the power loom (1785), and the cotton gin (1793). These devices enabled better cotton thread and cotton goods to be produced. By 1771, the new machines were brought together in huge factories known as cotton mills, and, with each subsequent invention, the manufacture of cotton goods became faster and less expensive. Mechanization and the factory system were also adapted to many other industries.

The second set of important developments involved new ways of working with iron. At the end of the eighteenth century, the British perfected the puddling process and were able to make a superior quality of iron. About the same time, the rolling mill was invented, which meant that iron could be mass-produced into different shapes. By the middle of the nineteenth century, British iron dominated the market.

James Watt, in 1769, was responsible for a critical innovation that led to the third important advance of the era—the improvement of the steam engine. His engine was not only used to pump water and drive machinery in factories, it was also adapted to provide a new means of transportation— the locomotive. It was George Stephenson's *Rocket* that demonstrated the possibilities of the railroad in 1825.

A high price was paid for the industrialization of Britain. The labourers who worked in the mines and the urban factories were exposed to working and living conditions that made their lives horrible and often killed them. Lower-class men, women, and even children were seen as resources to be exploited. Humanitarians and reformers fought for legislation that would bring improvements; from the 1830s onward, the British government passed a number of acts that alleviated some, but not all, of the injustices. These concessions were not won easily. Demonstrations, political organization, and violence were used to pressure the wealthy middle-class factory owners and the politicians who represented their interests.

Indeed, civil unrest of one kind or another was a central feature of European life in the first half of the nineteenth century. After Napoleon's France was defeated, the Congress of Vienna (1814-1815) was called to reorganize Europe. Metternich, Austria's chancellor, wanted to ensure that European states were controlled by the noble families who were the traditional leaders of society. But the forces of nationalism, liberalism, and democracy led to uprisings in Spain, Italy, and Greece. The issue of Greek independence shattered European solidarity, and each country turned to its domestic problems. In almost every nation, the middle classes were trying to wrest a share of power from the nobility. Governments often responded by enacting legislation that repressed freedom of speech and other rights. In the more industrialized nations (Britain, France, and Belgium), the middle classes had enough resources to make gains. Elsewhere (Germany, Italy, and Poland), they were unsuccessful.

The most serious threat to those in power came in 1848, when a revolution in France triggered others across Europe. These uprisings failed, but an impression had been made. The masses, who were becoming aware of their strength, were ready to listen to and act on the socialist ideas that were being developed and discussed.

Bibliography

THE ORIGINS OF HUMANS

Allman, William F. "Who We Were." *U.S. News & World Report*, 16 September 1991.

Aiello, Leslie. *The Concise Book of the Origins of Man.* Scarborough: Prentice-Hall Canada, Inc., 1982.

Allen, Frederick Lewis. *Only Yesterday.* New York: Harper and Row, 1964.

Bower, Bruce. "Neanderthals' Disappearing Act." *Science News*, 8 June 1991.

Brown, Michael H. *The Search for Eve.* New York: Harper & Row, 1990.

Claiborne, Robert. *The First Americans.* New York: Time-Life Books, 1974.

Constable, George. *The Neanderthals.* New York: Time-Life Books, 1973.

Darwin, Charles. *The Origin of Species.* New York: Penguin Books, 1982.

Edey, Maitland. *The Missing Link.* New York: Time-Life Books, 1977.

Fisher, Helen E. "Richard Leakey's Time Machine." *Omni*, March 1983

Heathcote, Graham. "Maybe We Walk Erect because It's Cool, Man." *The Toronto Star*, 1 December 1991.

Hitching, Francis. "Was Darwin Wrong?" *Life*, April 1982. *Hoaxes and Deceptions.* New York: Time-Life Books, 1991.

Howells, William. "Homo sapiens: 20 Million Years in the Making." *Unesco Courier*, October/November 1972.

Johanson, Donald, and Maitland Edey. *Lucy: The Beginnings of Humankind.* New York: Simon and Shuster, 1981.

Johanson, Donald, and Maitland Edey. *Blueprints: Solving the Mystery of Evolution.* Toronto: Little, Brown, and Company, 1989.

Johanson, Donald, and James Shreeve. *Lucy's Child.* New York: Early Man Publishing, Inc., 1989.

Kern, Edward P.H. "Battle of the Bones." *Life*, December 1981.

Lambert, David, and the Diagram Group. *The Field Guide to Early Man.* New York: Facts on File Publications, 1987.

Leakey, Louis B. "Our African Ancestors." *Unesco Courier*, August/September 1972

Leakey, Maeve, and Richard Leakey. *A Guide to Koobi Fora.* Kenya: The National Museums of Kenya, 1988.

Leakey, Richard. *The Making of Mankind.* New York: E.P. Dutton, 1981.

Leakey, Richard, and Roger Lewin. *Origins.* New York: E.P. Dutton, 1977.

McKie, Robin. "The Noah's Ark Theory." *The Geographical Magazine*, March 1989.

Milner, Richard. *The Encyclopedia of Evolution.* New York: Oxford, 1990.

Morell, Virginia. "My Brother, the Ape." *Equinox*, September/October 1983.

Napier, John. "The Evolution of the Hand." In *Human Ancestors: Readings from Scientific American.* San Francisco: W.H. Freeman Co., 1979.

Prideaux, Tom. *Cro-Magnon Man.* New York: Time-Life Books, 1979.

Resenberger, Boyce. "Ancestors." *Science Digest*, April 1981.

Shreeve, James. "Argument Over a Woman." *Discover*, August 1990.

Simons, Elwyn. "The Early Relatives of Man." In *Human Ancestors: Readings from Scientific American.* San Francisco: W.H. Freeman and Co., 1979.

———. "Ramapithecus." In *Human Ancestors: Readings from Scientific American.* San Francisco: W.H. Freeman Co., 1979.

Stoler, Peter. "Puzzling Out Man's Ascent." *Time*, 7 November 1977.

Walker, Alan, and Richard Leakey. "Hominids of East Turkana." In *Human Ancestors: Readings from Scientific American.* San Francisco: W.H. Freeman Co., 1979.

Ward, Olivia. "Darwin Scholars Gear Up for Fight." *The Toronto Star*, 14 March 1983.

Washburn, Sherwood. "Tools and Human Evolution." In *Human Ancestors: Readings from Scientific American.* San Francisco: W.H. Freeman Co., 1979.

White, Edmund, and Dale M. Brown. *The First Men.* New York: Time-Life Books, 1973.

York, Derek. "Ape-Like Creature Walked Upright—Counting to 4 Million B.C." *The Globe and Mail*, 10 June 1982.

———. "Man, Ape Parting May Have Been Late." *The Globe and Mail*, 22 September 1983.

THE RISE OF CIVILIZATION

Balsiger, David, and Charles Sellier. *In Search of Noah's Ark.* Los Angeles: Sun Classic Books, 1976.

"The Birth of Civilization." *Science Digest*, April 1981.

Canby, Courtland. *Archaeology of the World.* London: Chancellor Press, 1980.

Claiborne, Robert. *The Birth of Writing.* Alexandria, Virginia: Time-Life Books, 1977.

Cole, John R., and Laurie R. Godfrey. "The Paluxy River Footprint Mystery—Solved" in *Creation/Evolution*, 1985.

Cyr, Donald L. "Whose Canopy Model?" In *Stonehenge Viewpoint.* Santa Barbara: Stonehenge Viewpoint, 1985.

Dawkins, Richard. *The Blind Watchmaker.* New York: W.W. Norton & Company, 1986.

Fagan, Brian. *The Adventure of Archaeology.* Washington D.C.: The National Geographic Society, 1985.

Gowlatt, John A. *Ascent to Civilization.* London: William Collins Sons & Co Ltd., 1984.

Hamblin, Dora Jane. *The First Cities.* New York: Time-Life Books, 1973.

Herbert, David. *The Necessity of Creationism in Public Education.* London, Ontario: Hersil Publishing, 1986.

Herbert, David. *The Rise of Evolutionism: The Escape From God.* London, Ontario: Hersil Publishing, 1987.

Howe, Helen, and Robert T. Howe. *The Ancient World.* New York: Longman, 1992.

Hyslop, Stephen G., Ray Hones, and Davis S. Thomson, eds. *The Age of the God-Kings.* Alexandria, Virginia: Time-Life Books, 1987.

Kite, Patricia. *Noah's Ark.* San Diego: Greenhaven Press, Inc., 1989.

Kuban, Glen. "A Summary of the Taylor Site Evidence." *Creation/Evolution*, Spring 1986.

MacDonald, David. "The Flood: Mesopotamian Archaeological Evidence." *Creation/Evolution*, Spring 1988.

McDonald, Robert. "Soviet Bear Snorts at Ark Hunt." *The Toronto Star.* 23 July 1988.

McGowan, Chris. *In the Beginning ...* Toronto: Macmilan of Canada, 1983.

McIntosh, Jane. *The Practical Archaeologist.* New York: Oxford, 1986.

Milner, Richard. *The Encyclopedia of Evolution.* New York: Oxford, 1990.

Moore, Robert A. "The Impossible Voyage of Noah's Ark." *Creation/Evolution*, Winter 1983.

Moore, Robert A. "Arkeology: A New Science in Support of Creation?" *Creation/Evolution*, Fall 1981.

Morris, H.M. *Scientific Creationism.* Toronto: Macmillan of Canada, 1974.

———. Interview in *In Search of Noah's Ark.* Sun Classic Pictures, Inc., 1976. Film.

Schadewald, Robert. "Scientific Creationists and Error." In *Creation/Evolution*, Spring 1986.

Stearns, Peter N., Donald R. Schwartz, and Barry K. Beyer. *World History.* Don Mills, Ontario: Addison-Wesley Publishing Company, 1989.

Stone, Merlin. *When God Was a Woman.* New York: Dorset Press, 1990.

Taylor, Ian. *In the Minds of Men.* Toronto: TFE Publishing, 1984.

Weber, Gregory. "Paluxy Man—The Creationist Piltdown." *Creation/Evolution*, Fall 1981.

Trueman, John H., and Dawn C. Trueman. *The Enduring Past.* Toronto: McGraw-Hill Ryerson, Limited, 1982.

Wood, Michael. Foreward. *The World Atlas of Archaeology.* New York: Crown Publishers, 1988.

EGYPTIAN CIVILIZATION: PUZZLE OF THE PYRAMIDS

Beers, Burton F. *World History: Patterns of Civilization.* Englewood, New Jersey: Prentice Hall, 1991.

Casson, Lionel. *Ancient Egypt.* Alexandria, Virginia: Time-Life Books, 1978.

Cottrell, Leonard. *Lost Civilizations.* New York: Collins, Franklin Watts Inc., 1974.

Dunan, Marcel, and John Bowle, eds. *Ancient and Medieval History.* New York: Crown Publishers, 1972.

De Camp, L. Sprague. *Great Cities of the Ancient World.* New York: Dorset Press, 1990.

Edwards, I.E.S. *The Pyramids of Egypt.* Baltimore: Cardinal, Sphere Books Ltd., 1961.

El Mahdy, Christine. *Mummies, Myth and Magic in Ancient Egypt.* London: Thames and Hudson, 1989.

Grosvenor, Gilbert M. *Ancient Egypt.* Washington: National Geographic Society, 1978.

Hart, George. *Ancient Egypt.* Toronto: Stoddart Publishing Co., 1990.

Hitching, Francis. *The World Atlas of Mysteries.* Toronto: William Collins Sons and Company Limited, 1978.

Hobson, Christine. *The World of the Pharaohs.* New York: Thames and Hudson, 1987.

Hoffman, Michael A. *Egypt before the Pharaohs.* New York: Dorset Press, 1990.

Hyslop, Stephen G., Ray Jones, and Davis S. Thomson, eds. *The Age of the God-Kings.* Alexandria, Virginia: Time-Life Books, 1987. *Lost Civilizations.* Alexandria, Virginia: Time-Life Books, 1992.

Mendelssohn, Kurt. *The Riddle of the Pyramids.* London: Cardinal, Sphere Books Ltd., 1976.

Murnane, William J. Ancient Egypt. London: Penguin Books, 1983.

Reeves, Nicholas. *The Complete Tutankhamun.* London: Thames and Hudson, 1990.

Sears, Margaret. "Who Built the Great Pyramid?" in *Rotunda*, Spring 1990.

Starr, Douglas. "Plastic Megaliths." *Omni*, February 1983.

Trueman, John H., and Dawn C. Trueman. *The Enduring Past*. Toronto: McGraw-Hill Ryerson Limited, 1982.

von Däniken, Erich. *Chariots of the Gods?* London: Souvenir Press Ltd.

Wilson, Clifford. *The Chariots Still Crash*. Scarborough: Signet Books, 1975.

BRONZE AGE GREECE AND THE MYSTERY OF ATLANTIS

Bacon, Edward. "Atlantis." In *Man, Myth and Magic*, part 6. Hicksville: Marshall Cavendish USA Ltd., 1974.

Casson, Lionel. "Where Did Homer's Heroes Come From?" In *Mysteries of the Past*, Joseph J. Thorndike, ed. New York: American Heritage Publishing Company, 1977.

Cottrell, Leonard. *Lost Civilizations*. New York: Collins, Franklin Watts Inc., 1974.

Edey, Maitland. *Lost World of the Aegean*. New York: Time-Life Books, 1975.

Hitching, Francis. *The World Atlas of Mysteries*. Toronto: William Collins Sons and Company Ltd., 1978.

Muck, Otto. *The Secret of Atlantis*. Toronto: William Collins Sons and Company Ltd., 1976.

Plato, *Timaeus and Critias*. Translated by Desmond Lee. New York: Penguin Books Ltd., 1977.

Sakellarakis, Yannis, and Efi Sapouna-Sakellarakis. "Drama of Death in a Minoan Temple." *National Geographic*, February 1981.

THE IDEALS OF SPARTA AND ATHENS

Agard, W.R. "What Democracy Meant to the Greeks." In *Civilization in Perspective*, John Patton, ed. Toronto: Macmillan of Canada, 1972.

Andronicos, Manolis. "Athenian Democracy's Grand Design." *UNESCO Courier*, October 1977.

Canby, Courtland. *Archaeology of the World*. Amsterdam: Chancellor Press, 1980.

Dunan, Marcel, and John Bowle, eds. *Ancient and Medieval History*. New York: Crown Publishers, 1972.

Edie, John, and Ivan Krakowsky. *Athens: The Parthenon*. Study Print no. 10-6010. Encyclopedia Britannica Educational Corp., 1968.

Greece, the Golden Age. Life Educational Reprint, no. 66. 1963.

Greece, Pride and Fall. Life Educational Reprint, no. 67. 1962.

Hicks, Jim. *The Persians*. Alexandria: Time-Life Books, 1978.

Parry, Hugh. *The Individual and His Society: Alcibiades-Greek Patriot or Traitor?* Toronto: Macmillan of Canada, 1969.

———. *Ideals of Education: Spartan Warrior and Athenian All-Round Man*. Toronto: Macmillan of Canada, 1969.

Ricker, John, and John Saywell. *The Emergence of Europe*. Toronto: Clarke, Irwin and Co., 1968.

Thucydides. *History of the Peloponnesian War*. Translated by Rex Warner. New York: Penguin Books Ltd., 1954.

Toynbee, Arnold. *A Study of History*. New York: Weathervane Books, 1972.

Trueman, John H., and Dawn C. Trueman. *The Enduring Past*. Toronto: McGraw-Hill Ryerson Ltd., 1982.

Warner, Rex. *World Mythology*. London: Royce Publications, 1983.

ALEXANDER, HANNIBAL, AND JULIUS CAESAR

Barzini, Luigi. *From Caesar to the Mafia*. La Salle, Ill.: Open Court Publishing Company, 1971.

Bowra, C.M. *Classical Greece*. New York: Time-Life Books, 1965.

Connolly, Peter. *Hannibal and the Enemies of Rome*. Morristown: Silver Burdett Co., 1979.

Dal Maso, Leonardo B. *Rome of the Caesars*. Rome: Bonechi-Edizione, 1976.

Dunan, Marcel, and John Bowle, eds. *Ancient and Medieval History*. New York: Crown Publishers, 1972.

Edey, Maitland. *The Sea Traders*. New York: Time-Life Books, 1974.

Hamblin, Dora Jane. *The Etruscans*. New York: Time-Life Books, 1976.

Lloyd, Alan. *Destroy Carthage*. London: Souvenir Press, 1977.

Parry, Hugh. *Julius Caesar: The Legend and the Man*. Toronto: Macmillan of Canada, 1972.

———. *People as Possessions: Master and Slave in the Roman World*. Toronto: Macmillan of Canada, 1972.

Porter, R.L. *Alexander the Great and His Partnership with the Persians*. Labyrinth Classical Studies, no. 28. University of Waterloo, January 1984.

Ricker, John, and John Saywell. *The Emergence of Europe*. Toronto: Clarke Irwin and Co., 1968.

Trueman, John H., and Dawn C. Trueman. *The Enduring Past*. Toronto: McGraw-Hill Ryerson Limited, 1982.

Vickers, Michael. *The Roman World*. Oxford: Elsevier-Phaidon, 1977.

Wells, H.G. *The Outline of History*. Revised edition. New York: Garden City Books, 1961.

THE TRIUMPH AND DECLINE OF ROME

Balsdon, J.V.D. "Life and Leisure." In *Civilization in Perspective*, John Patton, ed. Toronto: Macmillan Company of Canada, 1972.

Brooks, P.S., and N.Z. Walworth, *When the World Was Rome*. New York: J.B. Lippincott Company, 1972.

Buchanan, David. *Roman Sport and Entertainment*. Hong Kong: Longman, 1980.

Bury, J.B. "History of the Later Roman Empire." In *The Fall of Rome*, Mortimer Chambers, ed. Toronto: Holt, Rinehart and Winston, 1963.

Connolly, Peter. *Pompeii*. London: Macdonald Educational Ltd., 1979.

Dal Maso, Leonardo B. *Rome of the Caesars*. Rome: Bonechi-Edizione, 1976.

Dudley, Donald R. *The Civilization of Rome*. New York: New American Library, 1962.

Fenton, Edwin. *32 Problems in World History*. Glenview: Scott, Foresman and Company, 1964.

Forsyth, P.Y. *Setting the Record Straight: The Ancients and Mt. Vesuvius*. Labyrinth Classical Studies, no. 28, University of Waterloo, January 1984.

Gascoigne, Bamber, *The Christians*. London: Jonathan Cape Ltd., 1977.

Hadas, Moses. *Imperial Rome*. New York: Time-Life Books, 1971.

Kern, Edward. *Rome, Lively Hub of the Empire*. Life Educational Reprint no. 16. 1966.

Magi, Giovanna. *All Pompeii*. Naples: Bonechi Editore, 1977.

Matthews, Kenneth D. *The Early Romans*. Toronto: MacGraw-Hill Ryerson.

Parry, Hugh. *People as Possessions: Master and Slave in the Roman World*. Toronto: Macmillan of Canada, 1972.

Quennell, Peter. *The Colosseum*. New York: The Reader's Digest Association Ltd. with Newsweek Book Division, 1971.

Ricker, John, and John Saywell. *The Emergence of Europe*. Toronto: Clarke, Irwin and Company, 1968.

Salmon, E. Togo. "The Roman Army and the Disintegration of the Empire." In *The Fall of Rome*, Mortimer Chambers, ed. Toronto: Holt, Rinehart and Winston, 1963.

Trueman, John H., and Dawn C. Trueman. *The Enduring Past*. Toronto: McGraw-Hill Ryerson Ltd., 1982.

Wells, H.G. *The Outline of History*. Revised edition. New York: Garden City Books, 1961.

EUROPE, MESOAMERICA, AND SOUTH AMERICA

Bray, W.M., E.H. Swanson, and I.S. Farrington. *The New World*. Belgium: Elsevier-Phaidon, 1975.

Brown, R. Allen, Michael Prestwich, and Charles Coulson. *Castles*. New York: Greenwich House, Blanford Press, 1982.

Burland, C.A. "Aztecs." In *Man, Myth and Magic*. London: BPC Publishing Ltd., 1970.

Canby, Courtland. *Archaeology of the World*. London: Chancellor Press, 1980.

Cantor, Norman F. *Medieval History*. London: The Macmillan Company, 1969.

Casson, Lionel. "Who First Crossed the Oceans?" In *Mysteries of the Past*, Joseph C. Thorndike, ed. New York: American Heritage Publishing Company, 1977.

Dunan, Marcel, and John Bowle, eds. *Ancient and Medieval History*. New York: Crown Publishers, 1972.

Eliade, M. "Patterns in Comparative Religion." In *Man, Myth and Magic*. London: BPC Publishing, 1970.

Fitzgerald, M.P., and D.R. Rayburn. *Eratosthenes of Cyrene*. In Labyrinth Classical Studies. University of Waterloo, January 1981.

Furneaux, Rupert. *Ancient Mysteries*. London: Futura Publications, 1976.

Gimpel, Jean. "The Cathedral Builders." In *32 Problems in World History*, Edwin Fenton, ed. Glenview: Scott, Foresman and Company, 1969.

Hale, John R. *Age of Exploration*. New York: Time Inc., 1966.

Hartt, Frederick. *Art*. vol. 1. New York: Harry N. Abrams Inc., 1976.

Heyerdahl, Thor. *The Ra Expeditions*. New York: The New American Heritage Library Inc., 1971.

Hitching, Francis. *The World Atlas of Mysteries*. Toronto: William Collins Sons and Company Ltd., 1978.

Major, J.R, R. Scranton, and G.P. Cuttino. *Civilization in the Western World*. Toronto: J.B. Lippincott Company, 1971.

Mariott, J.A.R. *The Eastern Question*. London: Oxford, 1969.

Mendelssohn, Kurt. *The Riddle of the Pyramids*. London: Cardinal, 1974.

McDowell, Bart. "The Aztecs." *National Geographic*, December 1980.

Reid, Richard. *Buildings*. London: Michael Joseph, 1980.

Ricker, John, and John Saywell. *The Emergence of Europe*. Clark, Irwin and Company, 1968.

Sellman, R.R. *The Crusades*. New York: Roy Publishing Inc., 1955.

Setton, Kenneth M. "The Norman Conquest." *National Geographic*, August 1966.

Sherrard, Philip. *Byzantium*. New York: Time-Life Books, 1966.

Simons, Gerald. *Barbarian Europe*. New York: Time-Life Books, 1968.

Stuart, Gene S. *The Mighty Aztecs*. Washington, D.C.: The National Geographic Society, 1981.

Trueman, John H., and Dawn C. Trueman. *The Enduring Past*. Toronto: McGraw-Hill Ryerson Limited, 1982.

Wells, H.G. *The Outline of History.* Revised edition. New York: Garden City Books, 1961.

Wolf, John B. *The Emergence of European Civilization.* New York: Harper and Row, 1962.

EUROPE AND THE SUN KING

Bertelli, Carlo. "The Last Supper." *National Geographic,* November 1983.

Blitzer, Charles. *Age of Kings.* New York: Time Incorporated, 1967.

Chamberlin, E.R. *Renaissance Times.* New York: Perigee Books, 1980.

Cruickshank, J.E. *The Modern Age 1500-1763.* Toronto: Longmans Canada Limited, 1963.

Guizot, François. "History of Civilization in Europe." Translated by William Hazlitt. In *The Greatness of Louis XIV,* William F. Church, ed. Toronto: D.C. Heath and Company, 1972.

Hale, John R. *Renaissance.* New York: Time-Life Inc., 1965.

Hartt, Frederick. *Art.* vol. 2. New York: Harry N. Abrams, 1976.

Hemming, John. *The Search for El Dorado.* London: Michael Joseph, 1978.

Lavender, E.F.B. Lewis, and N. Sheffe. *A Thousand Ages.* Toronto: McGraw-Hill Company of Canada, 1961.

Mackirdy, K.A., J.S. Moir, and Y.F. Zoltvany. *Changing Perspectives in Canadian History.* Don Mills, Ontario: J.M. Dent & Sons, 1971.

Ricker, John, and John Saywell. *Europe and the Modern World.* Toronto: Clark, Irwin & Company Ltd., 1976.

Ripley, Elizabeth. *Michelangelo.* New York: Oxford University Press, 1953.

Seller, Charles, and Henry May. *A Synopsis of American History.* Chicago: Rand McNally and Company, 1969.

Saint-Simon, Duc de. *The Memoirs of the Duke of Saint-Simon of Louis XIV and the Regency.* Translated by Bayle St. John. In *The Greatness of Louis XIV,* William F. Church, ed. Toronto: D.C. Heath and Company, 1972.

Stamp, Kenneth M. *The Peculiar Institution.* New York: Vintage Books, 1956.

Trueman, John, and Dawn C. Trueman. *The Enduring Past.* Toronto: McGraw-Hill Ryerson Ltd., 1982.

Wells, H.G. *The Outline of History.* Revised edition. New York: Garden City Books, 1961.

Wolf, John B. *The Emergence of European Civilization.* New York: Harper & Row, 1962.

EUROPE AND THE FRENCH REVOLUTION

Blum, Jerome, Rondo Cameron, and Thomas G. Barnes. *The European World.* Boston: Little, Brown, and Company, 1970.

Bury, J.B. *The Idea of Progress.* New York: Dover Publications Inc., 1960.

Craig, Gordon A., *Europe Since 1815.* Toronto: Holt, Rinehart and Winston, 1966.

Creal, Michael. *The Idea of Progress: The Origins of Modern Optimism.* Toronto: Macmillan of Canada, 1970.

——. *The Dynamics of Revolution: France 1789-94.* Toronto: Macmillan of Canada, 1970.

——. *Voltaire: Passionate Fighter for Liberty.* Toronto: Macmillan of Canada, 1970.

Cruickshank, J.E. *The Modern Age.* Toronto: Longmans Canada Ltd., 1963.

Curtis, Michael, ed. *The Great Political Theories.* New York: Avon Books, 1973.

Fenton, Edwin. *32 Problems in World History.* Chicago: Scott, Foresman and Company, 1969.

Fessenden, Nicholas B. *The Impact of the Industrial Revolution.* New York: Harcourt Brace Jovanovich, 1978.

Gingerich, Owen. "The Foundation of Modern Science." *UNESCO Courier,* April 1973.

Herold, Christopher J. *The Age of Napoleon.* New York: American Heritage Publishing Co. Inc., 1983.

Hux, Allan D., and Frederick E. Jarman. *The French Revolution.* Toronto: Academic Press Canada, 1982.

Kick, H.W. *The Rise of Modern Warfare.* New York: Crescent Books, 1982.

Mendenhall, Thomas, Basil D. Henning, and Archibald S. Foord. *The Quest for a Principle of Authority in Europe 1715-Present.* Toronto: Holt, Rinehart and Winston, 1965.

Merton, Robert K. *Science, Technology and Society in Seventeenth Century England.* New York: Harper and Row, 1970.

Ricker, John, and John Saywell. *Europe and the Modern World.* Toronto: Clarke, Irwin and Company, 1976.

Spencer, Robert. *The West and a Wider World.* Toronto: Clarke, Irwin and Company, 1966.

Wells, H.G. *The Outline of History.* Revised edition. New York: Garden City Books, 1961.

Wolf, John B. *The Emergence of European Civilization.* New York: Harper and Row, 1962.

Photo Credits

ABBREVIATIONS

Bettmann = The Bettmann Archive

Granger = The Granger Collection, New York

ROM = Royal Ontario Museum, Toronto, Canada

Davis = Dale Davis

KEY: (t) = top; (b) = bottom; (l) = left; (r) = right

3 Granger; 16 Adespoten Photo Service; 25 Davis; 26 Davis; 34 Museum of Art and Archaeology, University of Missouri—Columbia, Gift of Dr. and Mrs. Saul S. Weinberg; 36 The University Museum, University of Pennsylvania (neg. G59249); 37 The University Museum, University of Pennsylvania (neg. S4-28745); 41 Robert Fried/Stock Boston; 46 Granger; 54 ROM; 58 ROM; 79 ROM; 81 Granger; 90 (t and b) Davis; 92 (t and b) Davis; 104 Davis; 117 Davis; 119 M&M Fulmer, Toronto; 129 (t and b) ROM; 136 ROM; 147 Alinari/Art Resource, New York; 166 (t and b) ROM; 175 Susan Hider; 176 Davis; 178 (l) Davis, (r) C. Coulter; 179 Davis; 181 Davis; 203 By permission of the British Library; 205 Davis; 207 ROM; 210 Davis; 220 By permission of the British Library; 221 Bodleian Library, University of Oxford, Ms. Gough Liturg. 2, fol. 30r; 222 Victoria and Albert Museum/neg. no. V.65; 228 © Charlotte Kahler; 229 First Light/Gerry Kobalenko; 231 British Tourist Authority; 238 Bettmann; 256 (t and b) Matthew J. Richmond; 257 Davis; 258 Davis; 259 Davis; 261 Davis; 265 (l and r) Alan Hirsch; 266 Alan Hirsch; 276 Granger; 278 – 279 © OLIVETTI with the permission of Soprintendenta and Beni Artistica e Storici—Milan; 280 Alinari/Art Resource, New York; 281 (t) Alinari/Art Resource, New York, (b) Davis; 282 Davis; 283 Davis; 285 The Royal Collection © 1993 Her Majesty the Queen; 287 ROM; 289 Bettmann; 294 ROM; 295 *Country Life*; 308 National Archives of Canada/C-034183; 310 Davis; 324 Davis; 344 Goldschmidt/Locke/Versailles © Photo R.M.N.; 346 Xuvie/Voltaire/Versailles © Photo R.M.N; 349 (all) Granger; 351 Escot/J.J. Rousseau/Versailles © Photo R.M.N; 354 Giraudon/Art Resource; 358 Bettmann; 369 Granger; 374 Granger; 385 Giraudon/Art Resource, New York; 390 Bettmann; 401 Granger; 404 Granger

Text Credits

BACON, EDWARD: adapted from "Atlantis," in *Man, Myth and Magic, Part 6*. By permission of Little, Brown & Co. (UK) Ltd.

BARZINI, LUIGI: adapted from "The Enigma of Caesar," in *From Caesar to the Mafia* by Luigi Barzini, by permission of Open Court Publishing Company, La Salle, Illinois. Copyright © 1971 by Luigi Barzini.

BOWRA, C M: adapted from *Great Ages of Man/Classical Greece* by C.M. Bowra and the Editors of Time–Life Books. Copyright © 1965 Time–Life Books Inc.

DUDLEY, DONALD R: adapted from *The Civilization of Rome* by Donald R. Dudley. Copyright © 1960, 1962 by Donald R. Dudley. Used by permission of Dutton Signet, a division of Penguin Books USA Inc.

HERODOTUS: from *The History of Herodotus, Book II* translated by George Rawlinson (Everyman's Library, 1964). Reprinted by permission of J.M. Dent.

SALMON, E TOGO: adapted from "The Roman Army and the Disintegration of The Empire." Original text printed in *Transactions of the Royal Society of Canada*, Third Series, Volume LII, 1958.

THORNE, ALAN G, and MILFORD WOLPOFF: from "The Multiregional Evolution of Humans" by A.G. Thorne and M. Wolpoff, *Scientific American*, April 1992.

THUCYDIDES: adapted from *History of the Peloponnesian War* translated by Rex Warner (Penguin Classics, 1954). Copyright © Rex Warner, 1954. Reprinted by permission of Penguin Books Ltd.

VON DÄNIKEN, ERICH: adapted from Chapter 7, "Ancient Marvels or Space Travel Centres?" from *Chariots of the Gods?*, by permission of Souvenir Press Ltd.

WILSON, ALLAN C, and REBECCA L CANN: from "The Recent African Genesis of Humans" by A.C. Wilson and R.L. Cann, *Scientific American*, April 1992.

Index